Rosario+Vampire
Season II

11

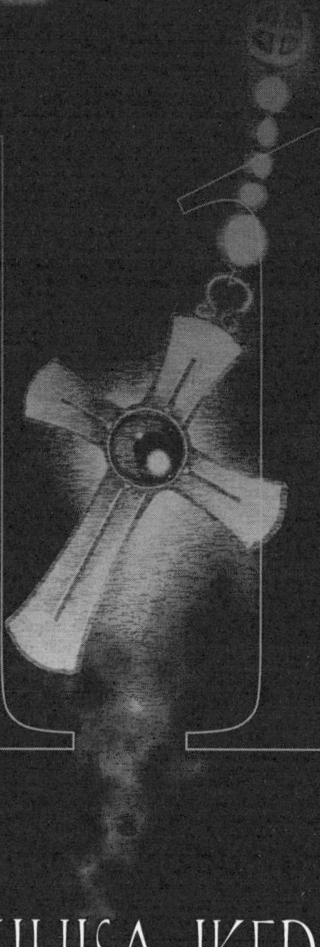

AKIHISA IKEDA

Horror Story Thus Far

Tsukune Aono accidentally enrolls in Yokai Academy, a high school for monsters! After befriending the school's cutest girl, Moka Akashiya, he decides to stay...even though Yokai has a zero-tolerance policy towards humans. (A *fatal* policy.) Tsukune has to hide his true identity while fending off attacks by monster gangs. He survives with the help of his News Club friends—Moka, Kurumu, Yukari, and Mizore. Just as Tsukune and his friends begin contemplating their future after they graduate, the mysterious organization Fairy Tale starts to wreak havoc on the monster—and human—world. When Moka's Rosario seal weakens, she and her friends travel to their new friend Huang's home in Hong Kong to get it fixed. There, they learn of the tragic disappearance of Moka's mother, Akasha, and the existence of Alucard, the True Ancestor of the vampires, who seeks to destroy the human world. Then Moka is kidnapped by her sister Aqua, an operative of the evil organization Fairy Tale, which plans to resurrect Alucard! After intensive training, Moka's friends infiltrate the enemy's multi-level floating fortress to rescue her. But their path is blocked and our brave friends must battle their way down into the deepest depths where Moka is imprisoned...!

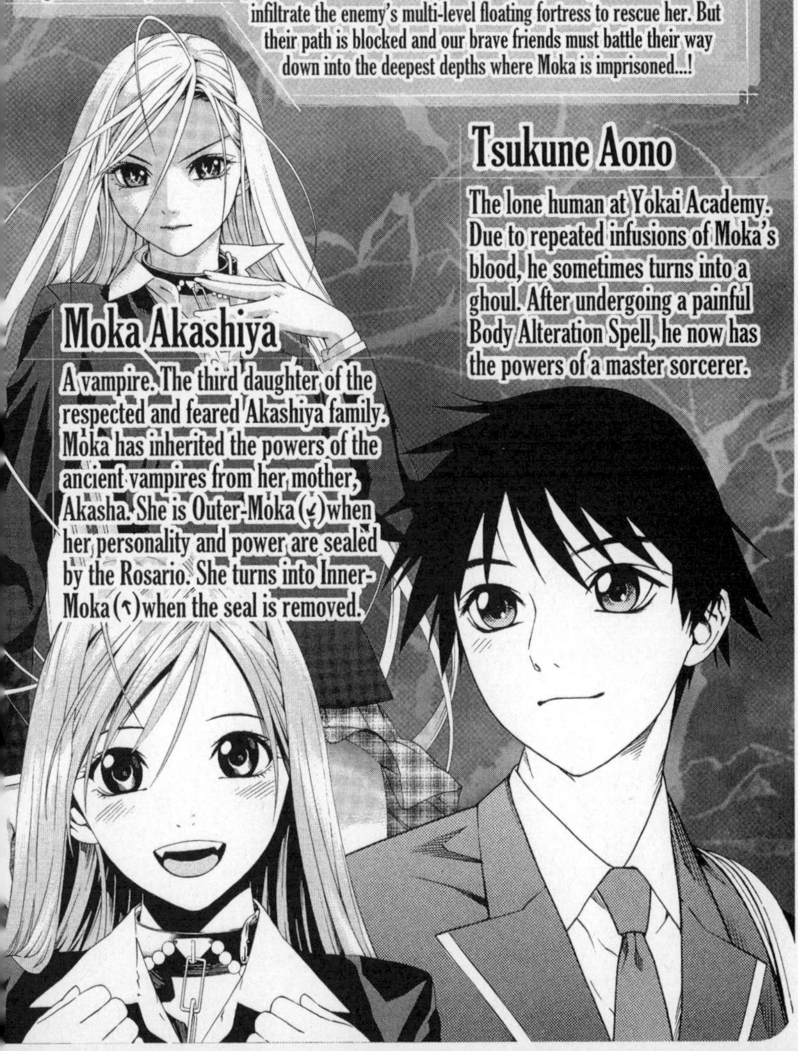

Tsukune Aono

The lone human at Yokai Academy. Due to repeated infusions of Moka's blood, he sometimes turns into a ghoul. After undergoing a painful Body Alteration Spell, he now has the powers of a master sorcerer.

Moka Akashiya

A vampire. The third daughter of the respected and feared Akashiya family. Moka has inherited the powers of the ancient vampires from her mother, Akasha. She is Outer-Moka (↙) when her personality and power are sealed by the Rosario. She turns into Inner-Moka (↖) when the seal is removed.

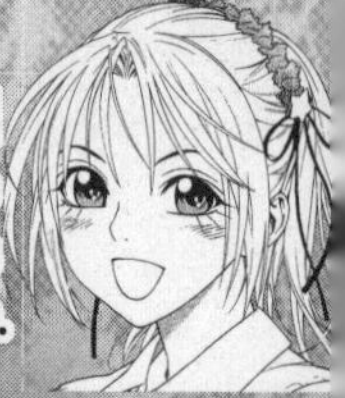

Kurumu Kurono

A succubus. Also adored by all the boys—for two obvious reasons. Fights with Moka over Tsukune.

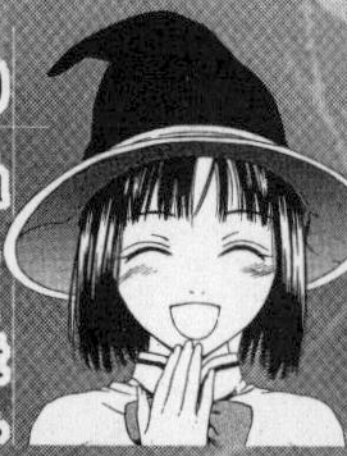

Yukari Sendo

A mischievous witch. Much younger than the others. A genius who skipped several grades. Cute, but has a sharp tongue.

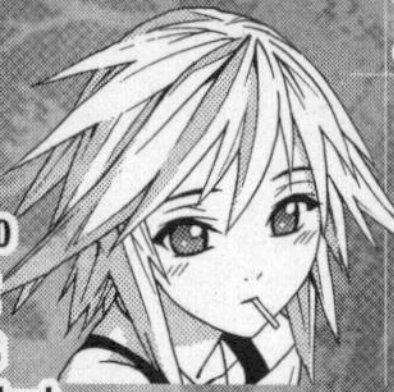

Mizore Shirayuki

A snow fairy who manipul ice. She fell in love with Tsukune after reading his newspaper articles.♡ It s her parents have accepted love for outsider Tsukune.

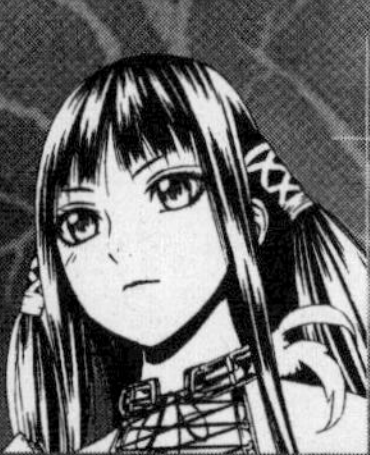

Ruby Tojo

A witch who only learned to trust humans after meeting Tsukune. Now employed as Yokai's headmaster's assistant. A bit of a masochist.

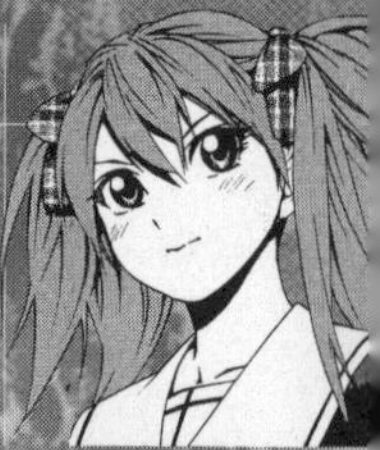

Koko Shuzen

Moka's stubborn little sister. Koko worships Moka's inner vampiric self but hates her sweet exterior. Koko's pet bat transforms into a weapon.

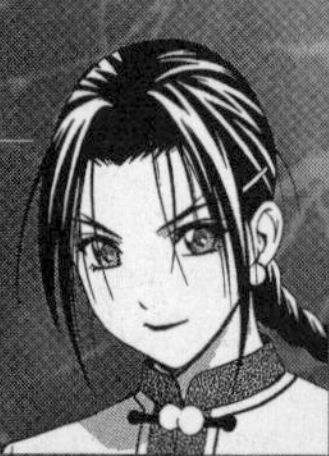

Huang Fangfang

Freshman at Yokai Academy, the only son of a Chinese Mafia family that controls China's most dangerous monsters. Also a "Yasha," a Chinese demon who excels at transformation and sorcery. In awe of Tsukune.

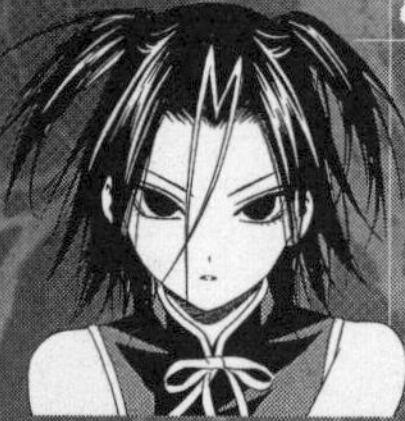

Aqua Shuzen

Moka's elder sister and the eldest daughter. Having lost her mother a a child, she was raised b relatives in China. A mas of Chinese martial arts.

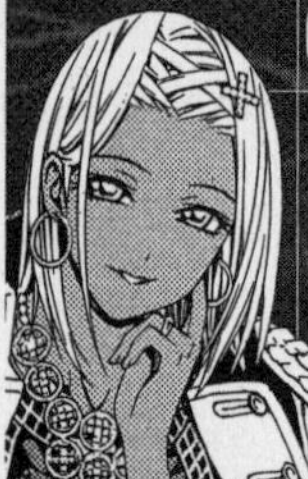

Gyokuro Shuzen

The current head of the Shuzen Family, and Kalua and Koko's birth mother. As the leader of Fairy Tale, she dreams of making chaos reign in the human world. Highly developed detection senses and...an otaku?!

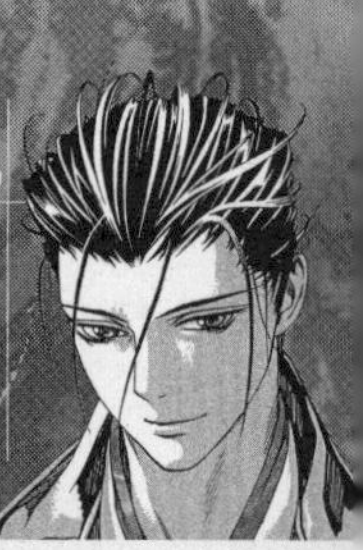

Miyabi Fujisaki

A mysterious executive member of Fairy Tale, a sinister group based in the human world.

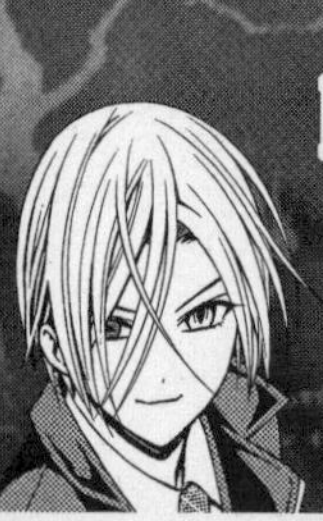

Kiria Yoshi

Tsukune's enemy at Yokai Academy is now a member of Fairy Tale, but acts independently when it suits him.

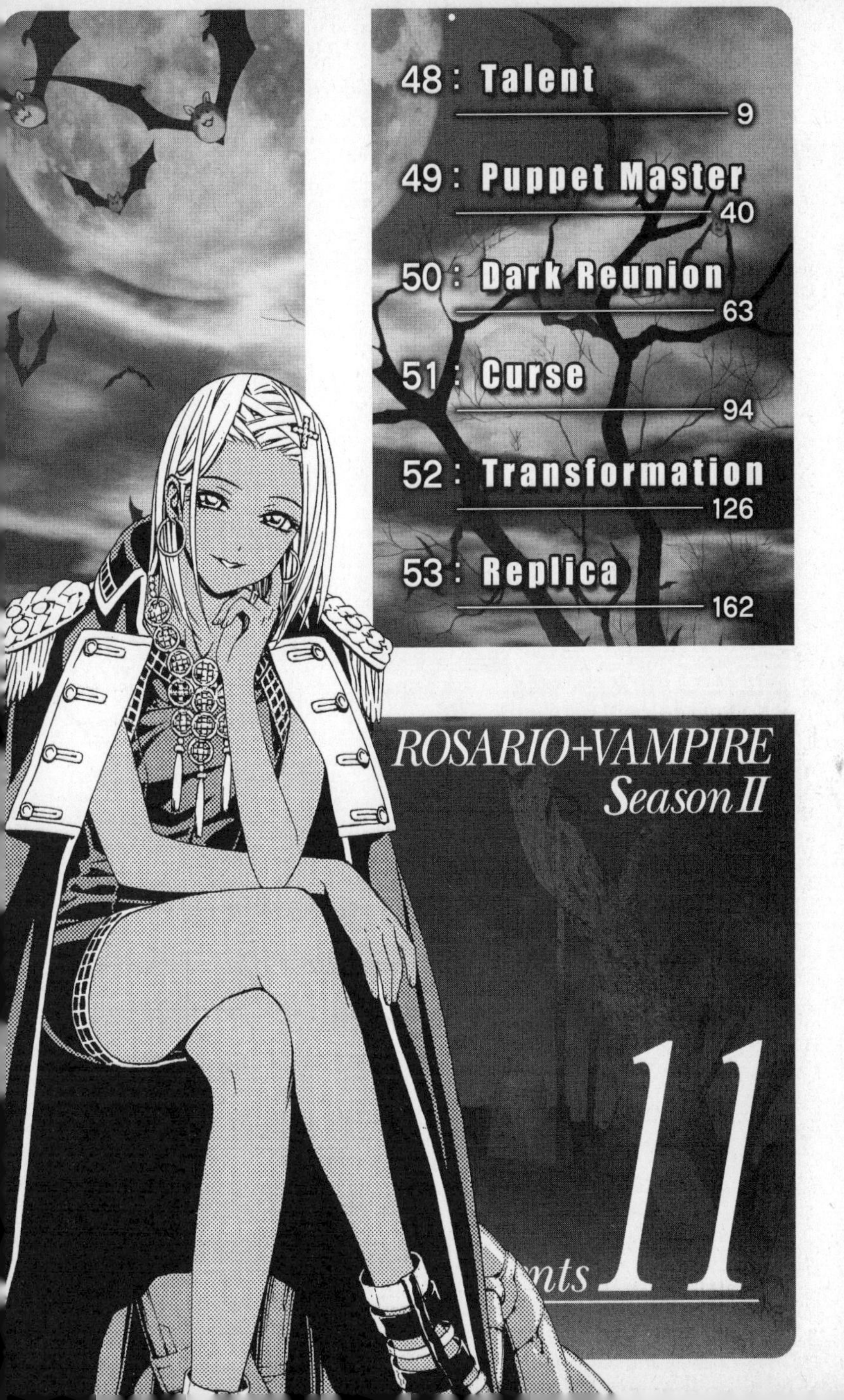

ROSARIO+VAMPIRE
Season II

nts 11

48: Talent

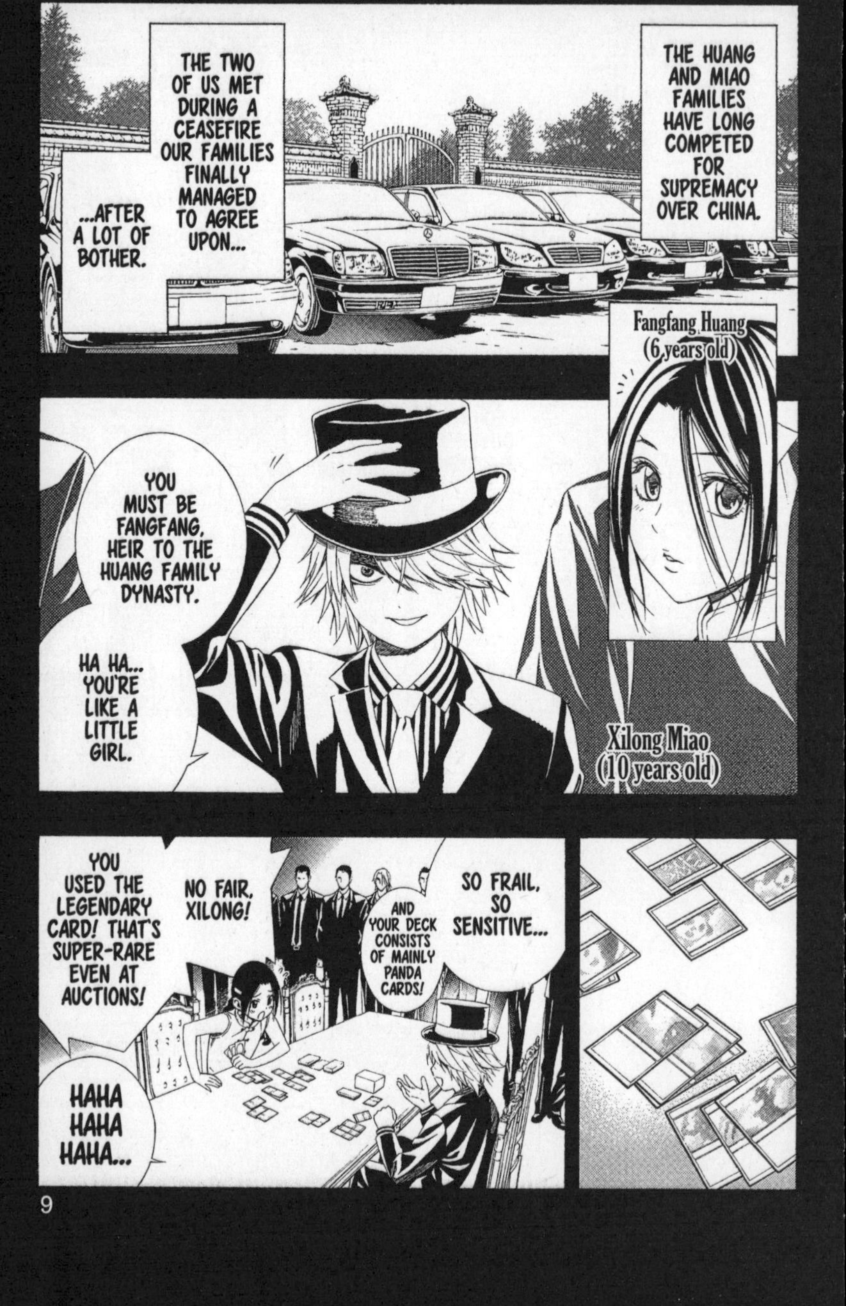
THE HUANG AND MIAO FAMILIES HAVE LONG COMPETED FOR SUPREMACY OVER CHINA.
THE TWO OF US MET DURING A CEASEFIRE OUR FAMILIES FINALLY MANAGED TO AGREE UPON...
...AFTER A LOT OF BOTHER.
Fangfang Huang (6 years old)
YOU MUST BE FANGFANG, HEIR TO THE HUANG FAMILY DYNASTY.
HA HA... YOU'RE LIKE A LITTLE GIRL.
Xilong Miao (10 years old)
SO FRAIL, SO SENSITIVE...
AND YOUR DECK CONSISTS OF MAINLY PANDA CARDS!
NO FAIR, XILONG!
YOU USED THE LEGENDARY CARD! THAT'S SUPER-RARE EVEN AT AUCTIONS!
HAHA HAHA HAHA...

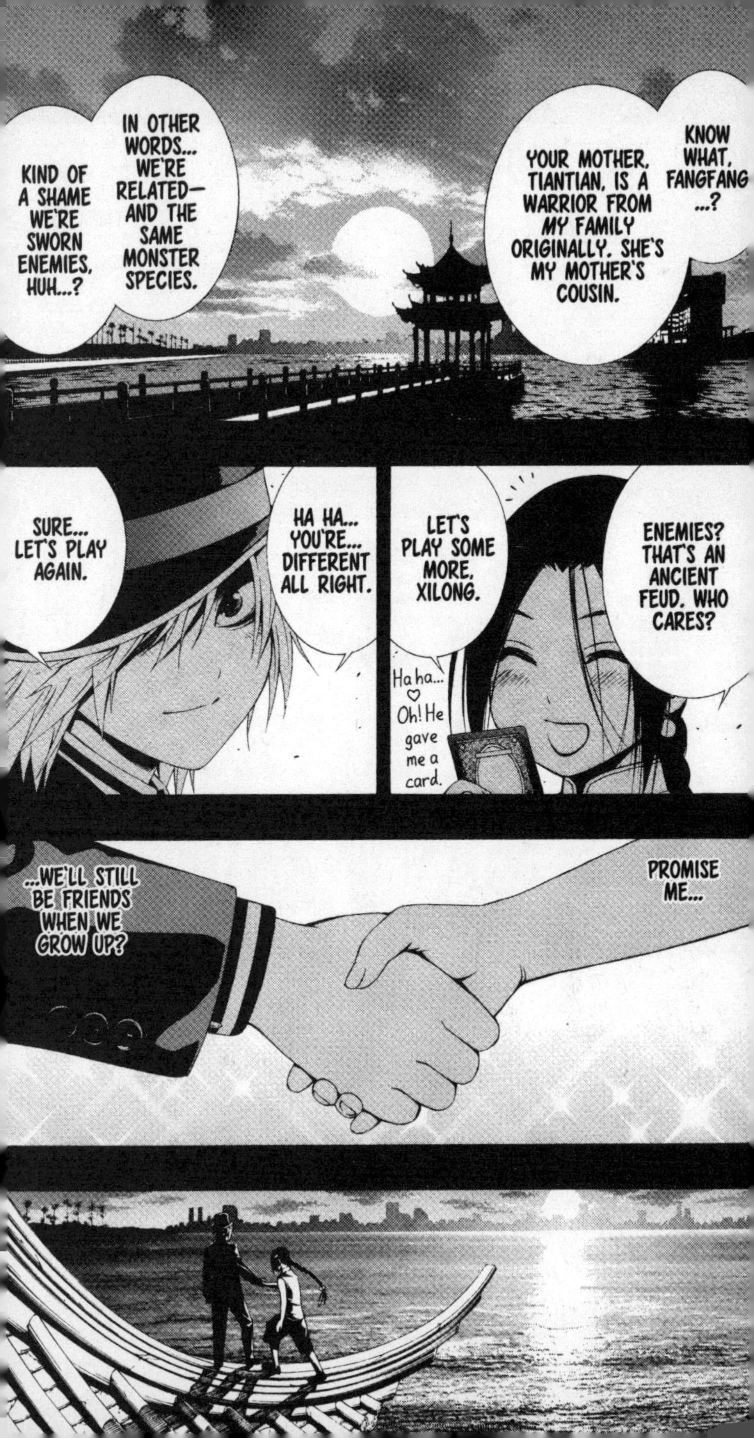
KNOW WHAT, FANGFANG ...?
YOUR MOTHER, TIANTIAN, IS A WARRIOR FROM MY FAMILY ORIGINALLY. SHE'S MY MOTHER'S COUSIN.
IN OTHER WORDS... WE'RE RELATED—AND THE SAME MONSTER SPECIES.
KIND OF A SHAME WE'RE SWORN ENEMIES, HUH...?
ENEMIES? THAT'S AN ANCIENT FEUD. WHO CARES?
LET'S PLAY SOME MORE, XILONG.
Ha ha... ♡ Oh! He gave me a card.
HA HA... YOU'RE... DIFFERENT ALL RIGHT.
SURE... LET'S PLAY AGAIN.
PROMISE ME...
...WE'LL STILL BE FRIENDS WHEN WE GROW UP?

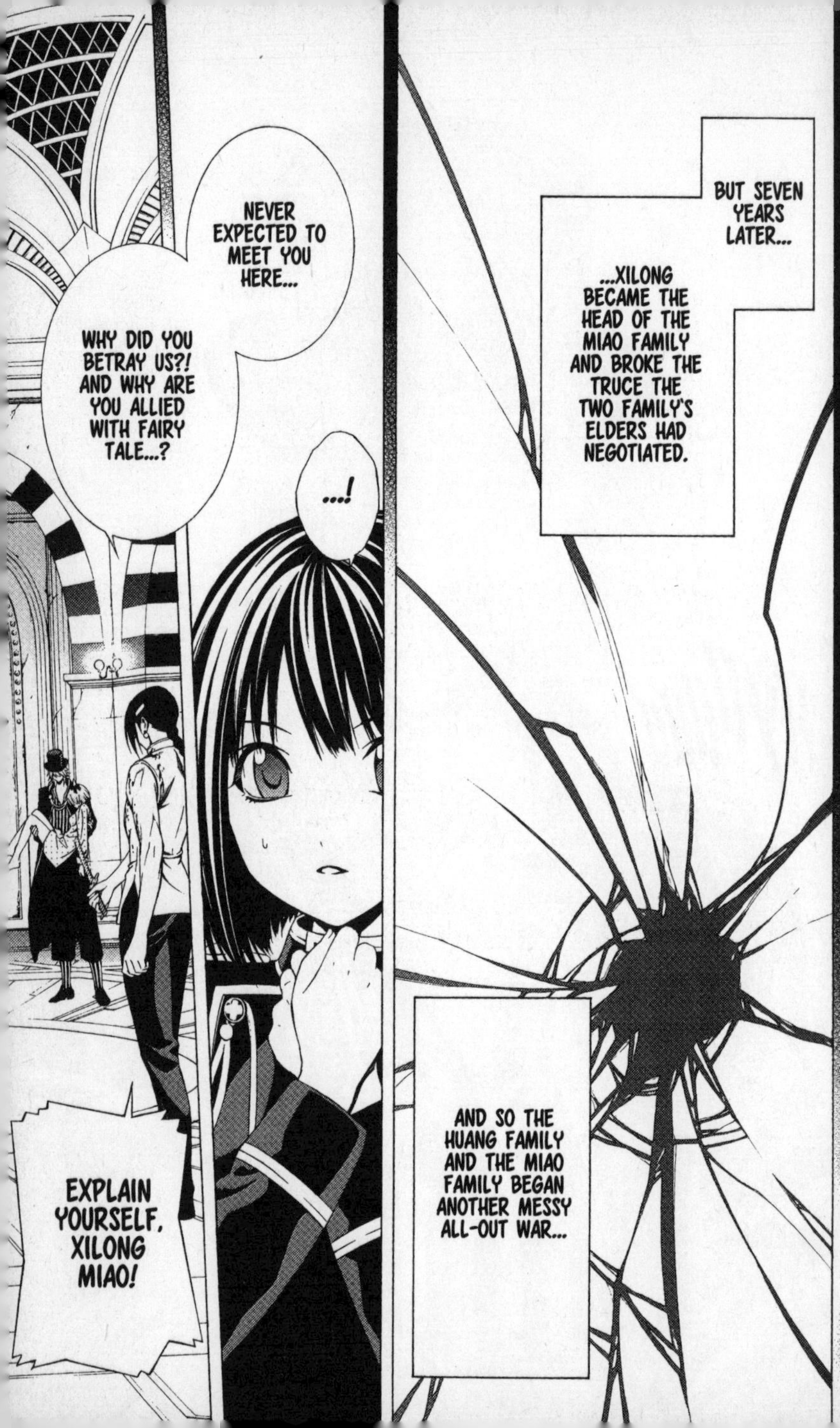
BUT SEVEN YEARS LATER...
...XILONG BECAME THE HEAD OF THE MIAO FAMILY AND BROKE THE TRUCE THE TWO FAMILY'S ELDERS HAD NEGOTIATED.
AND SO THE HUANG FAMILY AND THE MIAO FAMILY BEGAN ANOTHER MESSY ALL-OUT WAR...
NEVER EXPECTED TO MEET YOU HERE...
WHY DID YOU BETRAY US?! AND WHY ARE YOU ALLIED WITH FAIRY TALE...?
...!
EXPLAIN YOURSELF, XILONG MIAO!

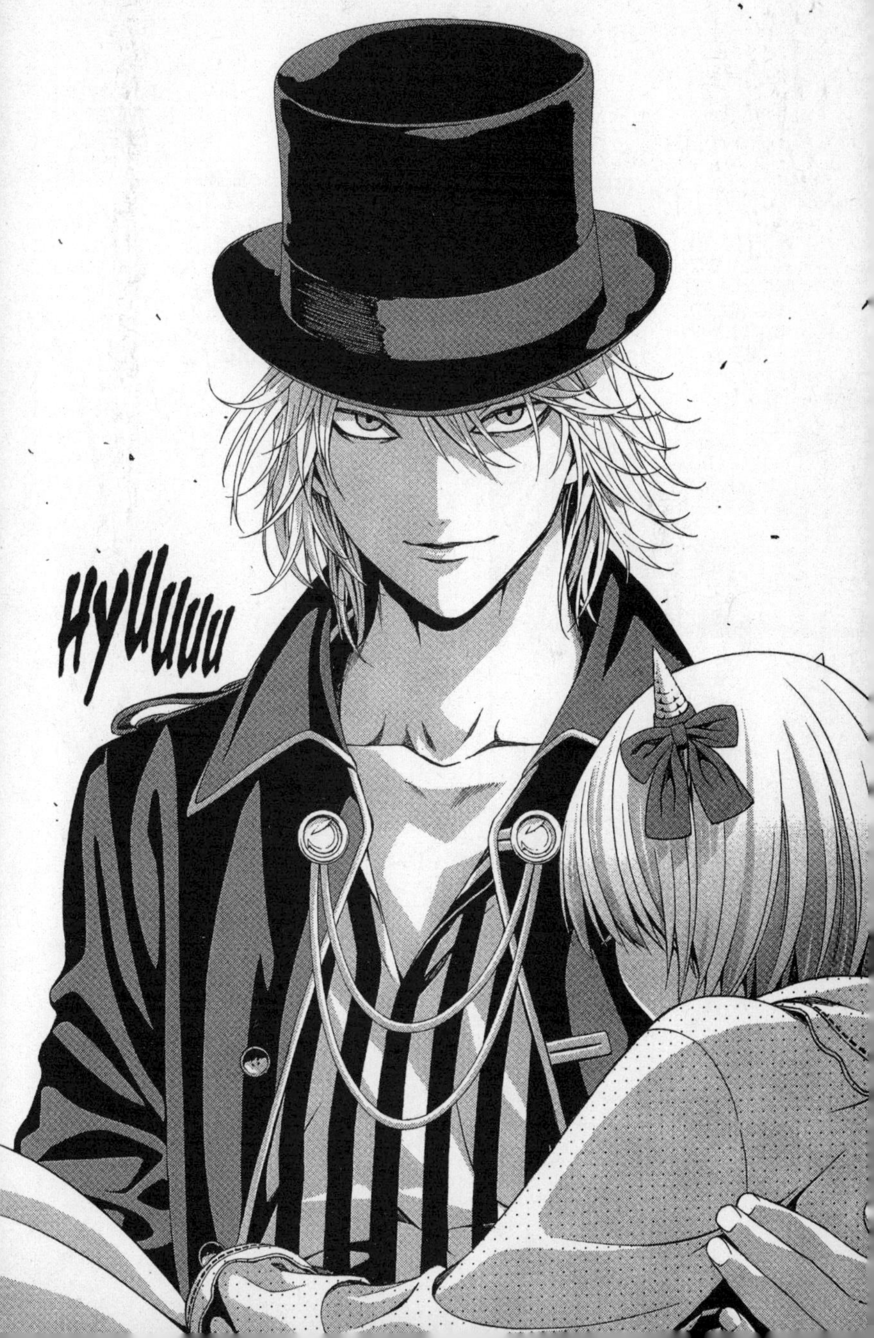
HYUUUU

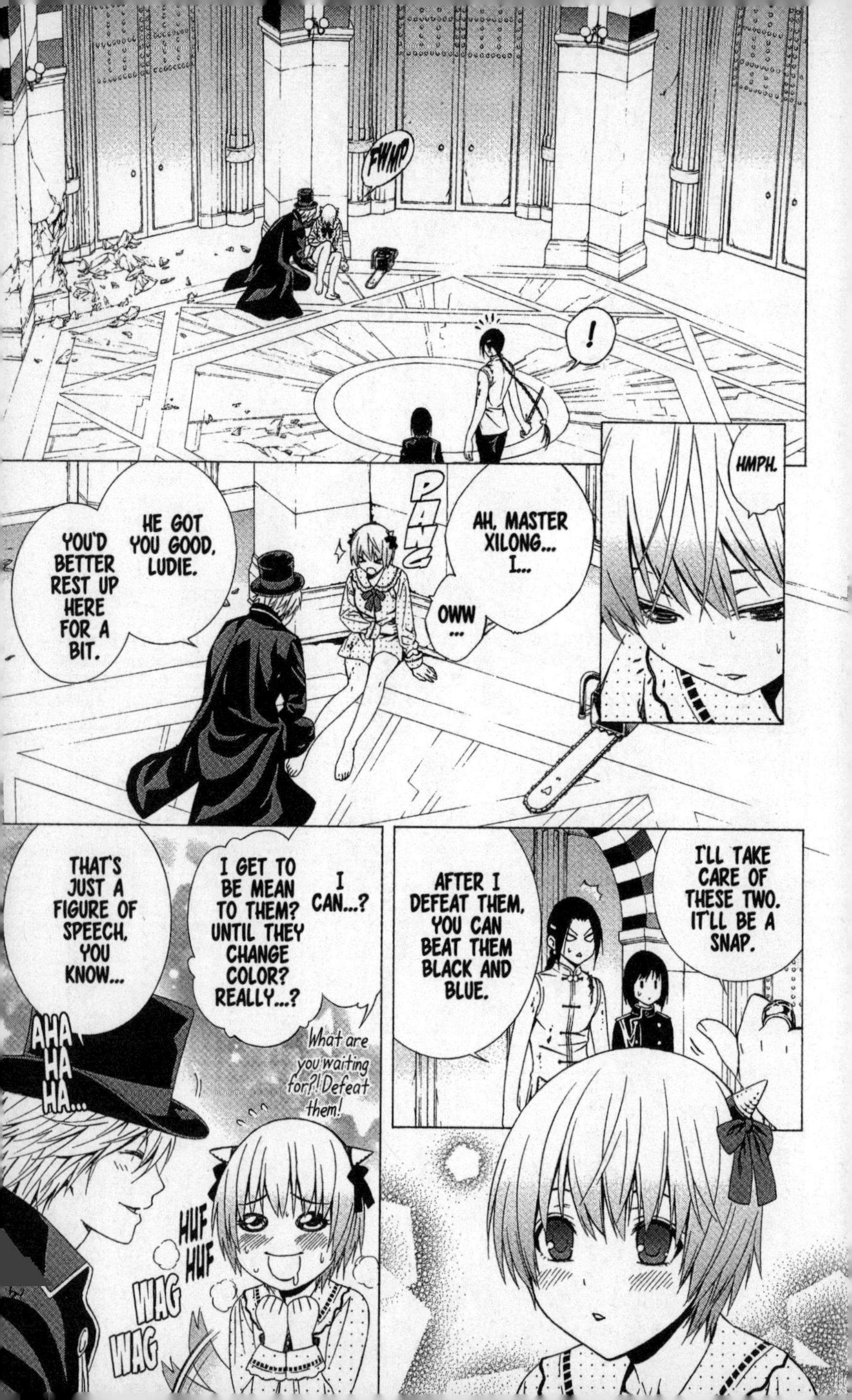

FWMP
!
HMPH.
PANG
AH, MASTER XILONG... I...
OWW...
HE GOT YOU GOOD, LUDIE.
YOU'D BETTER REST UP HERE FOR A BIT.
I'LL TAKE CARE OF THESE TWO. IT'LL BE A SNAP.
AFTER I DEFEAT THEM, YOU CAN BEAT THEM BLACK AND BLUE.
I CAN...?
I GET TO BE MEAN TO THEM? UNTIL THEY CHANGE COLOR? REALLY...?
What are you waiting for?! Defeat them!
THAT'S JUST A FIGURE OF SPEECH, YOU KNOW...
AHA HA HA...
HUF HUF
WAG WAG

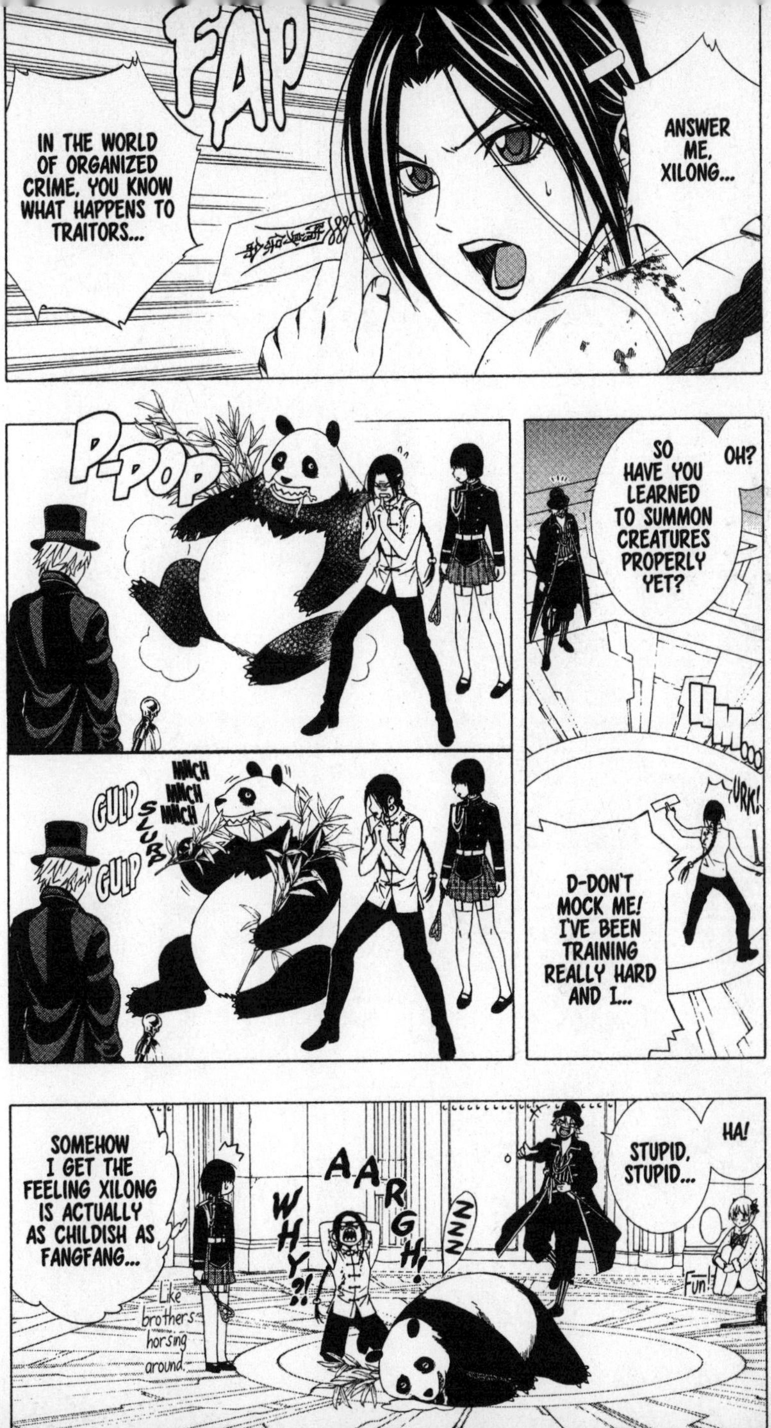
ANSWER ME, XILONG...
FAP
IN THE WORLD OF ORGANIZED CRIME, YOU KNOW WHAT HAPPENS TO TRAITORS...
OH?
SO HAVE YOU LEARNED TO SUMMON CREATURES PROPERLY YET?
UM...
URK!
D-DON'T MOCK ME! I'VE BEEN TRAINING REALLY HARD AND I...
P-POP
MNCH MNCH MNCH
SLURP
GULP
GULP
HA!
STUPID, STUPID...
Fun!
ZZZ
AARGH!
WHY?!
SOMEHOW I GET THE FEELING XILONG IS ACTUALLY AS CHILDISH AS FANGFANG...
Like brothers horsing around.

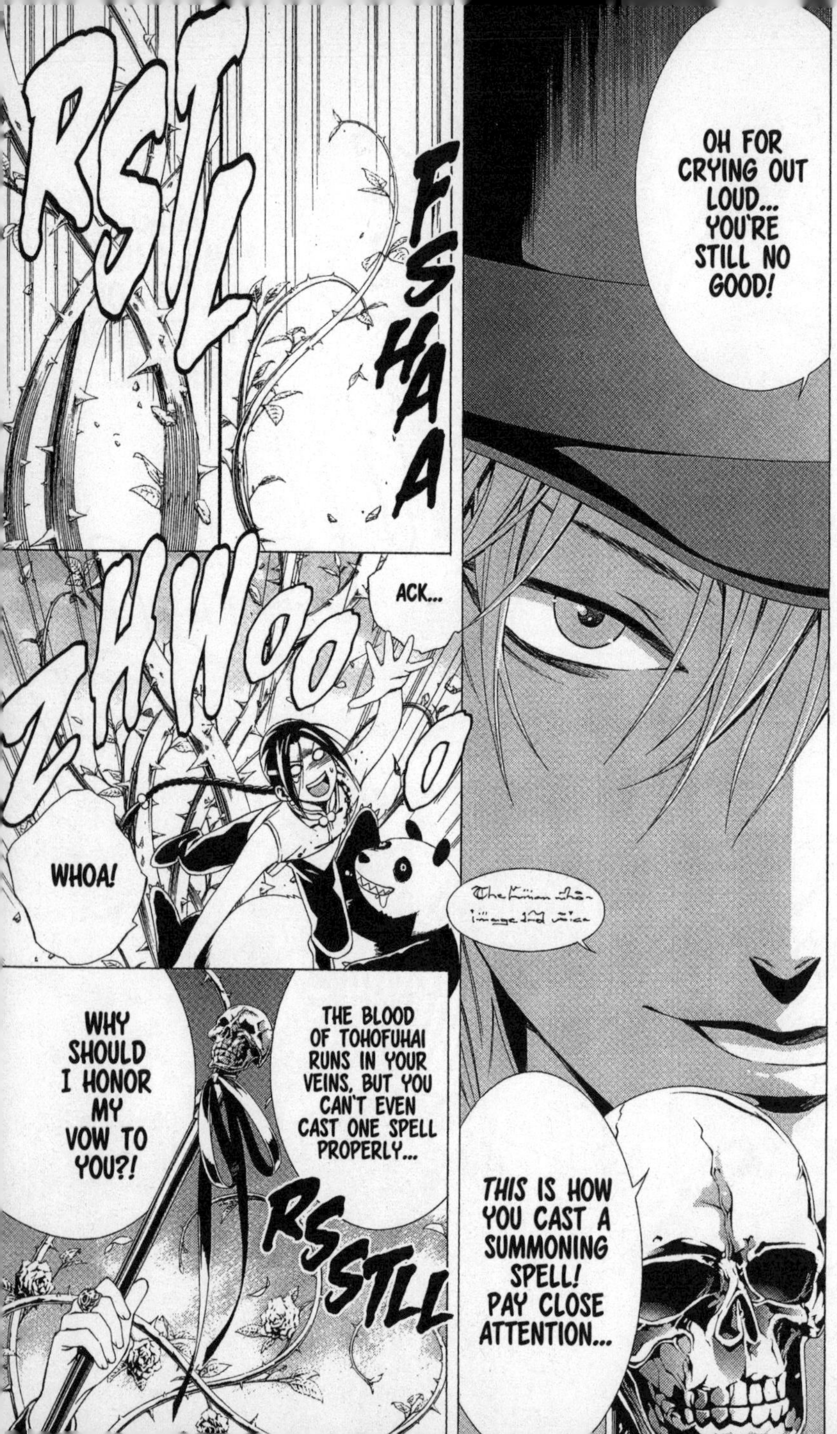
OH FOR CRYING OUT LOUD... YOU'RE STILL NO GOOD!
THIS IS HOW YOU CAST A SUMMONING SPELL! PAY CLOSE ATTENTION...
FSHAAA
RSTL
ACK...
ZHWOOOO
WHOA!
THE BLOOD OF TOHOFUHAI RUNS IN YOUR VEINS, BUT YOU CAN'T EVEN CAST ONE SPELL PROPERLY...
WHY SHOULD I HONOR MY VOW TO YOU?!
RSSTLL

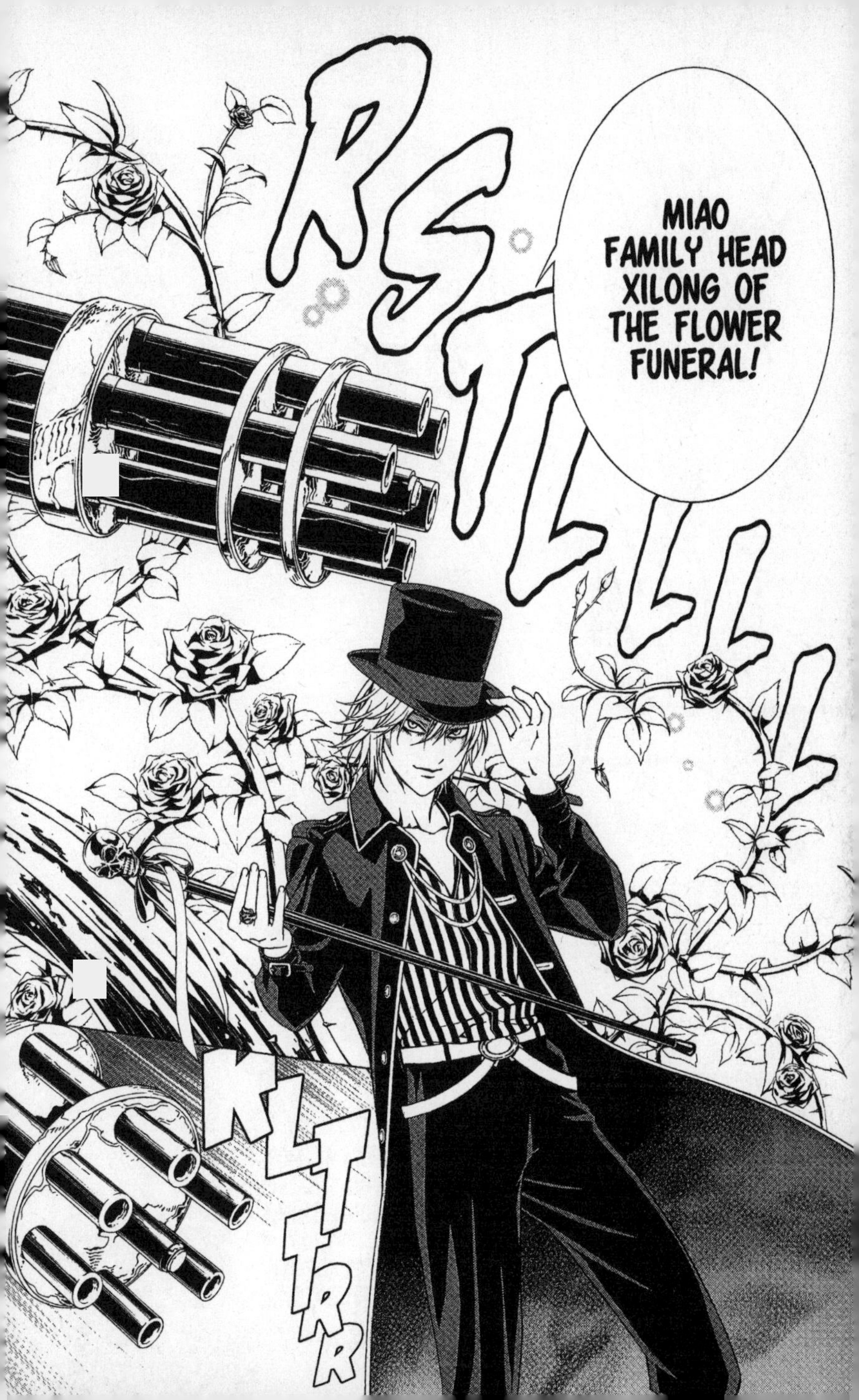
MIAO FAMILY HEAD XILONG OF THE FLOWER FUNERAL!
RSTLLLL
KLTTRR

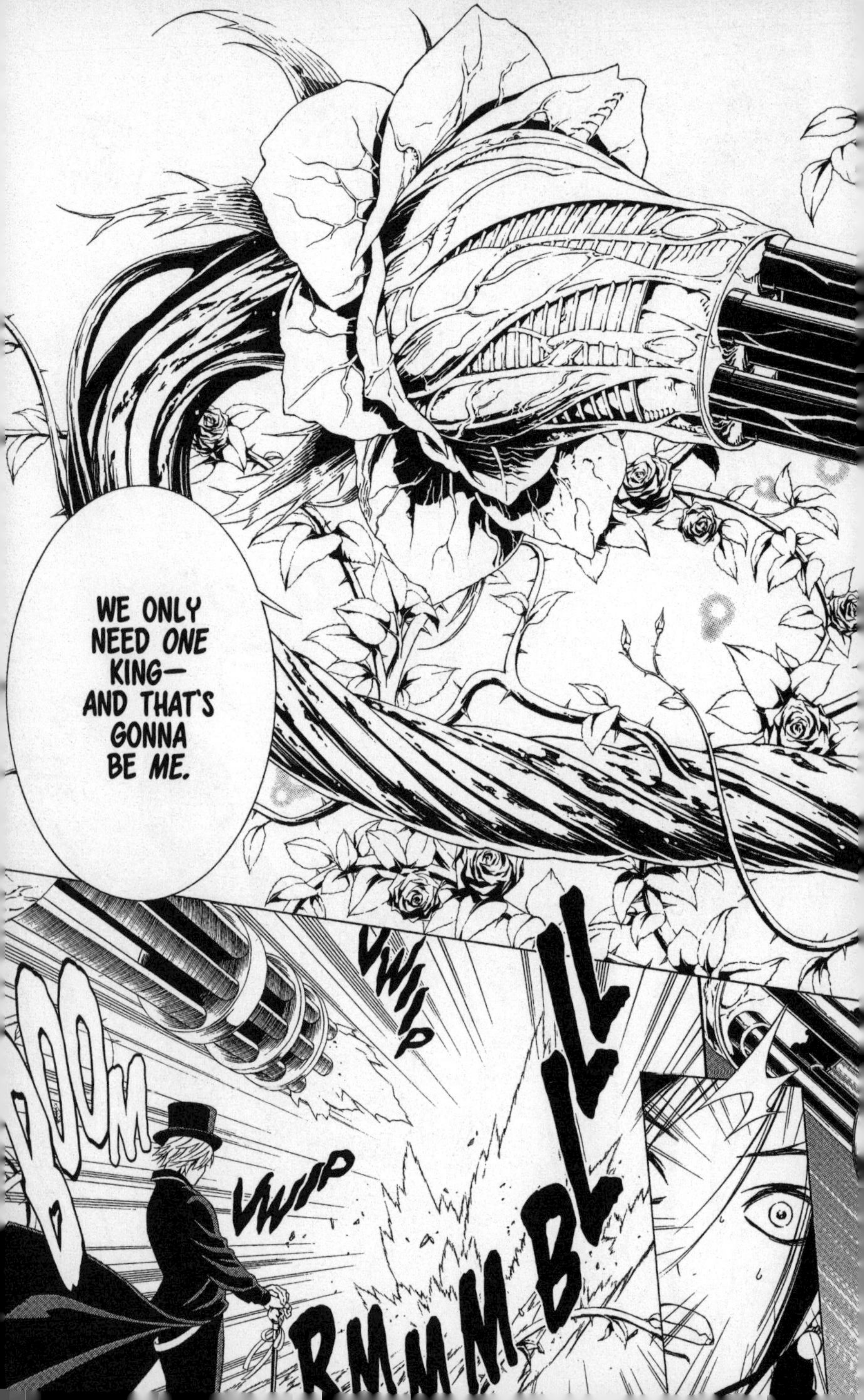
WE ONLY NEED ONE KING— AND THAT'S GONNA BE ME.
RMMMBLLL
VWIP
VWIP
BOOM

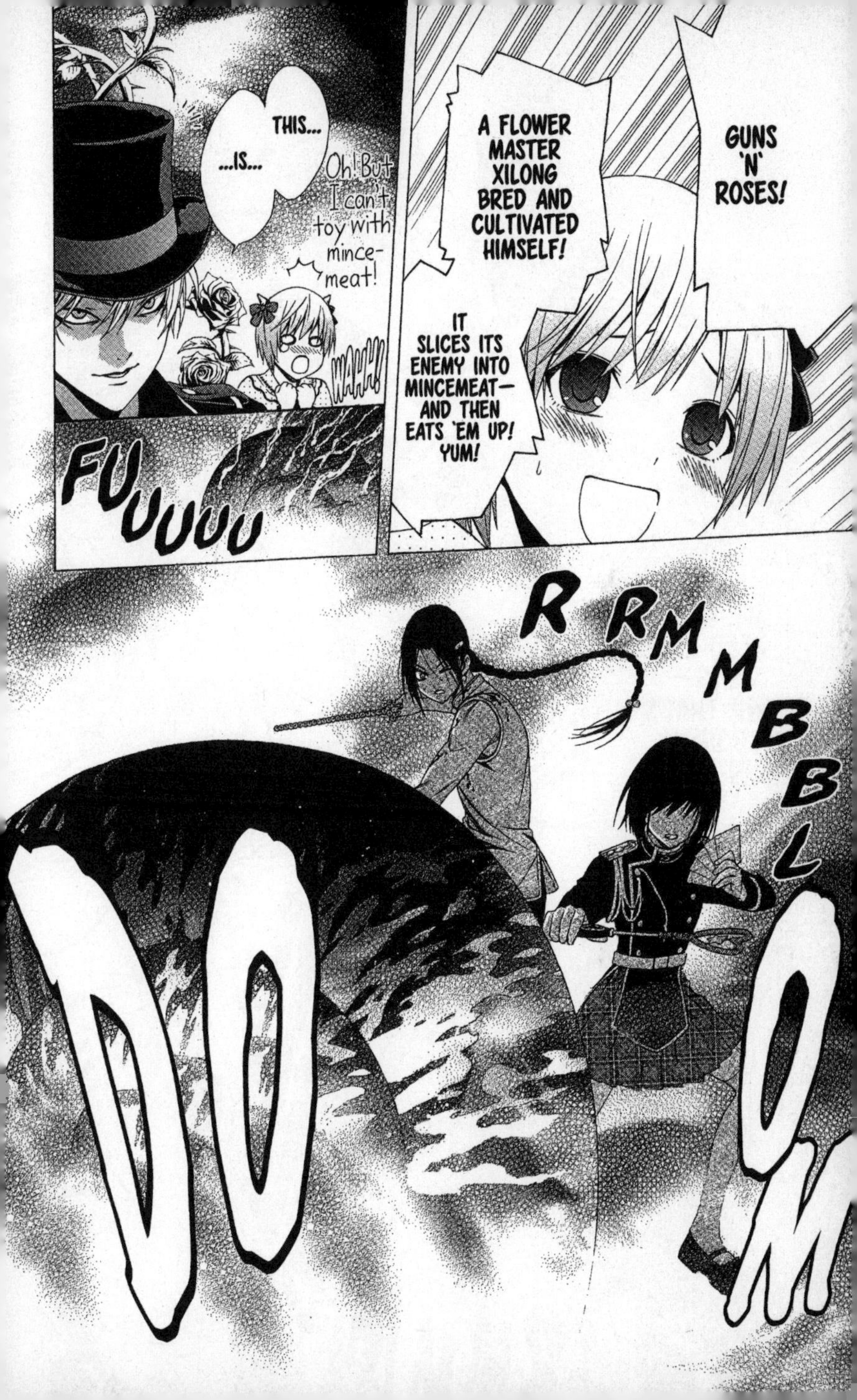
GUNS 'N' ROSES!
A FLOWER MASTER XILONG BRED AND CULTIVATED HIMSELF!
IT SLICES ITS ENEMY INTO MINCEMEAT—AND THEN EATS 'EM UP! YUM!
THIS...
...IS...
Oh! But I can't toy with mince-meat!
WAHH!
FUUUUUU
RRMMBBL
DOOM

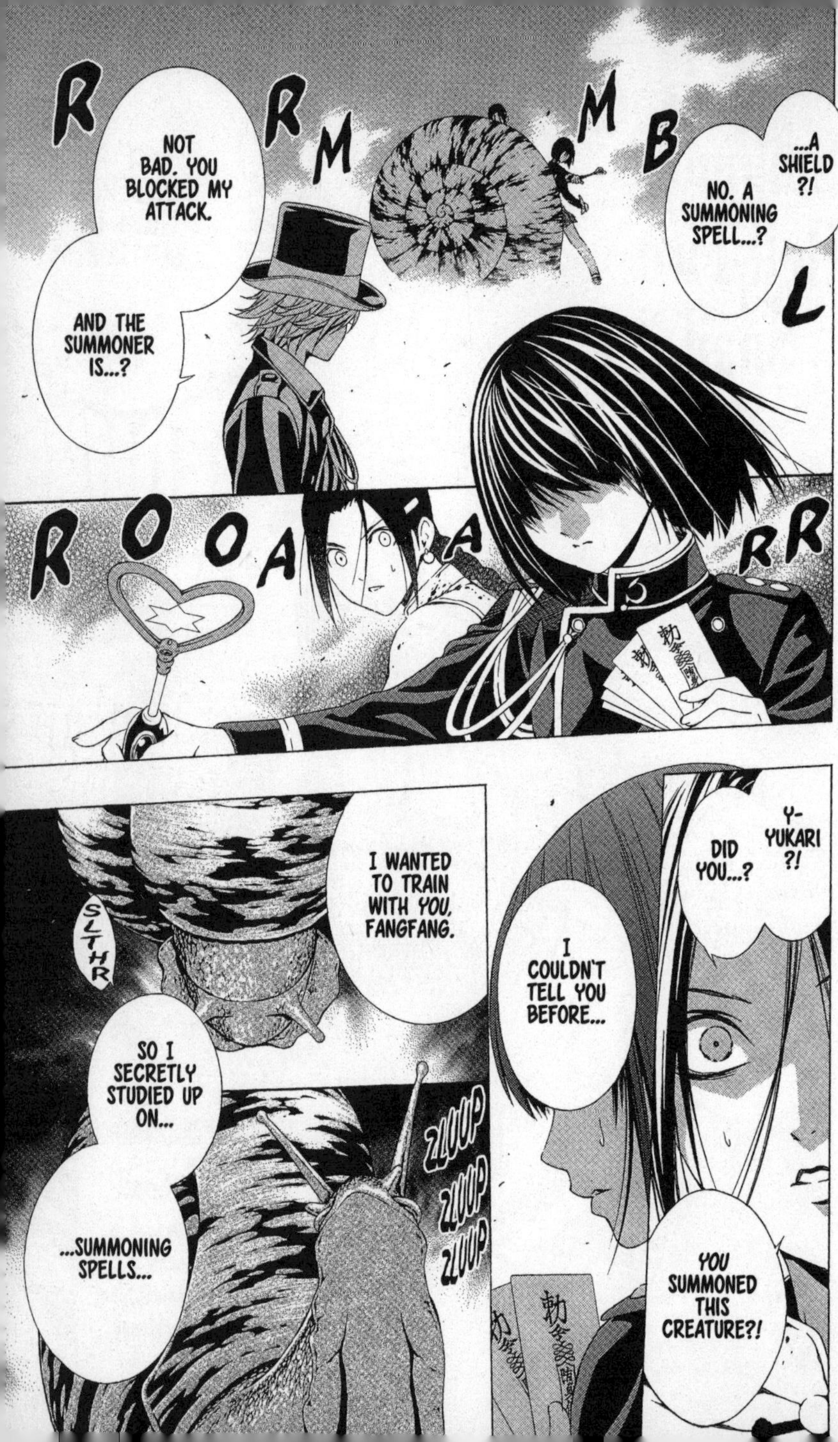
...A SHIELD ?!
NO. A SUMMONING SPELL...?
RRRMMBL
NOT BAD. YOU BLOCKED MY ATTACK.
AND THE SUMMONER IS...?
ROOAARR
Y-YUKARI ?!
DID YOU...?
YOU SUMMONED THIS CREATURE?!
I COULDN'T TELL YOU BEFORE...
I WANTED TO TRAIN WITH *YOU*, FANGFANG.
SLTHR
SO I SECRETLY STUDIED UP ON...
ZLUUP ZLUUP ZLUUP
...SUMMONING SPELLS...

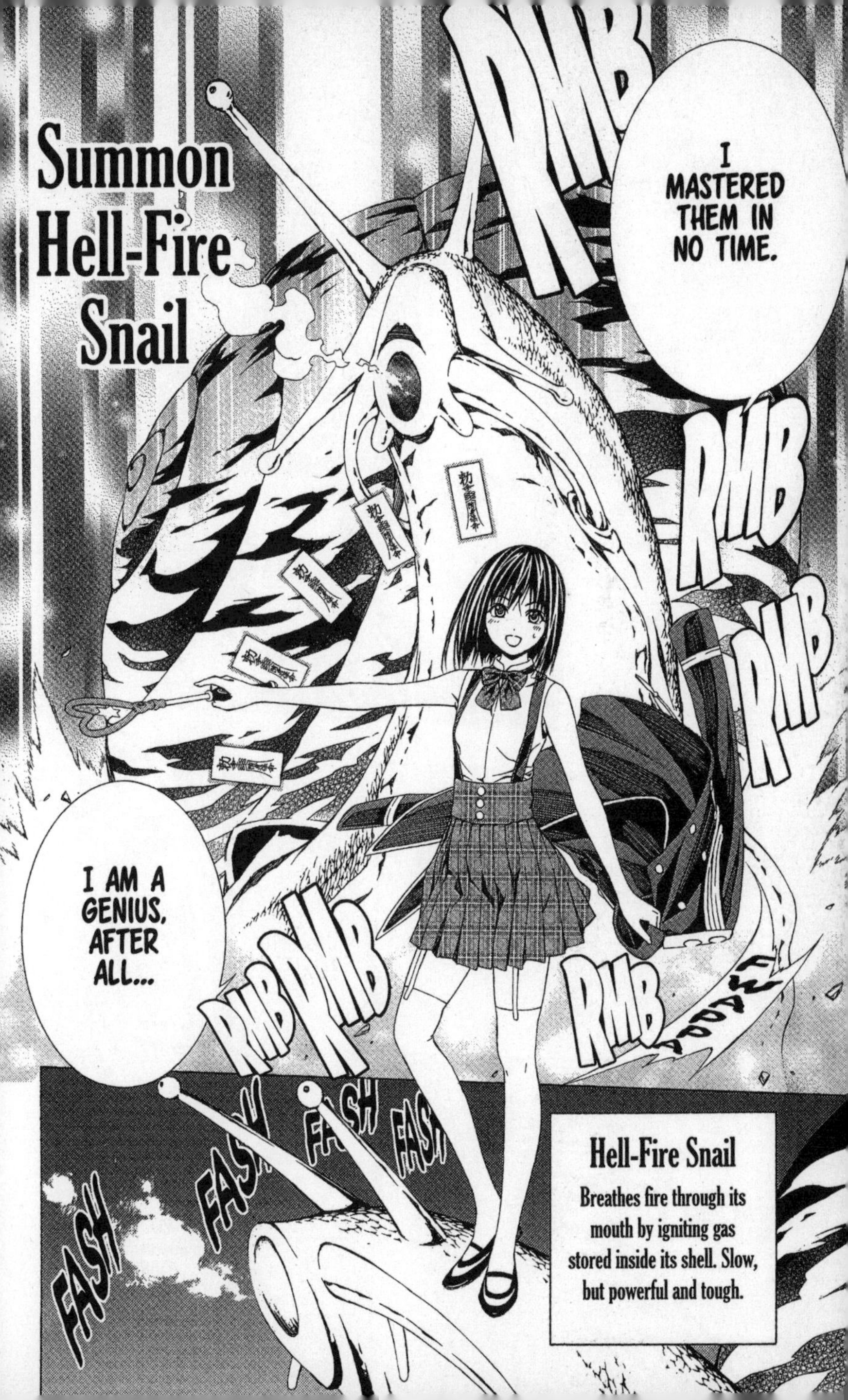

RMB
I MASTERED THEM IN NO TIME.
Summon Hell-Fire Snail
RMB
RMB
RMB
I AM A GENIUS, AFTER ALL...
RMB
RMB
RMB
Hell-Fire Snail
Breathes fire through its mouth by igniting gas stored inside its shell. Slow, but powerful and tough.
FASH
FASH
FASH
FASH

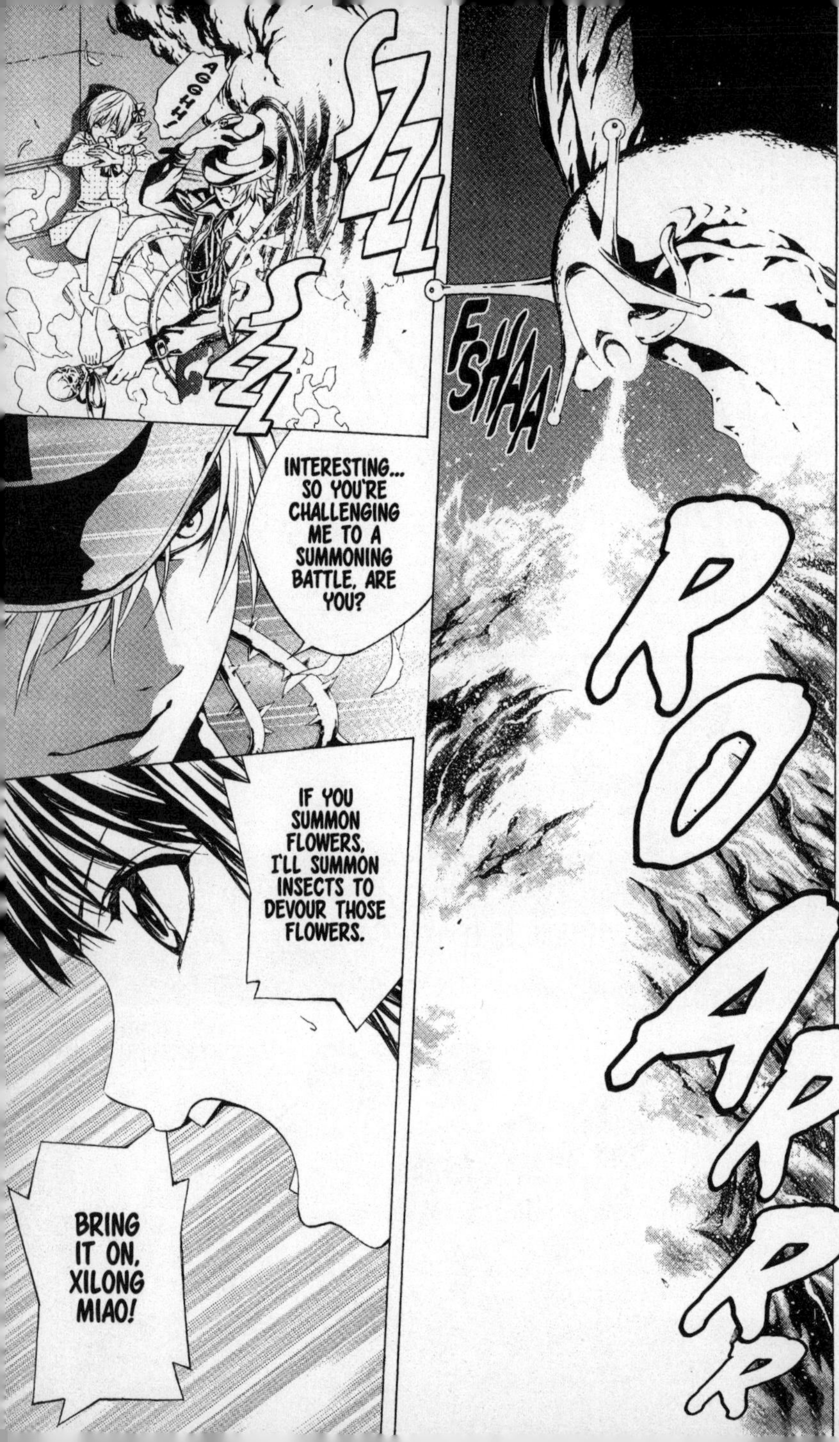

FSHAA
ROARRRR
AGGHH!
SZZZ
SZZZ
INTERESTING... SO YOU'RE CHALLENGING ME TO A SUMMONING BATTLE, ARE YOU?
IF YOU SUMMON FLOWERS, I'LL SUMMON INSECTS TO DEVOUR THOSE FLOWERS.
BRING IT ON, XILONG MIAO!

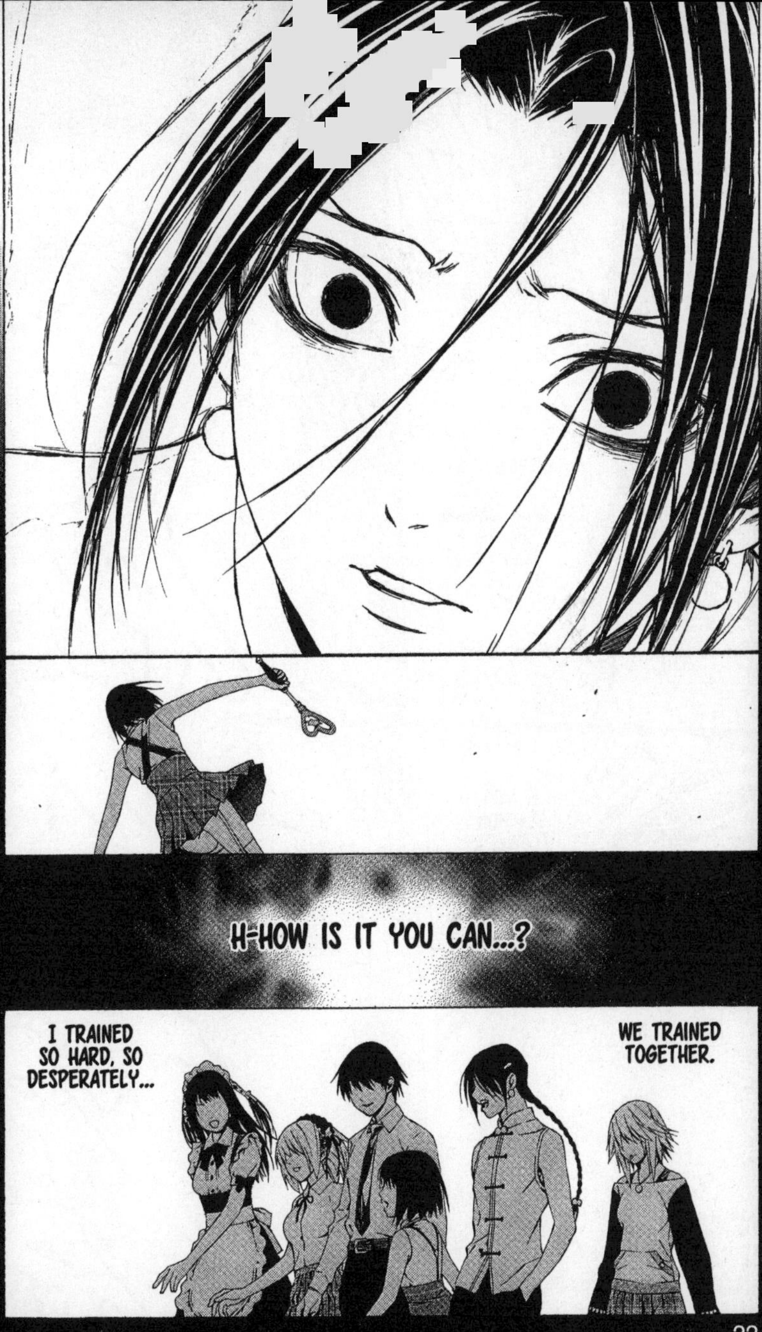
H-HOW IS IT YOU CAN...?
WE TRAINED TOGETHER.
I TRAINED SO HARD, SO DESPERATELY...

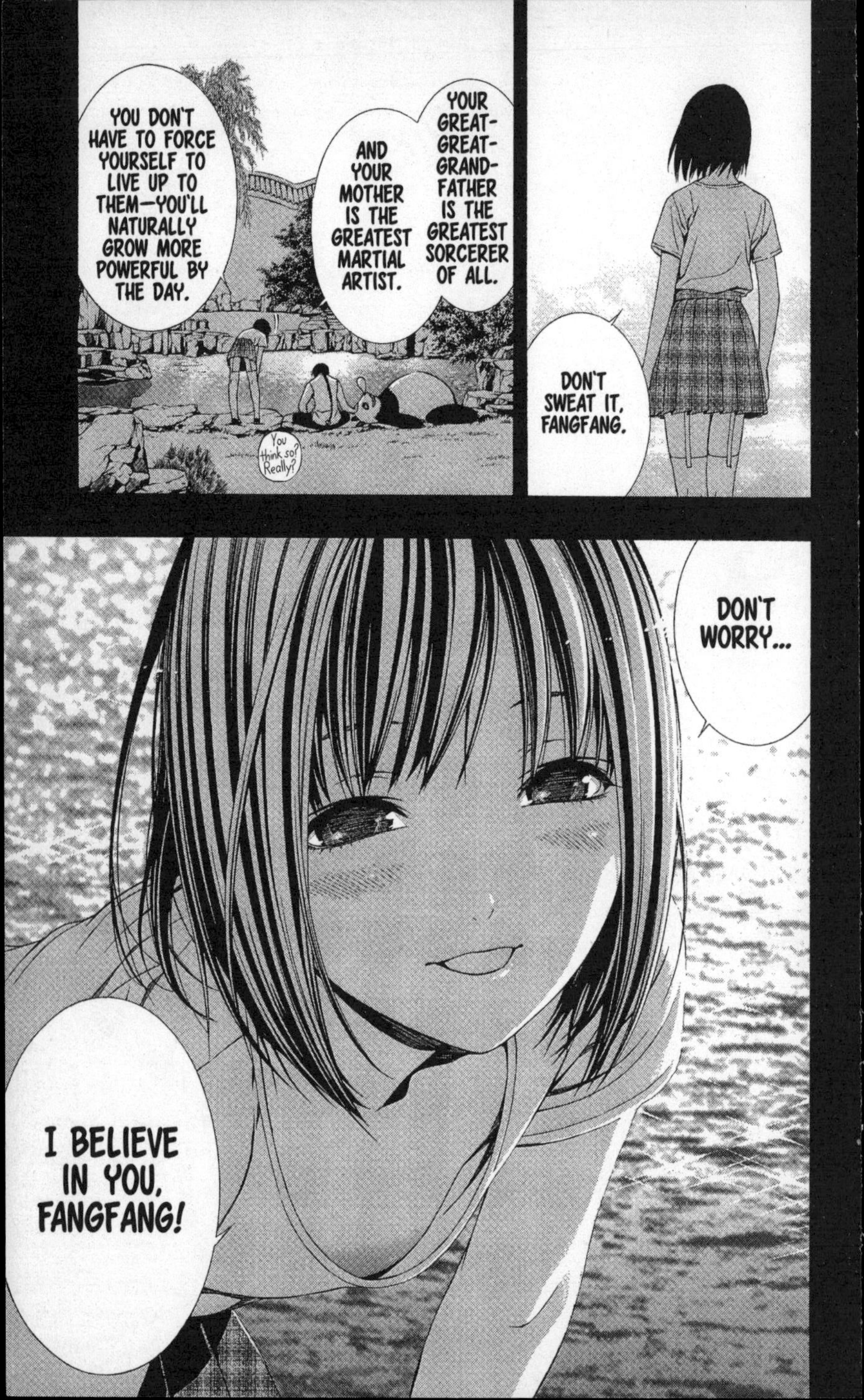
DON'T SWEAT IT, FANGFANG.
YOUR GREAT-GREAT-GRANDFATHER IS THE GREATEST SORCERER OF ALL.
AND YOUR MOTHER IS THE GREATEST MARTIAL ARTIST.
YOU DON'T HAVE TO FORCE YOURSELF TO LIVE UP TO THEM—YOU'LL NATURALLY GROW MORE POWERFUL BY THE DAY.
You think so? Really?
DON'T WORRY...
I BELIEVE IN YOU, FANGFANG!

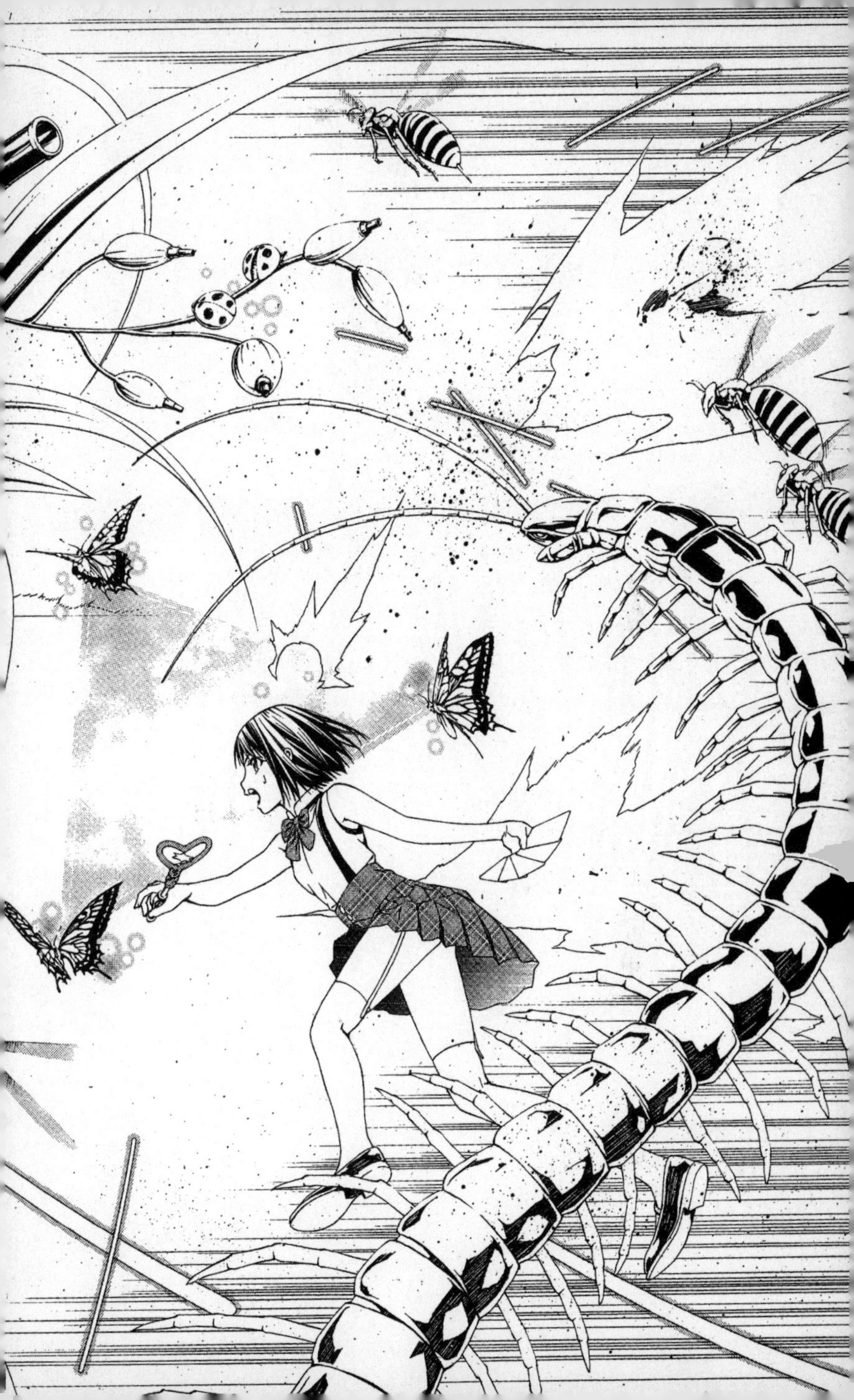

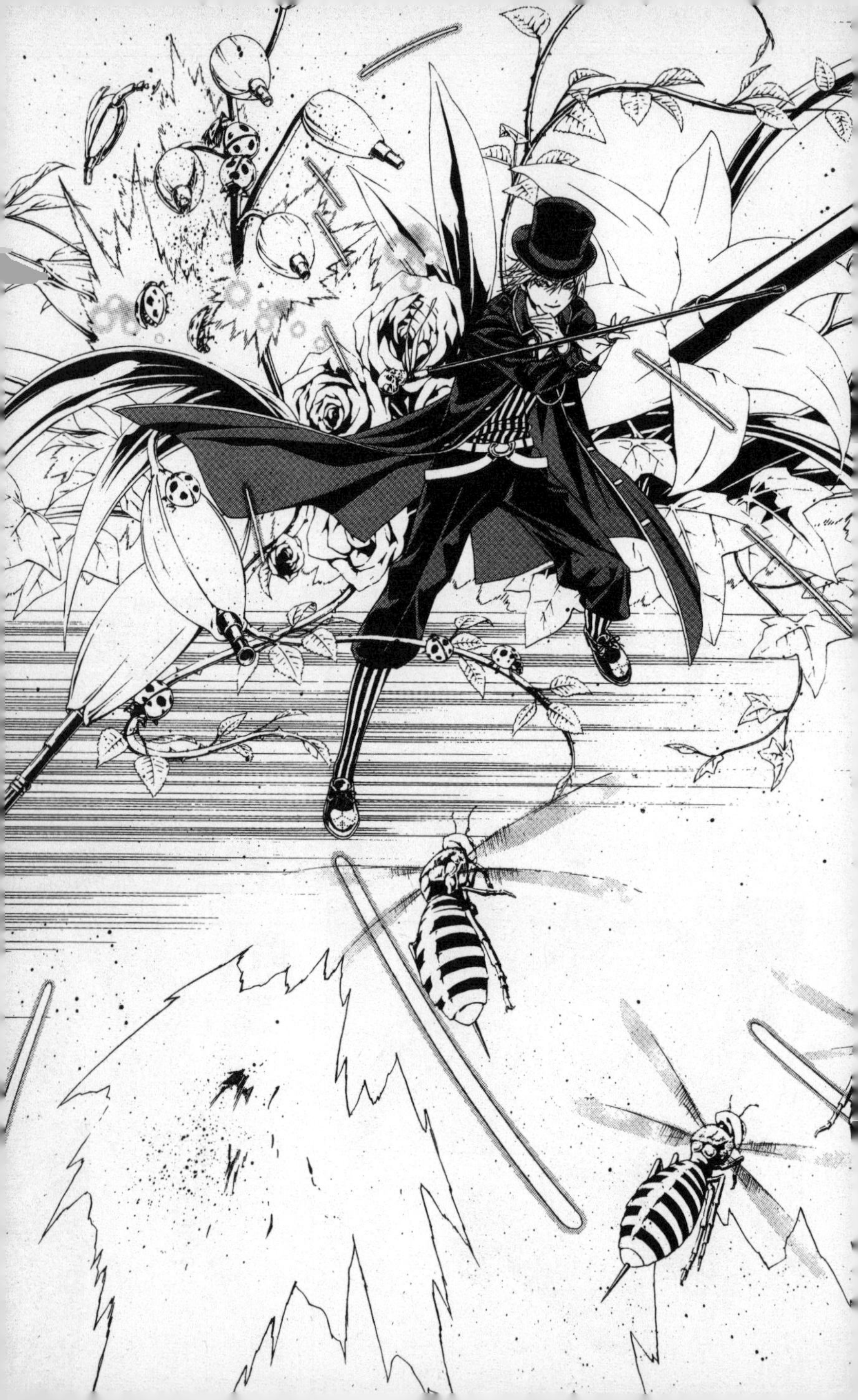

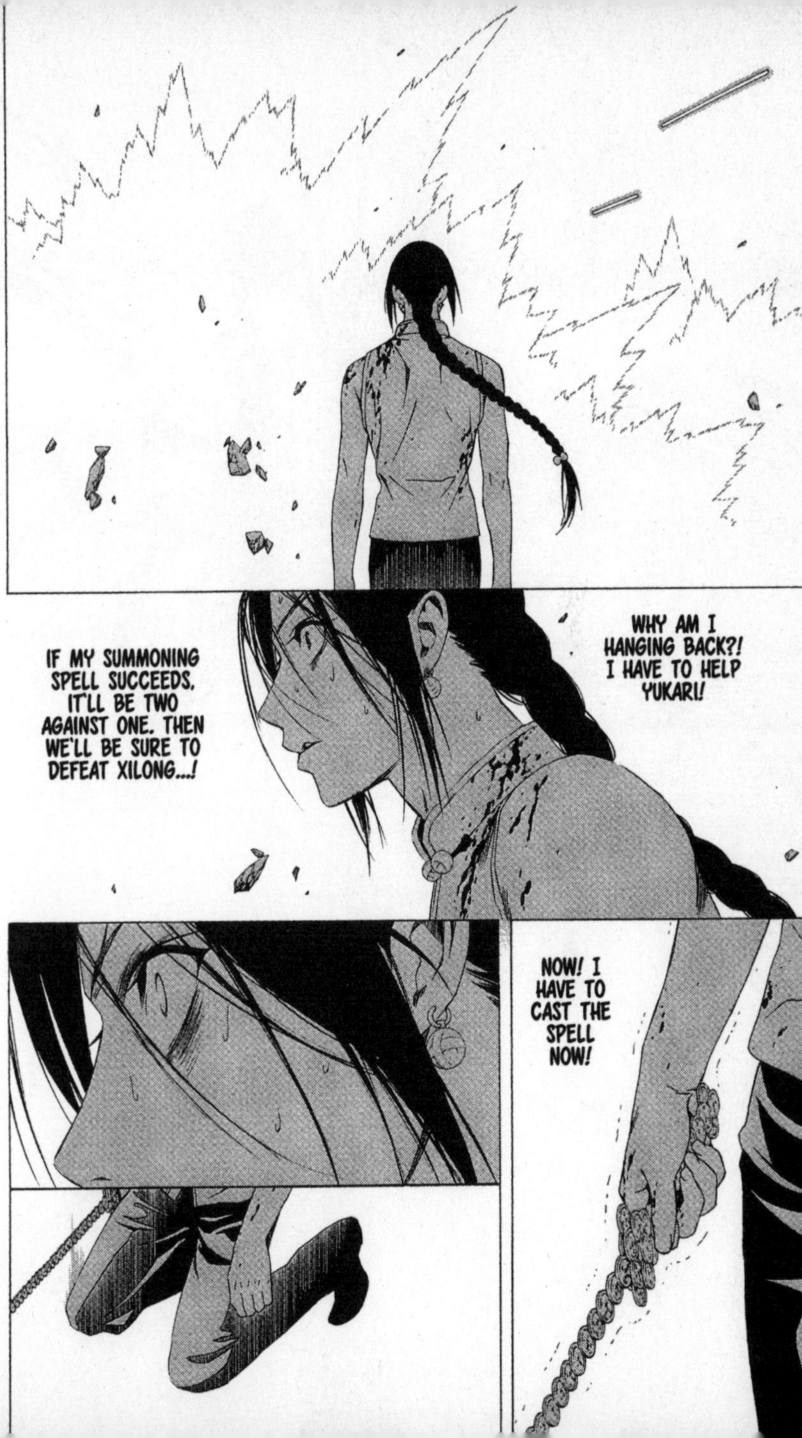
WHY AM I HANGING BACK?! I HAVE TO HELP YUKARI!
IF MY SUMMONING SPELL SUCCEEDS, IT'LL BE TWO AGAINST ONE. THEN WE'LL BE SURE TO DEFEAT XILONG...!
NOW! I HAVE TO CAST THE SPELL NOW!

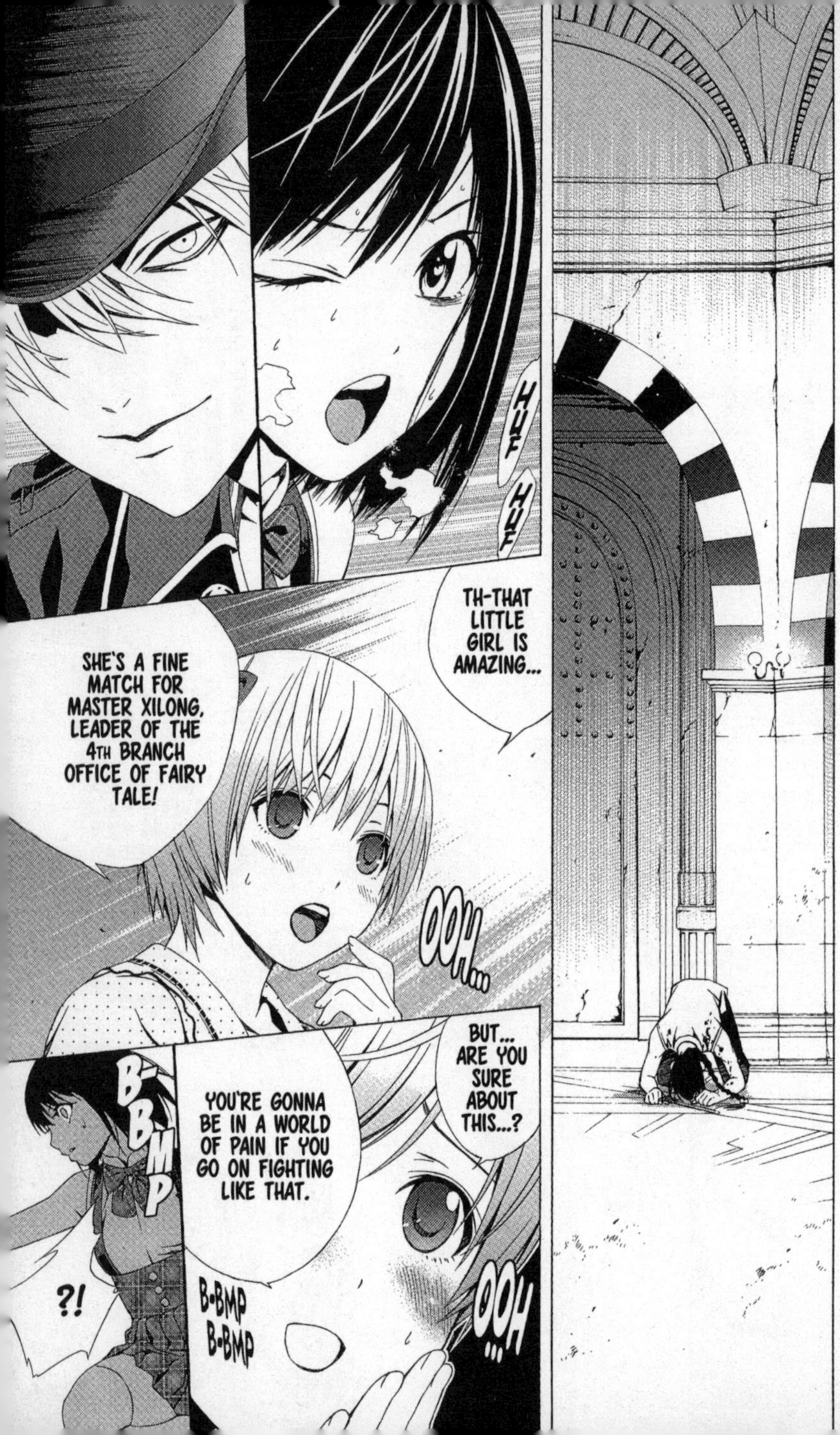
HUF HUF
TH-THAT LITTLE GIRL IS AMAZING...
SHE'S A FINE MATCH FOR MASTER XILONG, LEADER OF THE 4TH BRANCH OFFICE OF FAIRY TALE!
OOH...
BUT... ARE YOU SURE ABOUT THIS...?
YOU'RE GONNA BE IN A WORLD OF PAIN IF YOU GO ON FIGHTING LIKE THAT.
OOH...
B-BMP B-BMP
B-BMP
?!

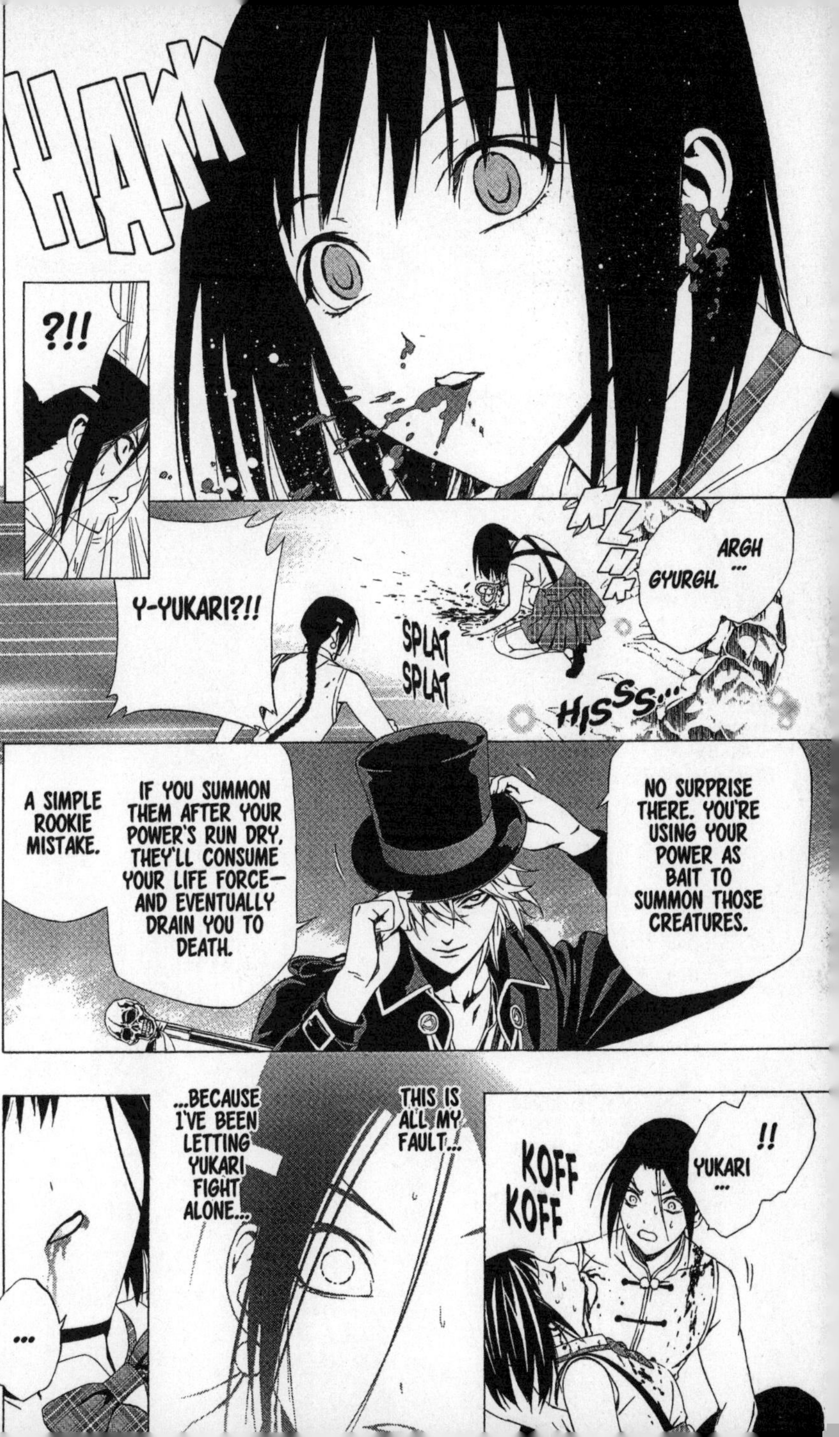
HAKK
?!!
ARGH... GYURGH.
KLINK
HISSS...
SPLAT SPLAT
Y-YUKARI?!!
NO SURPRISE THERE. YOU'RE USING YOUR POWER AS BAIT TO SUMMON THOSE CREATURES.
IF YOU SUMMON THEM AFTER YOUR POWER'S RUN DRY, THEY'LL CONSUME YOUR LIFE FORCE— AND EVENTUALLY DRAIN YOU TO DEATH.
A SIMPLE ROOKIE MISTAKE.
!!
YUKARI...
KOFF KOFF
THIS IS ALL MY FAULT...
...BECAUSE I'VE BEEN LETTING YUKARI FIGHT ALONE...
...

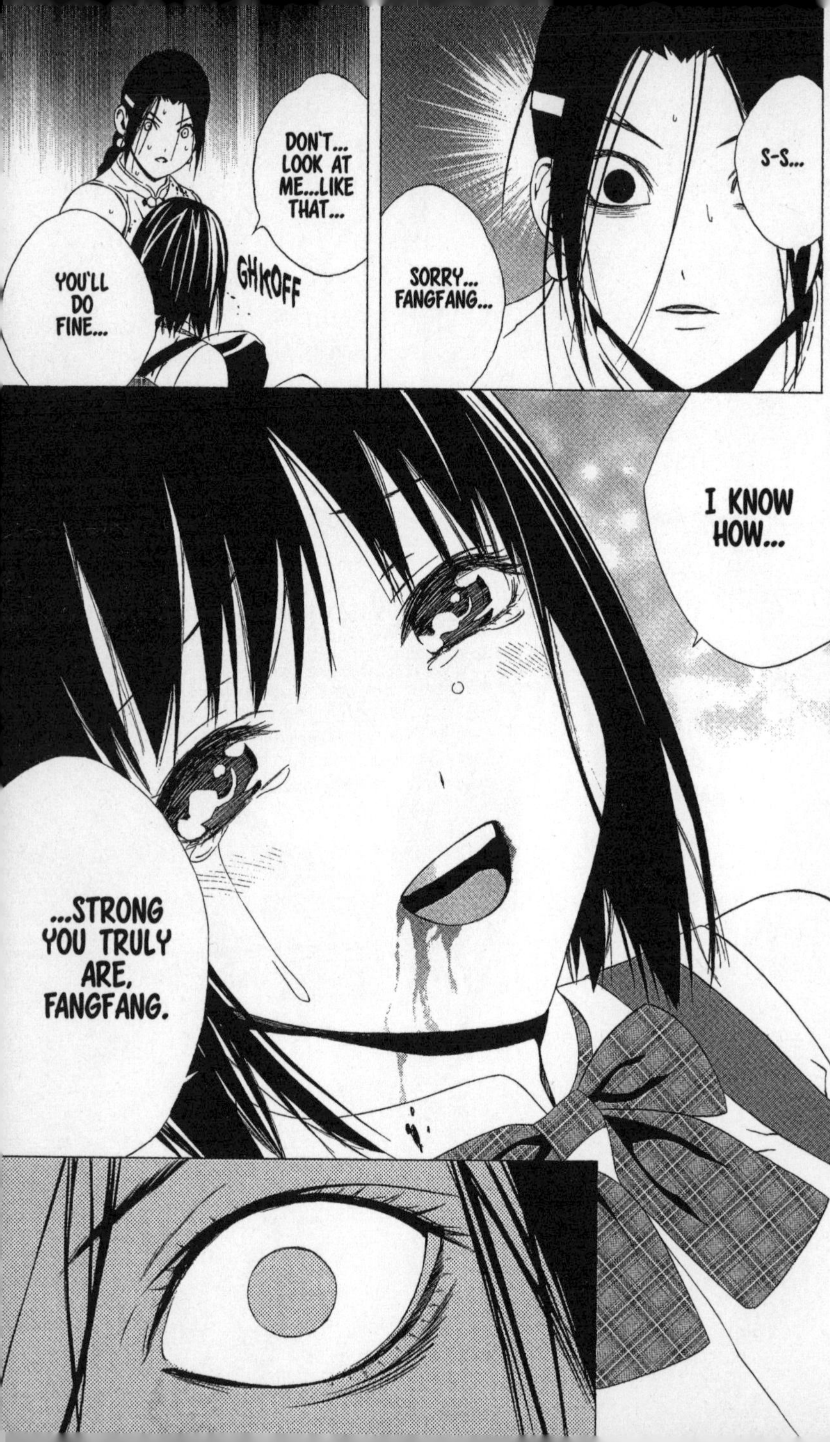
S-S...
SORRY... FANGFANG...
DON'T... LOOK AT ME...LIKE THAT...
GHKOFF
YOU'LL DO FINE...
I KNOW HOW...
...STRONG YOU TRULY ARE, FANGFANG.

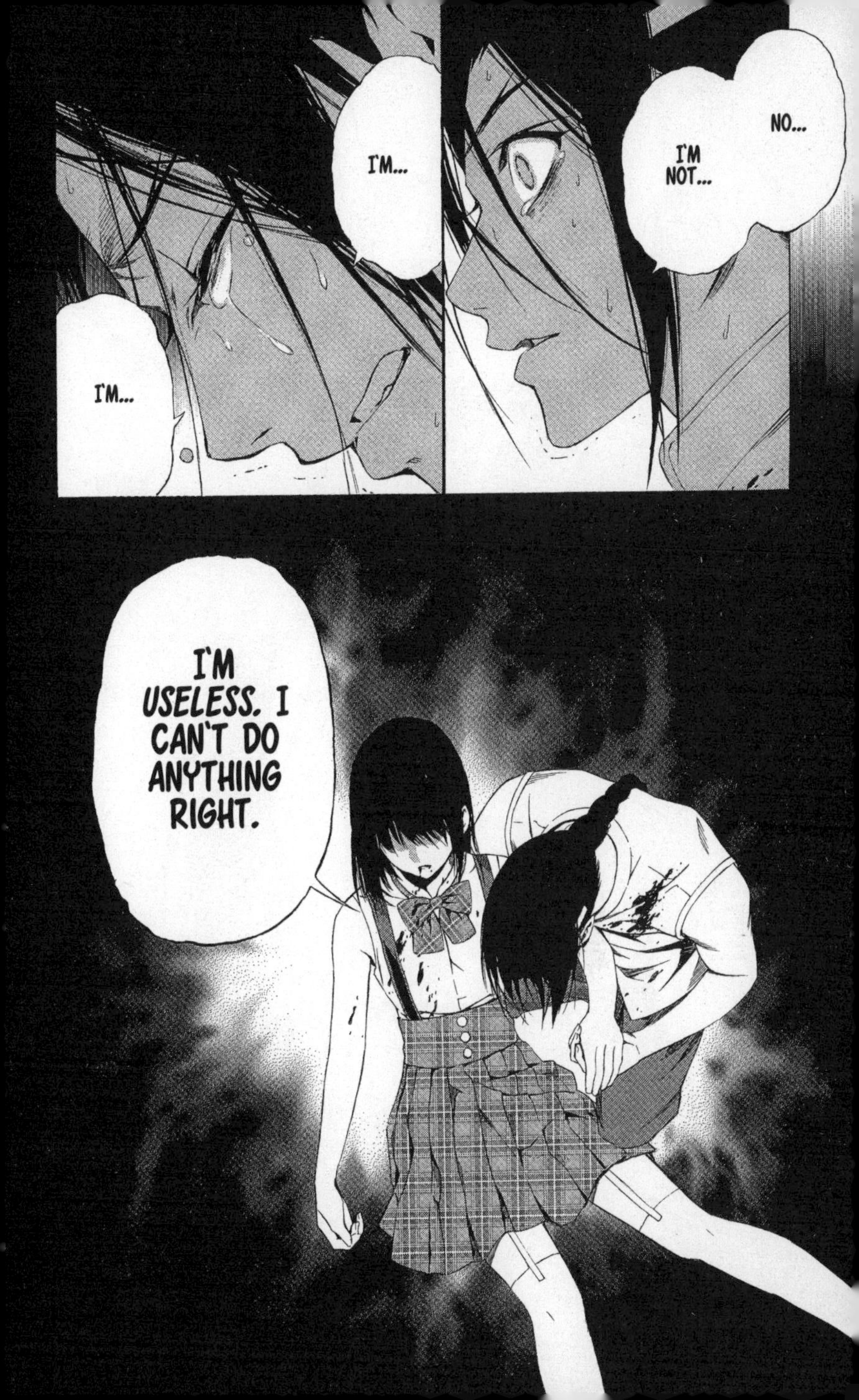
NO...
I'M NOT...
I'M...
I'M...
I'M USELESS. I CAN'T DO ANYTHING RIGHT.

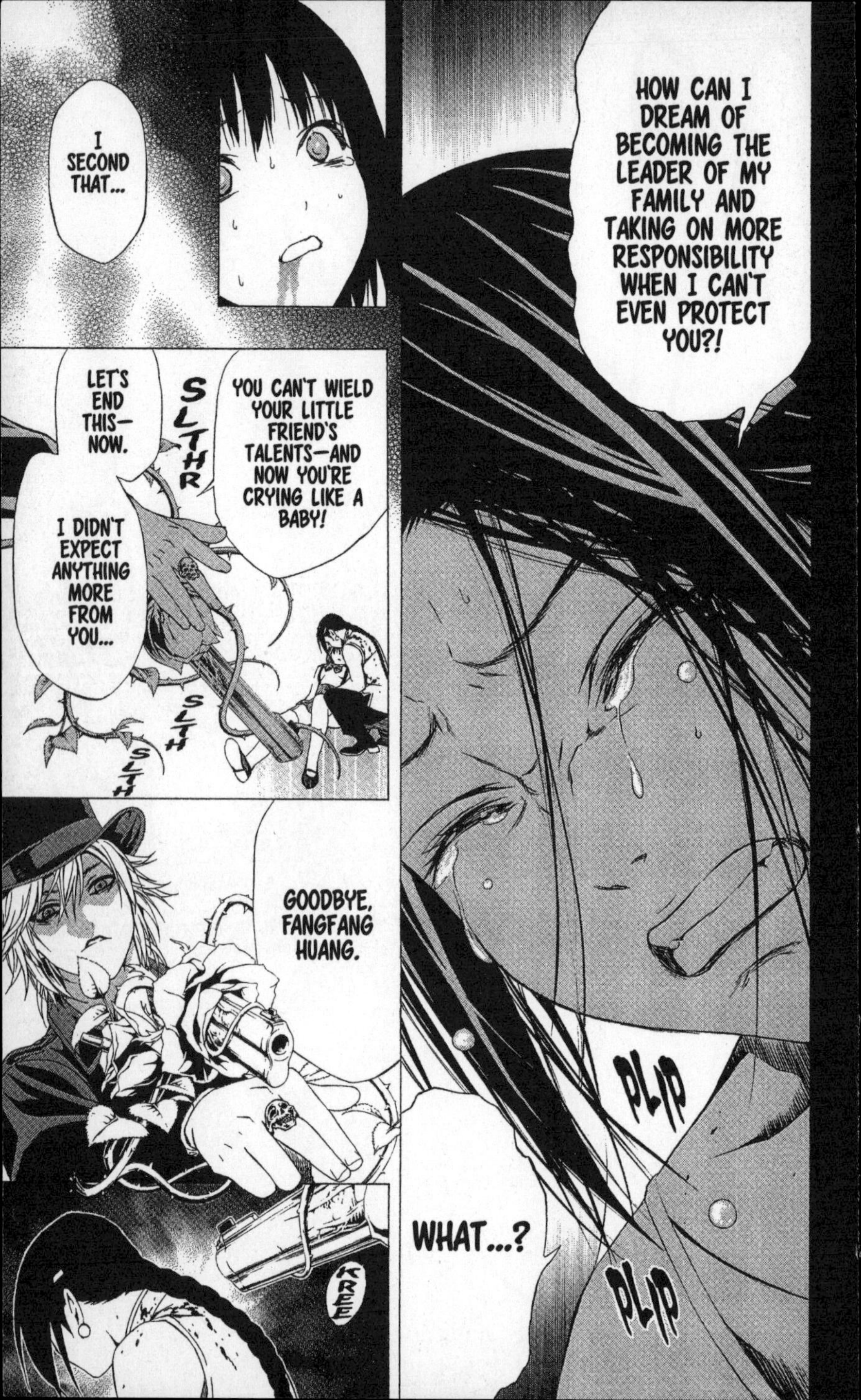
HOW CAN I DREAM OF BECOMING THE LEADER OF MY FAMILY AND TAKING ON MORE RESPONSIBILITY WHEN I CAN'T EVEN PROTECT YOU?!
PLIP
WHAT...?
PLIP
I SECOND THAT...
YOU CAN'T WIELD YOUR LITTLE FRIEND'S TALENTS—AND NOW YOU'RE CRYING LIKE A BABY!
SLTHR
LET'S END THIS—NOW.
I DIDN'T EXPECT ANYTHING MORE FROM YOU...
SLTH
SLTH
GOODBYE, FANGFANG HUANG.
KREE

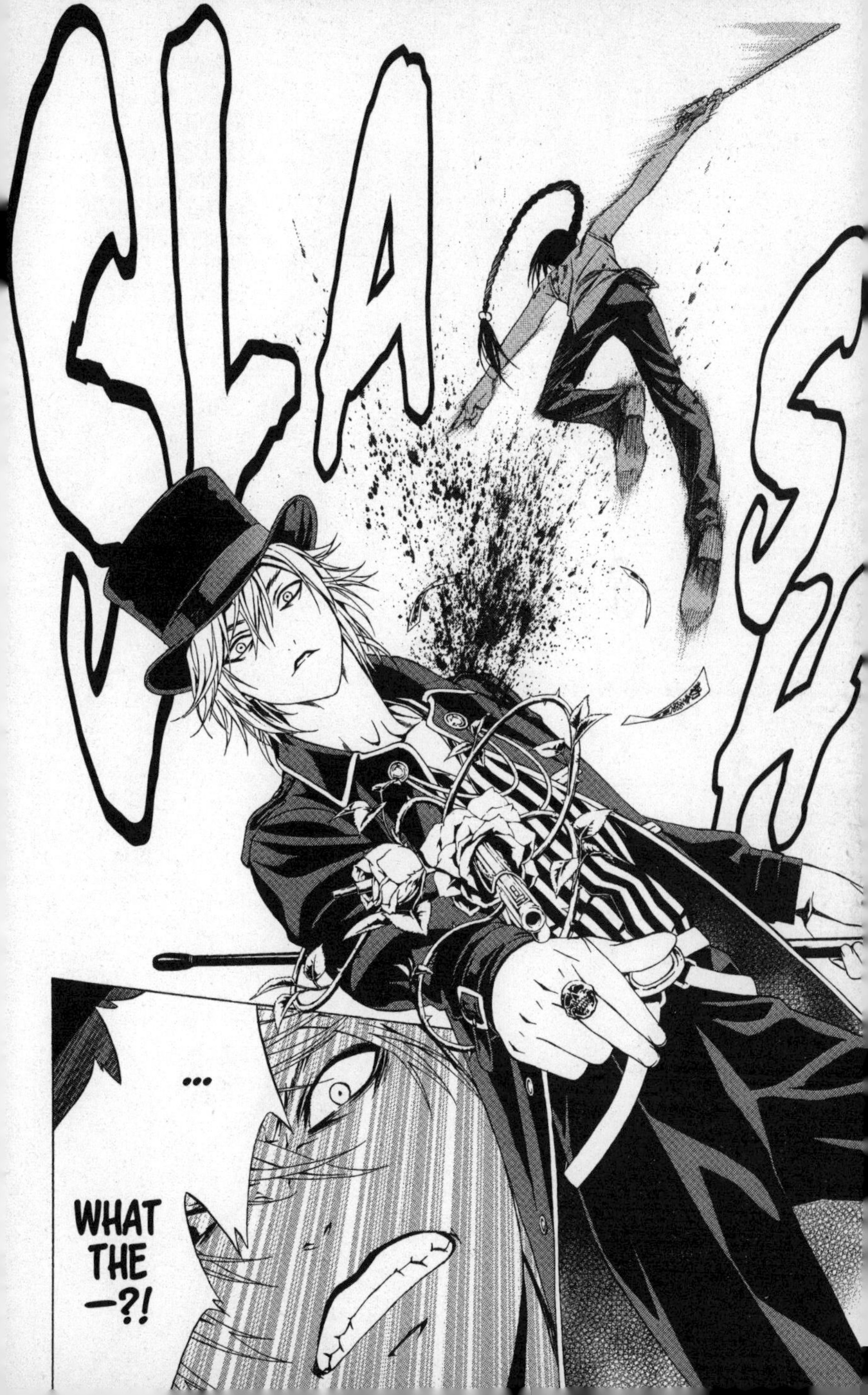
CLASH
...
WHAT THE —?!

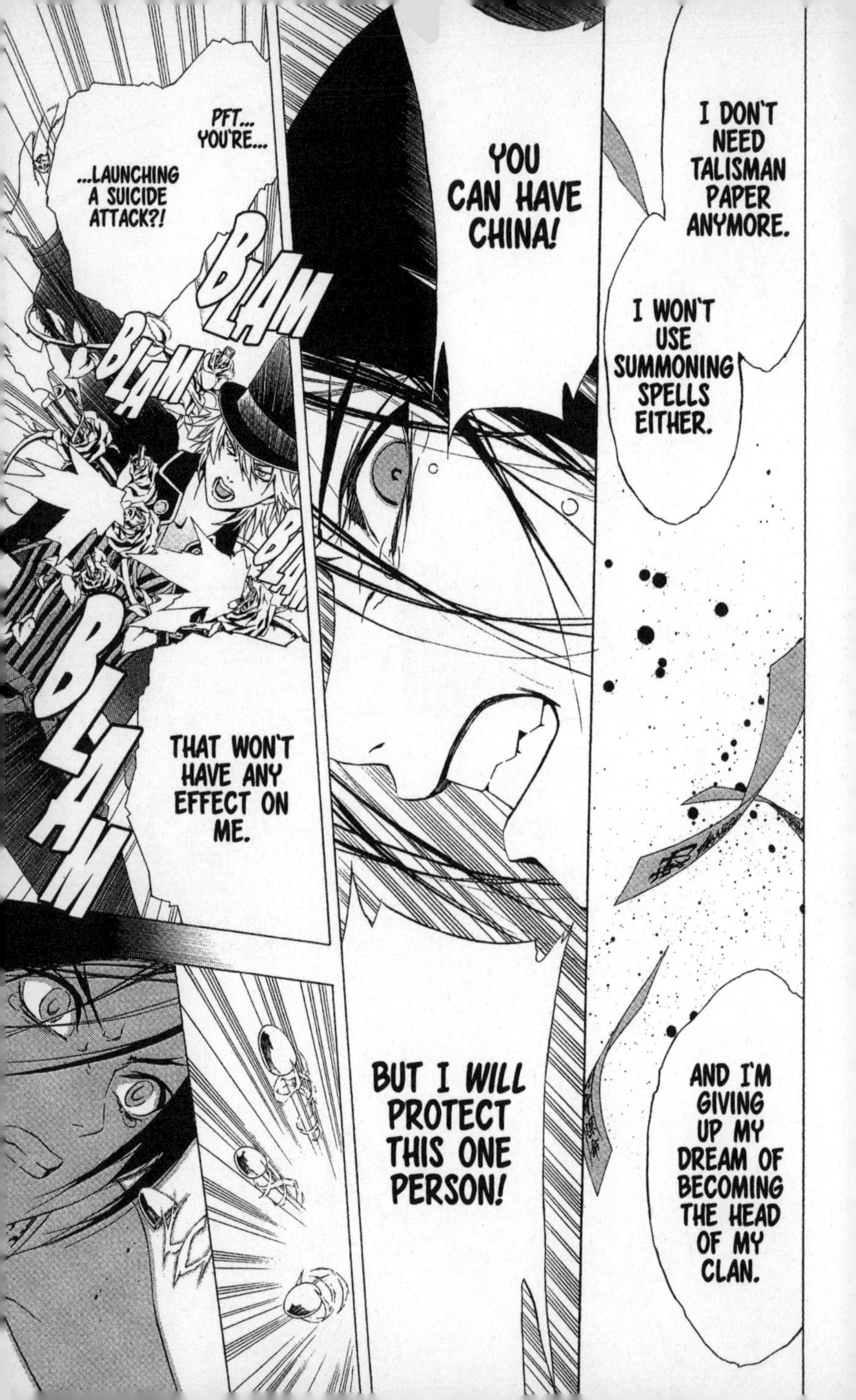
I DON'T NEED TALISMAN PAPER ANYMORE.
I WON'T USE SUMMONING SPELLS EITHER.
AND I'M GIVING UP MY DREAM OF BECOMING THE HEAD OF MY CLAN.
YOU CAN HAVE CHINA!
BUT I *WILL* PROTECT THIS ONE PERSON!
PFT... YOU'RE...
...LAUNCHING A SUICIDE ATTACK?!
BLAM
BLAM
BLAAM
THAT WON'T HAVE ANY EFFECT ON ME.

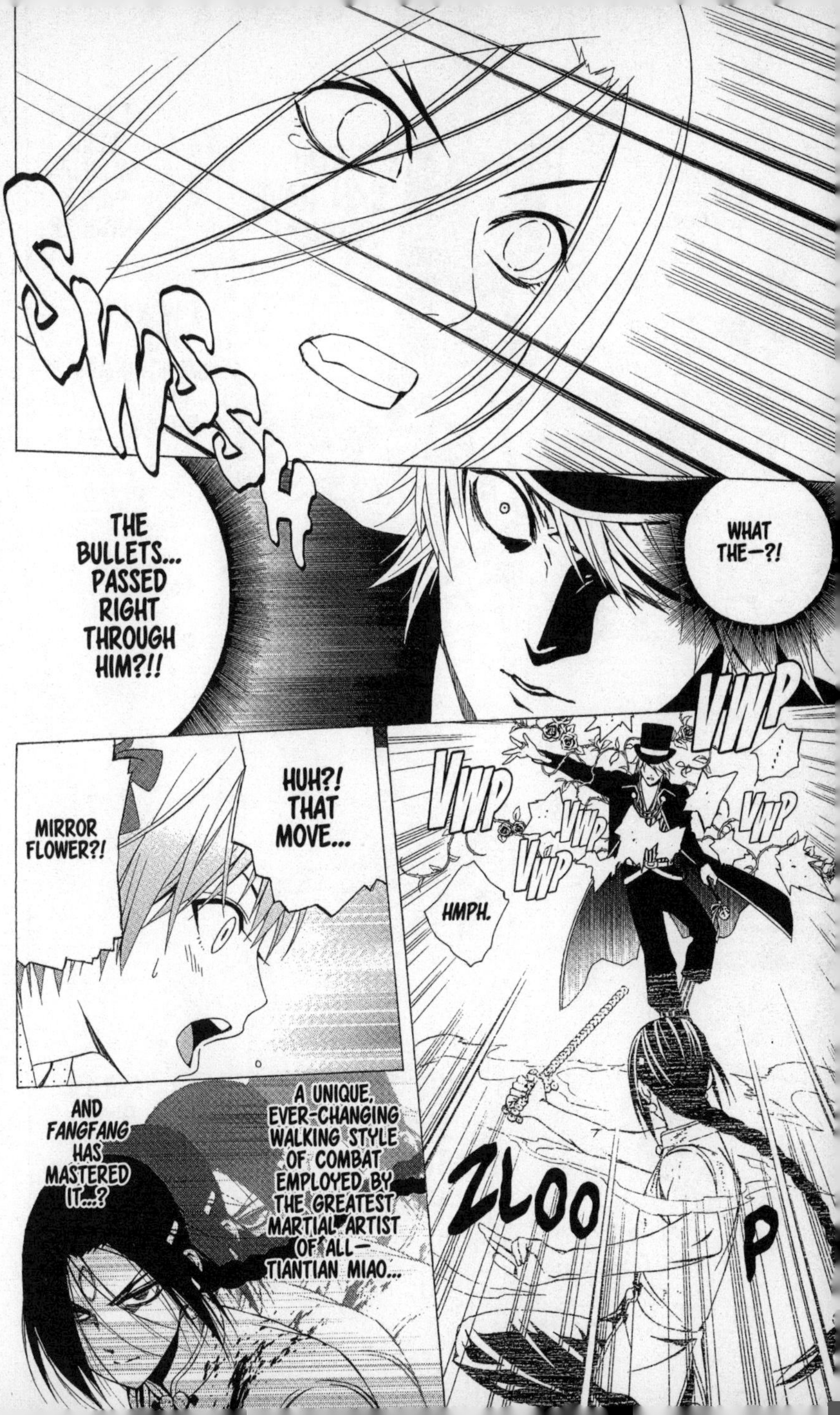
SWSSH
WHAT THE—?!
THE BULLETS... PASSED RIGHT THROUGH HIM?!!
VWP
VWP
VWP
VWP
VWP
HMPH.
HUH?! THAT MOVE...
MIRROR FLOWER?!
ZLOOP
A UNIQUE, EVER-CHANGING WALKING STYLE OF COMBAT EMPLOYED BY THE GREATEST MARTIAL ARTIST OF ALL— TIANTIAN MIAO...
AND FANGFANG HAS MASTERED IT...?

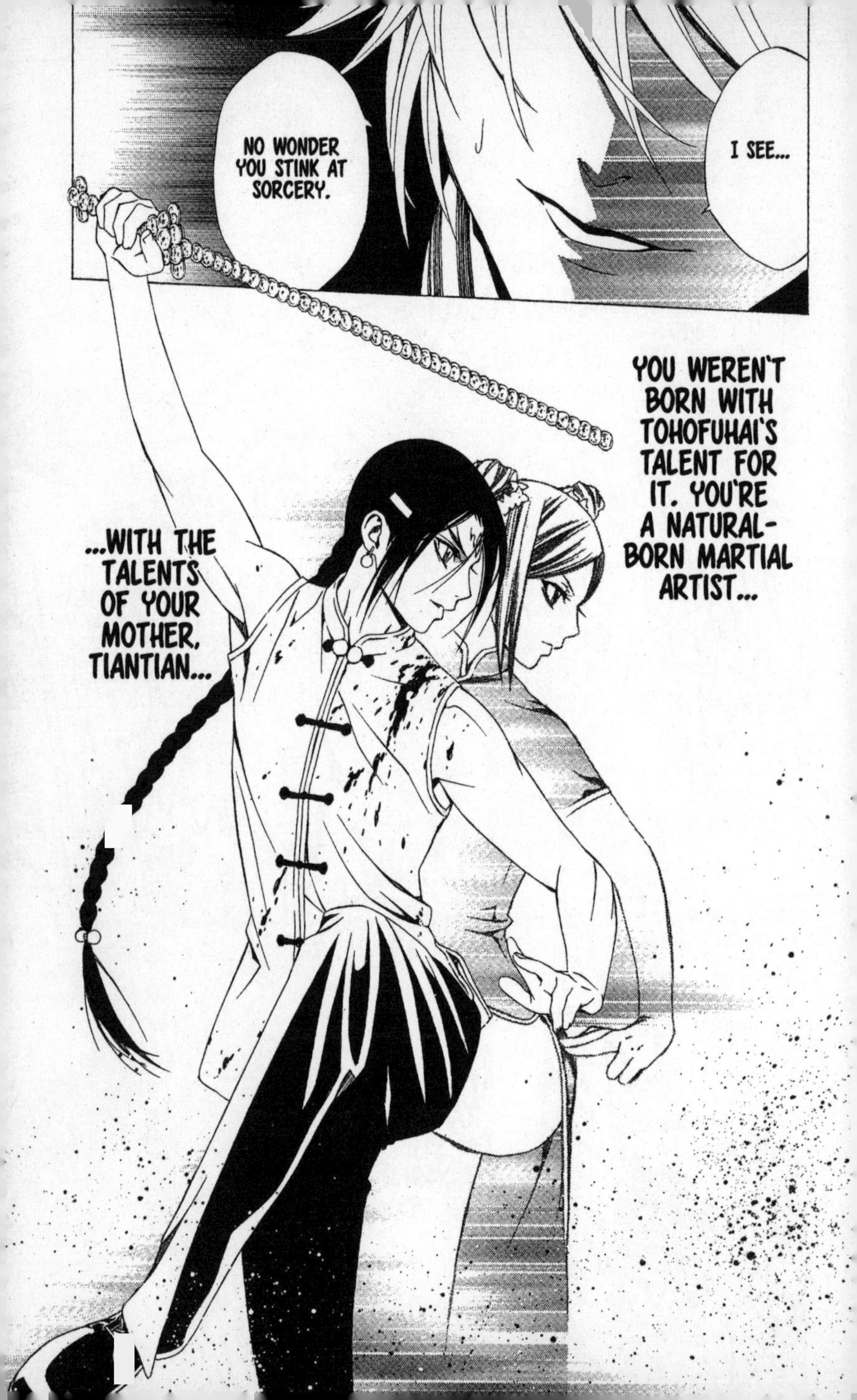
I SEE...
NO WONDER YOU STINK AT SORCERY.
YOU WEREN'T BORN WITH TOHOFUHAI'S TALENT FOR IT. YOU'RE A NATURAL-BORN MARTIAL ARTIST...
...WITH THE TALENTS OF YOUR MOTHER, TIANTIAN...

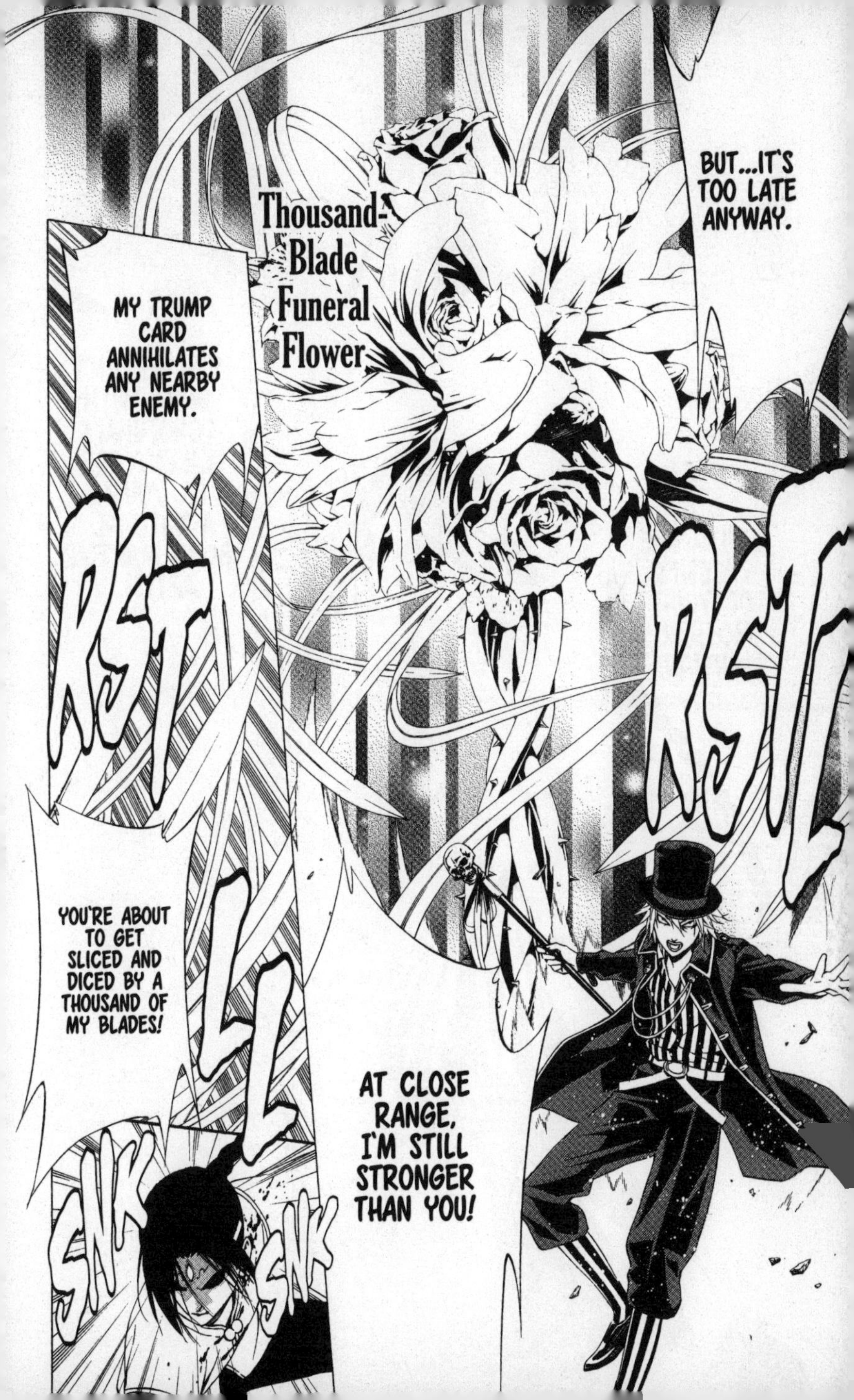
BUT...IT'S TOO LATE ANYWAY.
Thousand-Blade Funeral Flower
MY TRUMP CARD ANNIHILATES ANY NEARBY ENEMY.
RSTL
RSTL
AT CLOSE RANGE, I'M STILL STRONGER THAN YOU!
YOU'RE ABOUT TO GET SLICED AND DICED BY A THOUSAND OF MY BLADES!
SNK
SNK

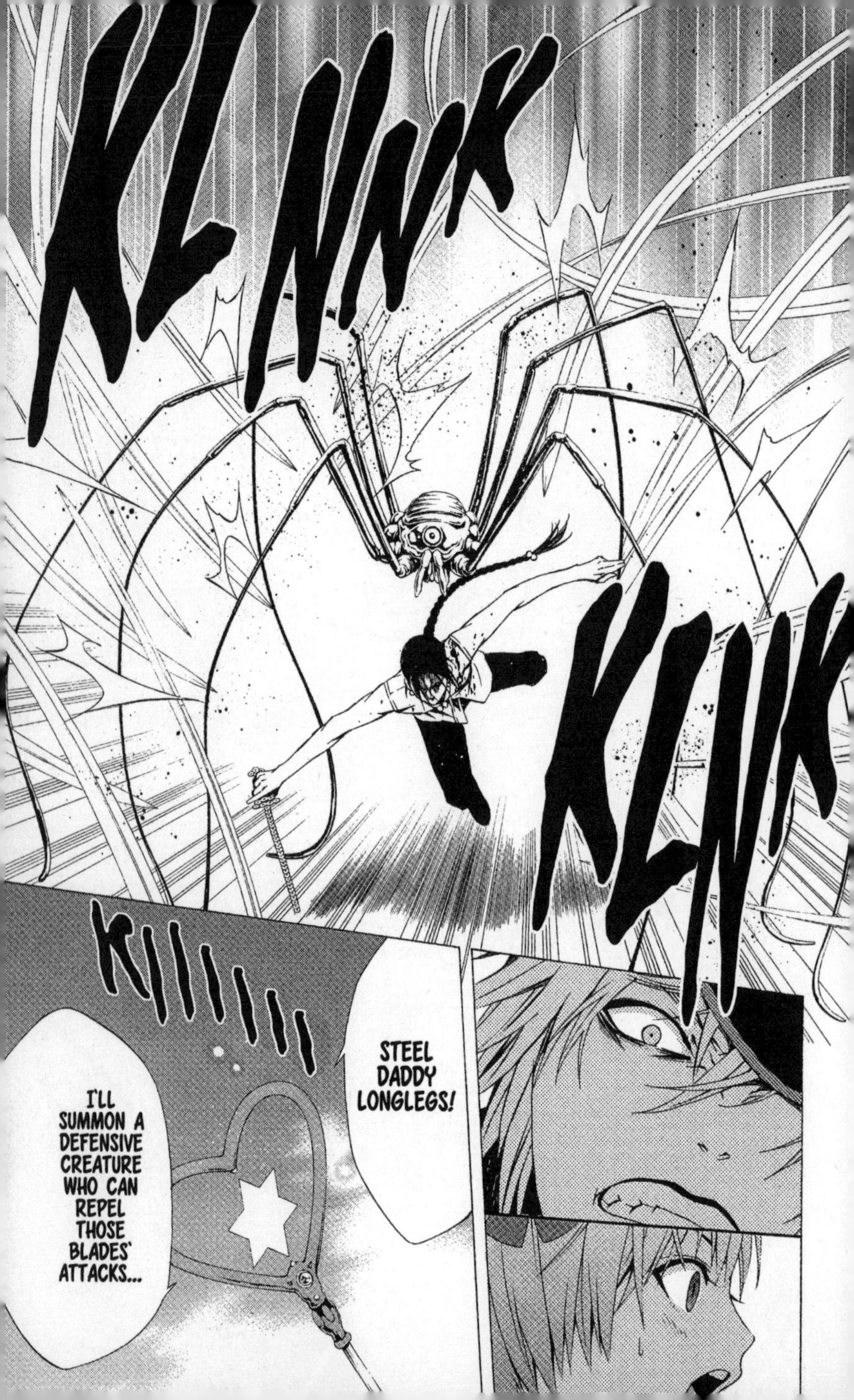
KLANK
KLANK
KIIIIIII
STEEL DADDY LONGLEGS!
I'LL SUMMON A DEFENSIVE CREATURE WHO CAN REPEL THOSE BLADES' ATTACKS...

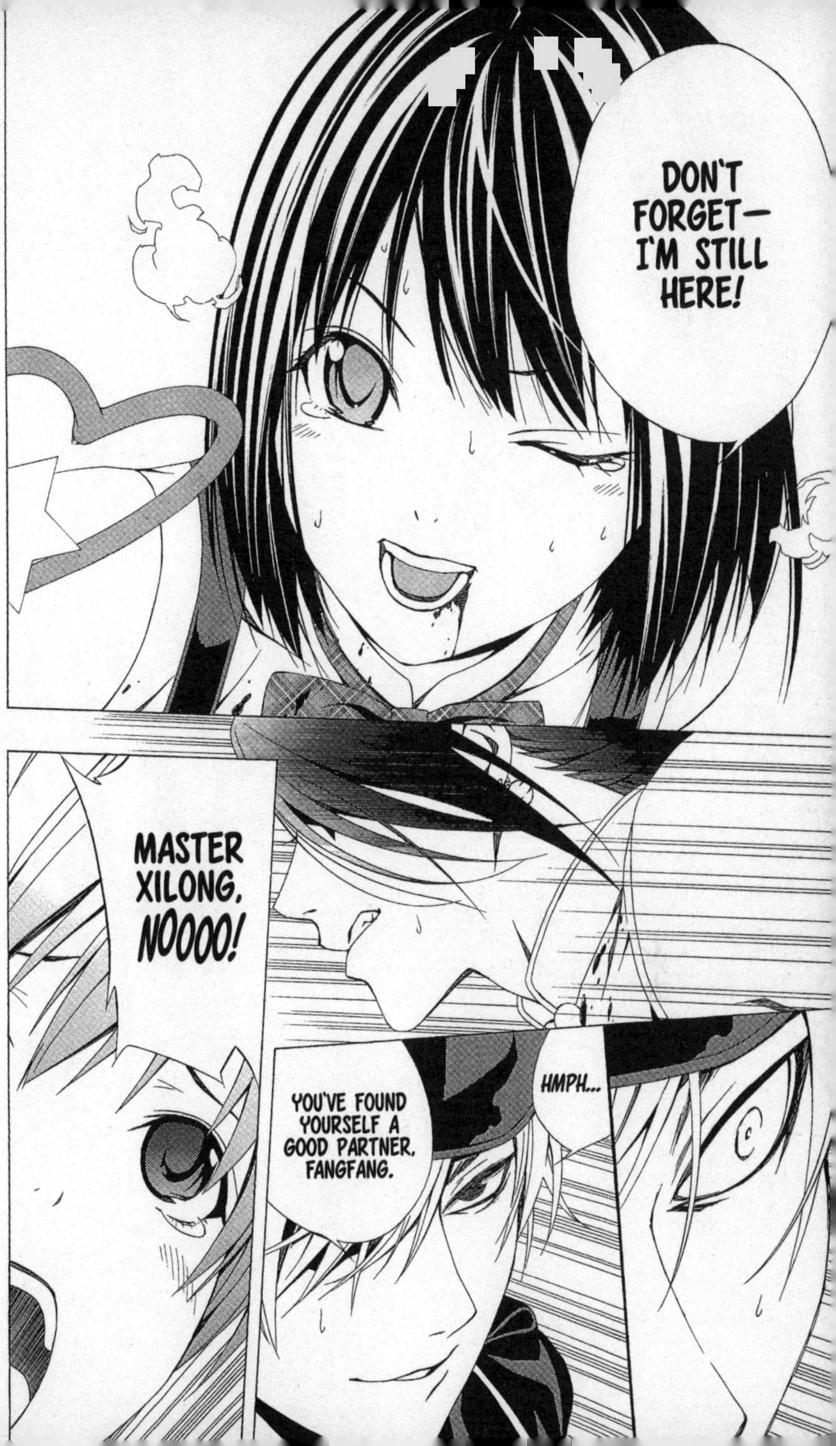
DON'T FORGET— I'M STILL HERE!
HMPH...
YOU'VE FOUND YOURSELF A GOOD PARTNER, FANGFANG.
MASTER XILONG, NOOOO!

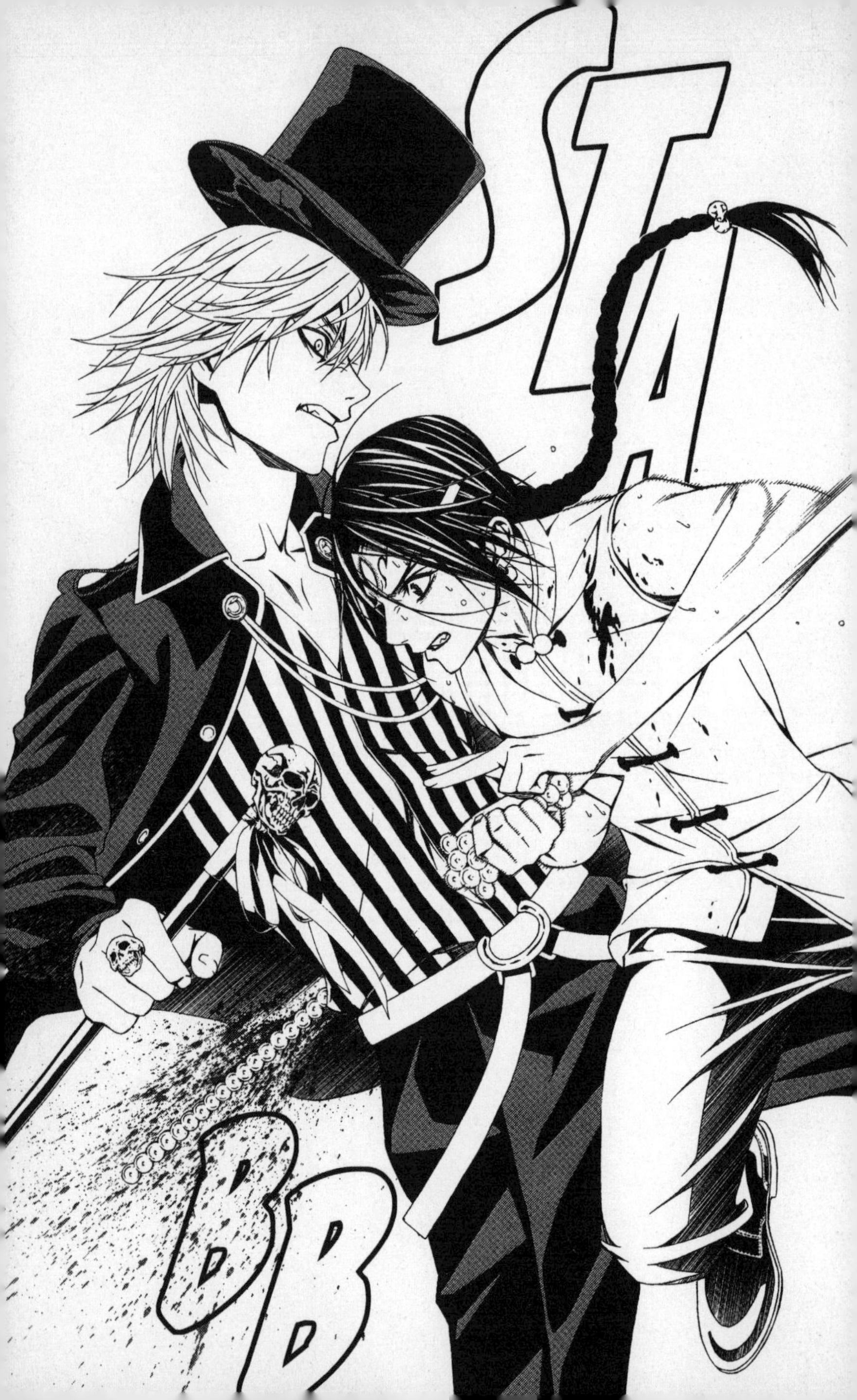
STABB

49: Puppet Master

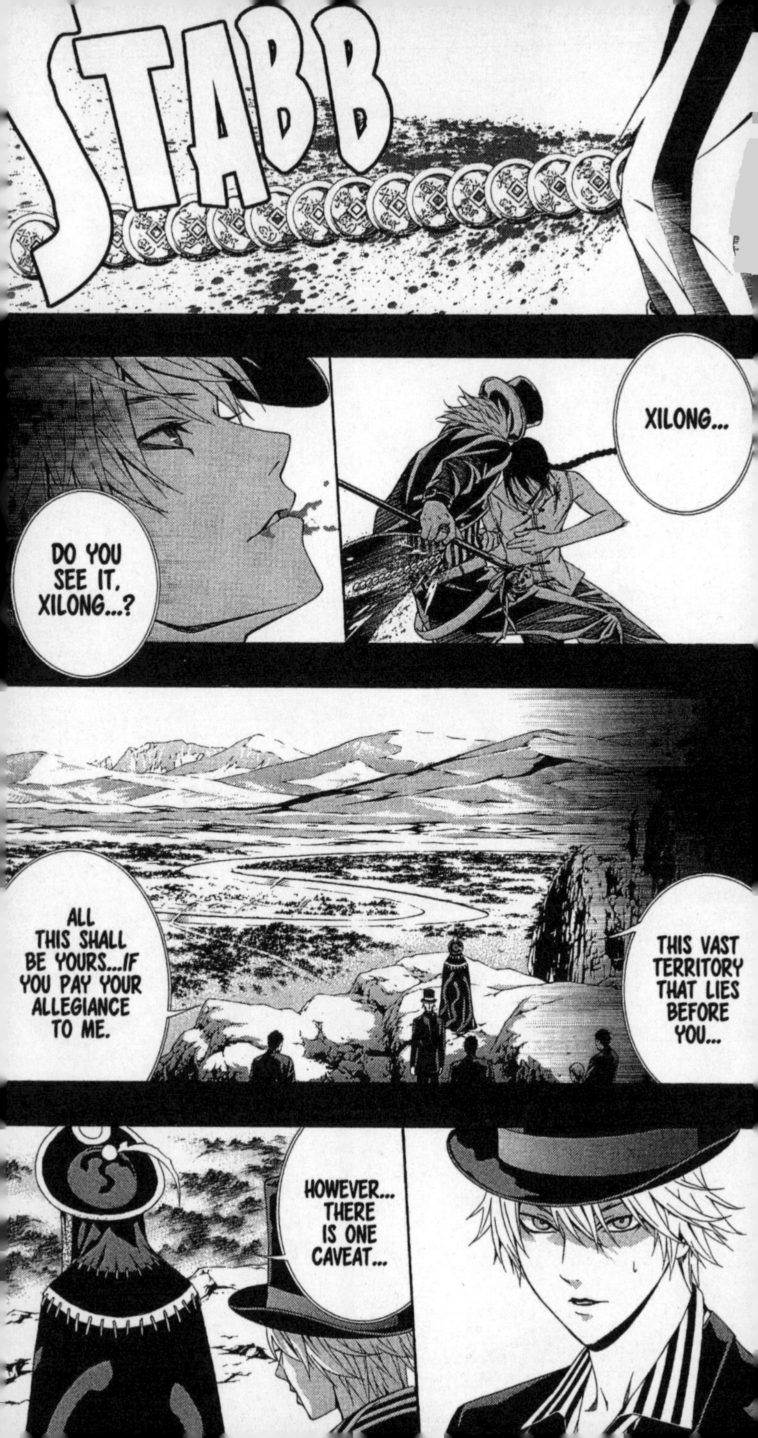
STABB
XILONG...
DO YOU SEE IT, XILONG...?
THIS VAST TERRITORY THAT LIES BEFORE YOU...
ALL THIS SHALL BE YOURS...IF YOU PAY YOUR ALLEGIANCE TO ME.
HOWEVER... THERE IS ONE CAVEAT...

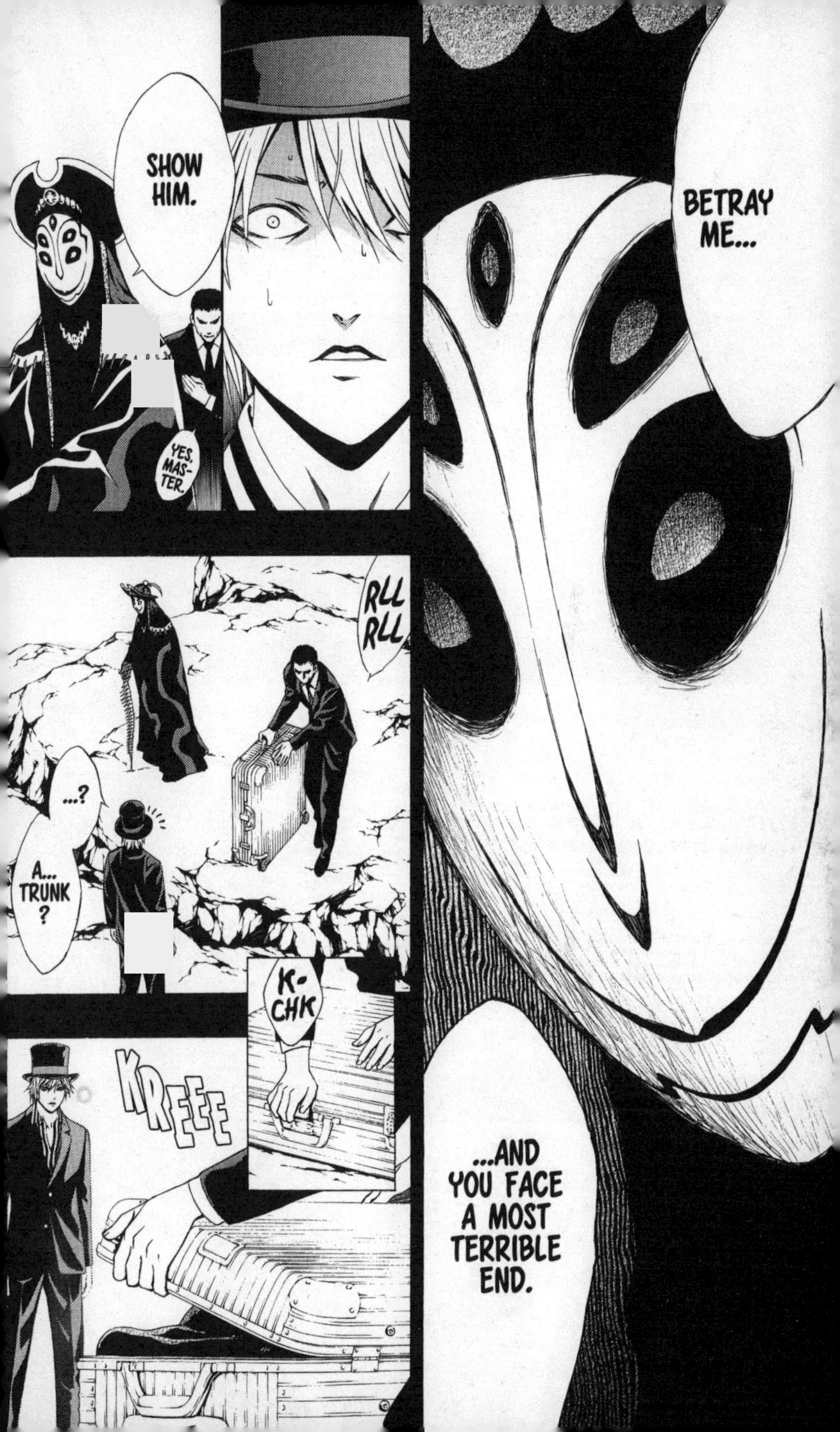
BETRAY ME...
...AND YOU FACE A MOST TERRIBLE END.
SHOW HIM.
YES, MASTER.
RLL RLL
...?
A... TRUNK?
K-CHK
KREEEE

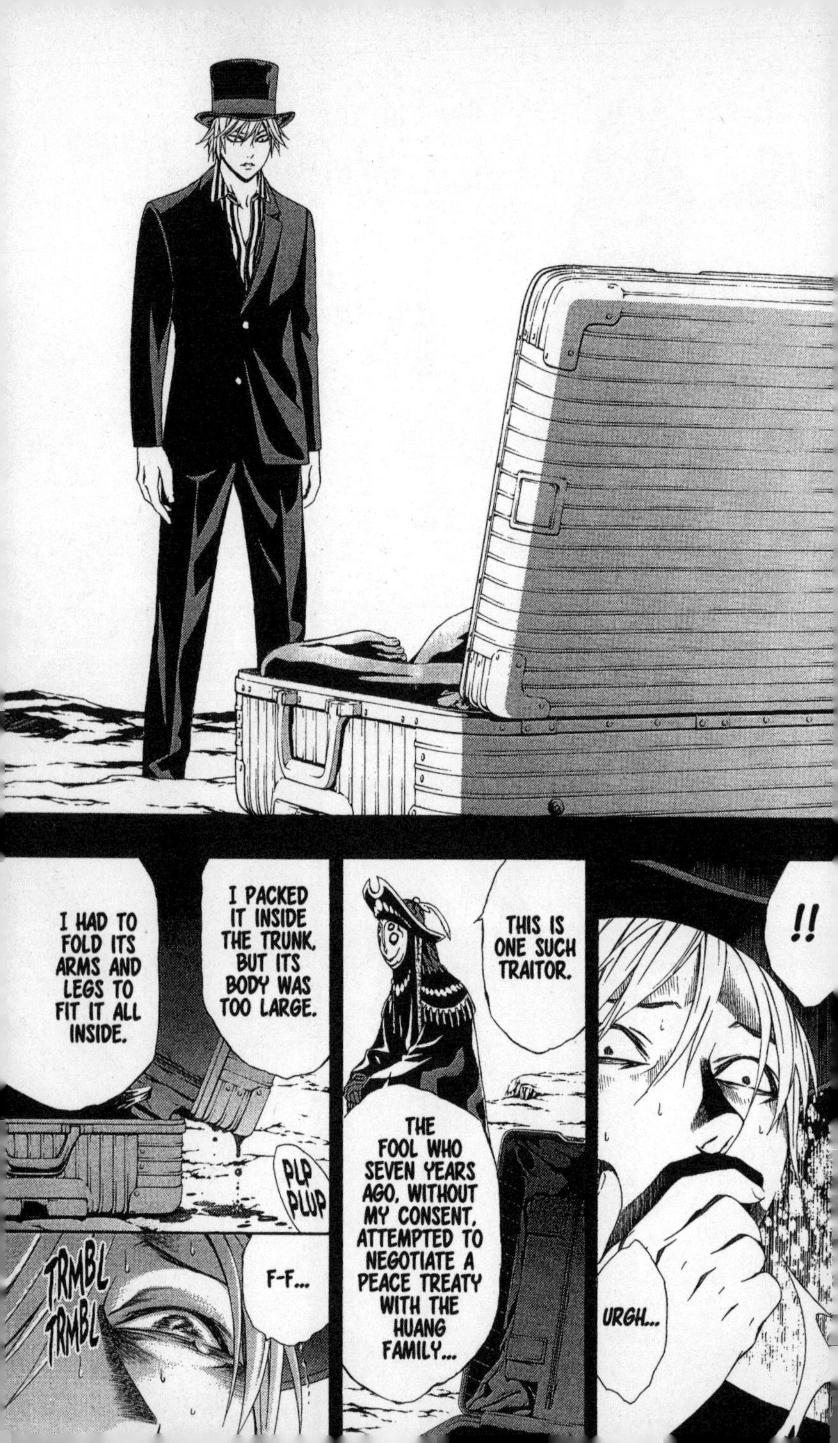
!!
URGH...
THIS IS ONE SUCH TRAITOR.
THE FOOL WHO SEVEN YEARS AGO, WITHOUT MY CONSENT, ATTEMPTED TO NEGOTIATE A PEACE TREATY WITH THE HUANG FAMILY...
I PACKED IT INSIDE THE TRUNK, BUT ITS BODY WAS TOO LARGE.
I HAD TO FOLD ITS ARMS AND LEGS TO FIT IT ALL INSIDE.
PLP PLUP
F-F...
TRMBL TRMBL

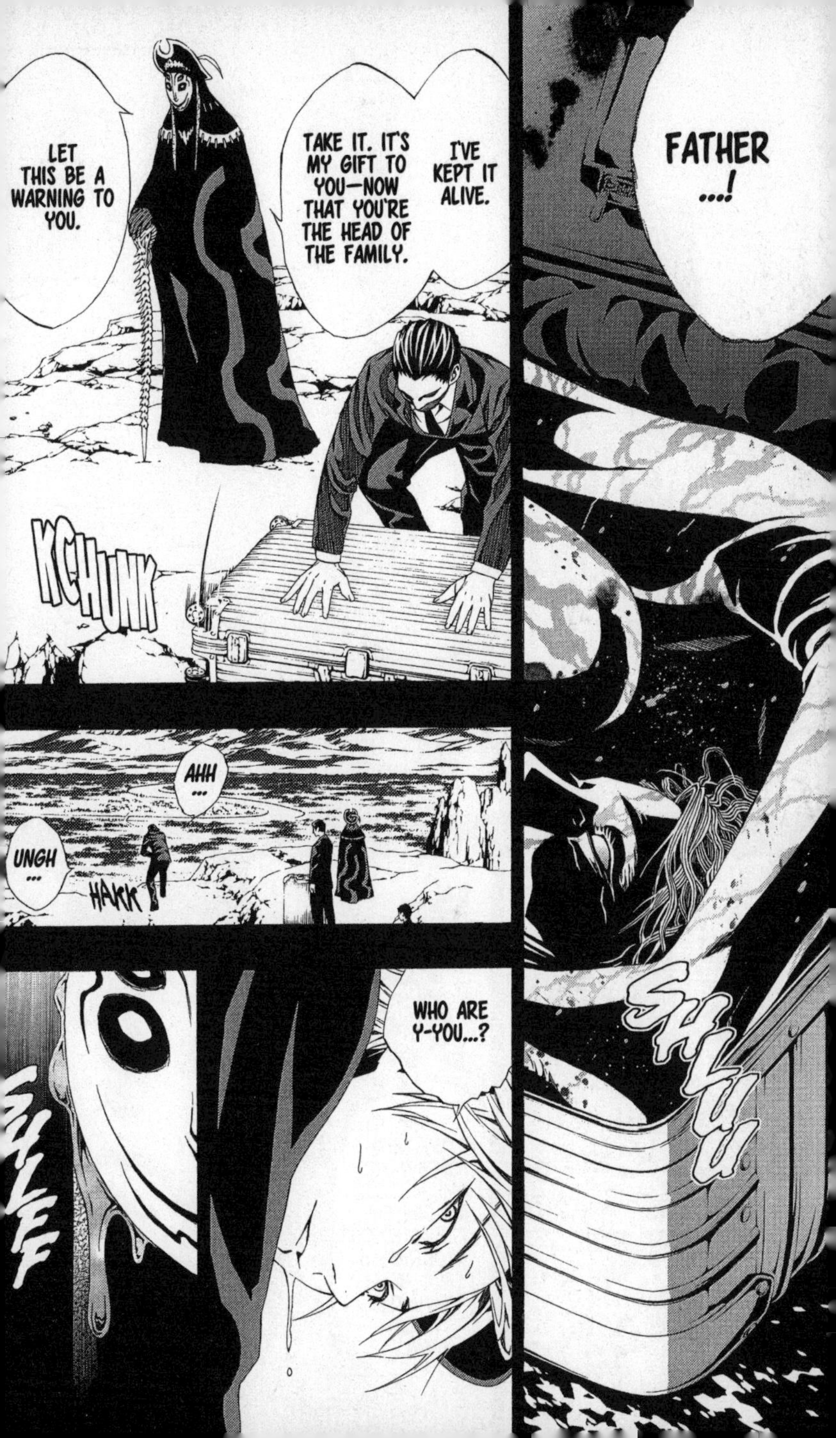
FATHER ...!
SHHUU
I'VE KEPT IT ALIVE.
TAKE IT. IT'S MY GIFT TO YOU—NOW THAT YOU'RE THE HEAD OF THE FAMILY.
LET THIS BE A WARNING TO YOU.
KCHUNK
AHH ...
UNGH ...
HAKK
WHO ARE Y-YOU...?
SHLEFF

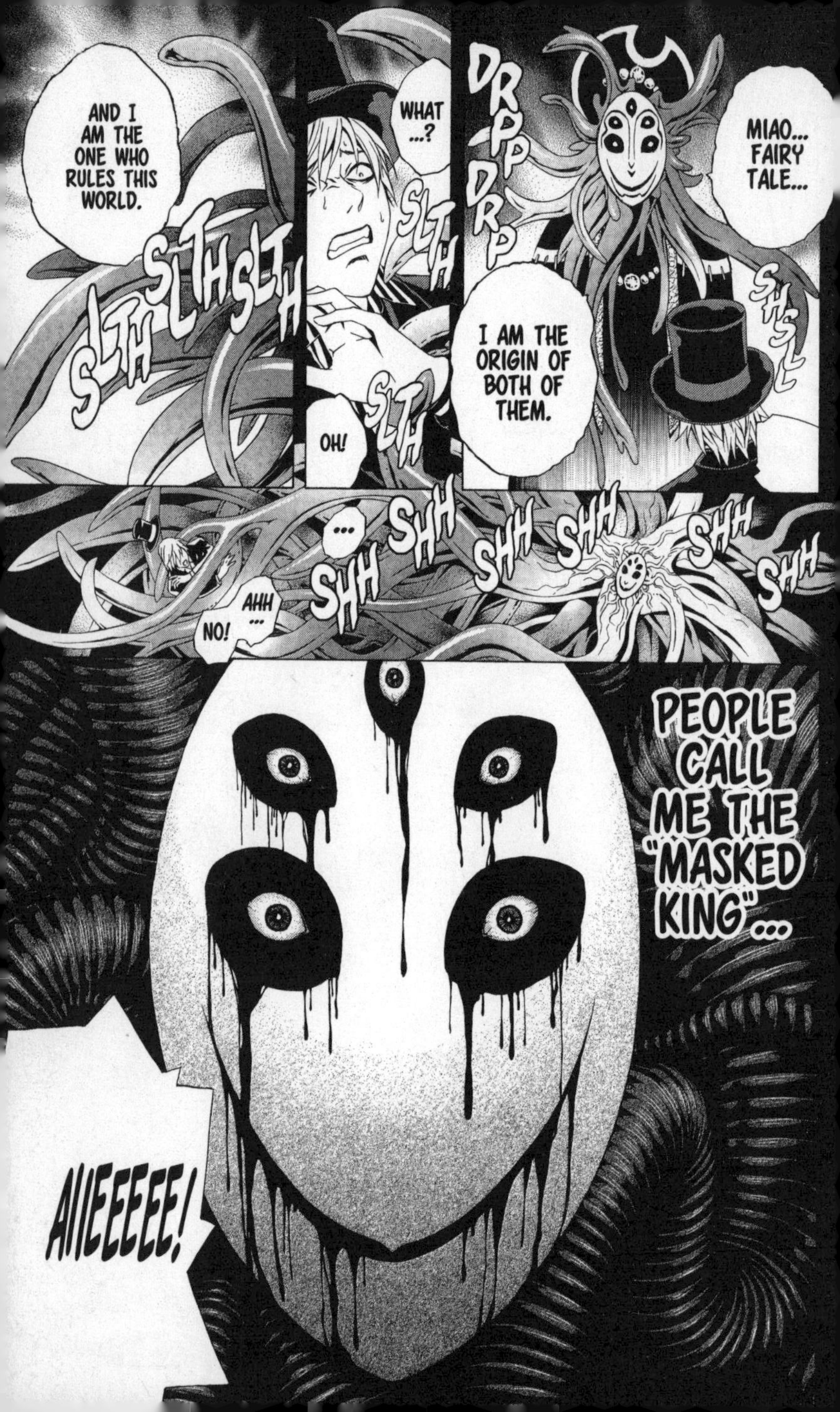
MIAO... FAIRY TALE...
DRPP DRP
I AM THE ORIGIN OF BOTH OF THEM.
WHAT ...?
SLTH
SLTH
OH!
AND I AM THE ONE WHO RULES THIS WORLD.
SLTH SLTH SLTH SLTH
SHH SHH SHH SHH SHH SHH
...
SHH
AHH ...
NO!
PEOPLE CALL ME THE "MASKED KING"...
AIIEEEEE!

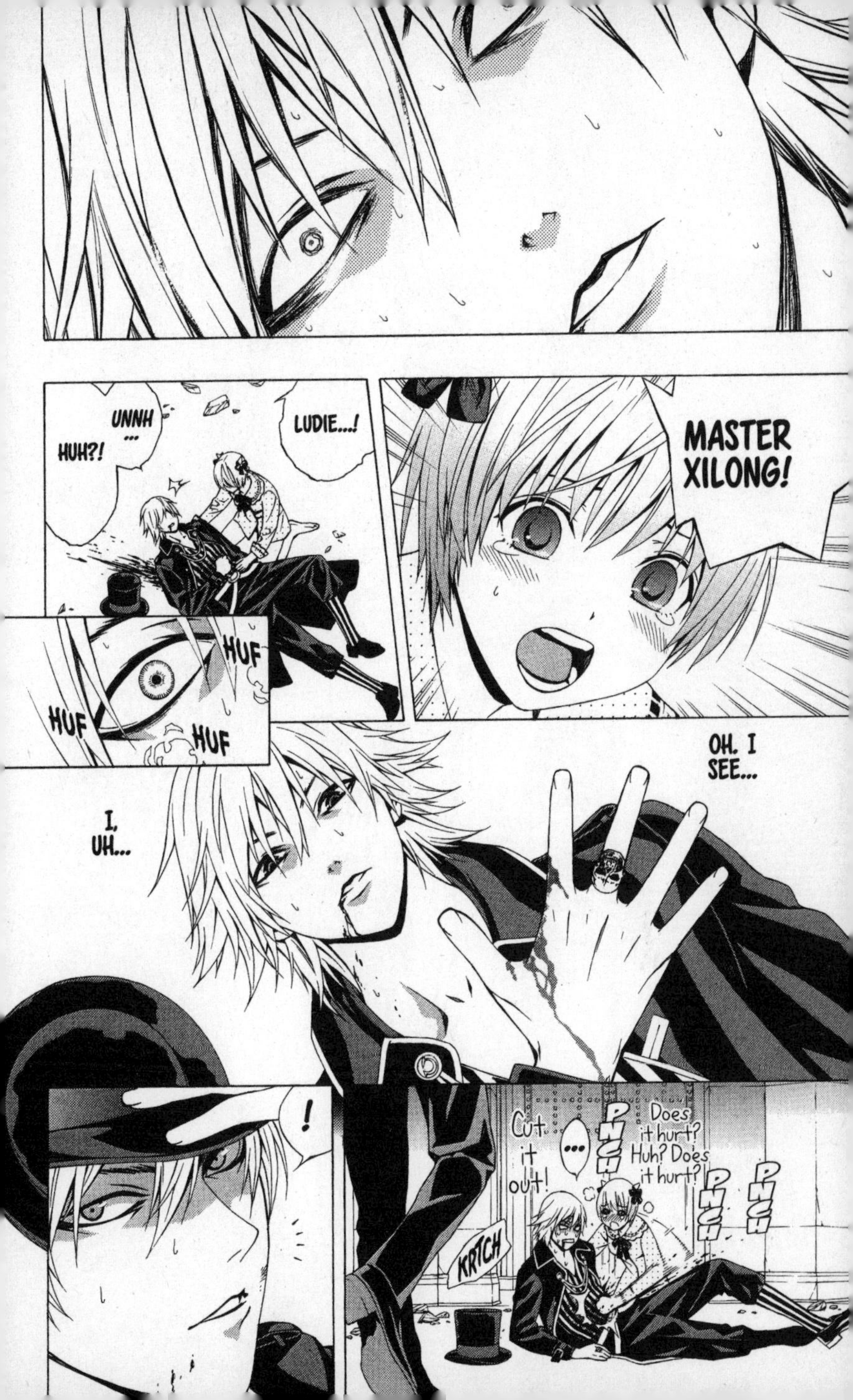
MASTER XILONG!
LUDIE...!
UNNH ...
HUH?!
HUF
HUF
HUF
OH. I SEE...
I, UH...
PNCH
PNCH
Does it hurt? Huh? Does it hurt?
PNCH
...
Cut it out!
KRTCH
!

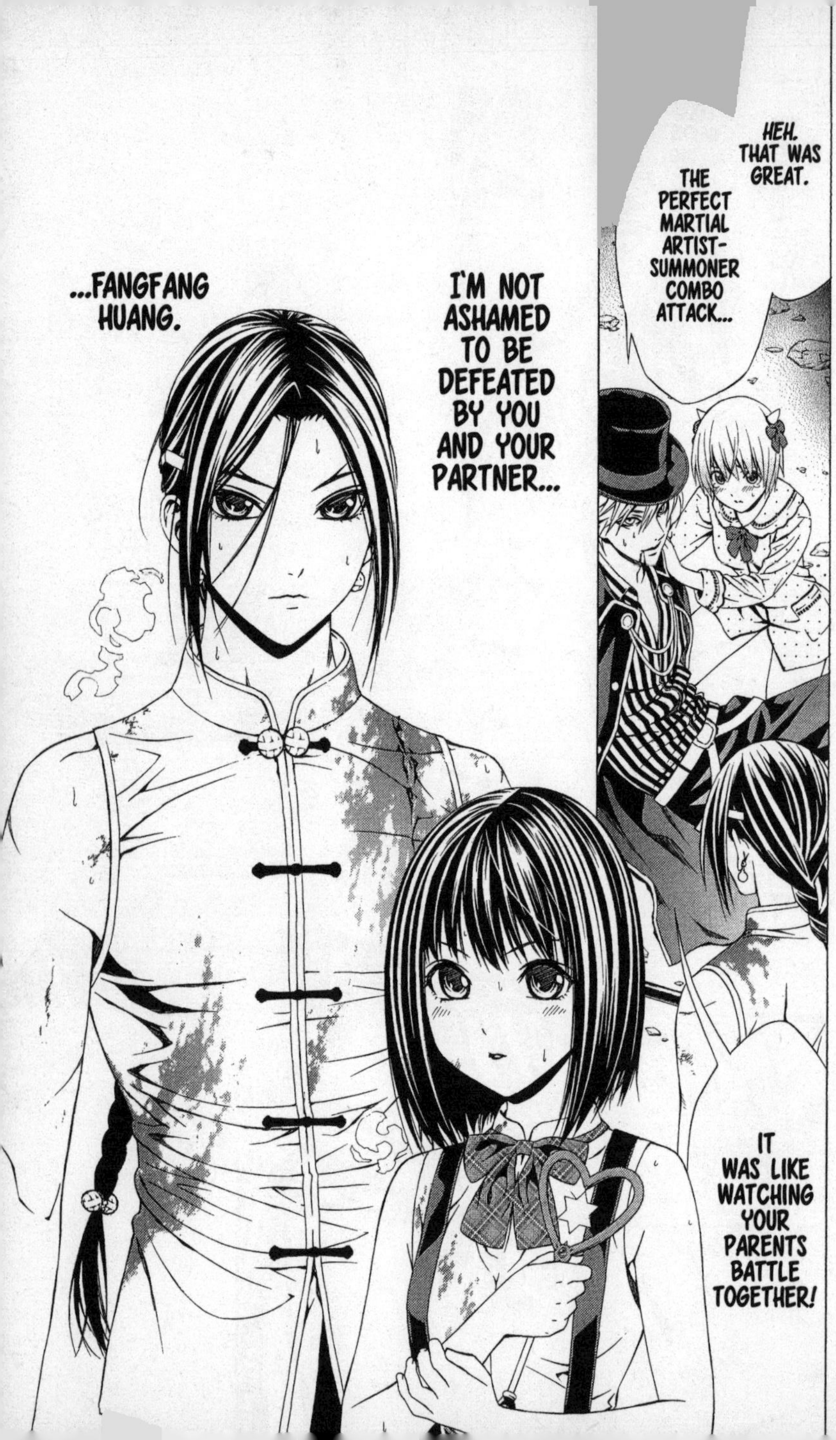
HEH. THAT WAS GREAT.
THE PERFECT MARTIAL ARTIST-SUMMONER COMBO ATTACK...
IT WAS LIKE WATCHING YOUR PARENTS BATTLE TOGETHER!
I'M NOT ASHAMED TO BE DEFEATED BY YOU AND YOUR PARTNER...
...FANGFANG HUANG.

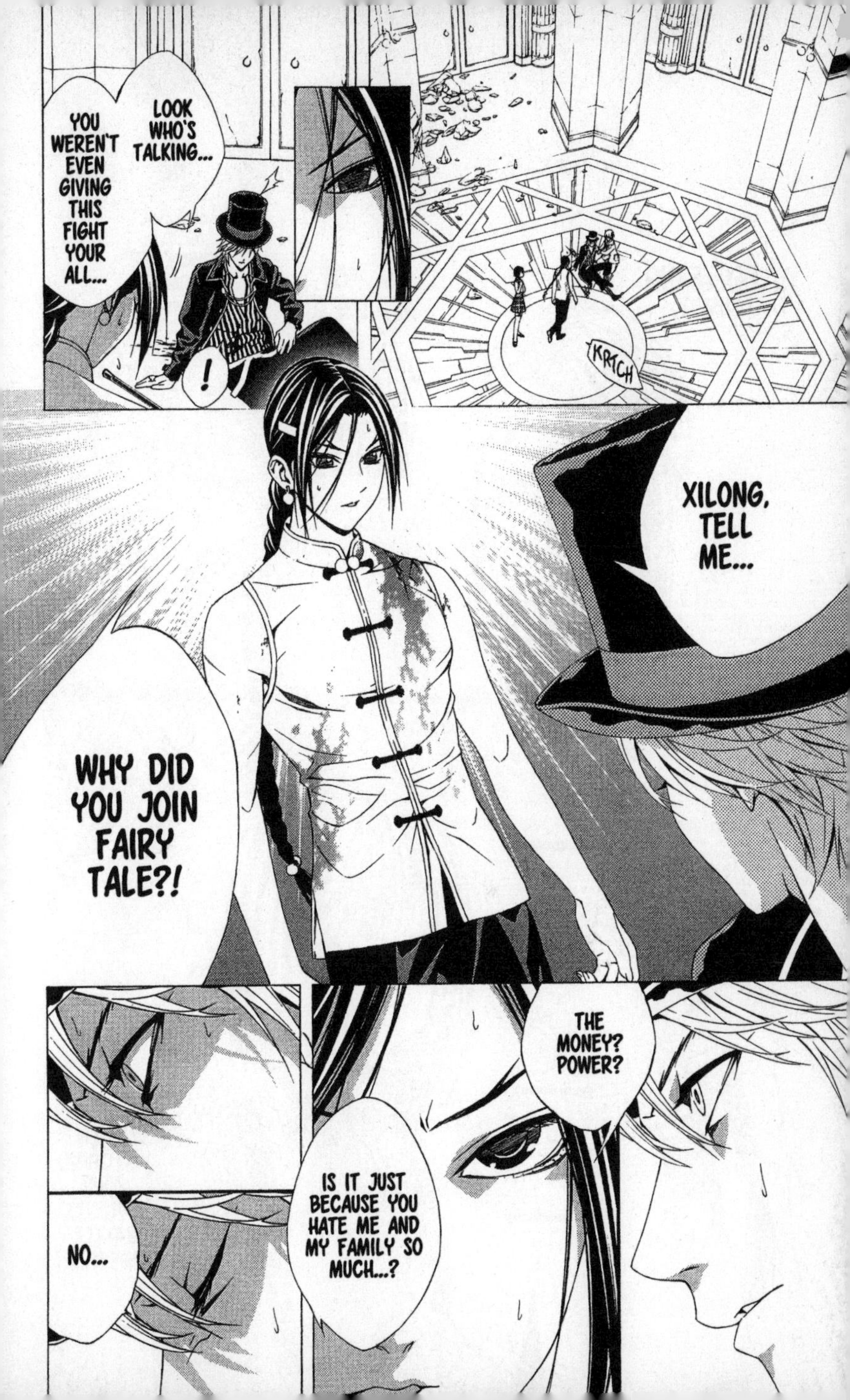
KRTCH
LOOK WHO'S TALKING...
YOU WEREN'T EVEN GIVING THIS FIGHT YOUR ALL...
!
XILONG, TELL ME...
WHY DID YOU JOIN FAIRY TALE?!
THE MONEY? POWER?
IS IT JUST BECAUSE YOU HATE ME AND MY FAMILY SO MUCH...?
NO...

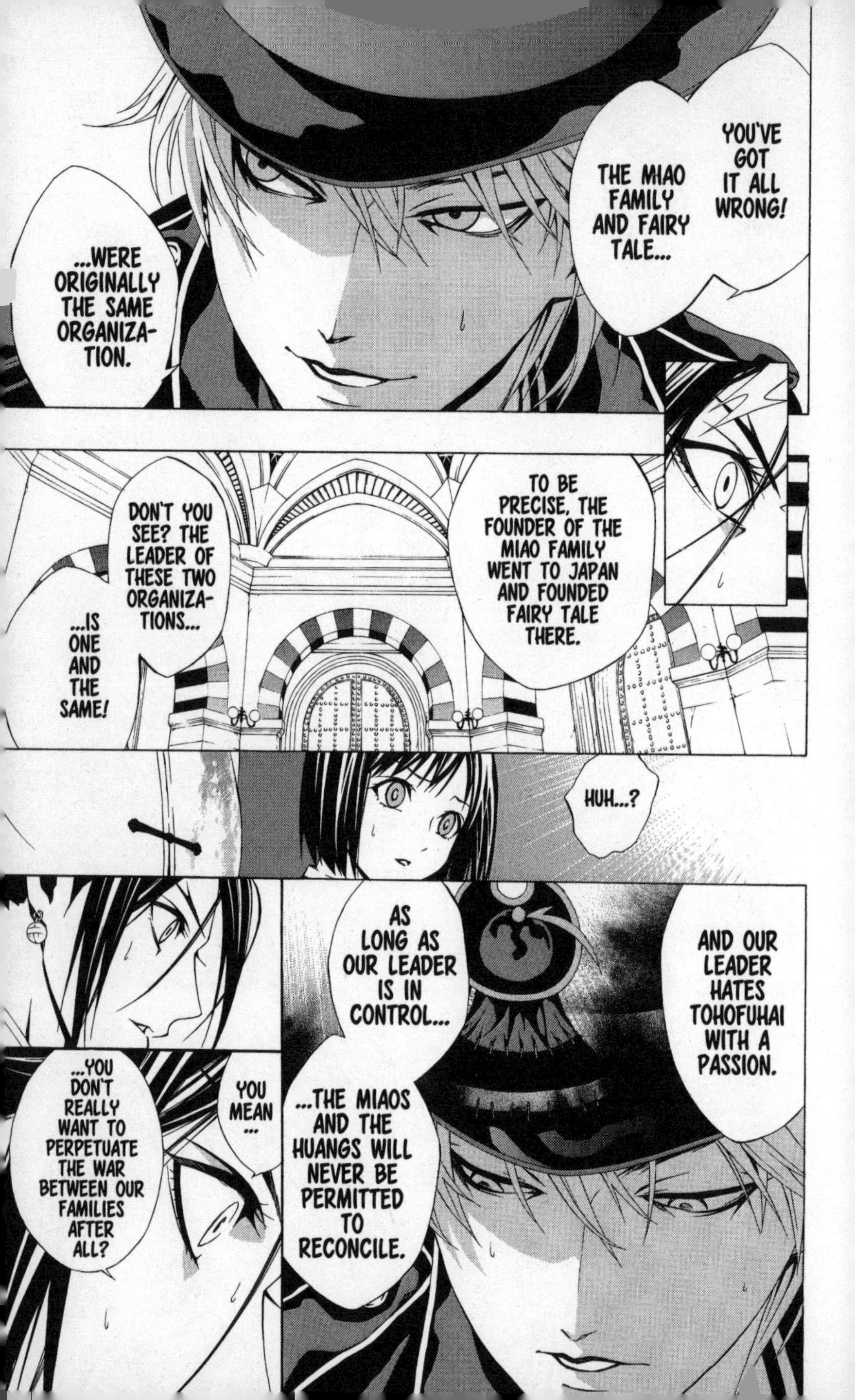
YOU'VE GOT IT ALL WRONG!
THE MIAO FAMILY AND FAIRY TALE...
...WERE ORIGINALLY THE SAME ORGANIZATION.
TO BE PRECISE, THE FOUNDER OF THE MIAO FAMILY WENT TO JAPAN AND FOUNDED FAIRY TALE THERE.
DON'T YOU SEE? THE LEADER OF THESE TWO ORGANIZATIONS...
...IS ONE AND THE SAME!
HUH...?
AND OUR LEADER HATES TOHOFUHAI WITH A PASSION.
AS LONG AS OUR LEADER IS IN CONTROL...
...THE MIAOS AND THE HUANGS WILL NEVER BE PERMITTED TO RECONCILE.
YOU MEAN...
...YOU DON'T REALLY WANT TO PERPETUATE THE WAR BETWEEN OUR FAMILIES AFTER ALL?

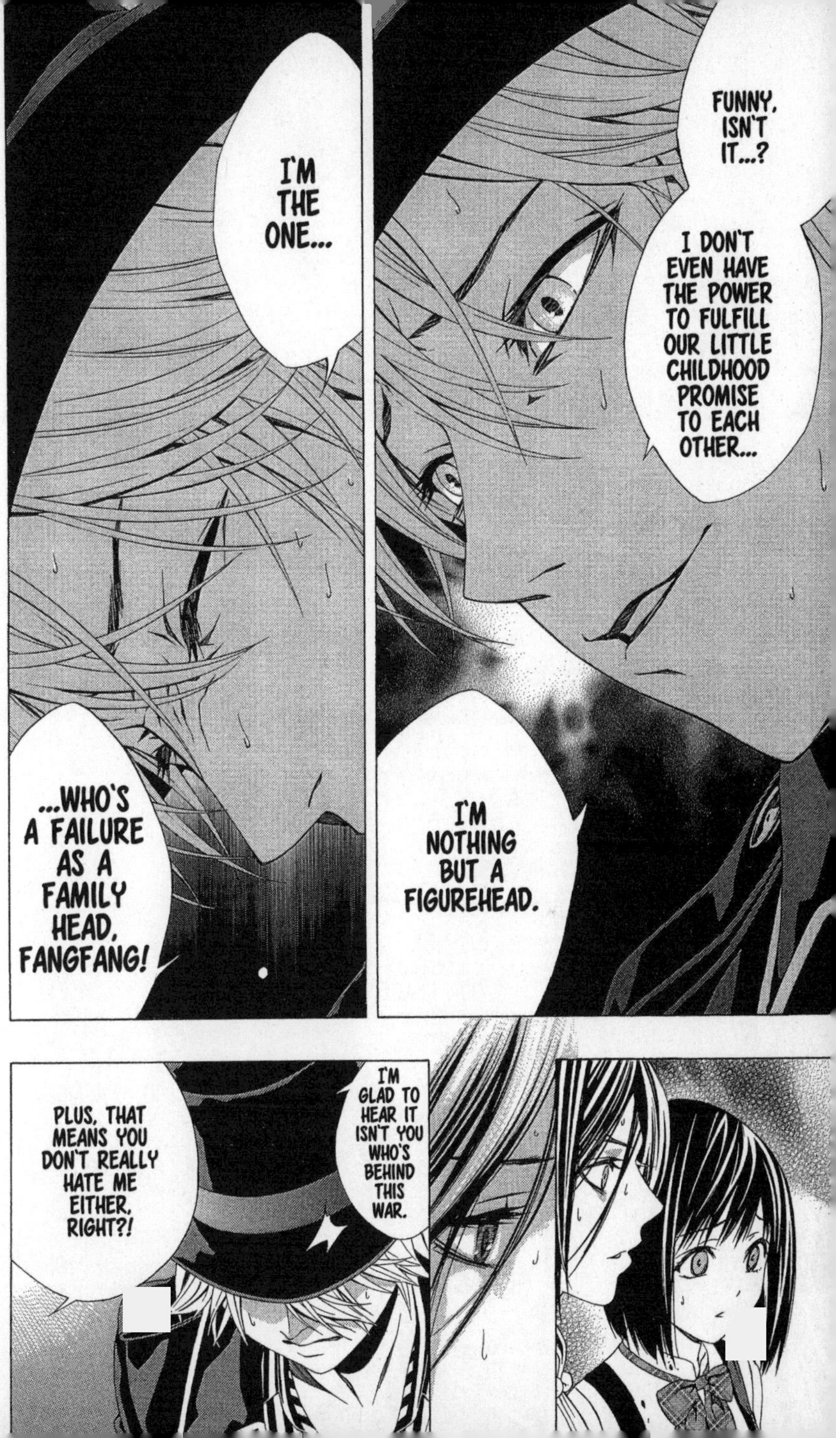
FUNNY, ISN'T IT...?
I DON'T EVEN HAVE THE POWER TO FULFILL OUR LITTLE CHILDHOOD PROMISE TO EACH OTHER...
I'M NOTHING BUT A FIGUREHEAD.
I'M THE ONE...
...WHO'S A FAILURE AS A FAMILY HEAD, FANGFANG!
I'M GLAD TO HEAR IT ISN'T YOU WHO'S BEHIND THIS WAR.
PLUS, THAT MEANS YOU DON'T REALLY HATE ME EITHER, RIGHT?!

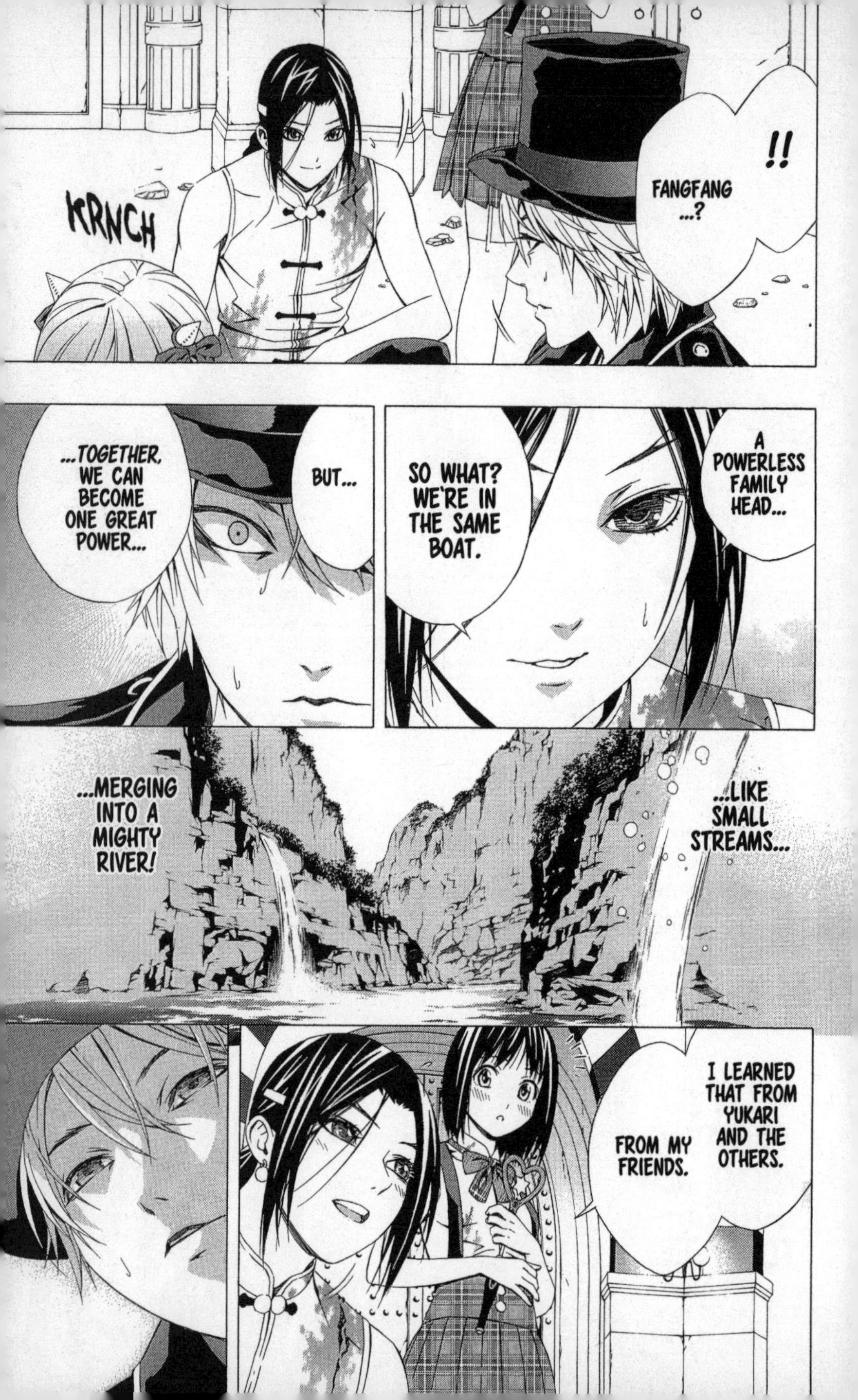
!!
FANGFANG ...?
KRNCH
A POWERLESS FAMILY HEAD...
SO WHAT? WE'RE IN THE SAME BOAT.
BUT...
...TOGETHER, WE CAN BECOME ONE GREAT POWER...
...LIKE SMALL STREAMS...
...MERGING INTO A MIGHTY RIVER!
I LEARNED THAT FROM YUKARI AND THE OTHERS.
FROM MY FRIENDS.

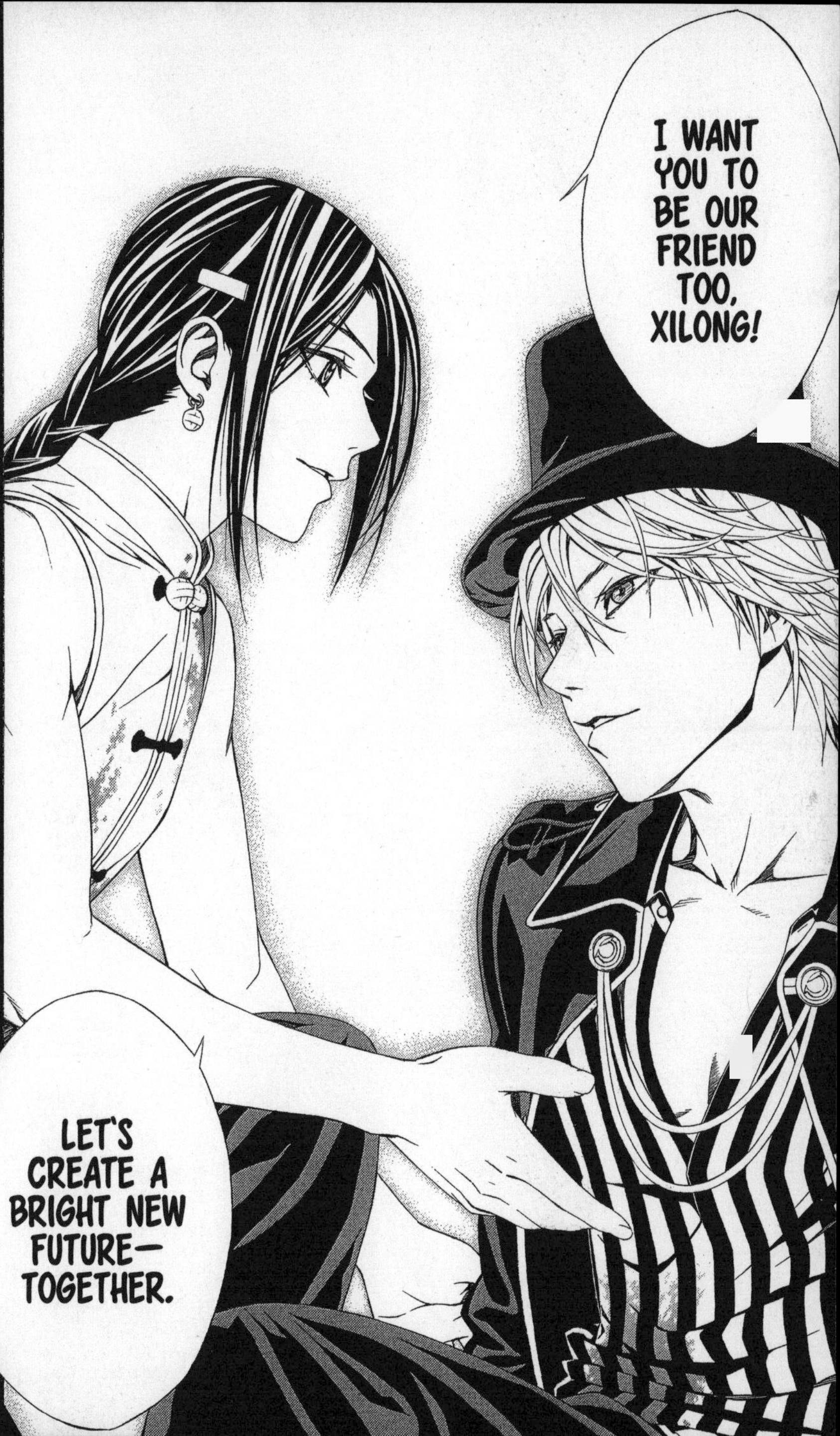
I WANT YOU TO BE OUR FRIEND TOO, XILONG!
LET'S CREATE A BRIGHT NEW FUTURE— TOGETHER.

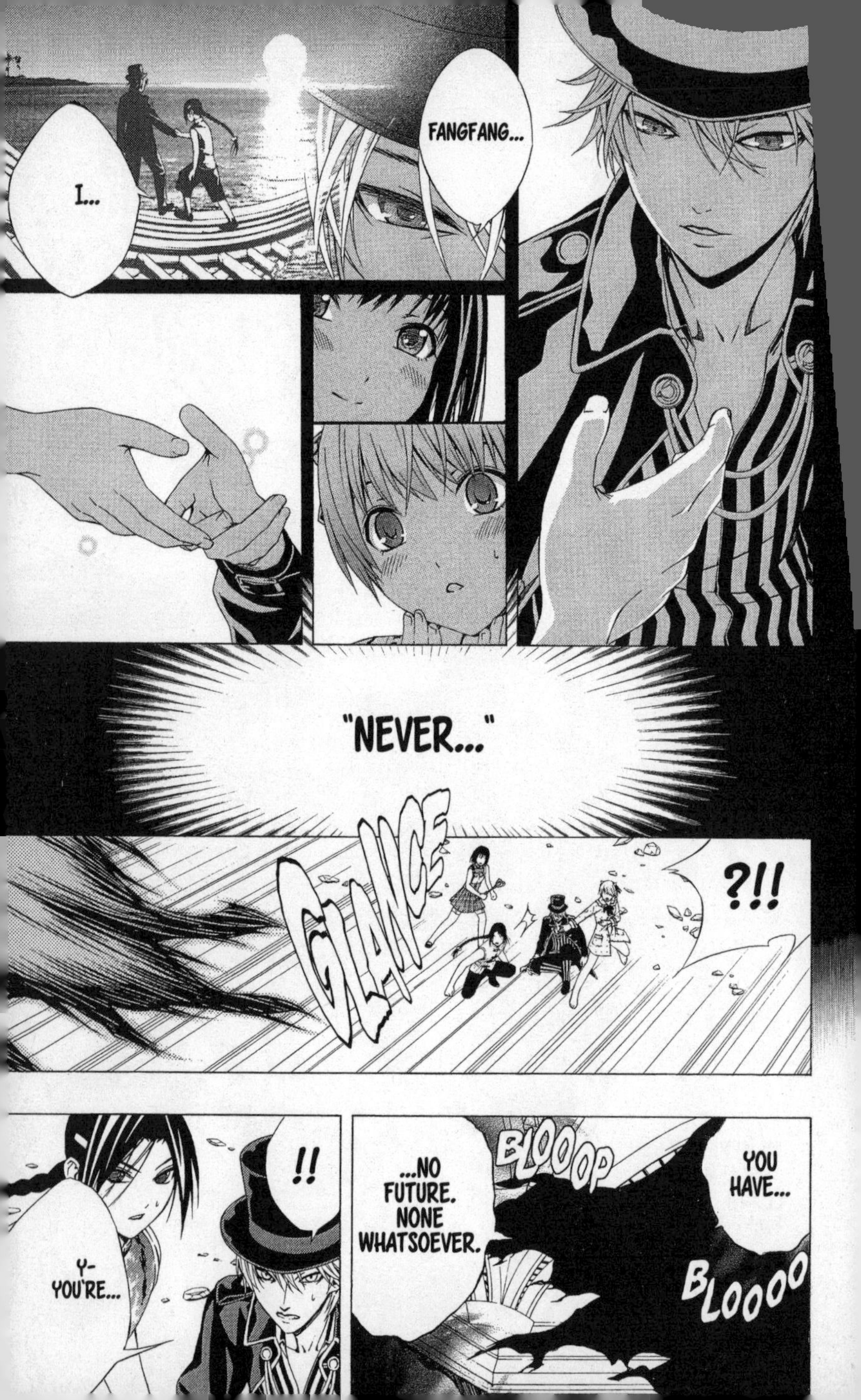
FANGFANG...
I...
"NEVER..."
?!!
GLANCE
YOU HAVE...
BLOOOP
...NO FUTURE. NONE WHATSOEVER.
BLOOOO
!!
Y- YOU'RE...

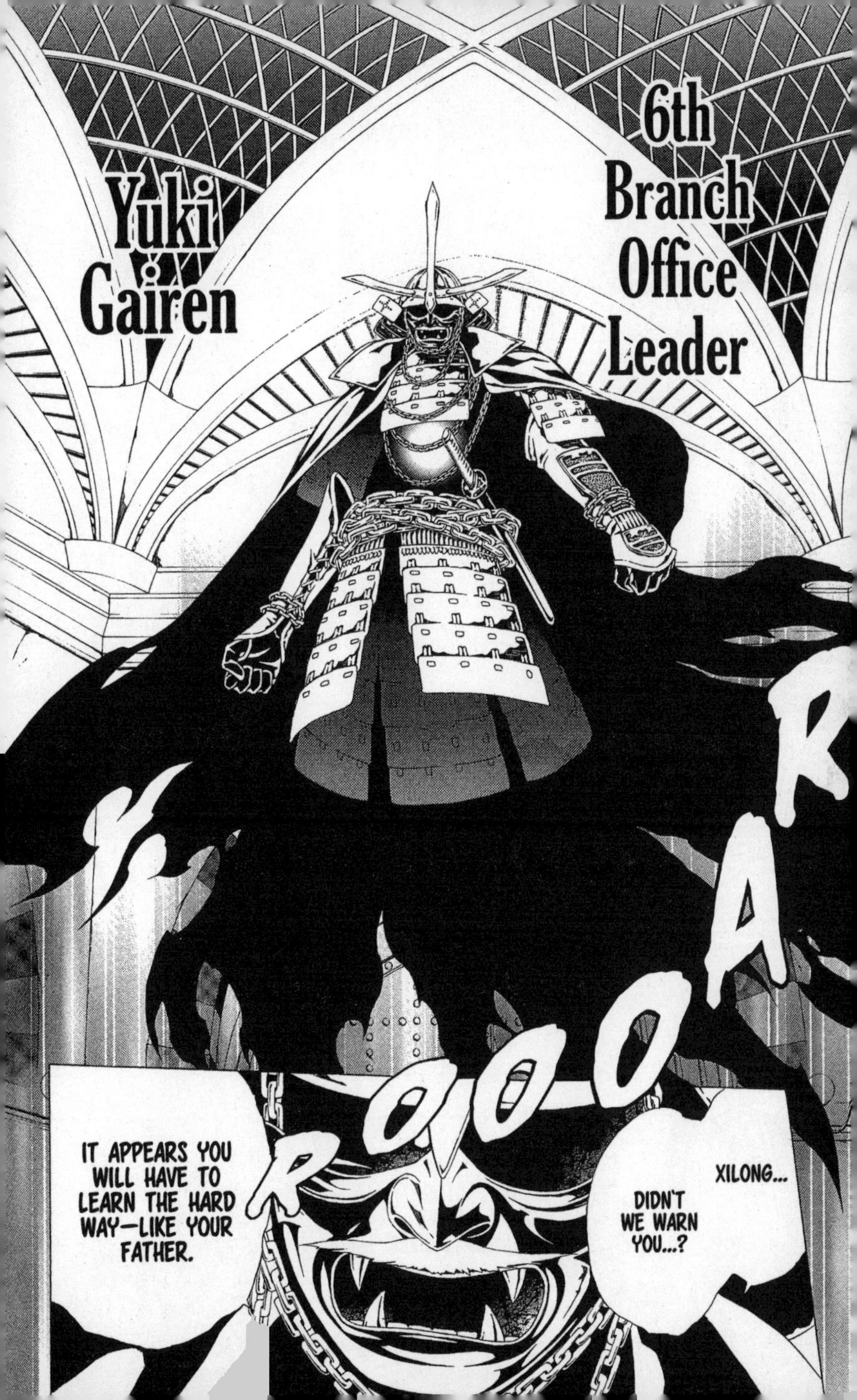

6th Branch Office Leader
Yuki Gairen
ROOOAR
XILONG...
DIDN'T WE WARN YOU...?
IT APPEARS YOU WILL HAVE TO LEARN THE HARD WAY—LIKE YOUR FATHER.

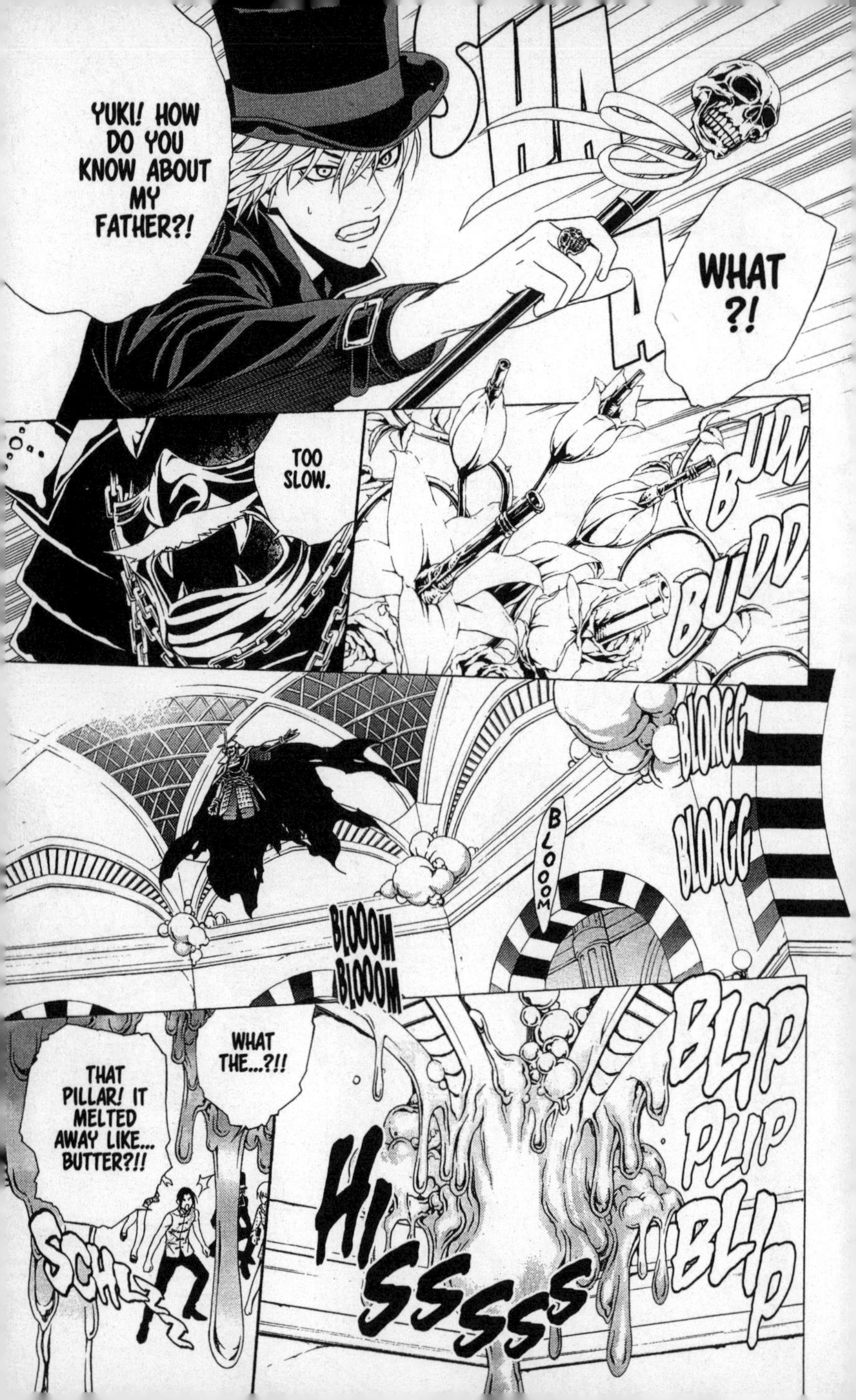
SHA
YUKI! HOW DO YOU KNOW ABOUT MY FATHER?!
WHAT?!
BUDD
BUDD
TOO SLOW.
BLORGG
BLORGG
BLOOOM
BLOOOM
BLOOOM
BLIP
PLIP
BLIP
HISSSSS
WHAT THE...?!!
THAT PILLAR! IT MELTED AWAY LIKE... BUTTER?!!
SCHL

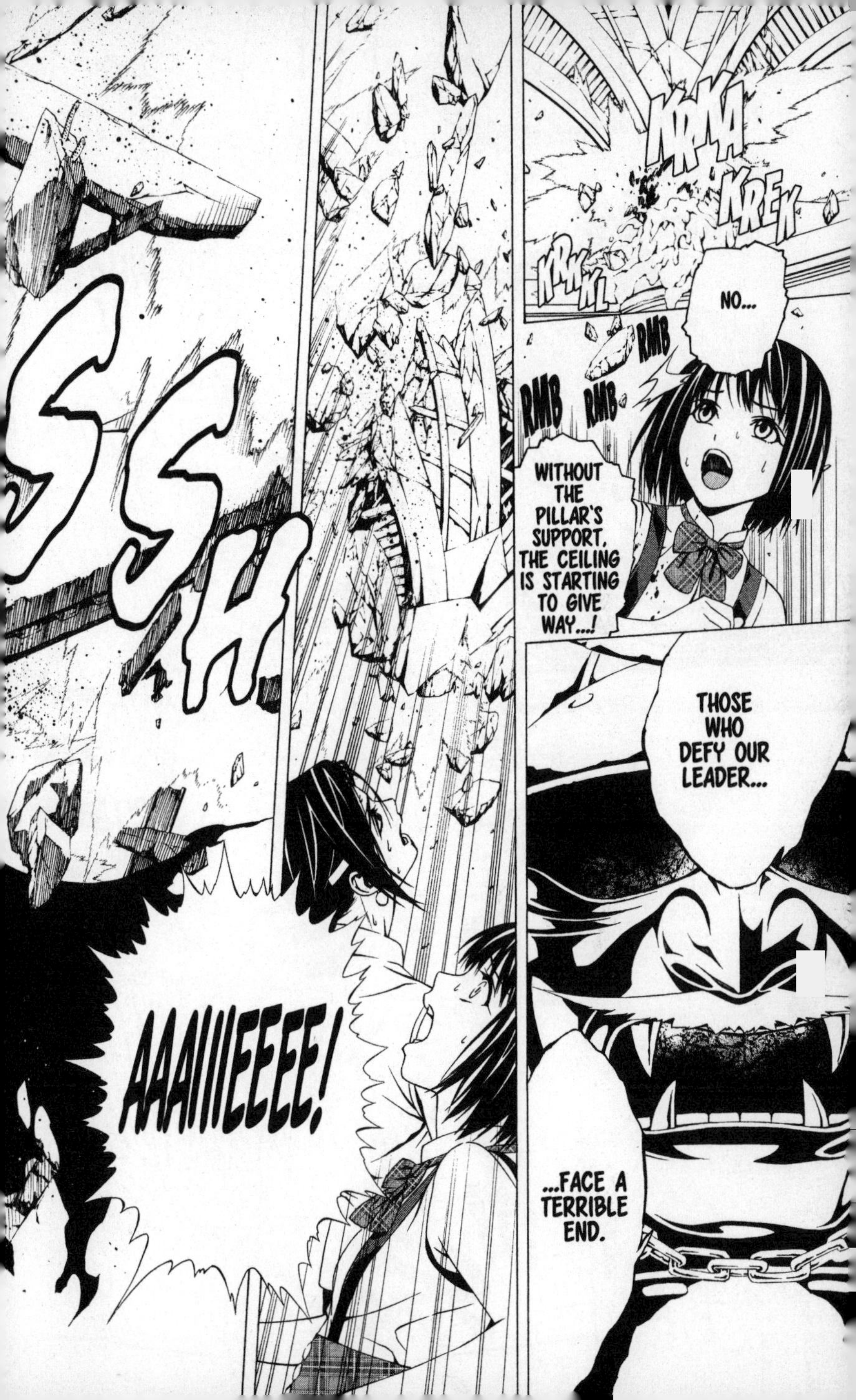
KRAKA
KREK
KRAKKL
RMB
RMB
RMB
NO...
WITHOUT THE PILLAR'S SUPPORT, THE CEILING IS STARTING TO GIVE WAY...!
THOSE WHO DEFY OUR LEADER...
...FACE A TERRIBLE END.
SSH
AAAIIIEEEE!

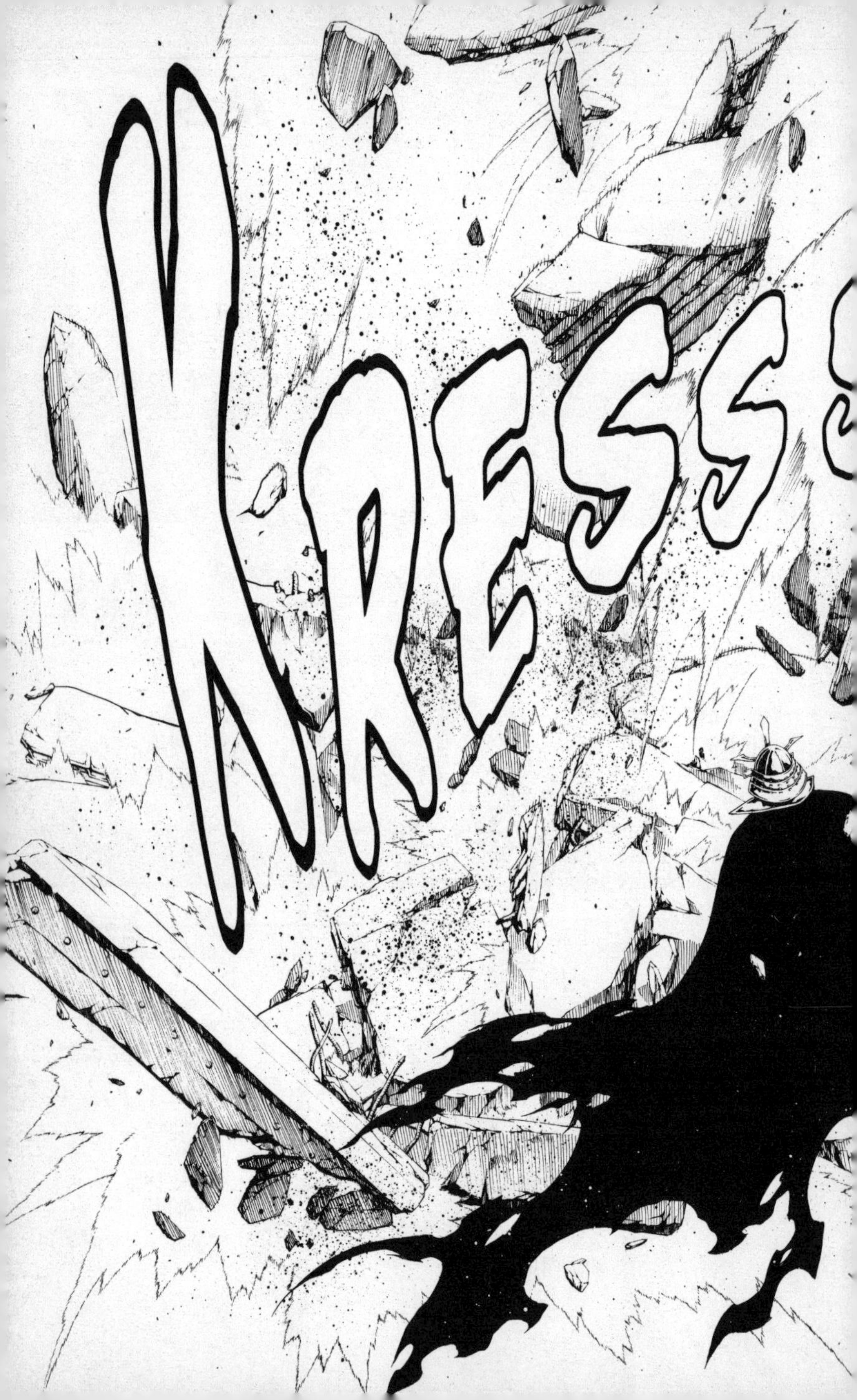
KRESSS

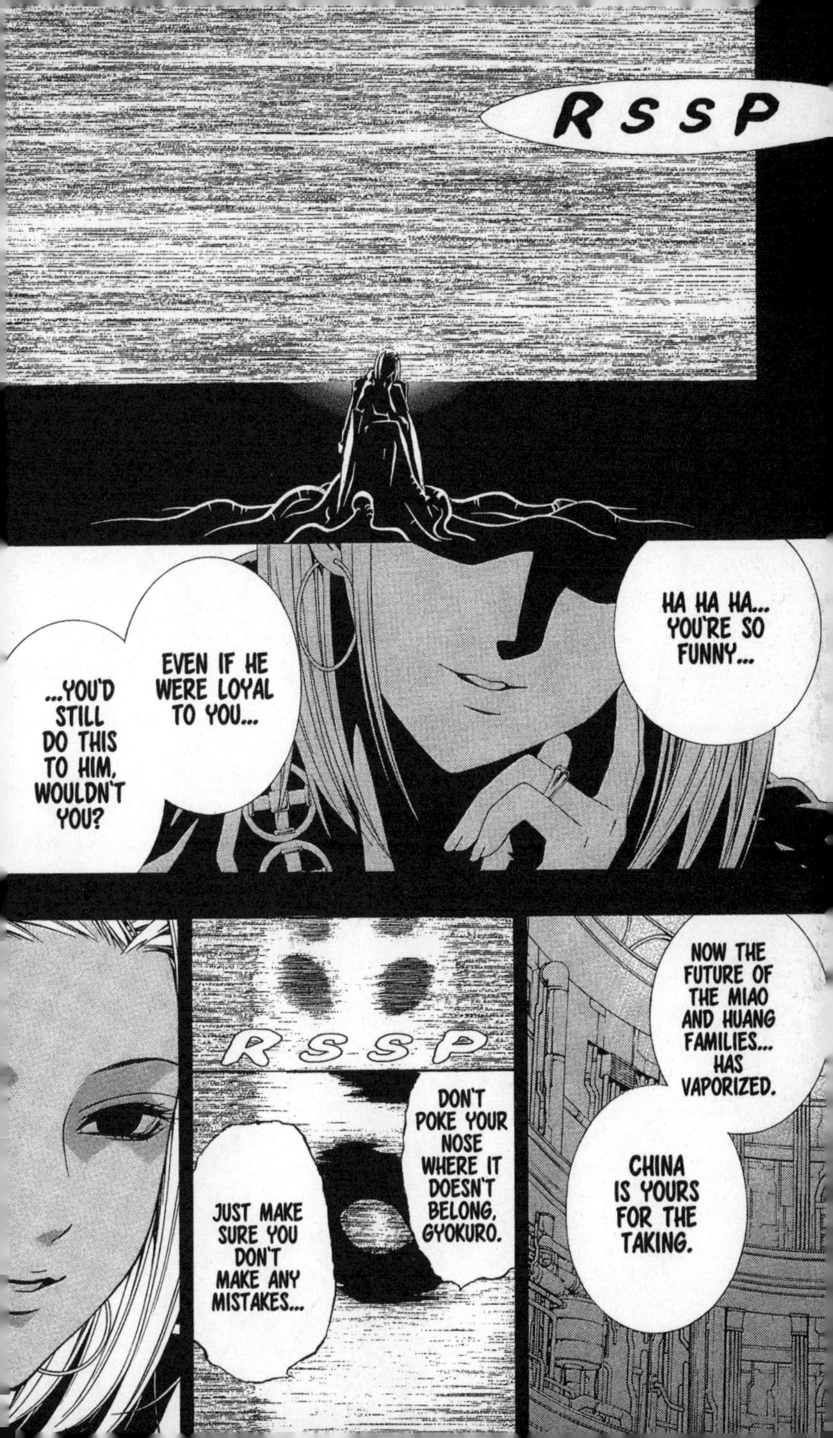
RSSP
HA HA HA... YOU'RE SO FUNNY...
EVEN IF HE WERE LOYAL TO YOU...
...YOU'D STILL DO THIS TO HIM, WOULDN'T YOU?
NOW THE FUTURE OF THE MIAO AND HUANG FAMILIES... HAS VAPORIZED.
CHINA IS YOURS FOR THE TAKING.
RSSP
DON'T POKE YOUR NOSE WHERE IT DOESN'T BELONG, GYOKURO.
JUST MAKE SURE YOU DON'T MAKE ANY MISTAKES...

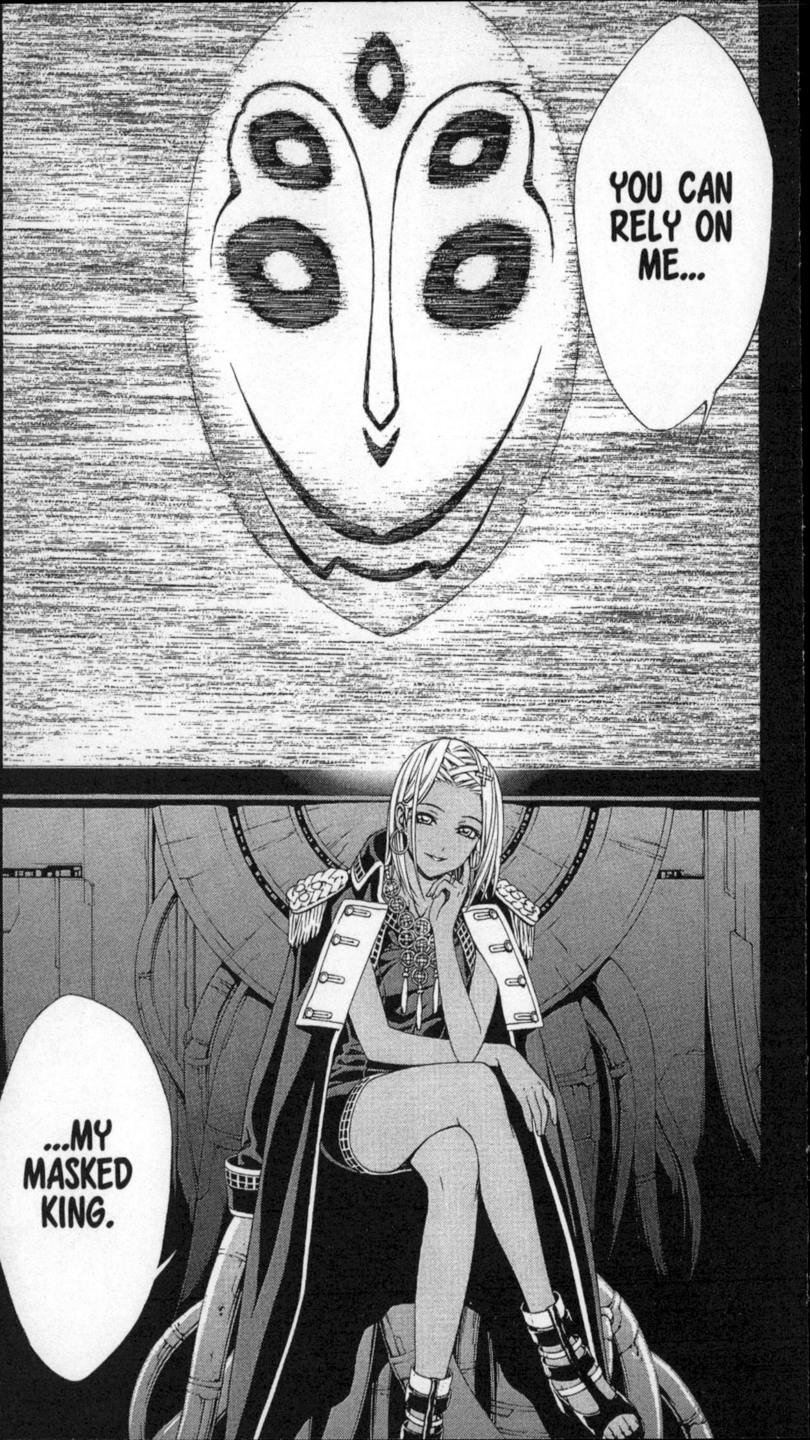
YOU CAN RELY ON ME...
...MY MASKED KING.

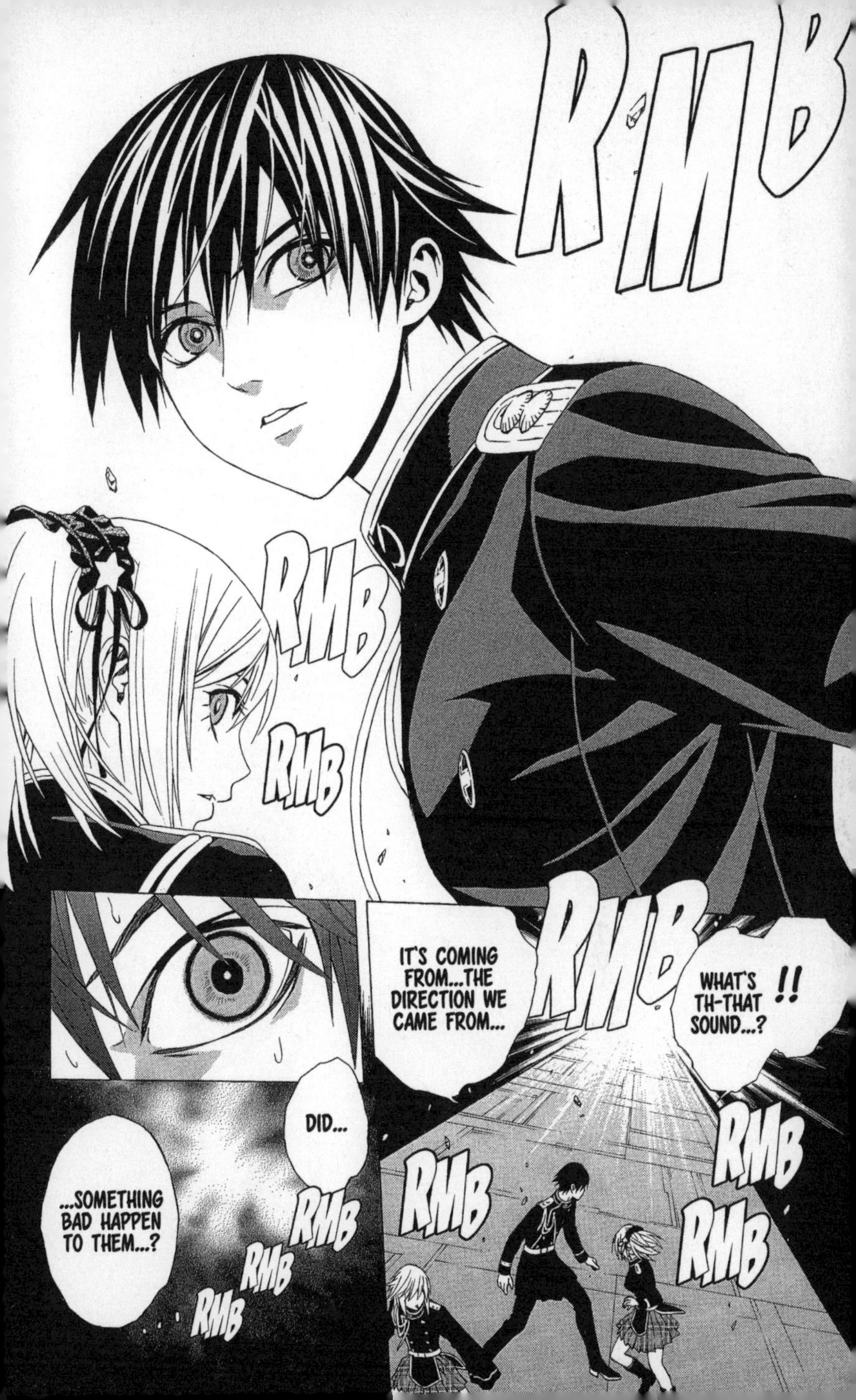
RMB
RMB
RMB
RMB
WHAT'S TH-THAT SOUND...? !!
IT'S COMING FROM...THE DIRECTION WE CAME FROM...
RMB
RMB
RMB
DID...
...SOMETHING BAD HAPPEN TO THEM...?
RMB
RMB
RMB

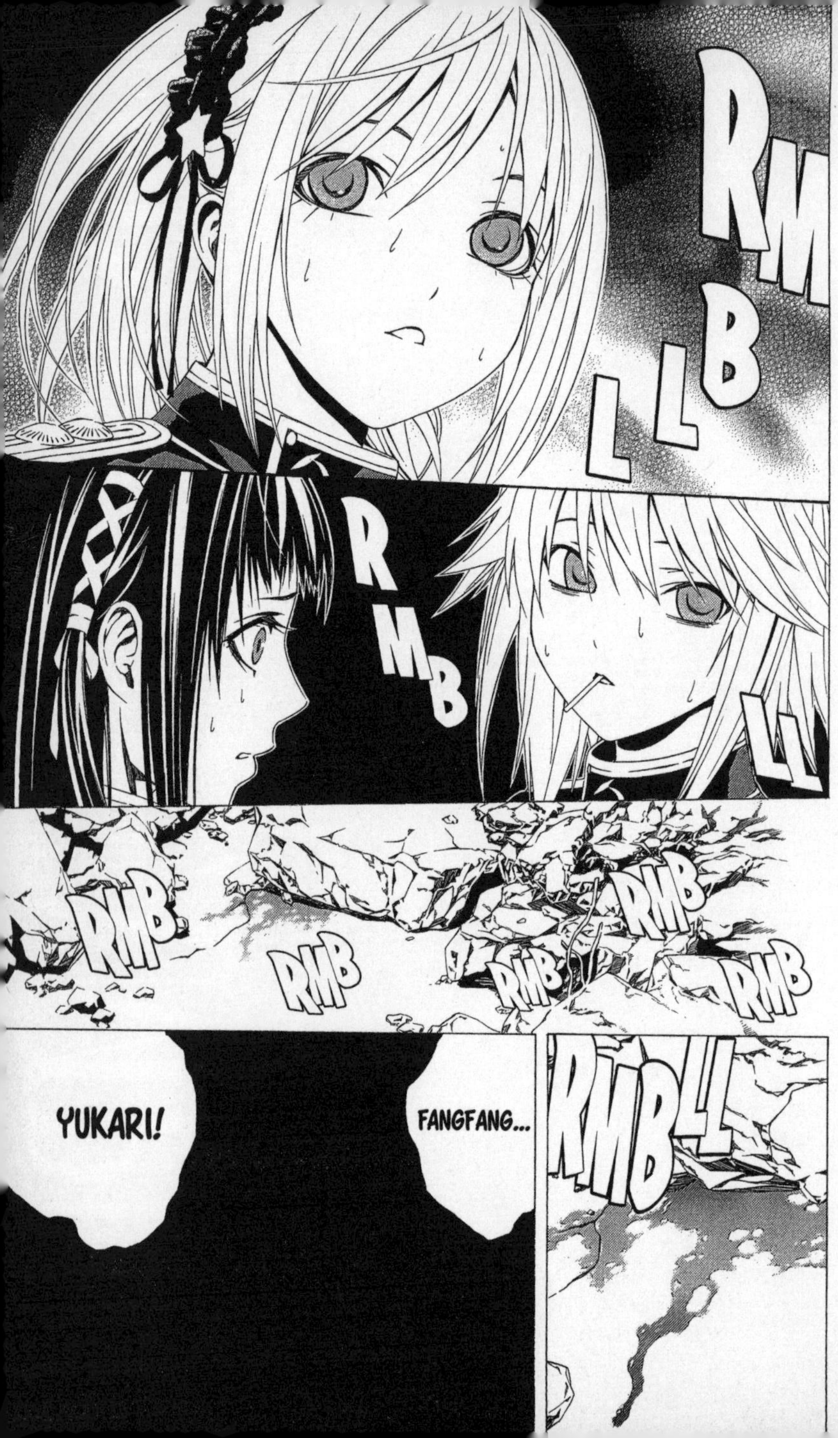
RMBLL
RMBLL
RMB
RMB
RMB
RMB
RMB
RMBLL
FANGFANG...
YUKARI!

ROSARIO+VAMPIRE

Season II

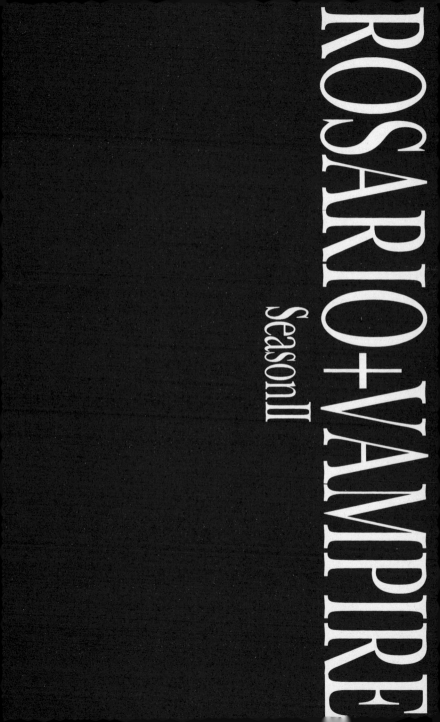

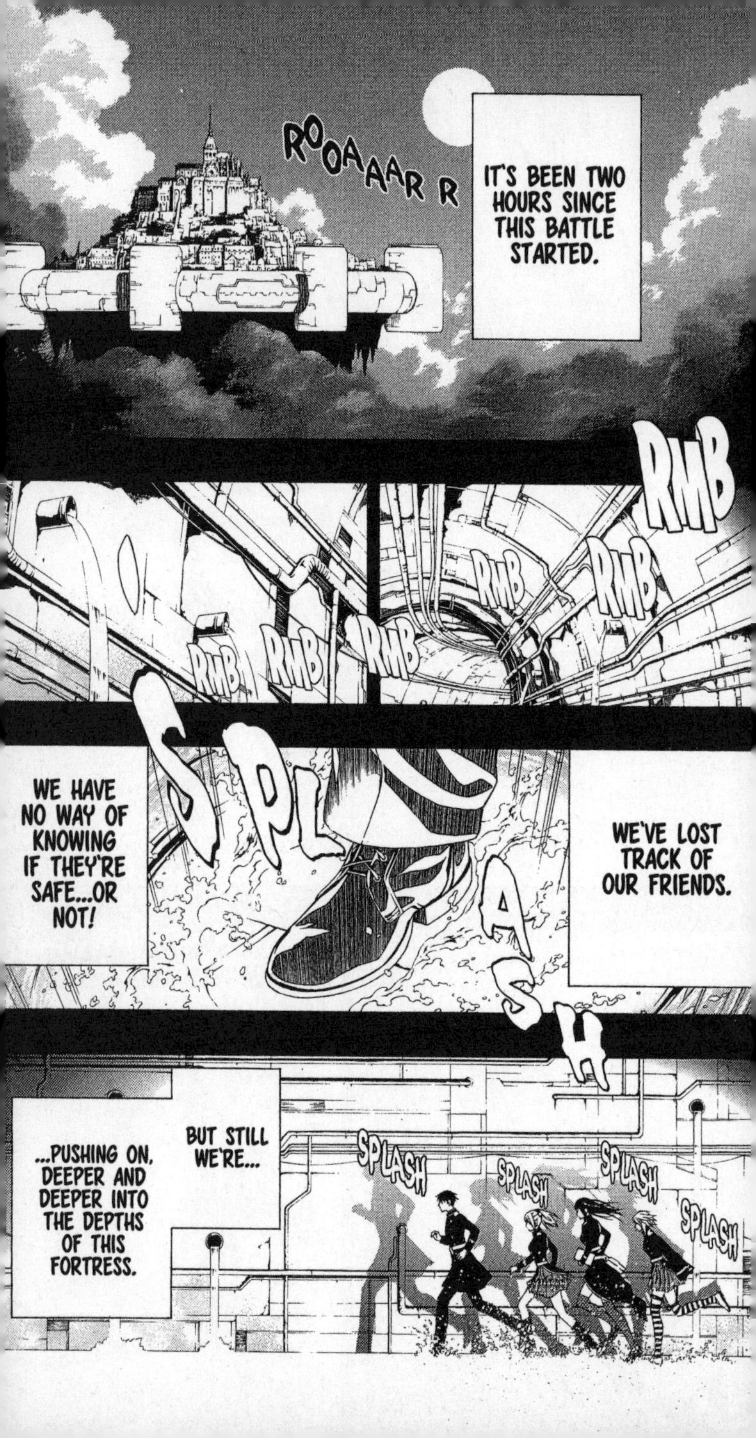

IT'S BEEN TWO HOURS SINCE THIS BATTLE STARTED.
ROOAAARR R
RMB
RMB
RMB
RMB
RMB
RMB
SPLASH
WE'VE LOST TRACK OF OUR FRIENDS.
WE HAVE NO WAY OF KNOWING IF THEY'RE SAFE...OR NOT!
SPLASH
SPLASH
SPLASH
SPLASH
BUT STILL WE'RE...
...PUSHING ON, DEEPER AND DEEPER INTO THE DEPTHS OF THIS FORTRESS.

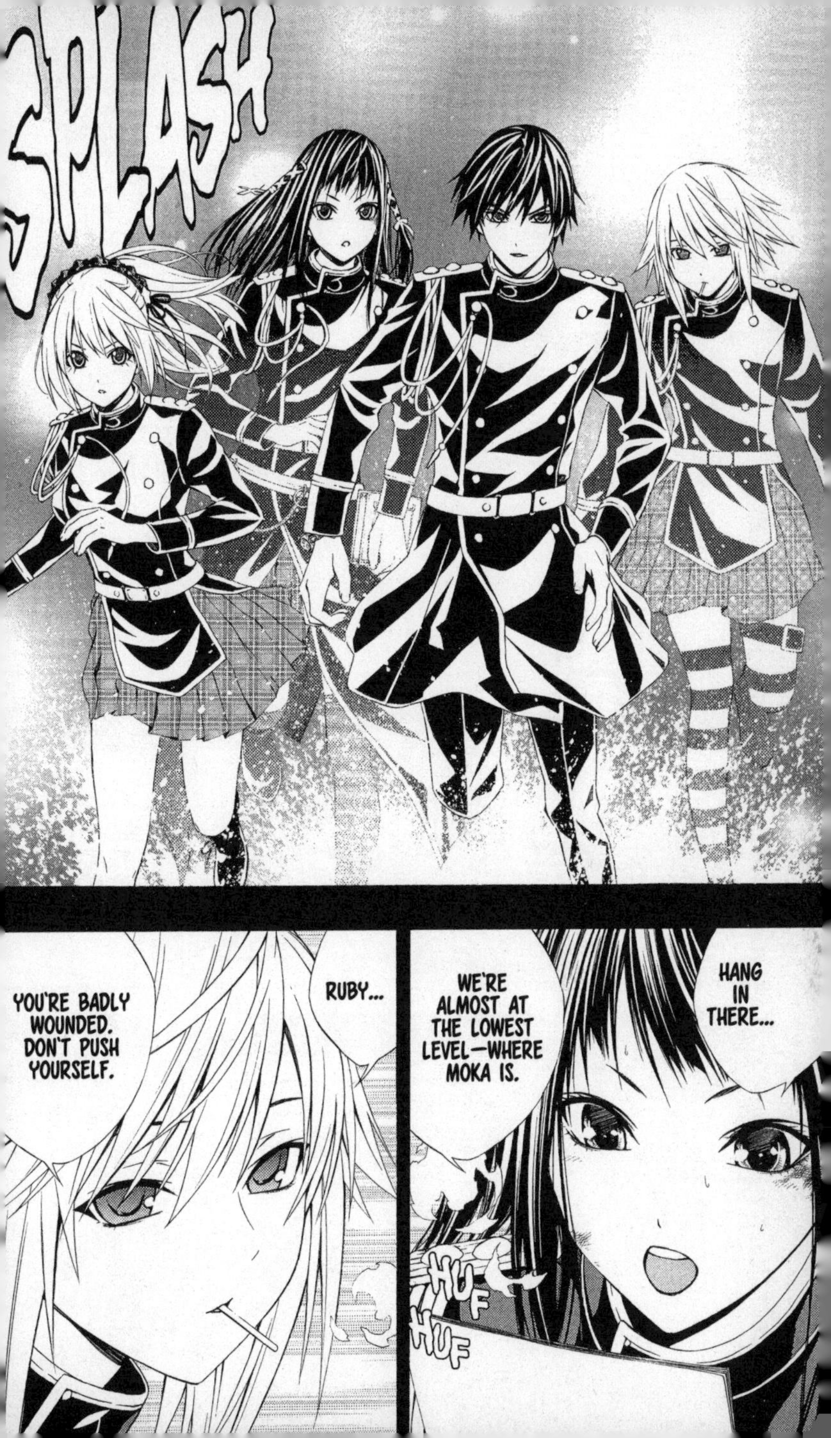
SPLASH
HANG IN THERE...
WE'RE ALMOST AT THE LOWEST LEVEL—WHERE MOKA IS.
HUF HUF
RUBY...
YOU'RE BADLY WOUNDED. DON'T PUSH YOURSELF.

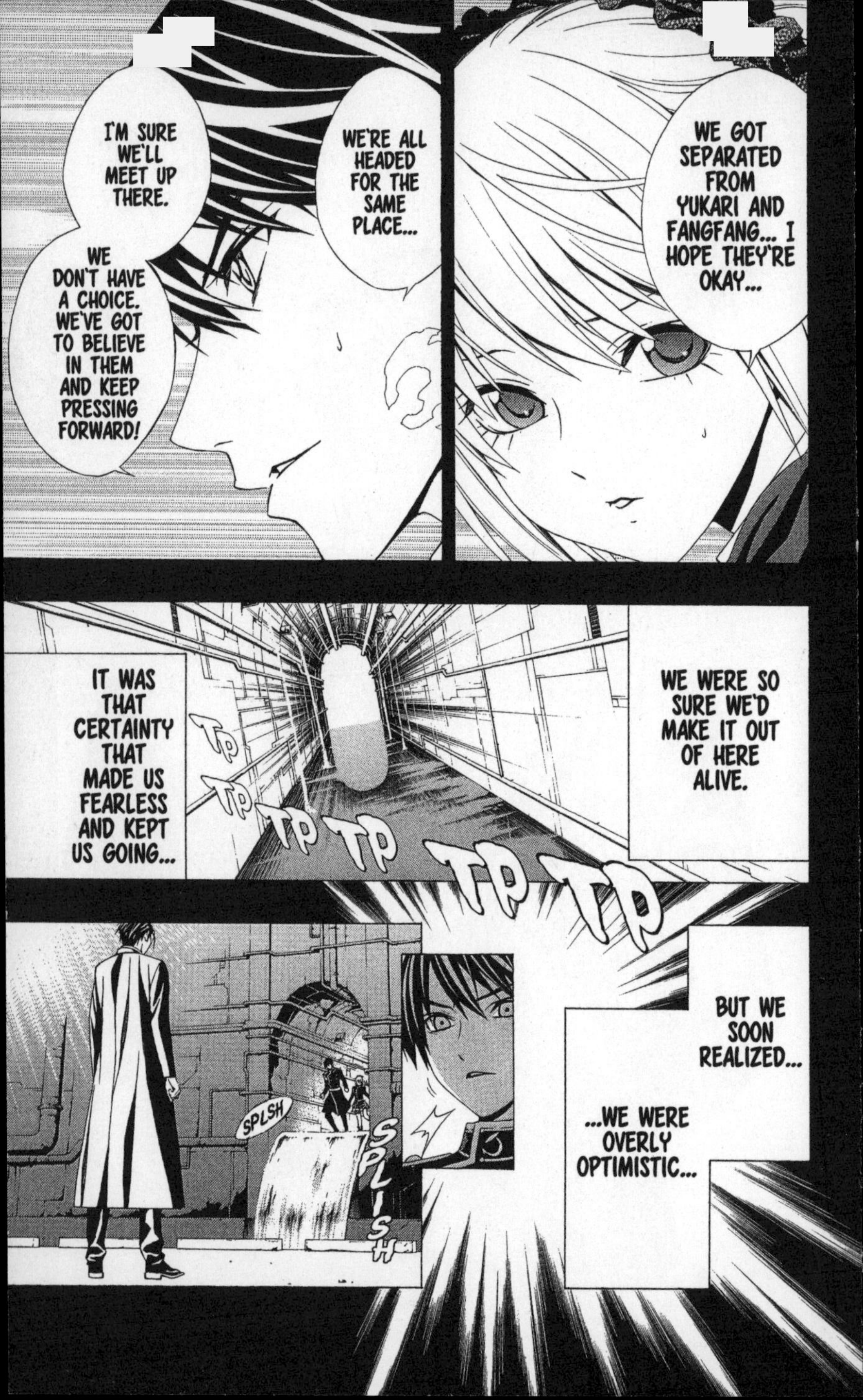
WE GOT SEPARATED FROM YUKARI AND FANGFANG... I HOPE THEY'RE OKAY...
WE'RE ALL HEADED FOR THE SAME PLACE...
I'M SURE WE'LL MEET UP THERE.
WE DON'T HAVE A CHOICE. WE'VE GOT TO BELIEVE IN THEM AND KEEP PRESSING FORWARD!
WE WERE SO SURE WE'D MAKE IT OUT OF HERE ALIVE.
IT WAS THAT CERTAINTY THAT MADE US FEARLESS AND KEPT US GOING...
TP TP TP TP TP TP TP
BUT WE SOON REALIZED...
...WE WERE OVERLY OPTIMISTIC...
SPLISH
SPLSH

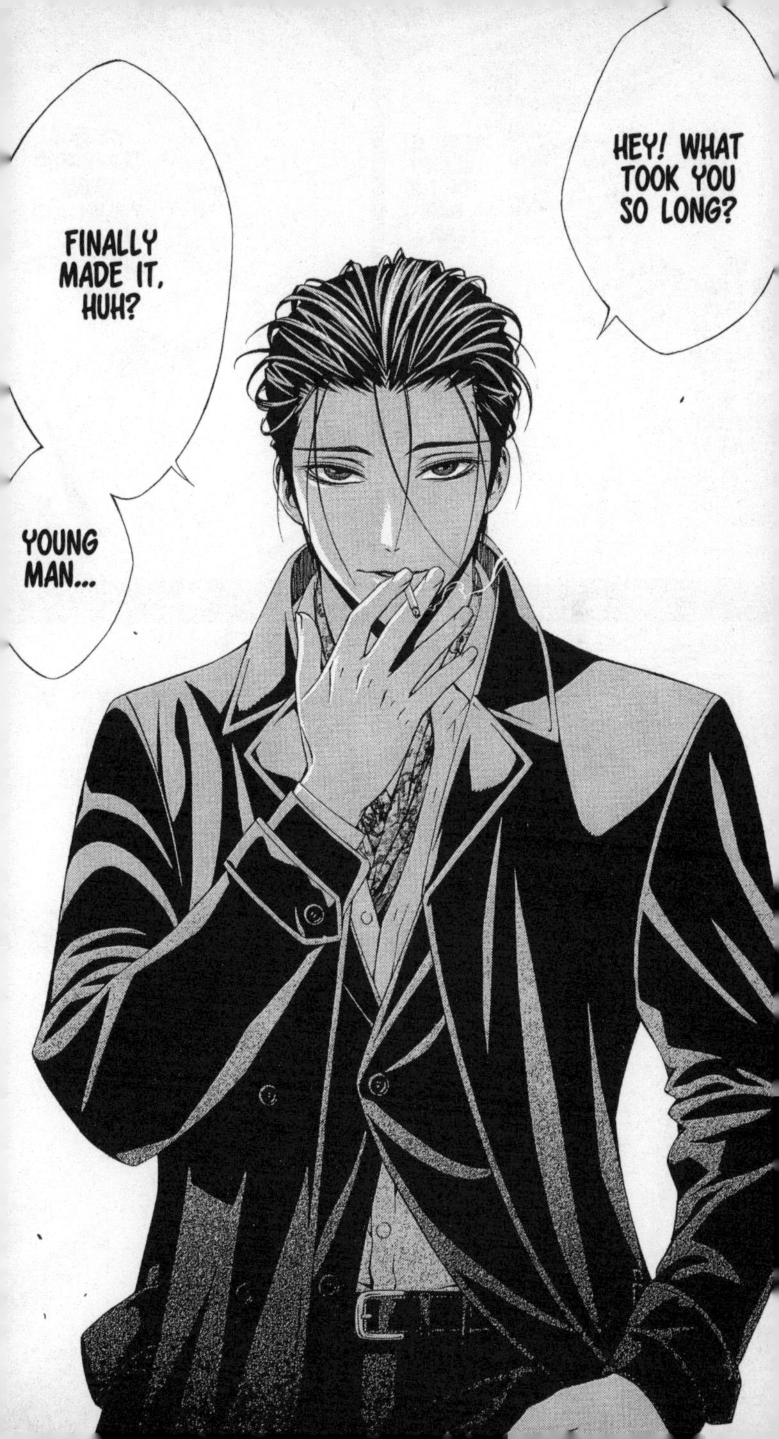
HEY! WHAT TOOK YOU SO LONG?
FINALLY MADE IT, HUH?
YOUNG MAN...

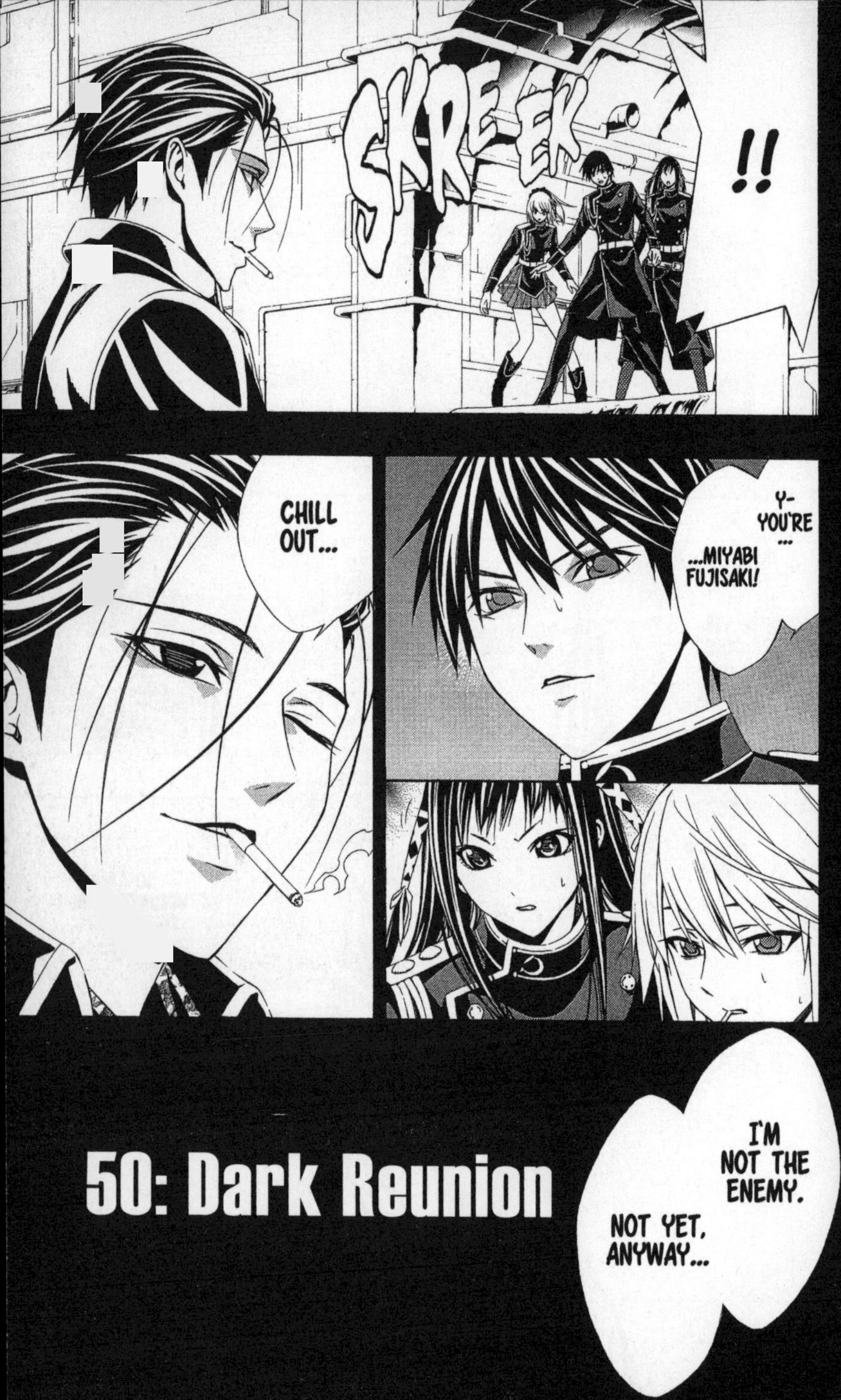
SKREEK
!!
Y- YOU'RE ...
...MIYABI FUJISAKI!
CHILL OUT...
I'M NOT THE ENEMY.
NOT YET, ANYWAY...
50: Dark Reunion

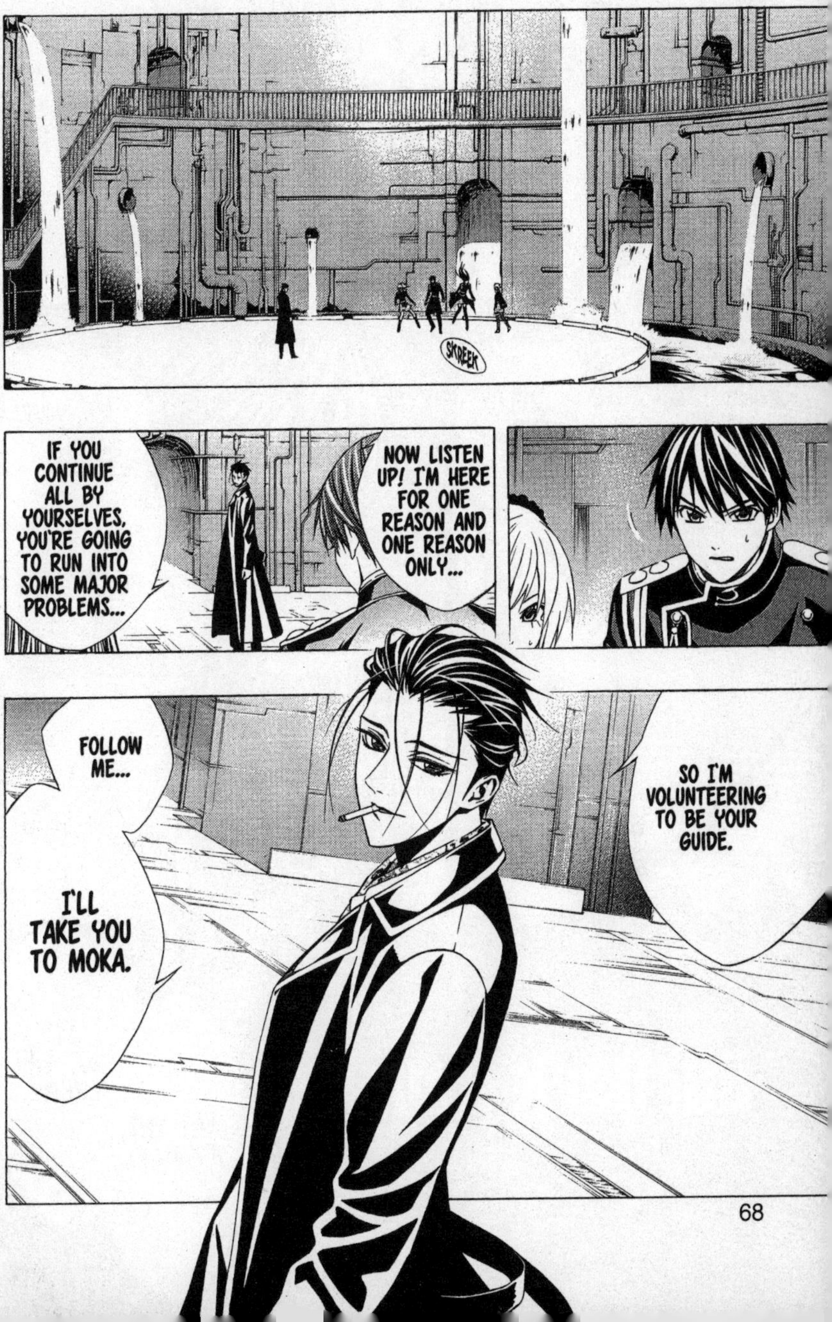
SKREEK
NOW LISTEN UP! I'M HERE FOR ONE REASON AND ONE REASON ONLY...
IF YOU CONTINUE ALL BY YOURSELVES, YOU'RE GOING TO RUN INTO SOME MAJOR PROBLEMS...
SO I'M VOLUNTEERING TO BE YOUR GUIDE.
FOLLOW ME...
I'LL TAKE YOU TO MOKA.

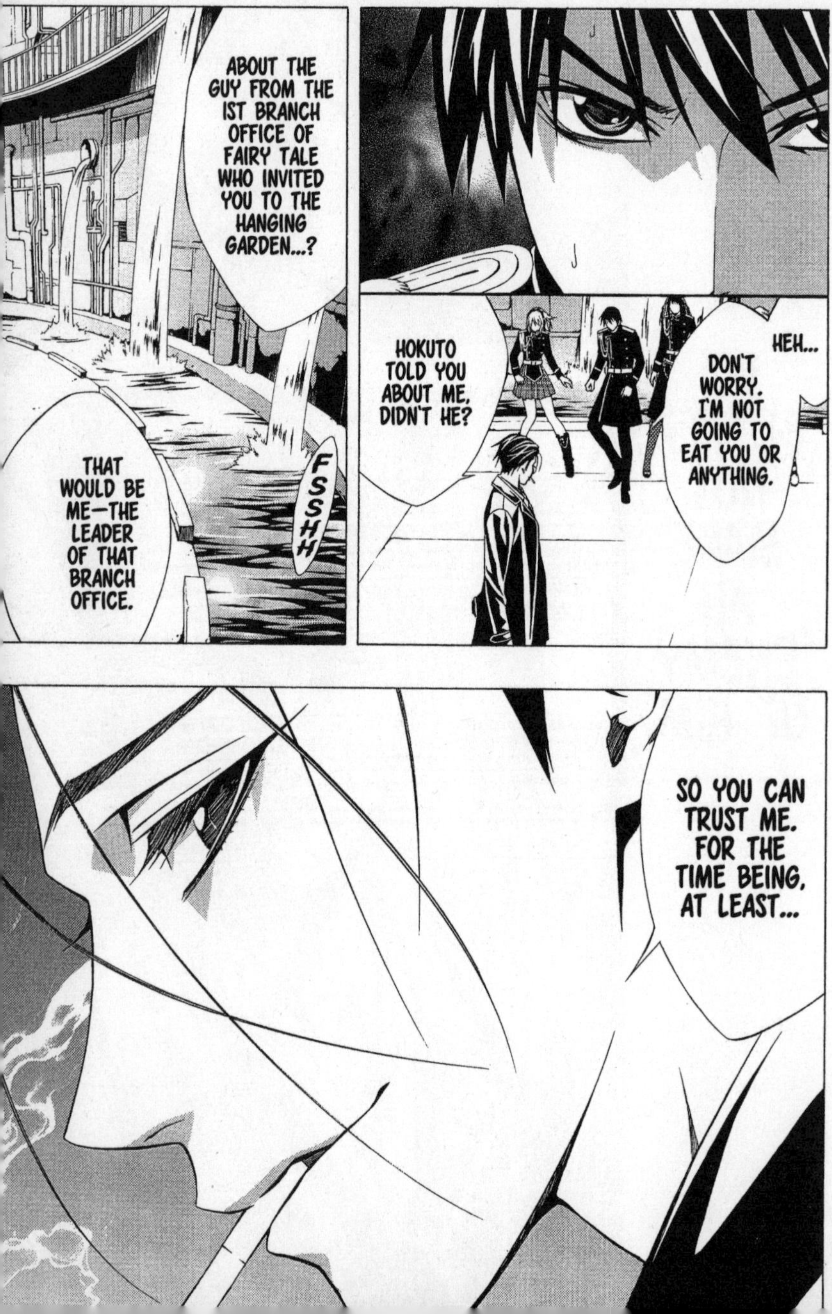
HEH...
DON'T WORRY. I'M NOT GOING TO EAT YOU OR ANYTHING.
HOKUTO TOLD YOU ABOUT ME, DIDN'T HE?
ABOUT THE GUY FROM THE 1ST BRANCH OFFICE OF FAIRY TALE WHO INVITED YOU TO THE HANGING GARDEN...?
FSSHH
THAT WOULD BE ME—THE LEADER OF THAT BRANCH OFFICE.
SO YOU CAN TRUST ME. FOR THE TIME BEING, AT LEAST...

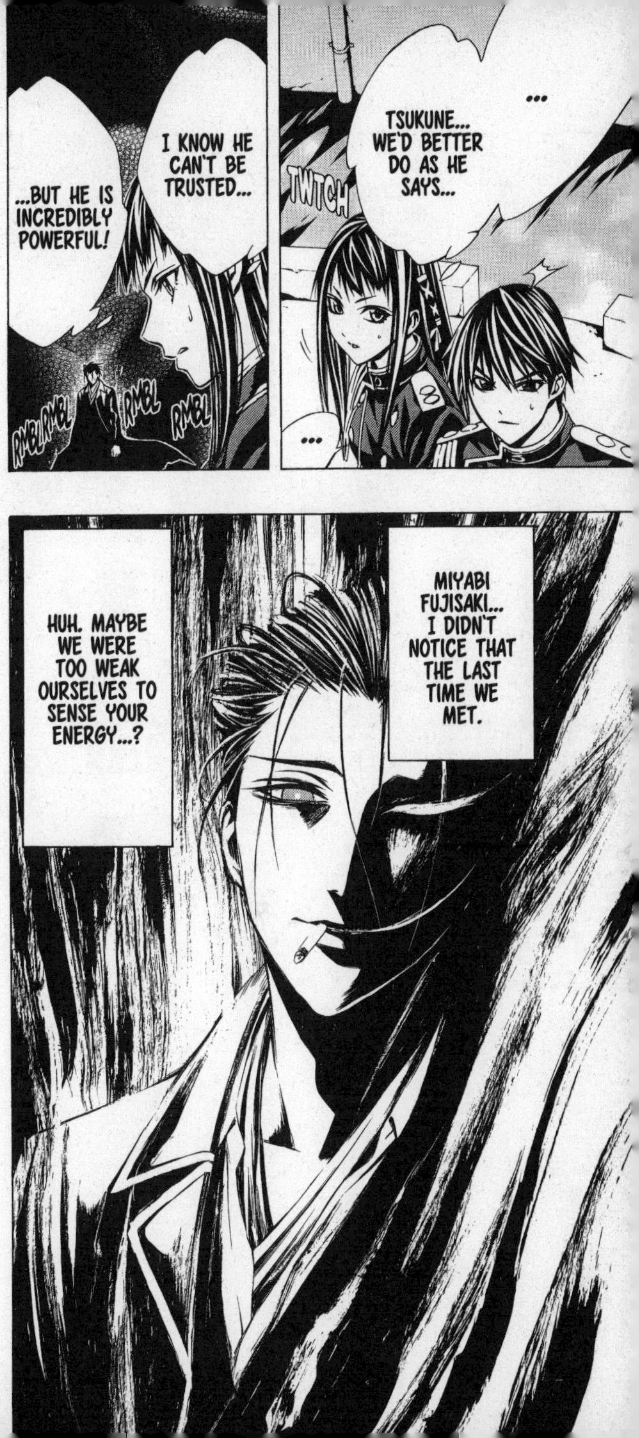
...
TSUKUNE... WE'D BETTER DO AS HE SAYS...
TWITCH
...
I KNOW HE CAN'T BE TRUSTED...
...BUT HE IS INCREDIBLY POWERFUL!
RMBL RMBL RMBL RMBL
MIYABI FUJISAKI... I DIDN'T NOTICE THAT THE LAST TIME WE MET.
HUH. MAYBE WE WERE TOO WEAK OURSELVES TO SENSE YOUR ENERGY...?

WE BETTER NOT MAKE AN ENEMY OF HIM.

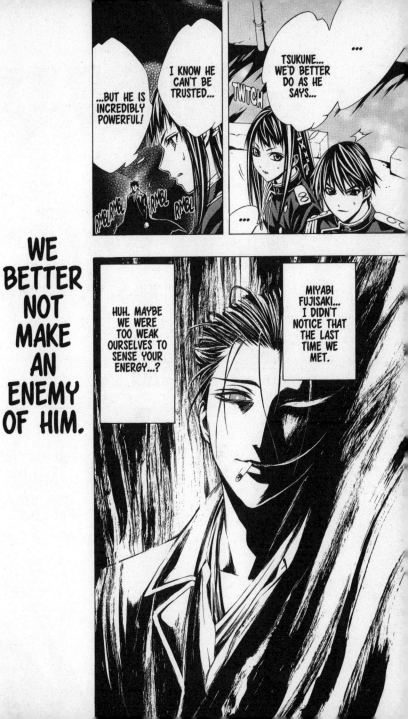

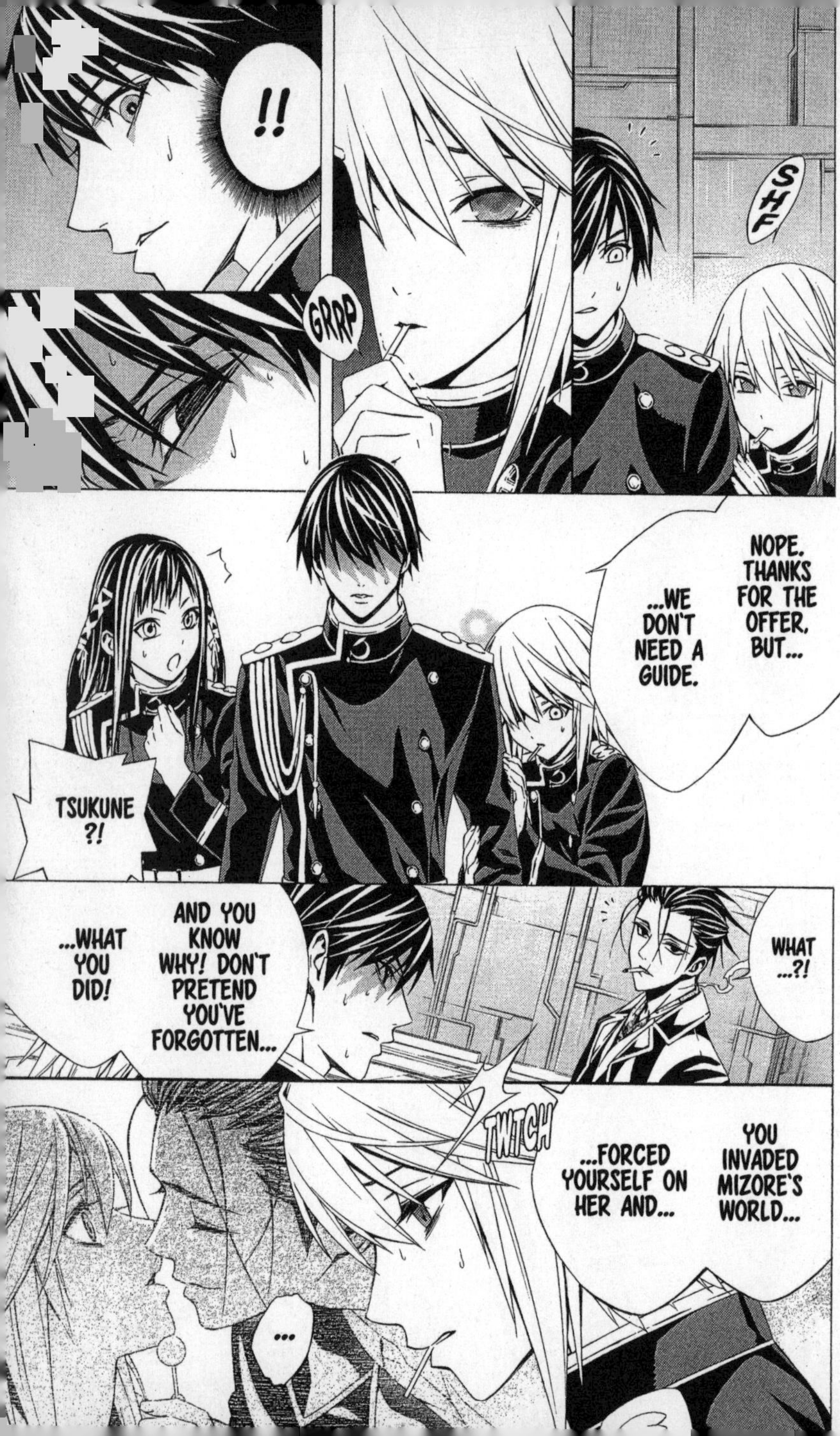
SHF
GRRP
!!
NOPE. THANKS FOR THE OFFER, BUT...
...WE DON'T NEED A GUIDE.
TSUKUNE ?!
WHAT ...?!
AND YOU KNOW WHY! DON'T PRETEND YOU'VE FORGOTTEN...
...WHAT YOU DID!
YOU INVADED MIZORE'S WORLD...
...FORCED YOURSELF ON HER AND...
TWITCH
...

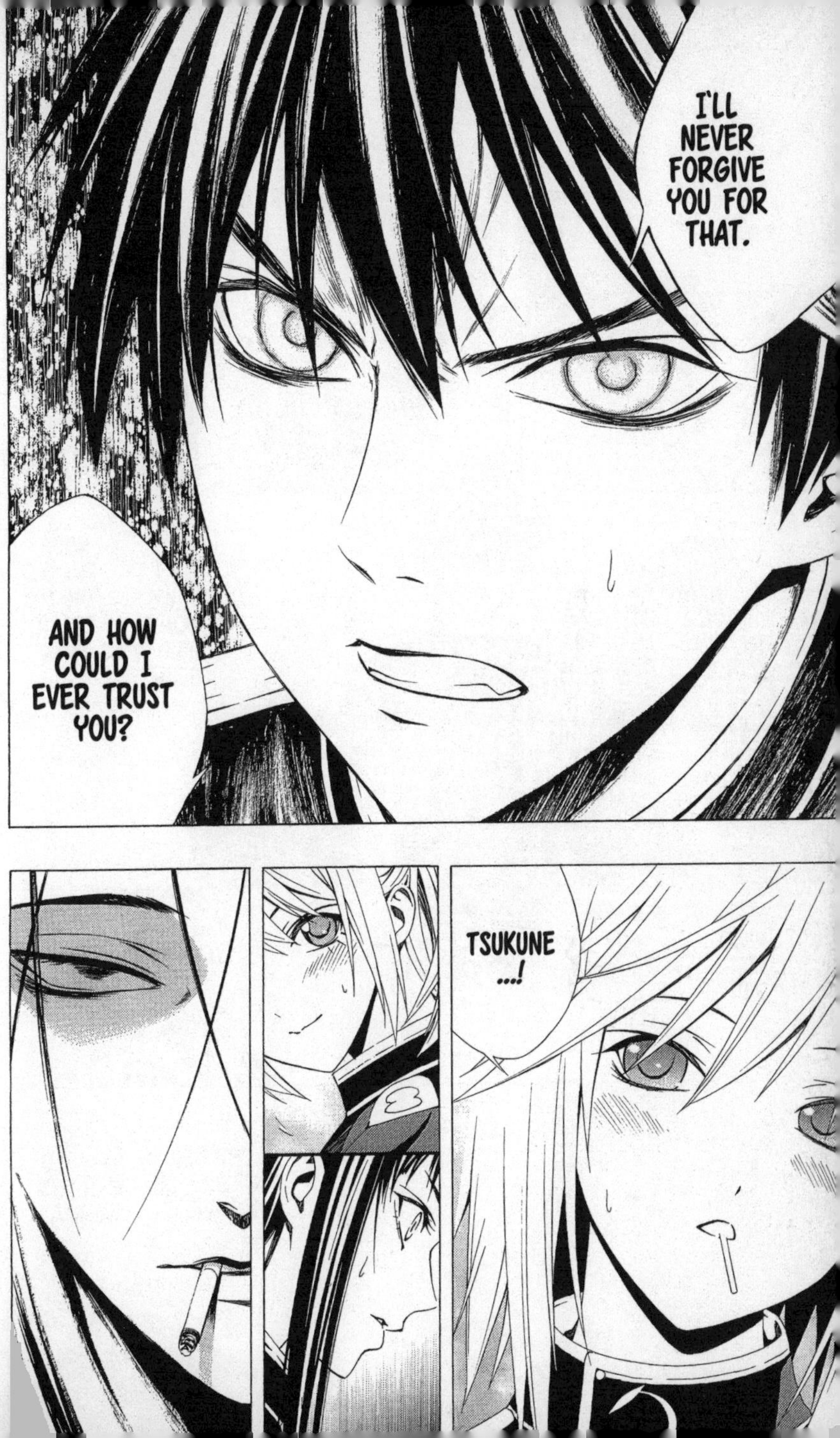
I'LL NEVER FORGIVE YOU FOR THAT.
AND HOW COULD I EVER TRUST YOU?
TSUKUNE ...!

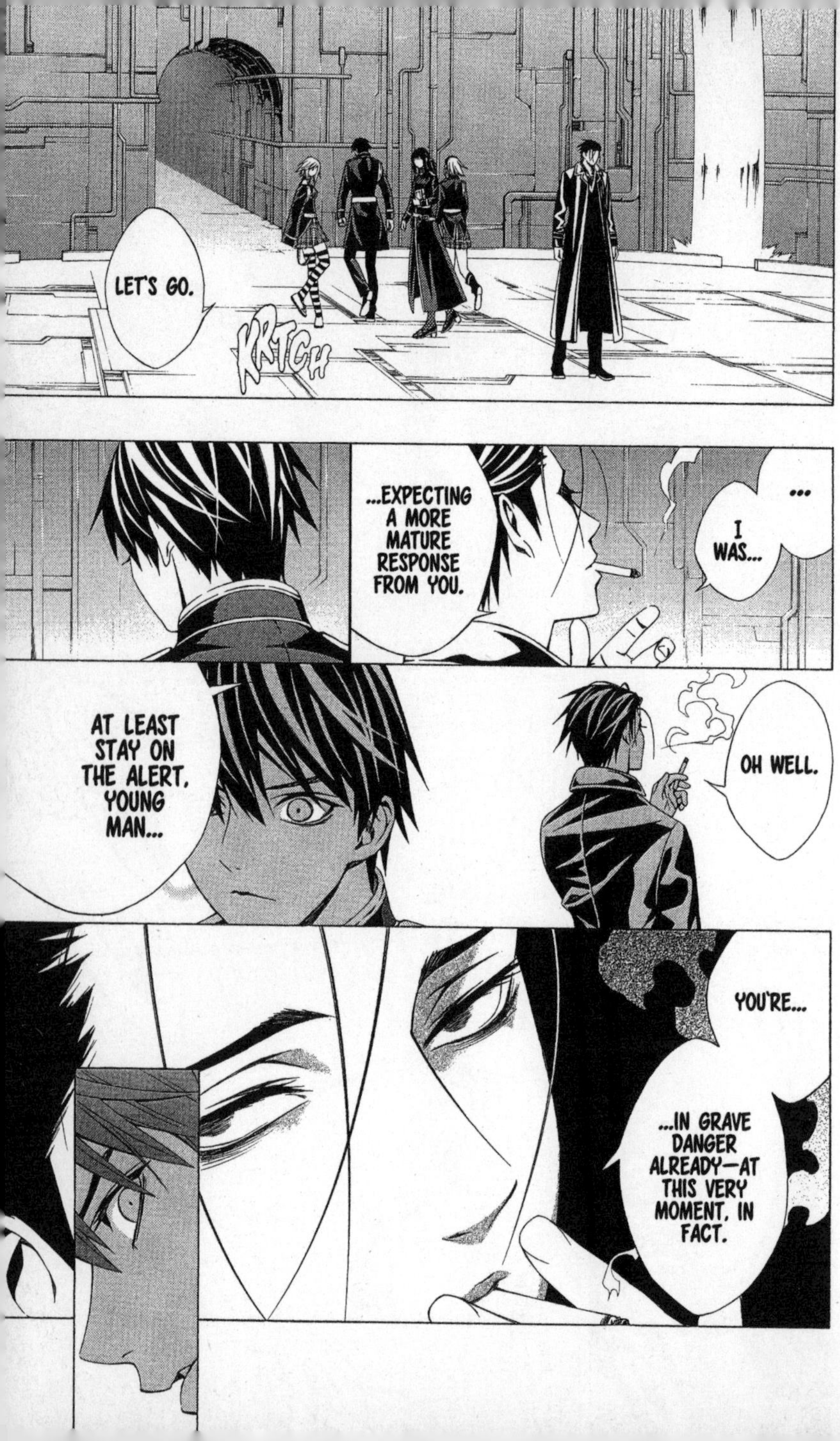
LET'S GO.
KRTCH
... I WAS...
...EXPECTING A MORE MATURE RESPONSE FROM YOU.
OH WELL.
AT LEAST STAY ON THE ALERT, YOUNG MAN...
YOU'RE...
...IN GRAVE DANGER ALREADY—AT THIS VERY MOMENT, IN FACT.

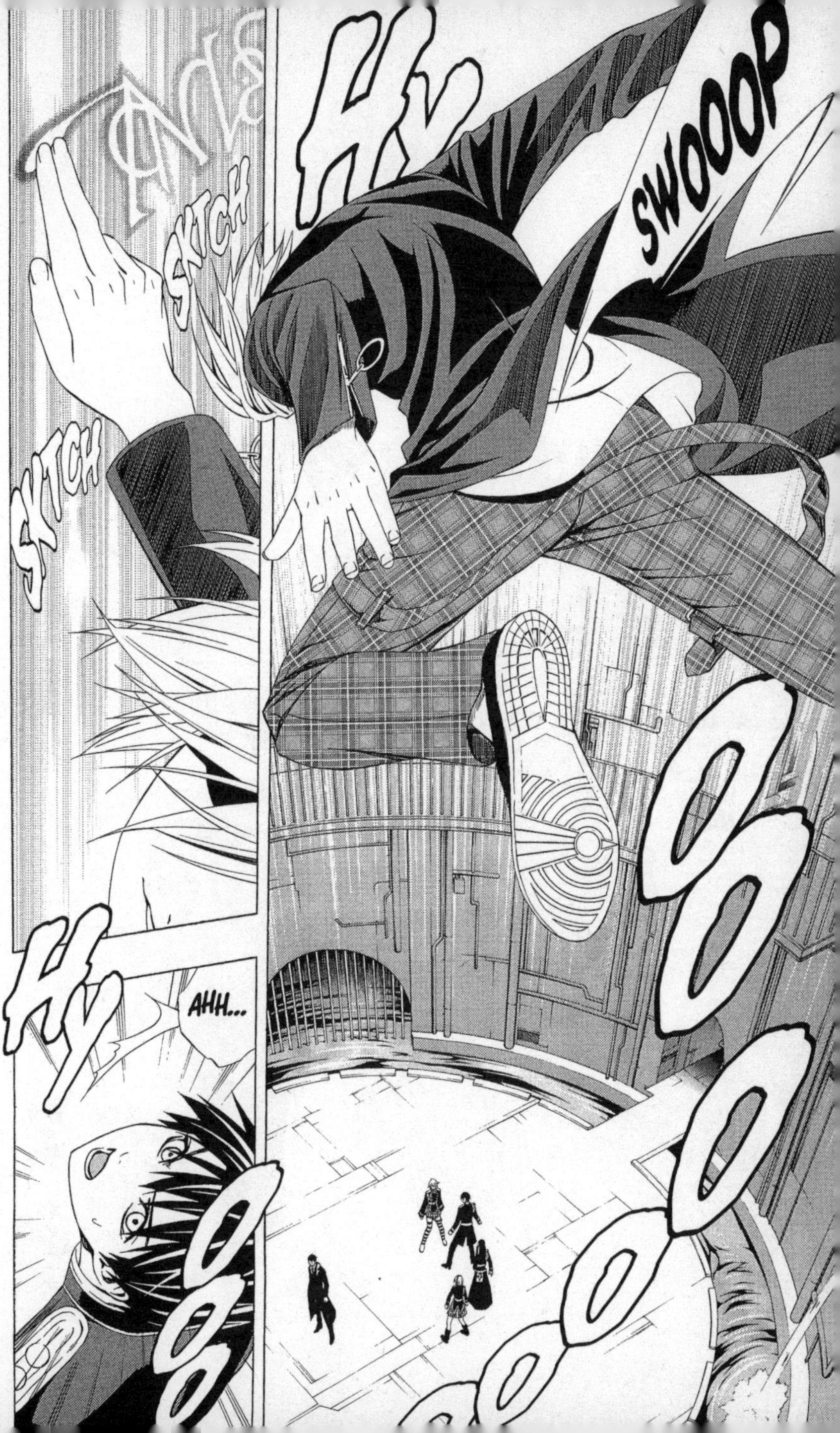
SWOOOP
SKTCH
SKTCH
AHH...

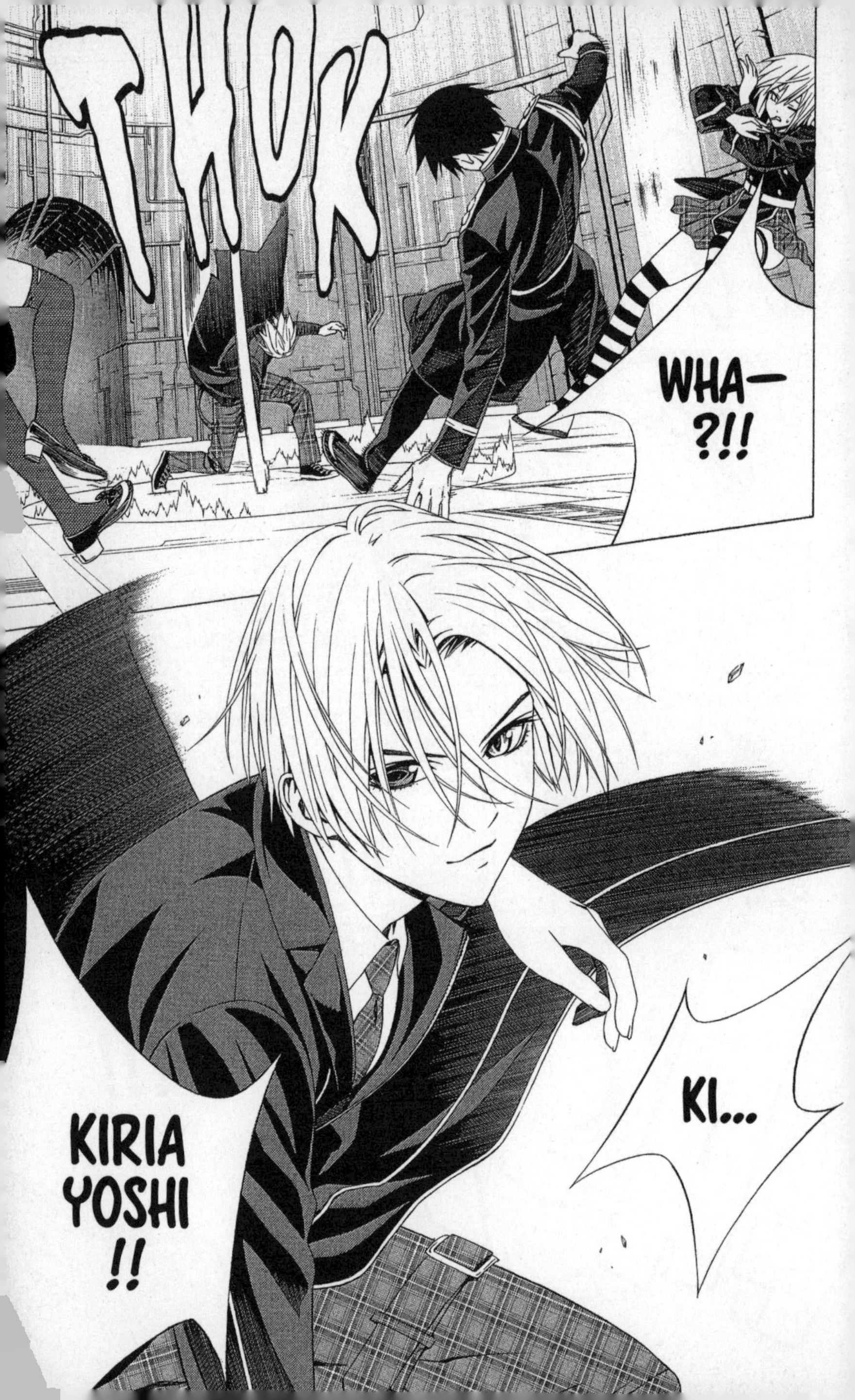
THOK
WHA— ?!!
KI...
KIRIA YOSHI !!

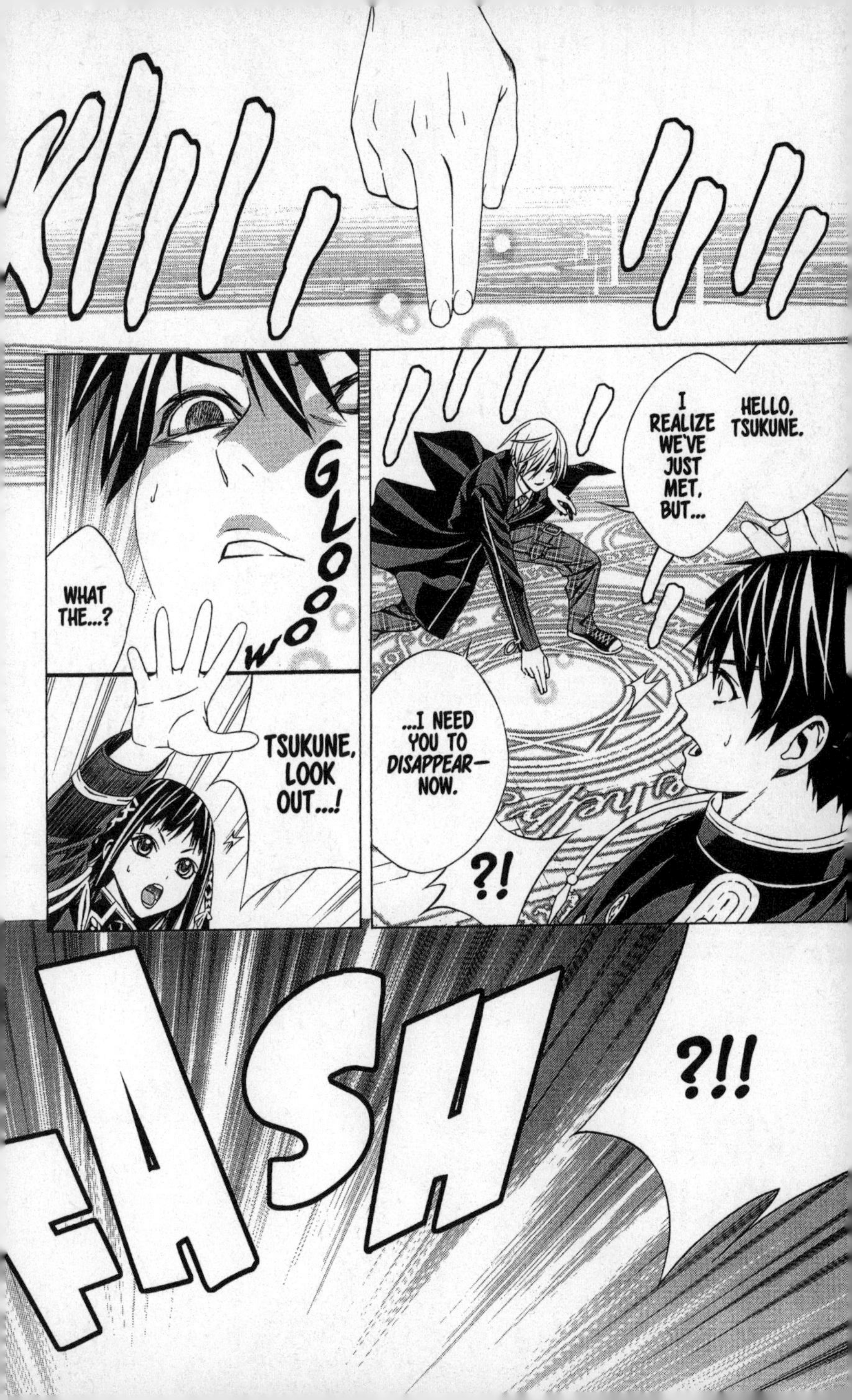
HELLO, TSUKUNE.
I REALIZE WE'VE JUST MET, BUT...
...I NEED YOU TO DISAPPEAR— NOW.
?!
WHAT THE...?
TSUKUNE, LOOK OUT...!
FASH
?!!

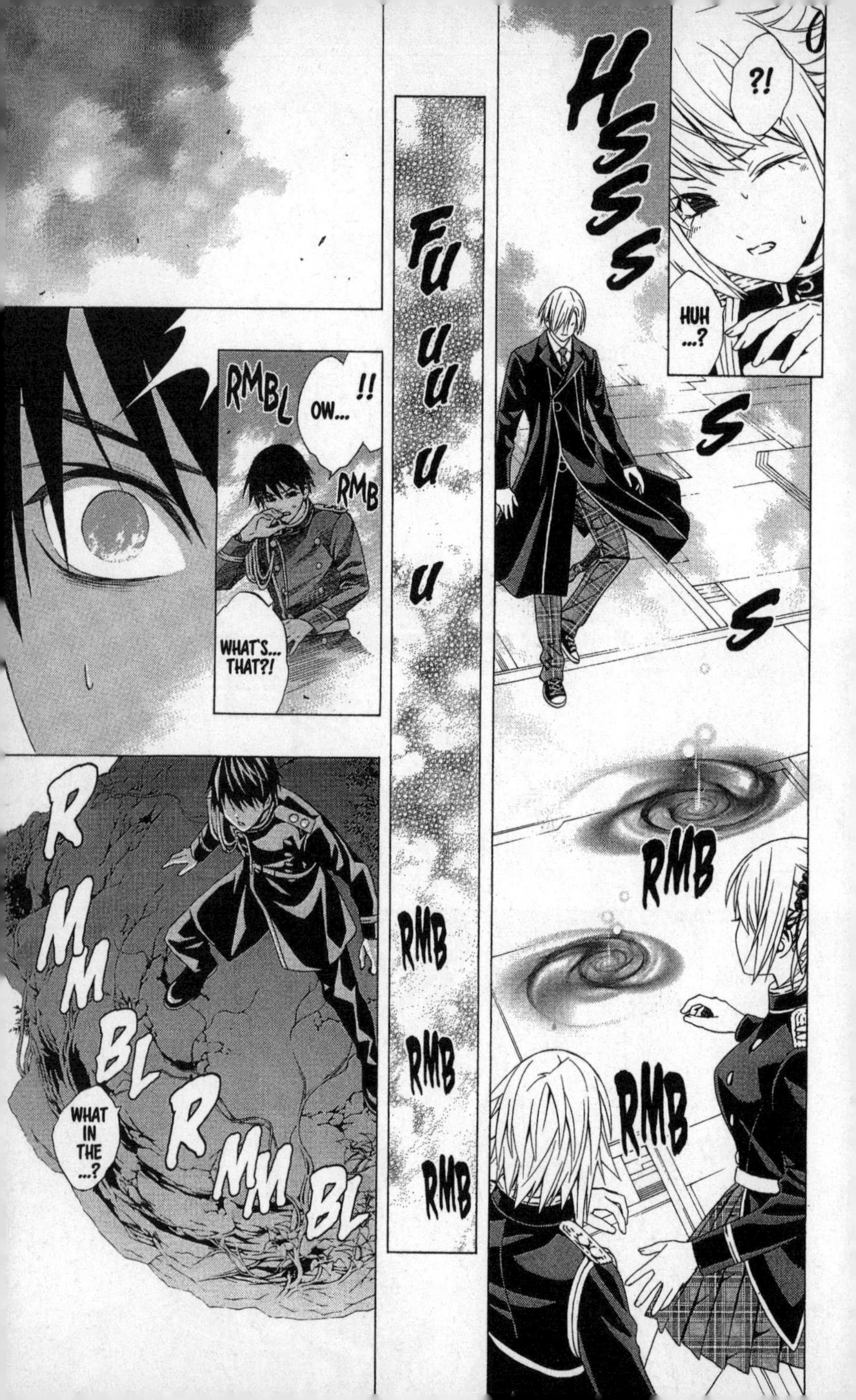
?!
HUH ...?
HSSSS
S
S
RMB
RMB
FUUUUUU
RMB
RMB
RMB
RMBL
OW... !!
RMB
WHAT'S... THAT?!
RMMBL
RMMBL
WHAT IN THE ...?

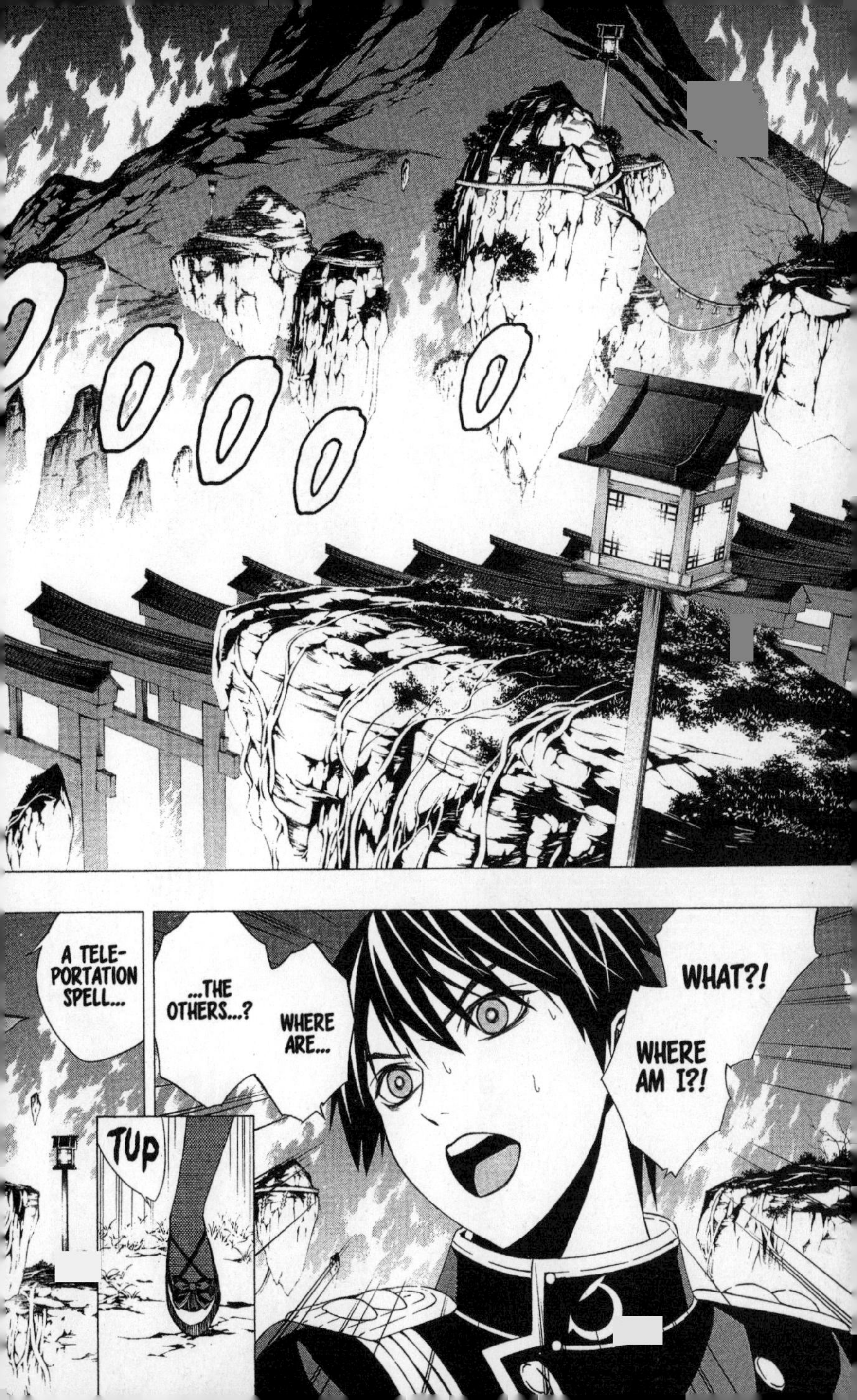
WHAT?!
WHERE AM I?!
WHERE ARE...
...THE OTHERS...?
A TELE-PORTATION SPELL...
TUP

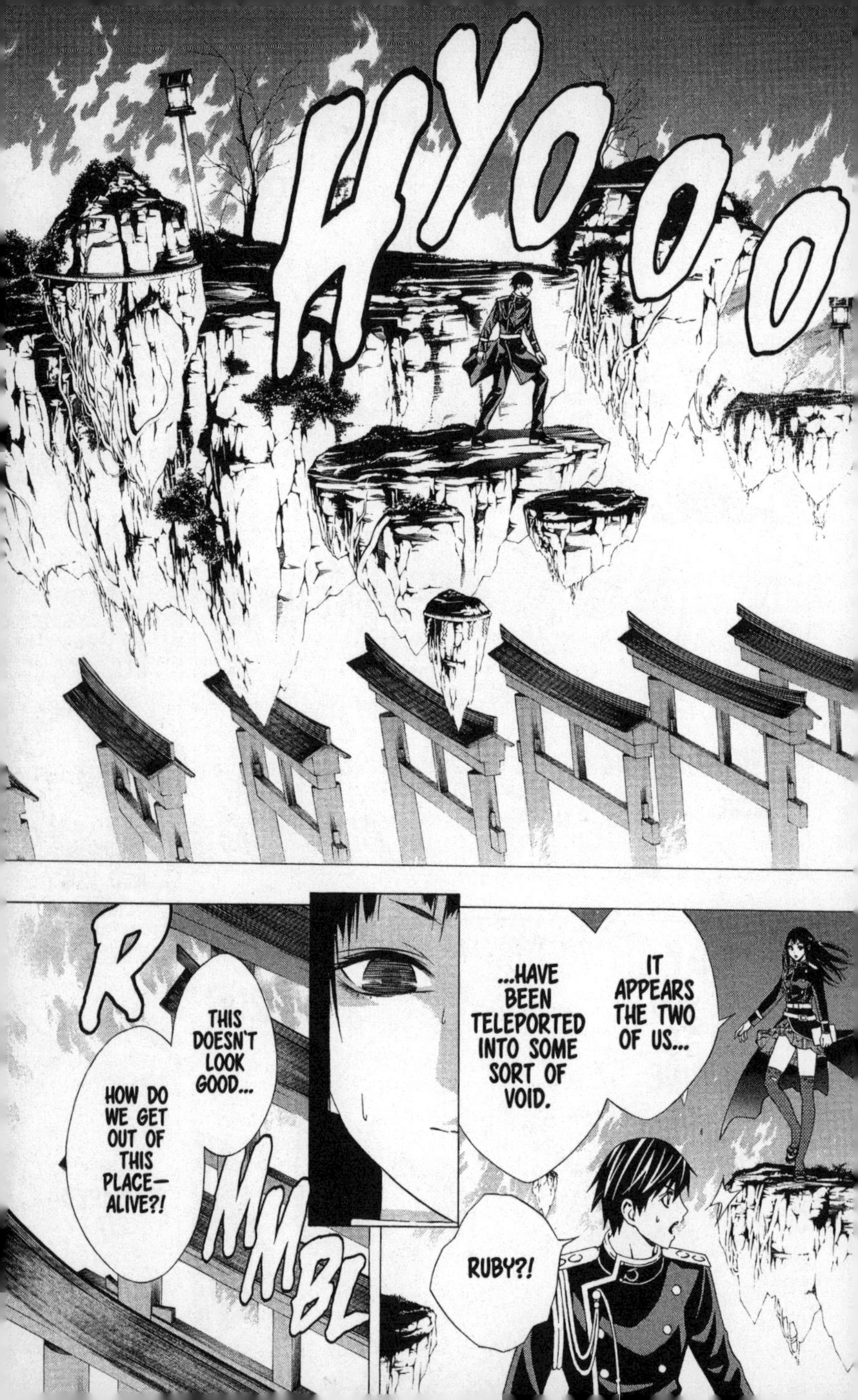
HYOOO
IT APPEARS THE TWO OF US...
...HAVE BEEN TELEPORTED INTO SOME SORT OF VOID.
RUBY?!
R
MMBL
THIS DOESN'T LOOK GOOD...
HOW DO WE GET OUT OF THIS PLACE—ALIVE?!

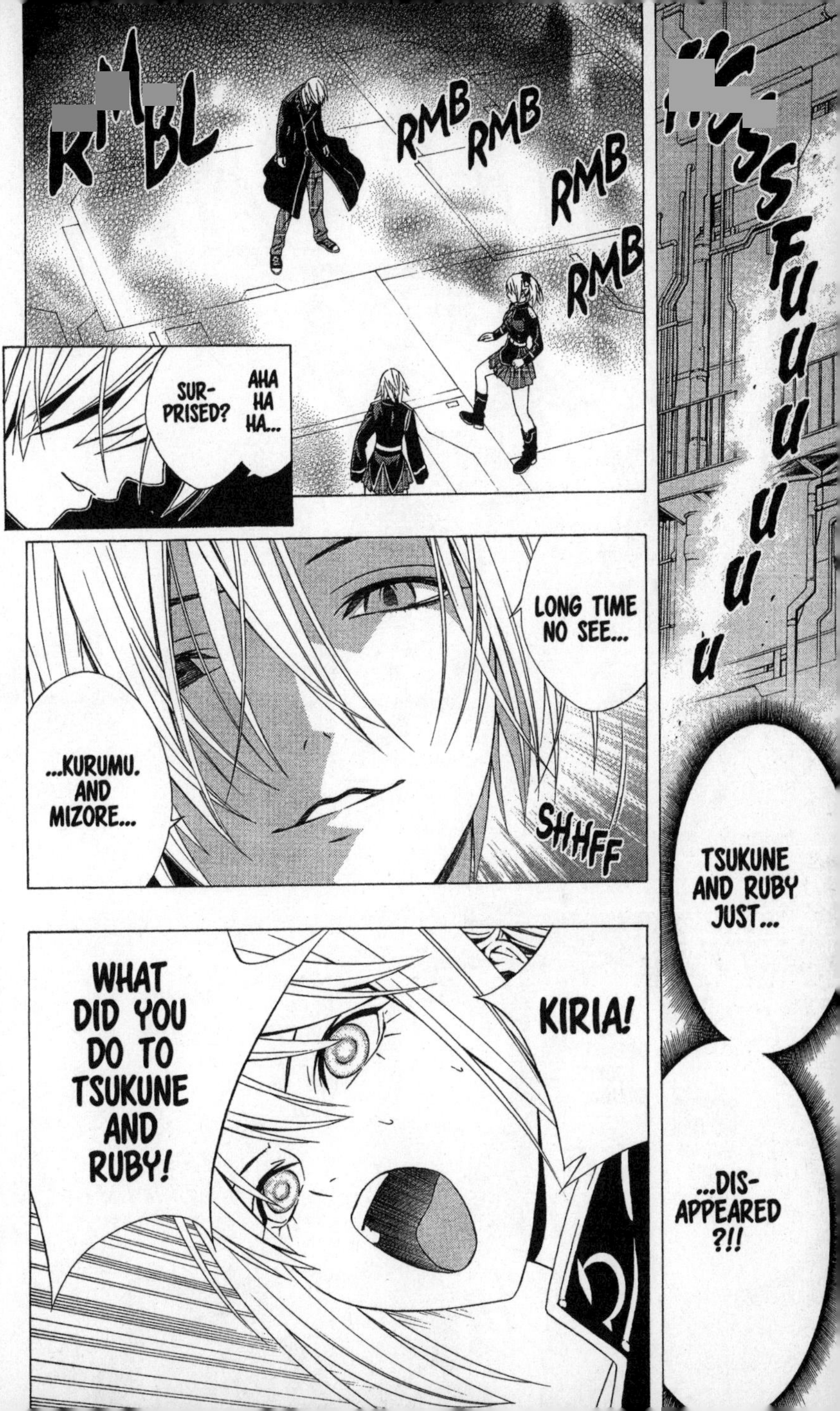
FUUUUUU
TSUKUNE AND RUBY JUST...
...DIS-APPEARED?!!
RMB RMB RMB RMB
AHA HA HA...
SUR-PRISED?
LONG TIME NO SEE...
SHHFF
...KURUMU. AND MIZORE...
KIRIA!
WHAT DID YOU DO TO TSUKUNE AND RUBY!

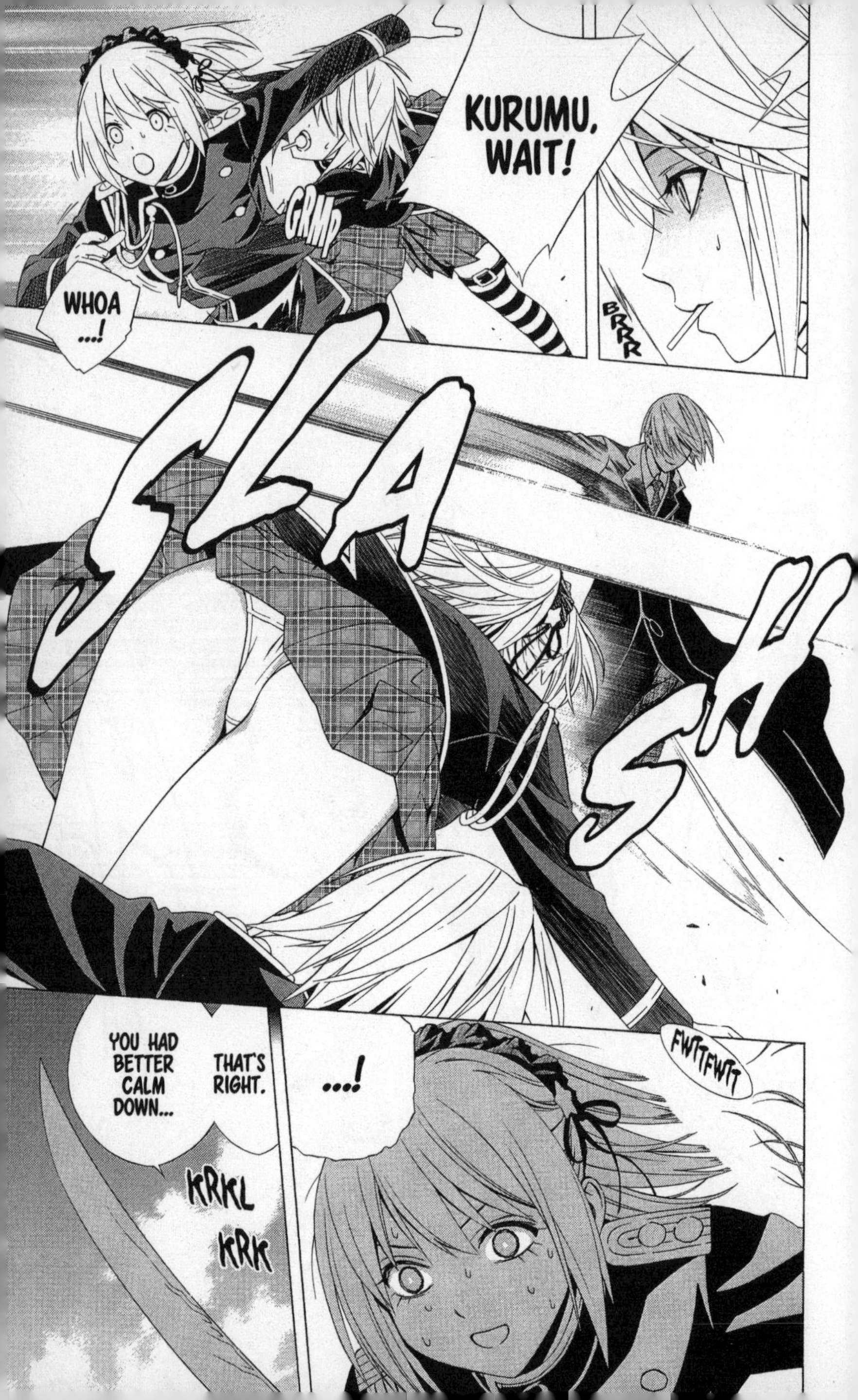
KURUMU, WAIT!
BRRRR
GRMP
WHOA ...!
CLASH
FWTTFWTT
...!
THAT'S RIGHT. YOU HAD BETTER CALM DOWN...
KRKL
KRK

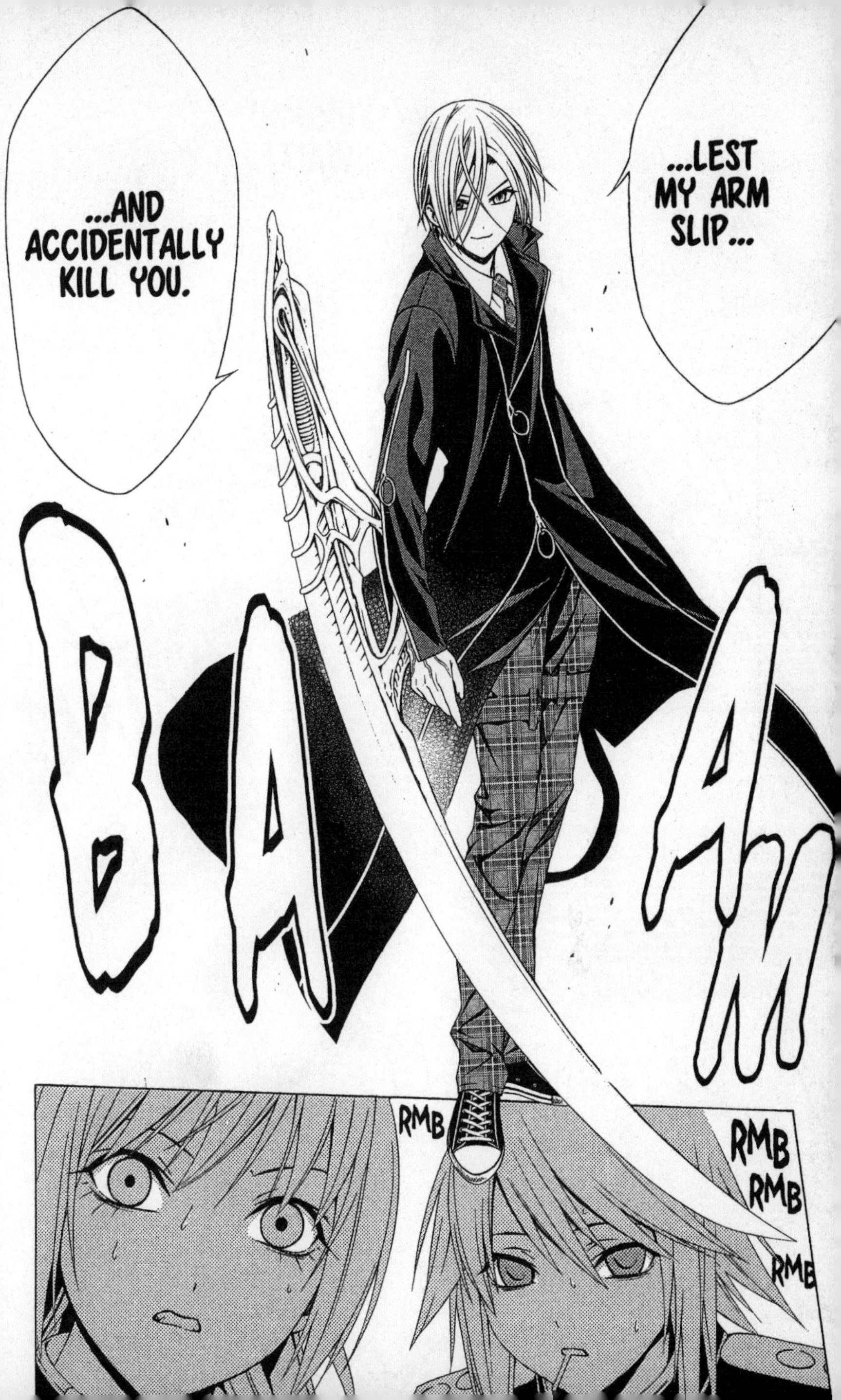
...LEST MY ARM SLIP...
...AND ACCIDENTALLY KILL YOU.
BAM
RMB
RMB
RMB
RMB

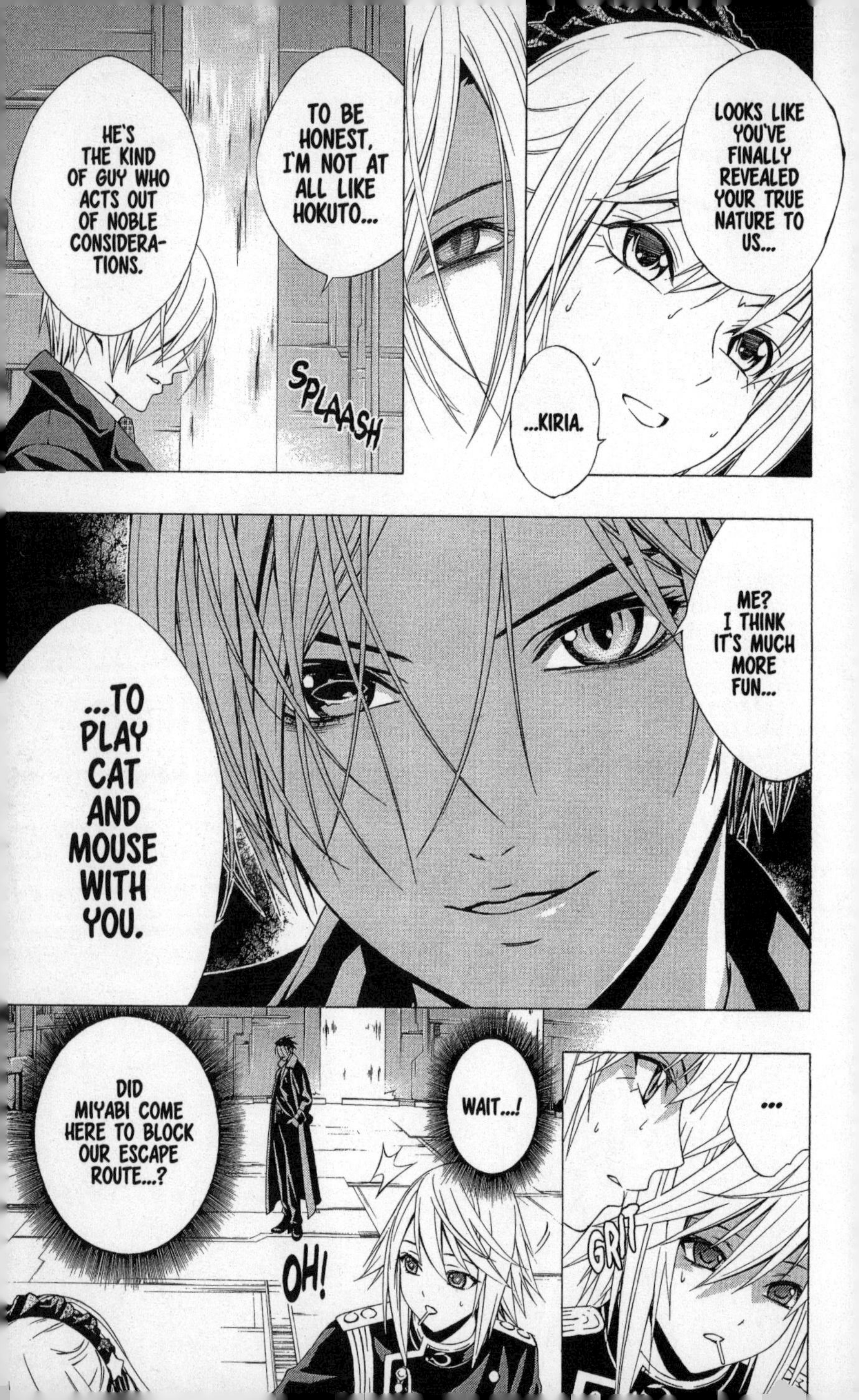
LOOKS LIKE YOU'VE FINALLY REVEALED YOUR TRUE NATURE TO US...
...KIRIA.
TO BE HONEST, I'M NOT AT ALL LIKE HOKUTO...
SPLAASH
HE'S THE KIND OF GUY WHO ACTS OUT OF NOBLE CONSIDERATIONS.
ME? I THINK IT'S MUCH MORE FUN...
...TO PLAY CAT AND MOUSE WITH YOU.
...
GRIT
WAIT...!
OH!
DID MIYABI COME HERE TO BLOCK OUR ESCAPE ROUTE...?

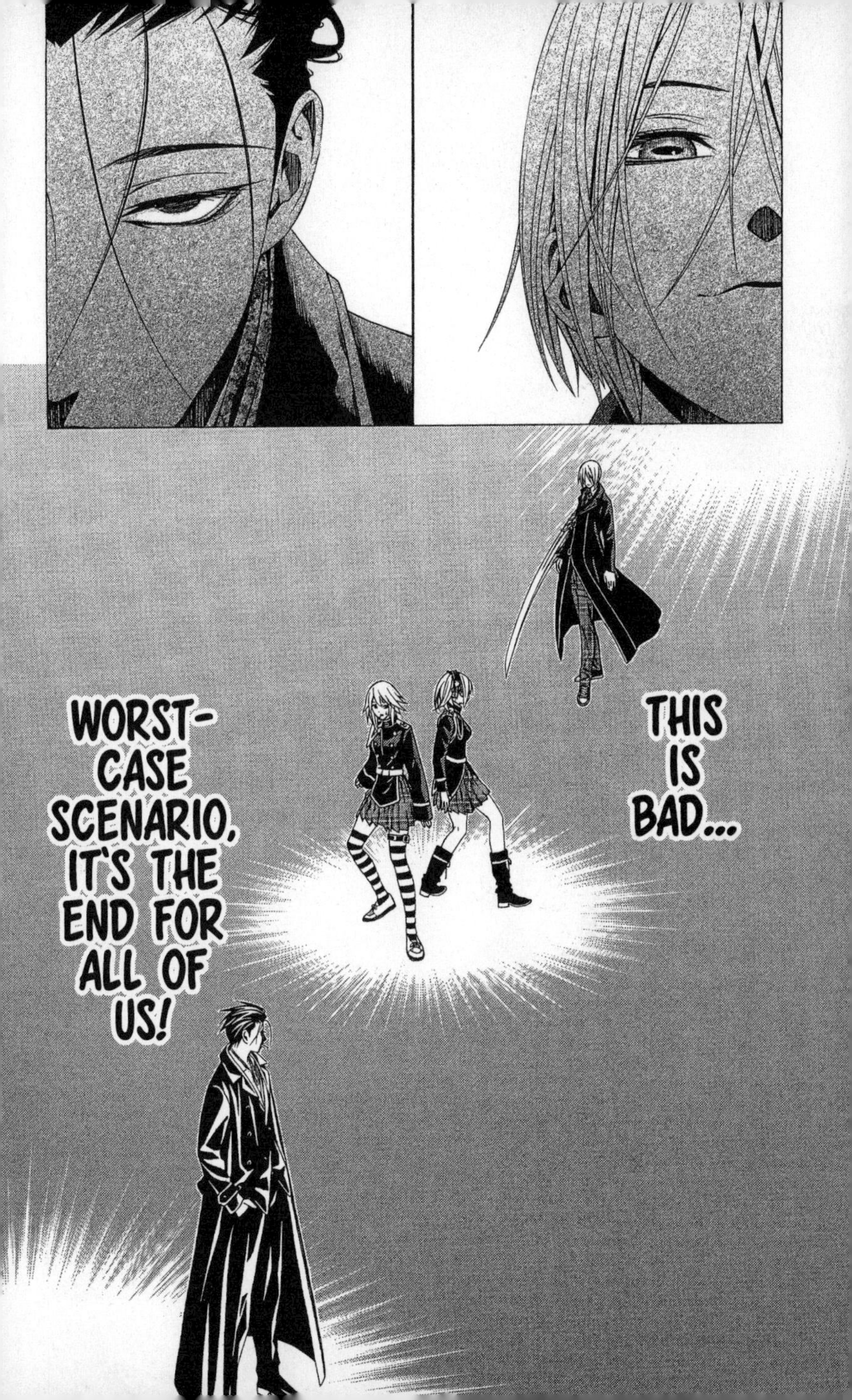
THIS IS BAD...
WORST-CASE SCENARIO. IT'S THE END FOR ALL OF US!

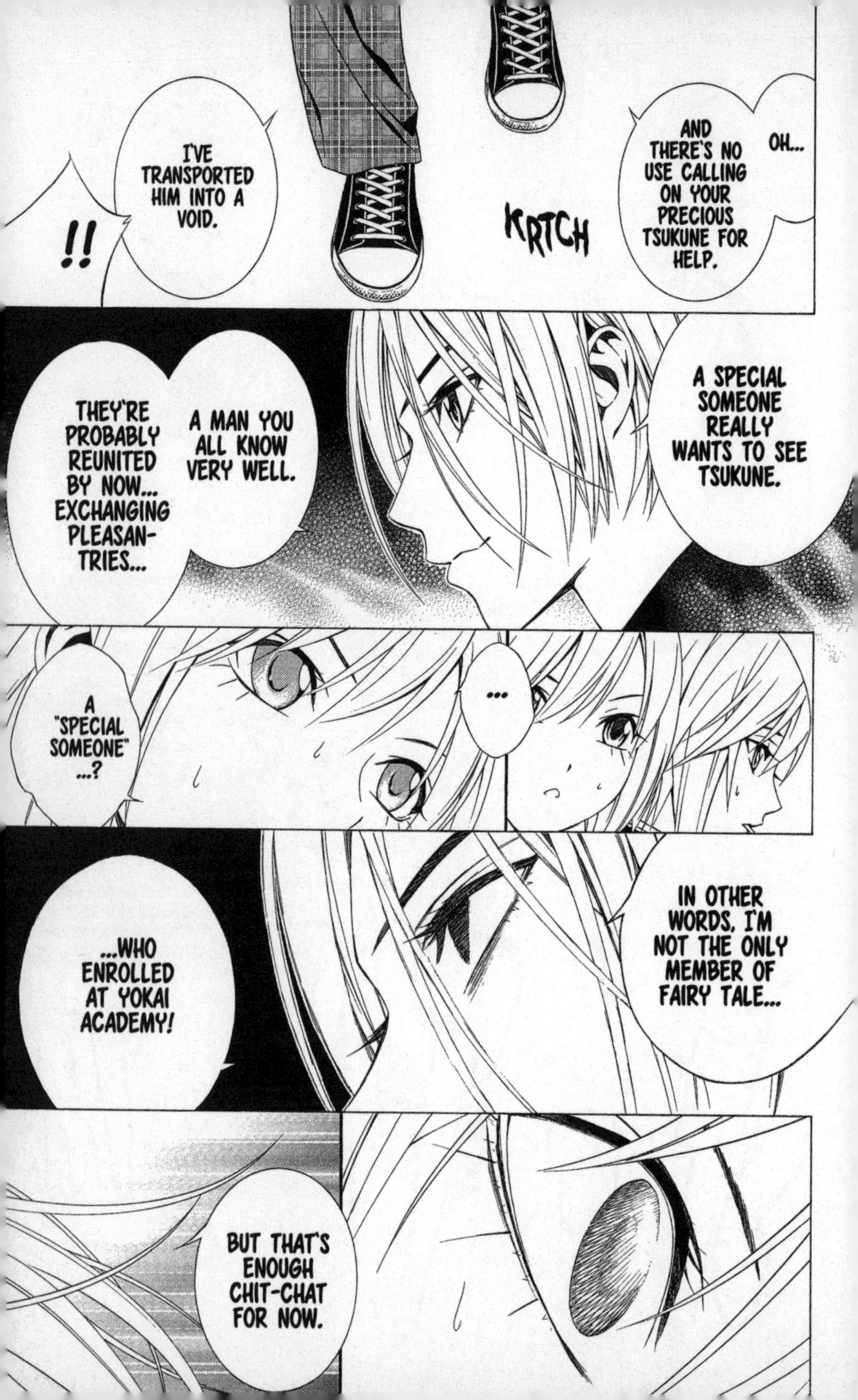
OH...
AND THERE'S NO USE CALLING ON YOUR PRECIOUS TSUKUNE FOR HELP.
KRTCH
I'VE TRANSPORTED HIM INTO A VOID.
!!
A SPECIAL SOMEONE REALLY WANTS TO SEE TSUKUNE.
A MAN YOU ALL KNOW VERY WELL.
THEY'RE PROBABLY REUNITED BY NOW... EXCHANGING PLEASAN-TRIES...
...
A "SPECIAL SOMEONE"...?
IN OTHER WORDS, I'M NOT THE ONLY MEMBER OF FAIRY TALE...
...WHO ENROLLED AT YOKAI ACADEMY!
BUT THAT'S ENOUGH CHIT-CHAT FOR NOW.

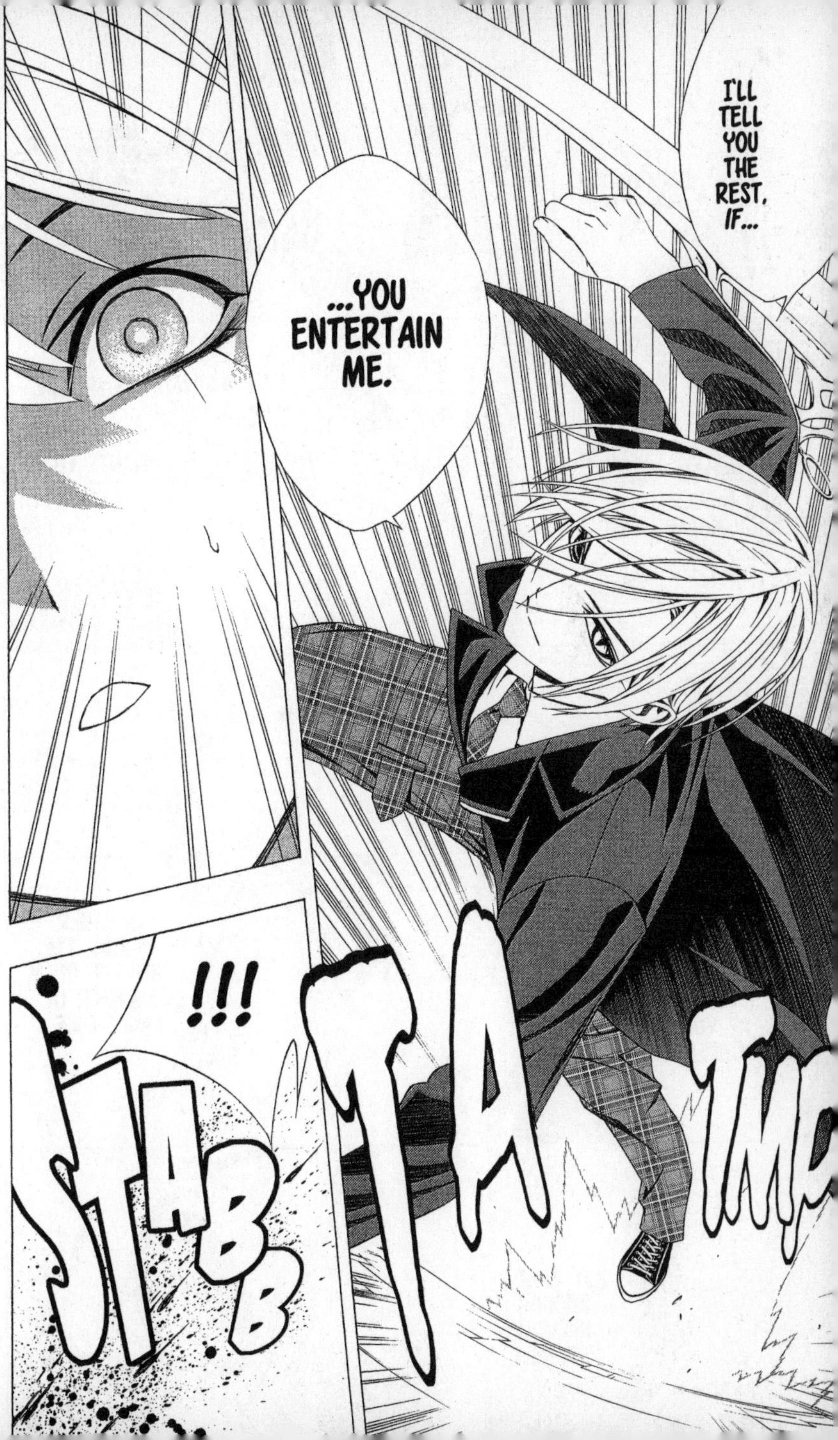
I'LL TELL YOU THE REST, IF...
...YOU ENTERTAIN ME.
TA TMP
!!!
STABB

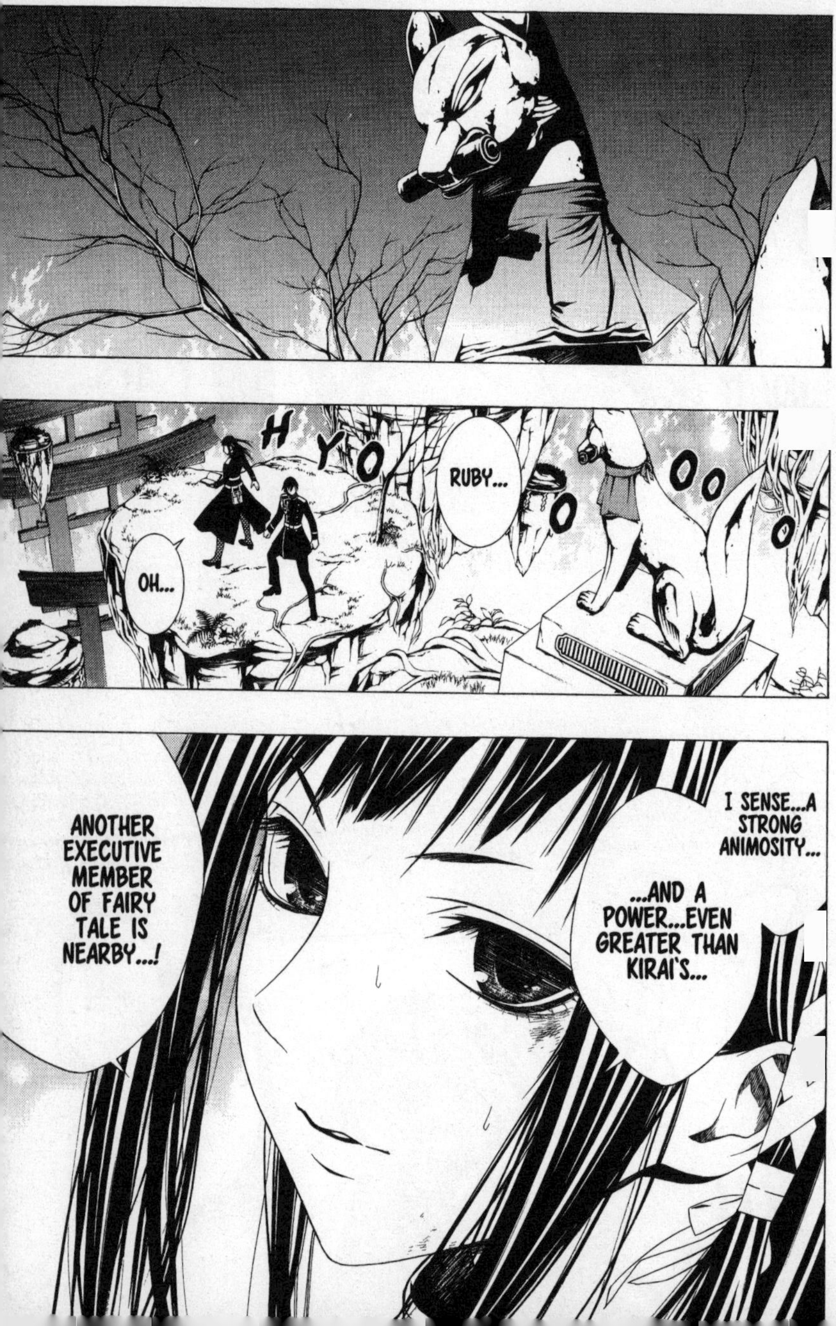
RUBY...
HYOOOOO
OH...
I SENSE...A STRONG ANIMOSITY...
...AND A POWER...EVEN GREATER THAN KIRAI'S...
ANOTHER EXECUTIVE MEMBER OF FAIRY TALE IS NEARBY...!

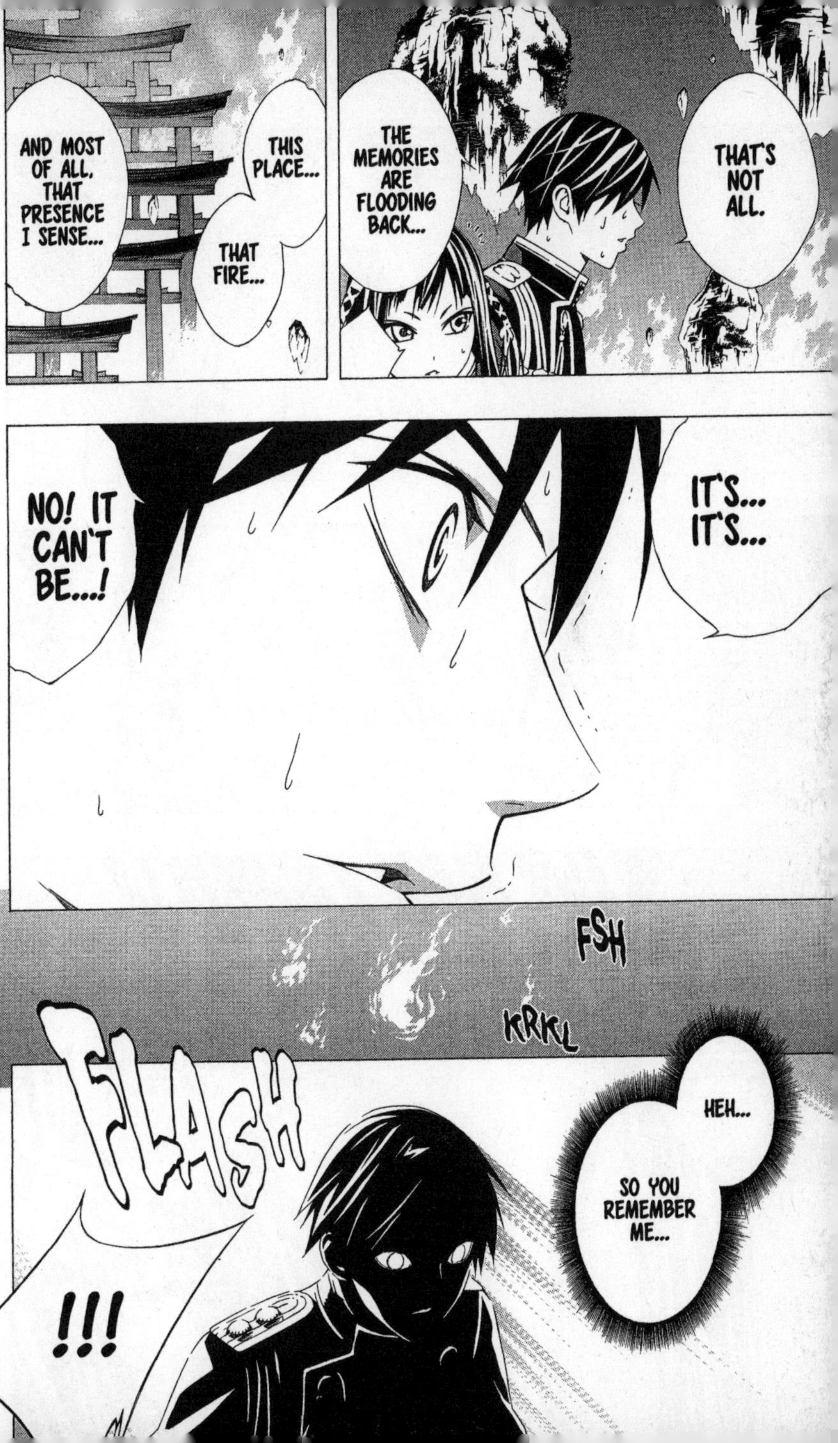
THAT'S NOT ALL.
THE MEMORIES ARE FLOODING BACK...
THIS PLACE...
THAT FIRE...
AND MOST OF ALL, THAT PRESENCE I SENSE...
IT'S... IT'S...
NO! IT CAN'T BE...!
FSH
KRKL
HEH...
SO YOU REMEMBER ME...
FLASH
!!!

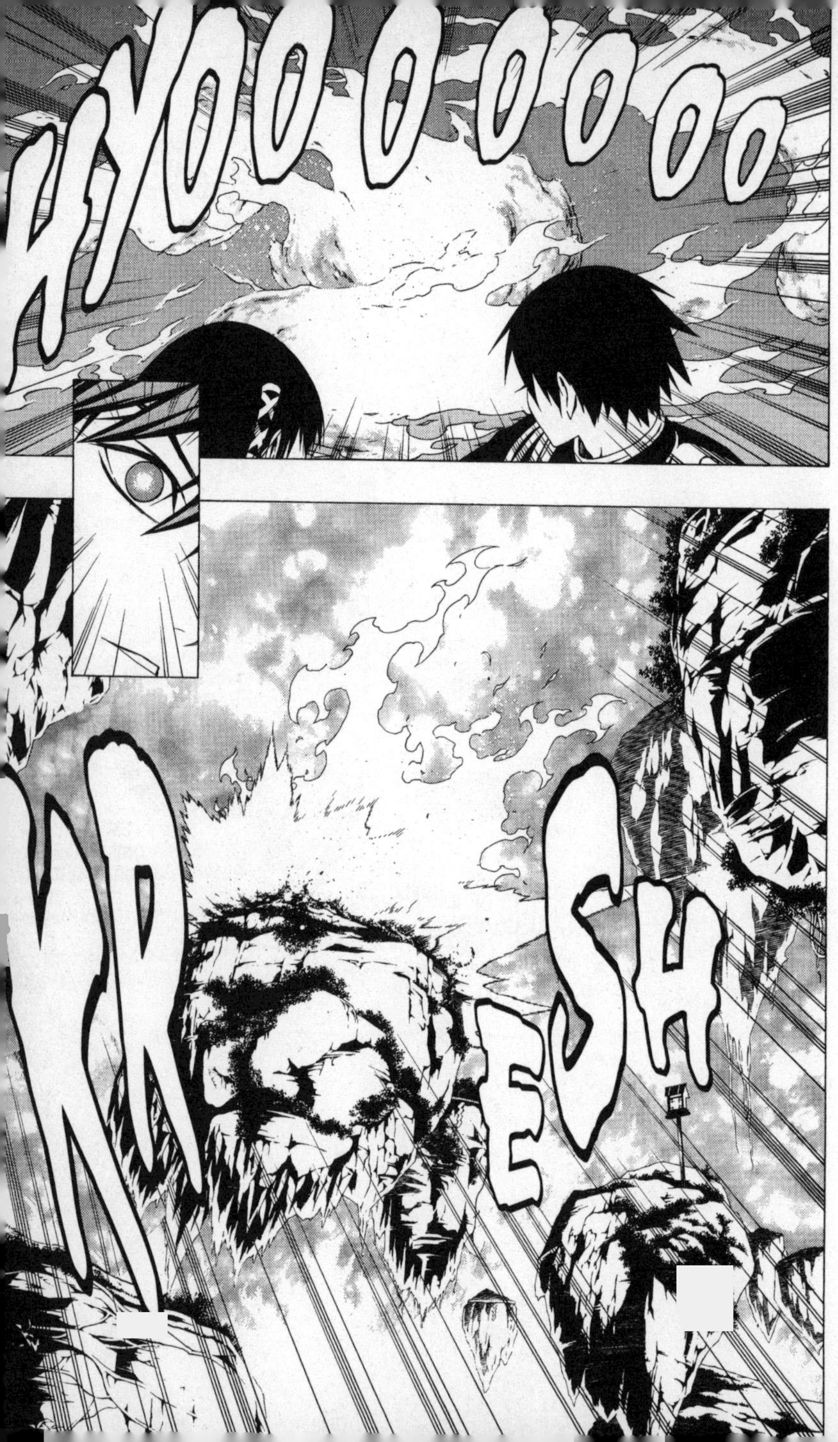

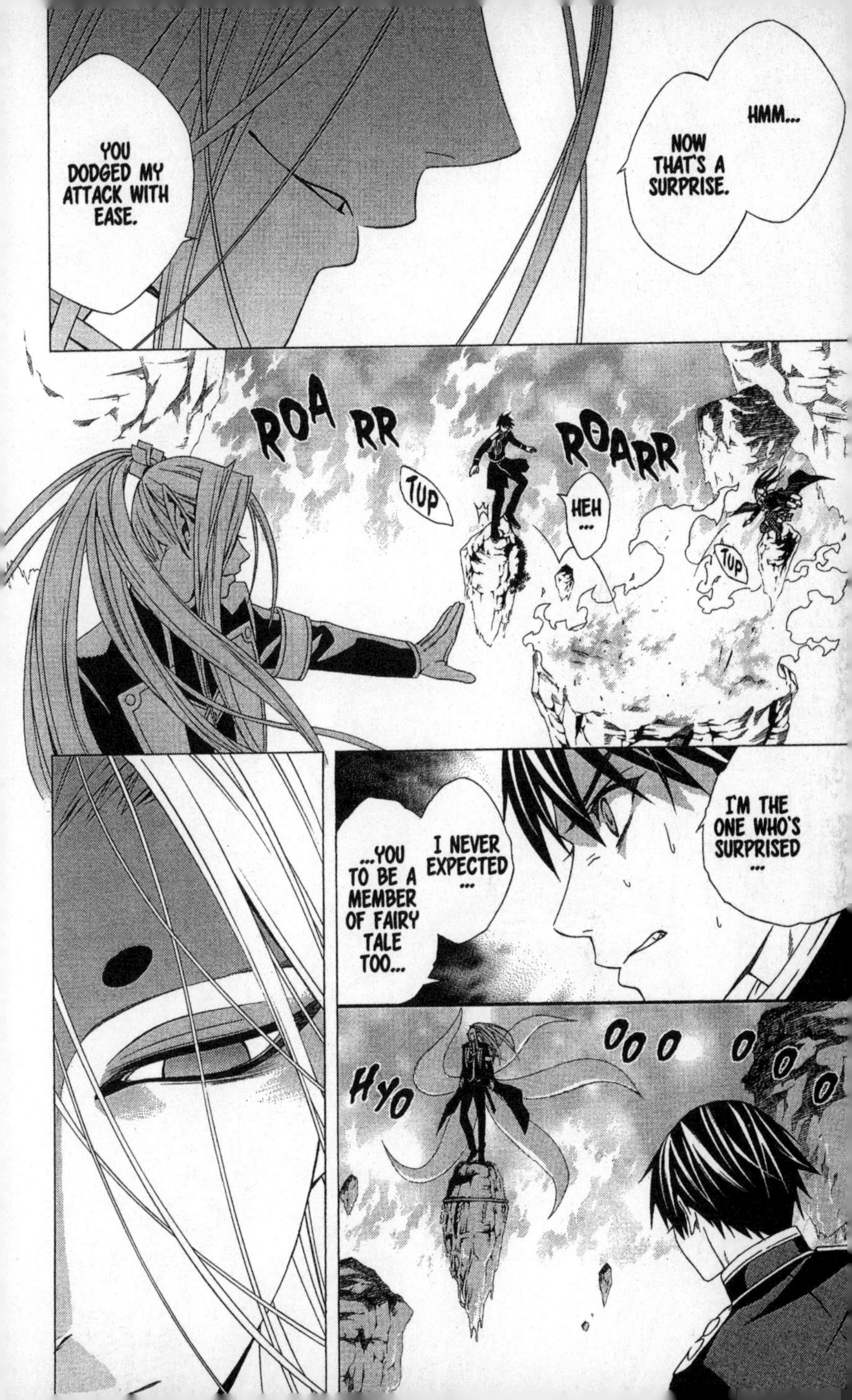
HMM...
NOW THAT'S A SURPRISE.
YOU DODGED MY ATTACK WITH EASE.
ROARR
HEH...
TUP
ROA RR
TUP
I'M THE ONE WHO'S SURPRISED...
I NEVER EXPECTED...
...YOU TO BE A MEMBER OF FAIRY TALE TOO...
OOOO
OOO O
HYO

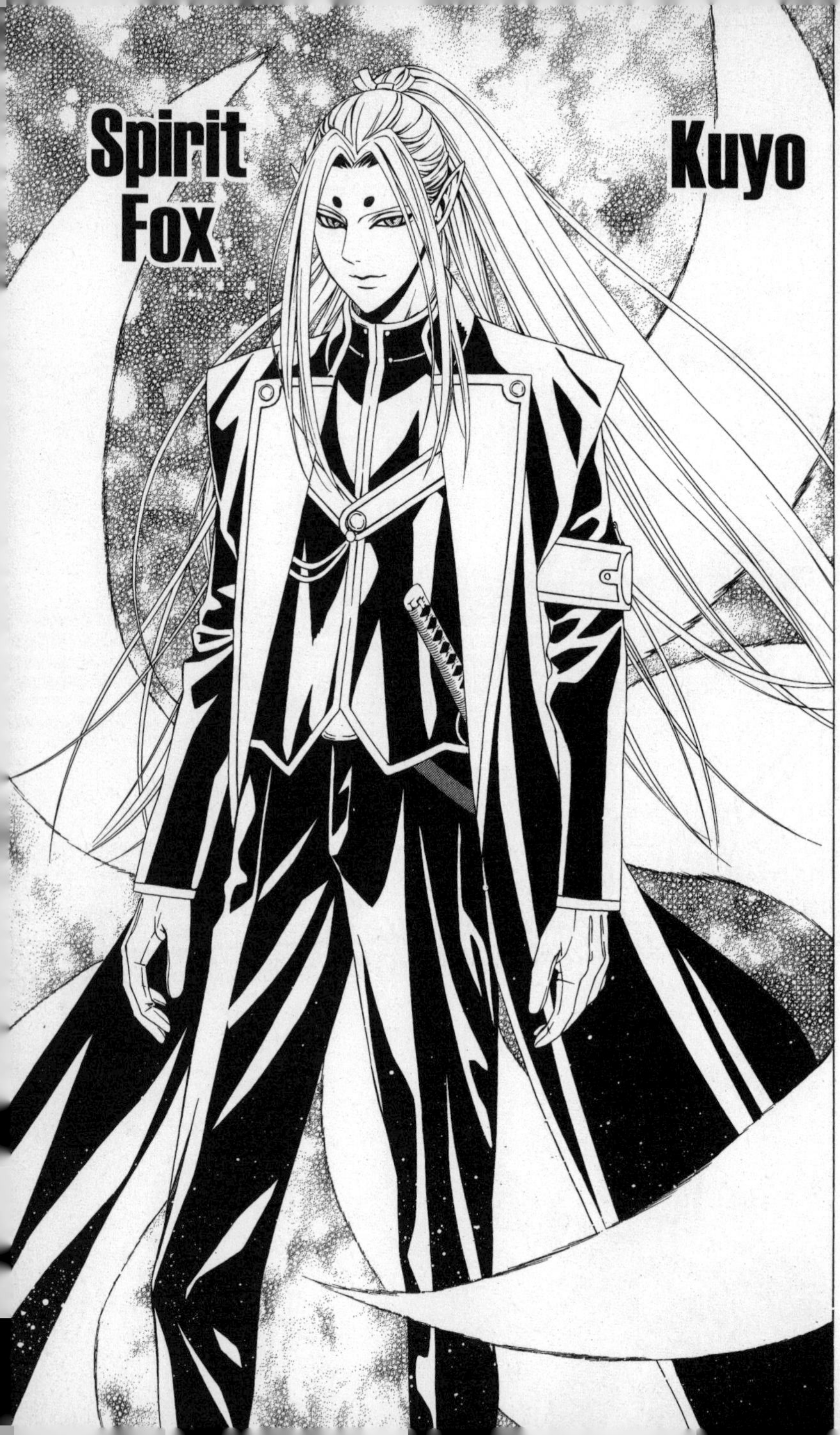
Kuyo
Spirit Fox

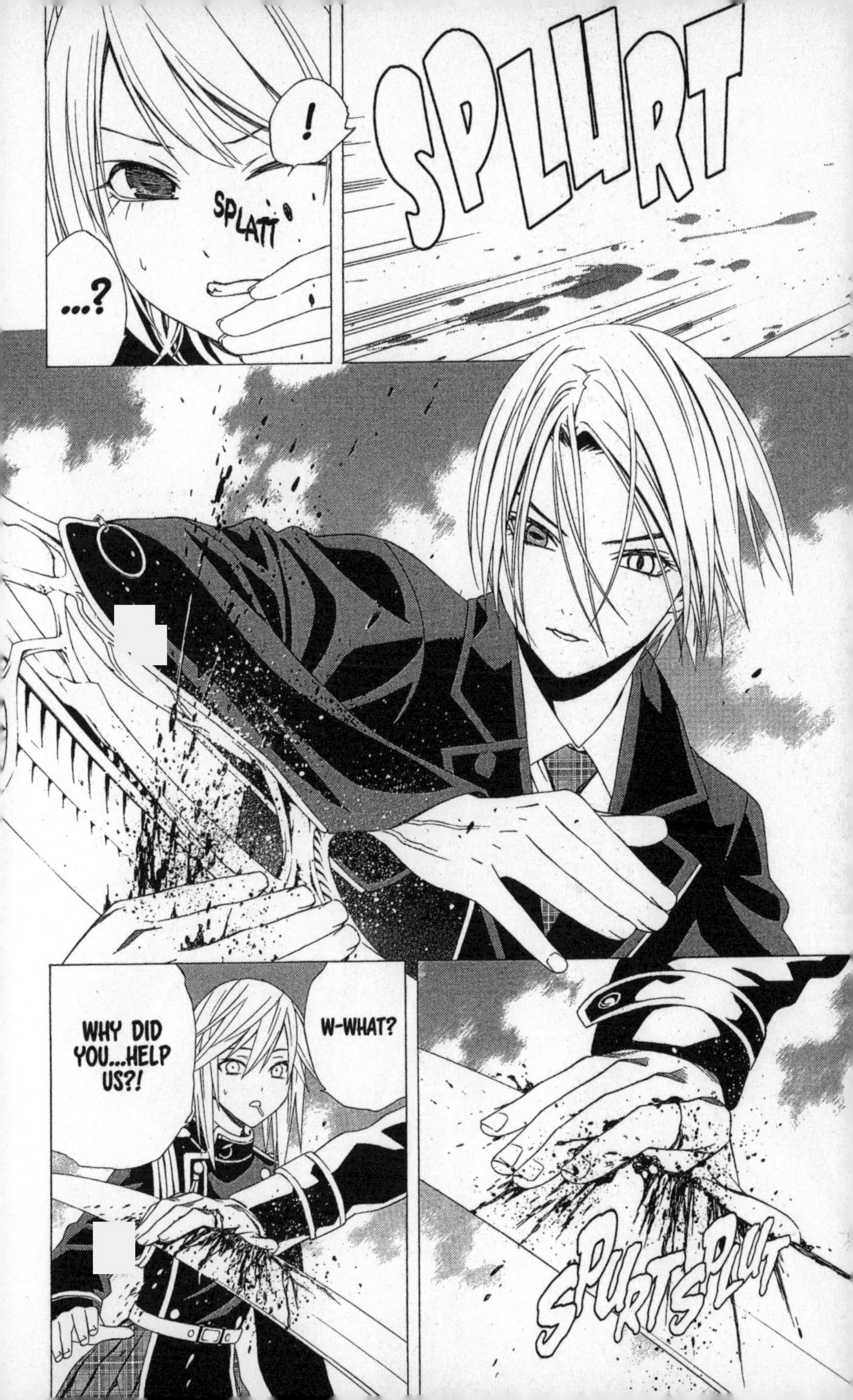
SPLURT
!
SPLATT
...?
SPURTSPLUT
W-WHAT?
WHY DID YOU...HELP US?!

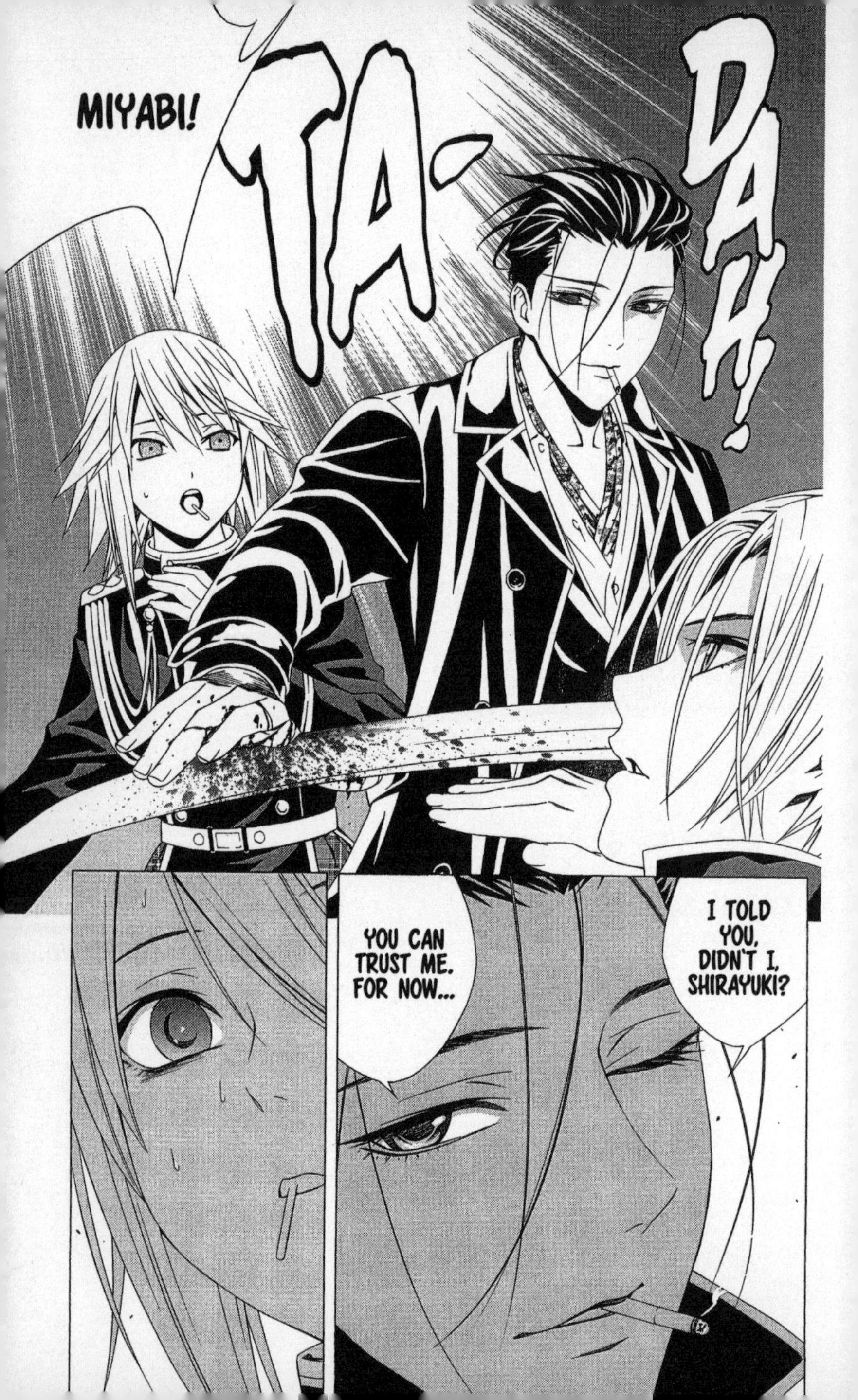
TA-DAH!
MIYABI!
I TOLD YOU, DIDN'T I, SHIRAYUKI?
YOU CAN TRUST ME. FOR NOW...

51: Curse

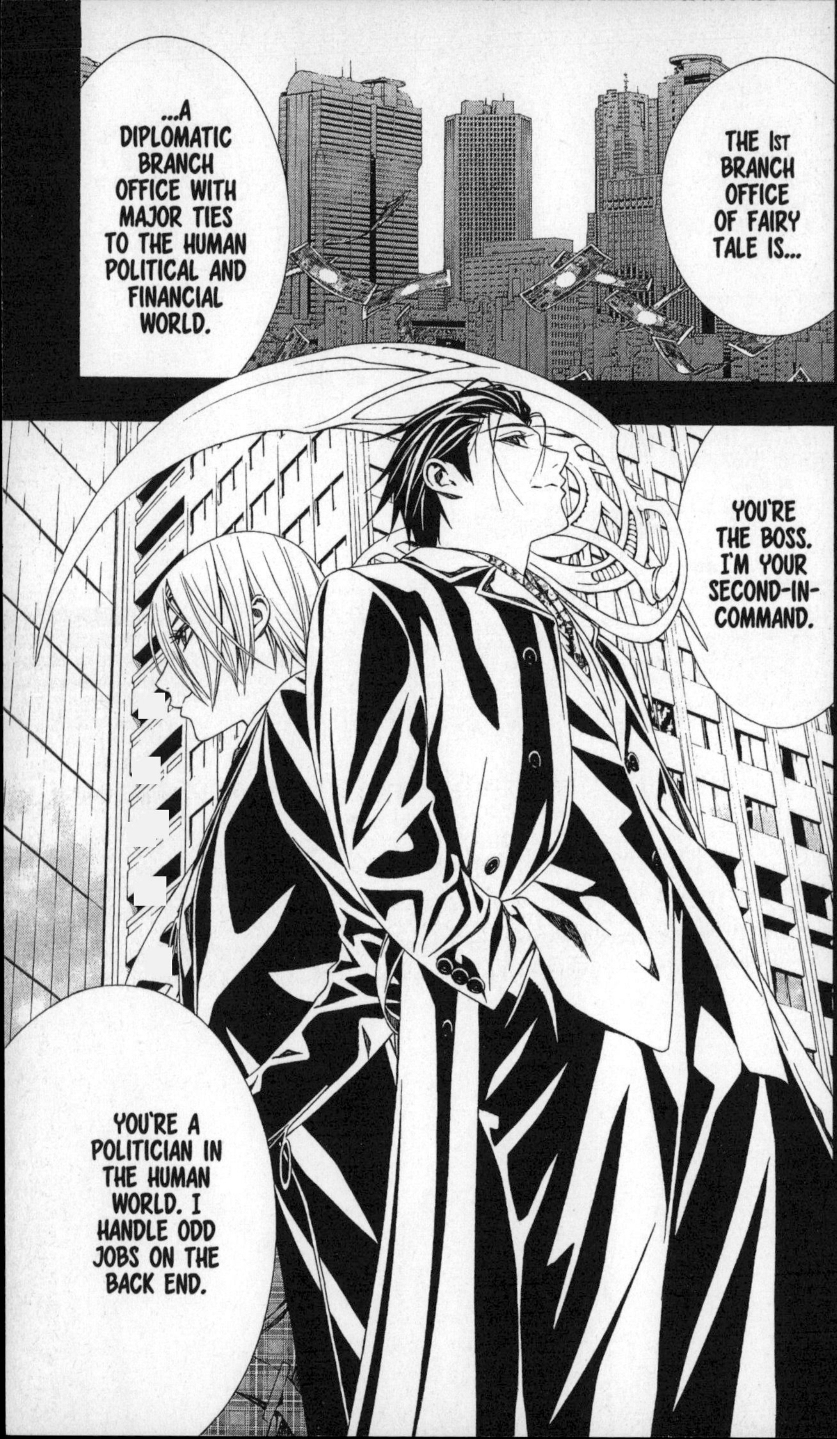
THE 1ST BRANCH OFFICE OF FAIRY TALE IS...
...A DIPLOMATIC BRANCH OFFICE WITH MAJOR TIES TO THE HUMAN POLITICAL AND FINANCIAL WORLD.
YOU'RE THE BOSS. I'M YOUR SECOND-IN-COMMAND.
YOU'RE A POLITICIAN IN THE HUMAN WORLD. I HANDLE ODD JOBS ON THE BACK END.

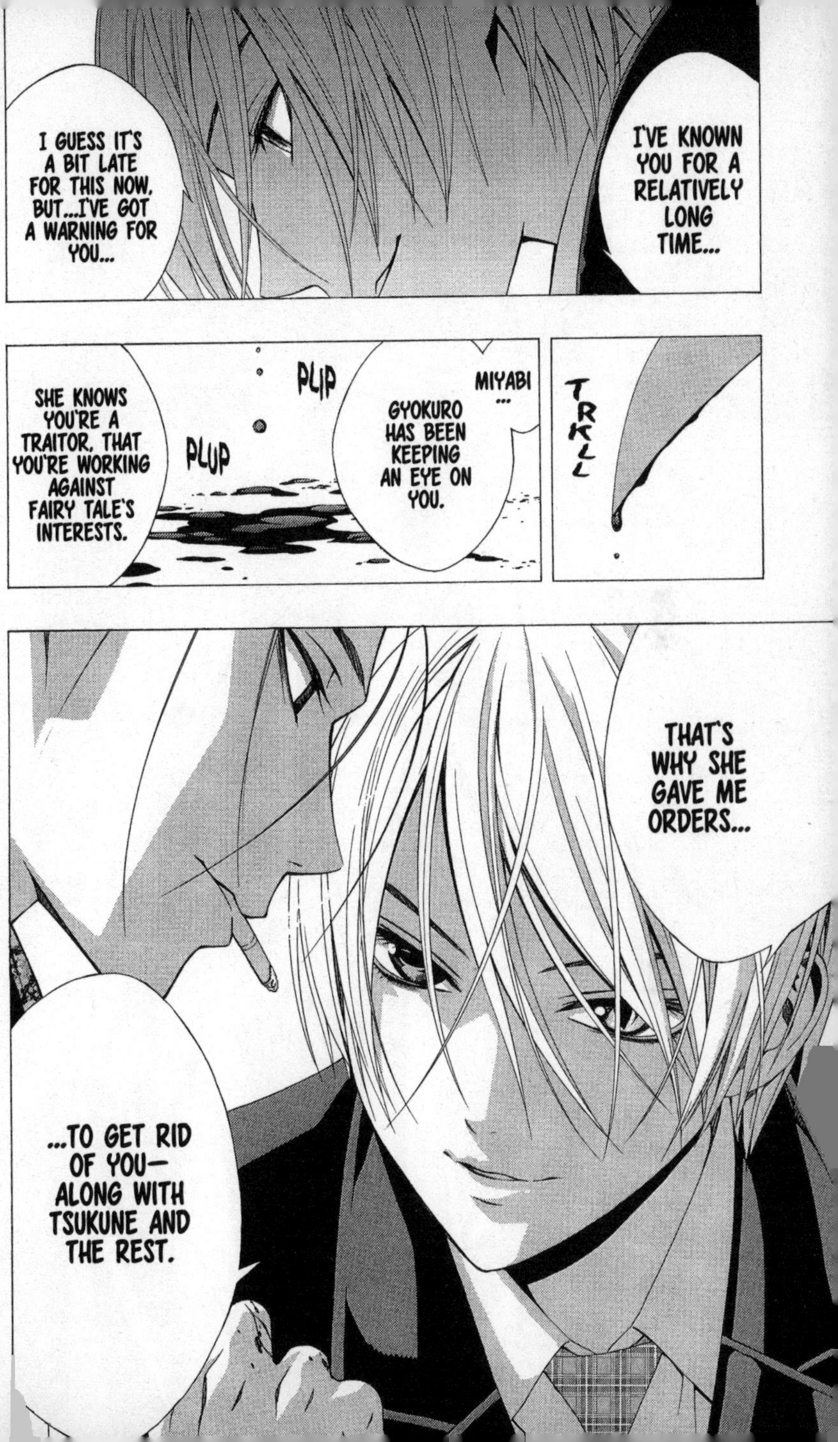
I'VE KNOWN YOU FOR A RELATIVELY LONG TIME...
I GUESS IT'S A BIT LATE FOR THIS NOW, BUT...I'VE GOT A WARNING FOR YOU...
TRKLL
MIYABI...
GYOKURO HAS BEEN KEEPING AN EYE ON YOU.
PLIP
PLUP
SHE KNOWS YOU'RE A TRAITOR, THAT YOU'RE WORKING AGAINST FAIRY TALE'S INTERESTS.
THAT'S WHY SHE GAVE ME ORDERS...
...TO GET RID OF YOU—ALONG WITH TSUKUNE AND THE REST.

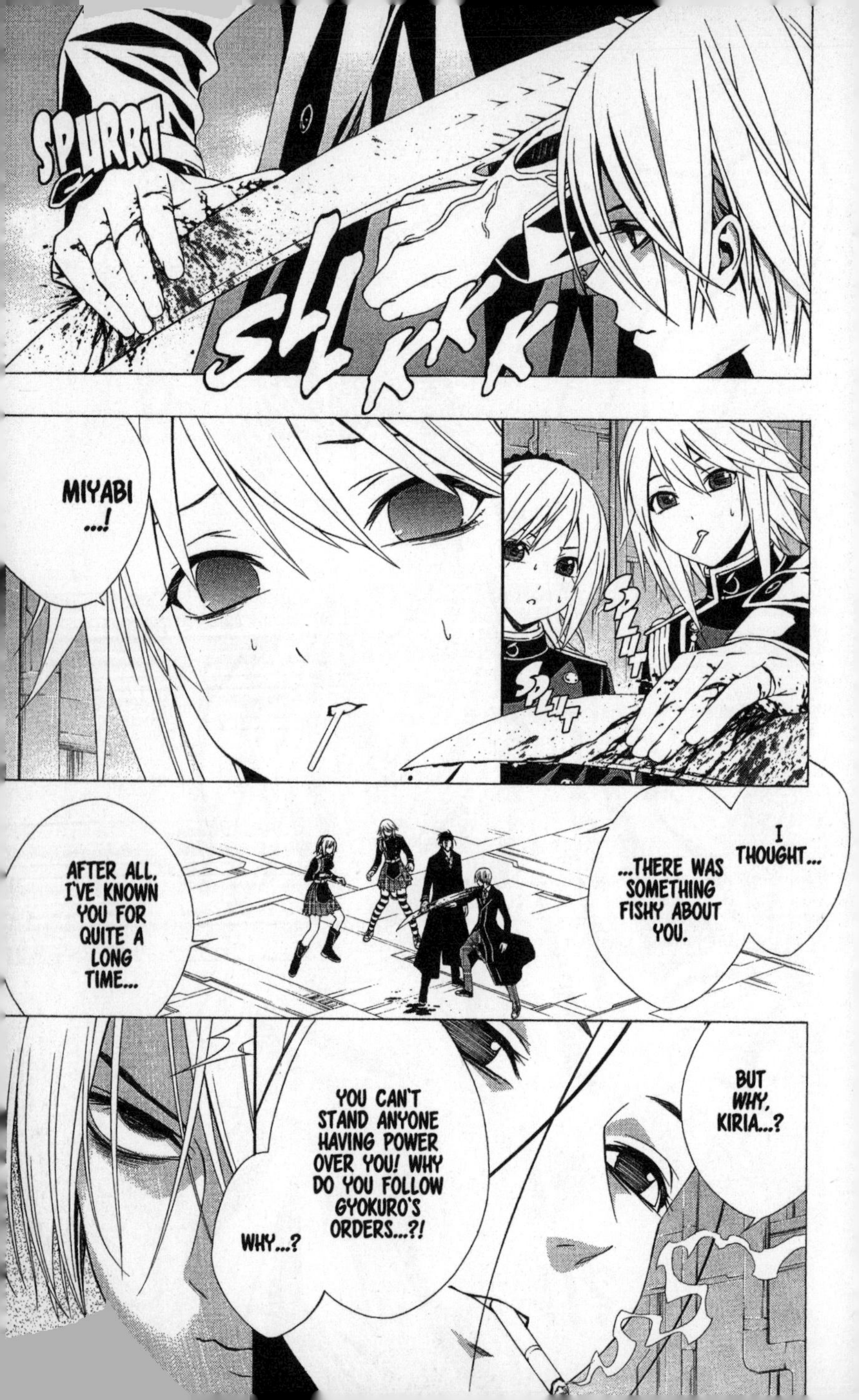
SPURRT
SLIKKK
SPLUT
SPLUT
MIYABI ...!
I THOUGHT...
...THERE WAS SOMETHING FISHY ABOUT YOU.
AFTER ALL, I'VE KNOWN YOU FOR QUITE A LONG TIME...
BUT WHY, KIRIA...?
YOU CAN'T STAND ANYONE HAVING POWER OVER YOU! WHY DO YOU FOLLOW GYOKURO'S ORDERS...?!
WHY...?

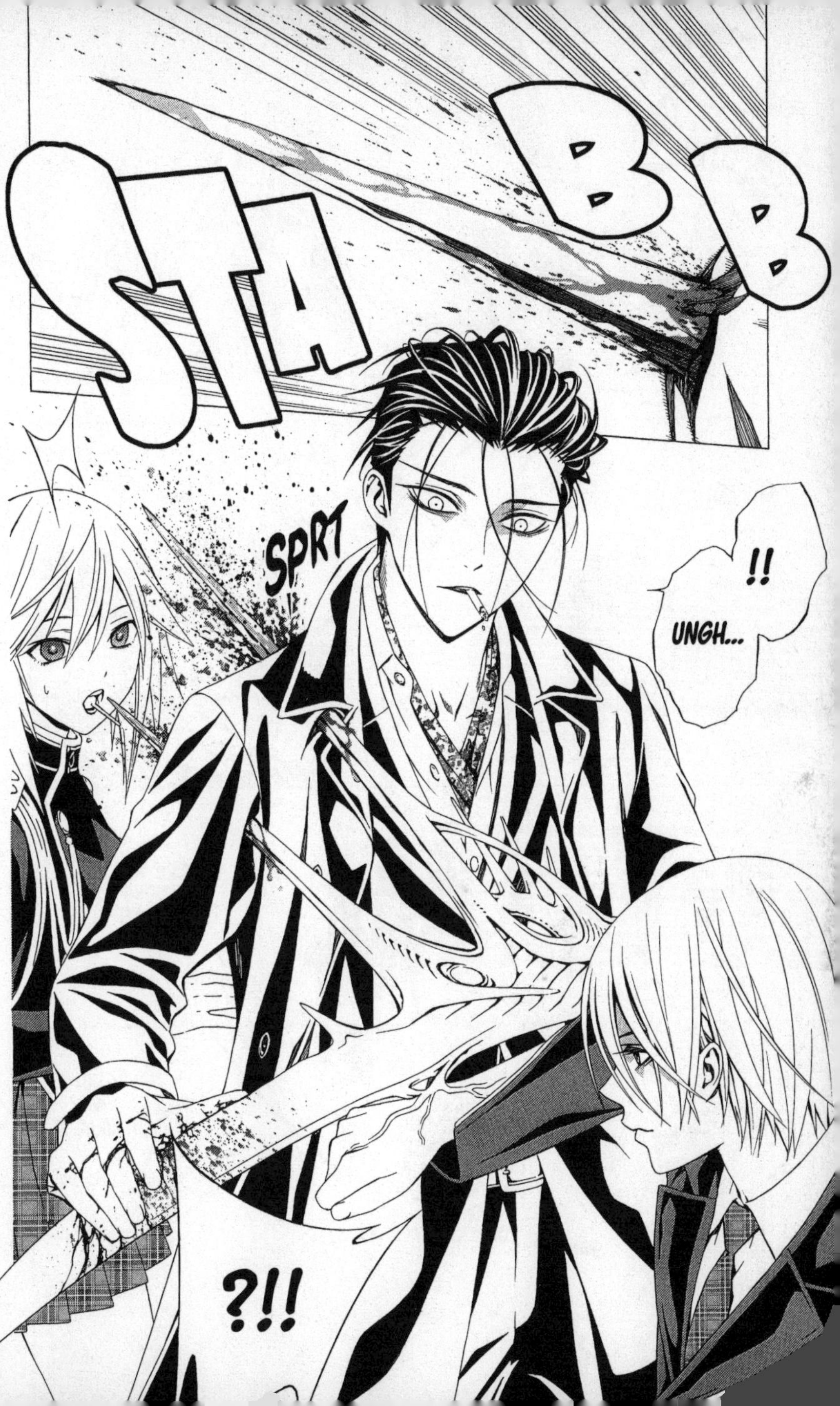
STABB
!!
UNGH...
SPRT
?!!

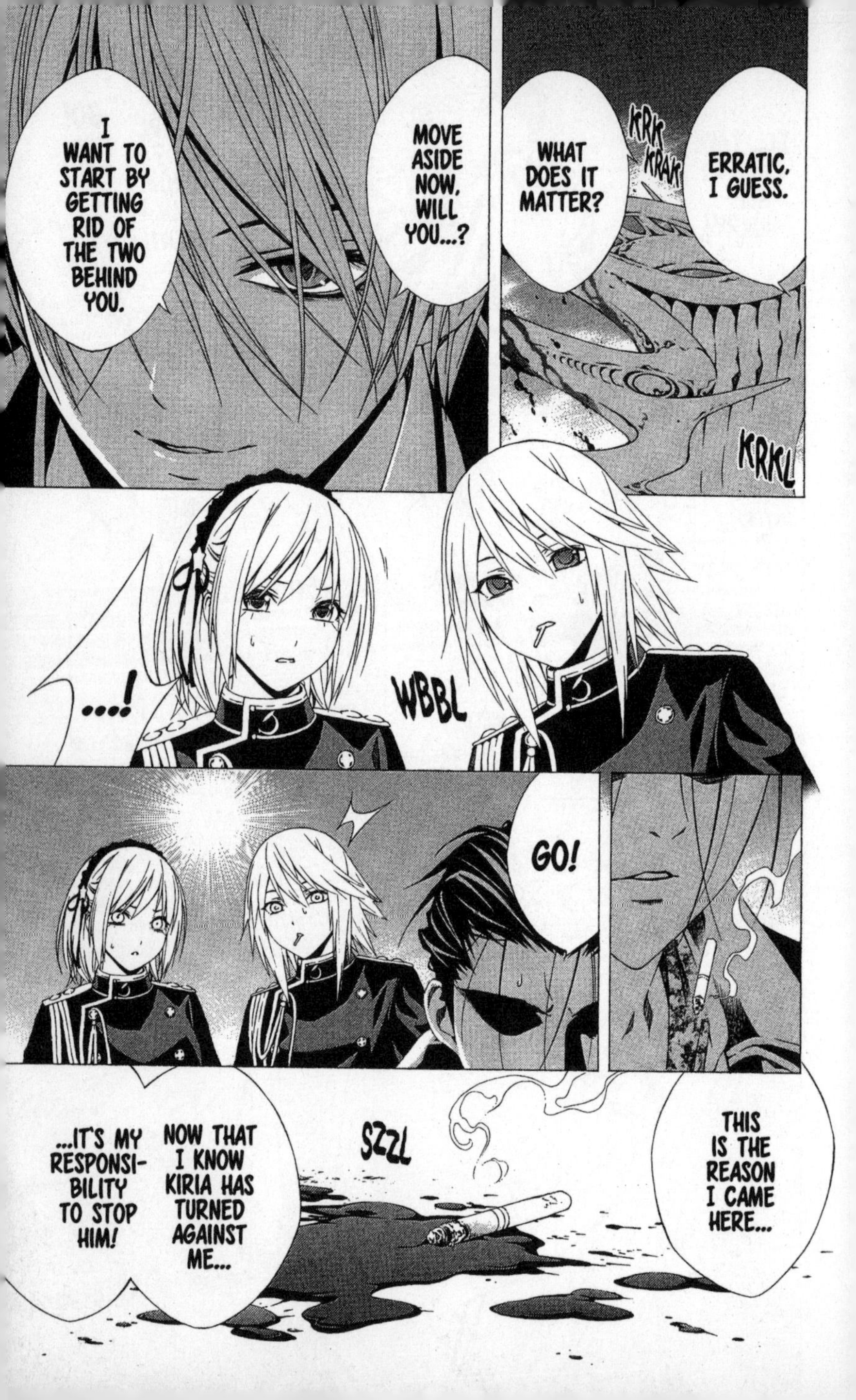
ERRATIC, I GUESS.
KRK KRAK
WHAT DOES IT MATTER?
KRKL
MOVE ASIDE NOW, WILL YOU...?
I WANT TO START BY GETTING RID OF THE TWO BEHIND YOU.
WBBL
...!
GO!
THIS IS THE REASON I CAME HERE...
SZZL
NOW THAT I KNOW KIRIA HAS TURNED AGAINST ME...
...IT'S MY RESPONSI-BILITY TO STOP HIM!

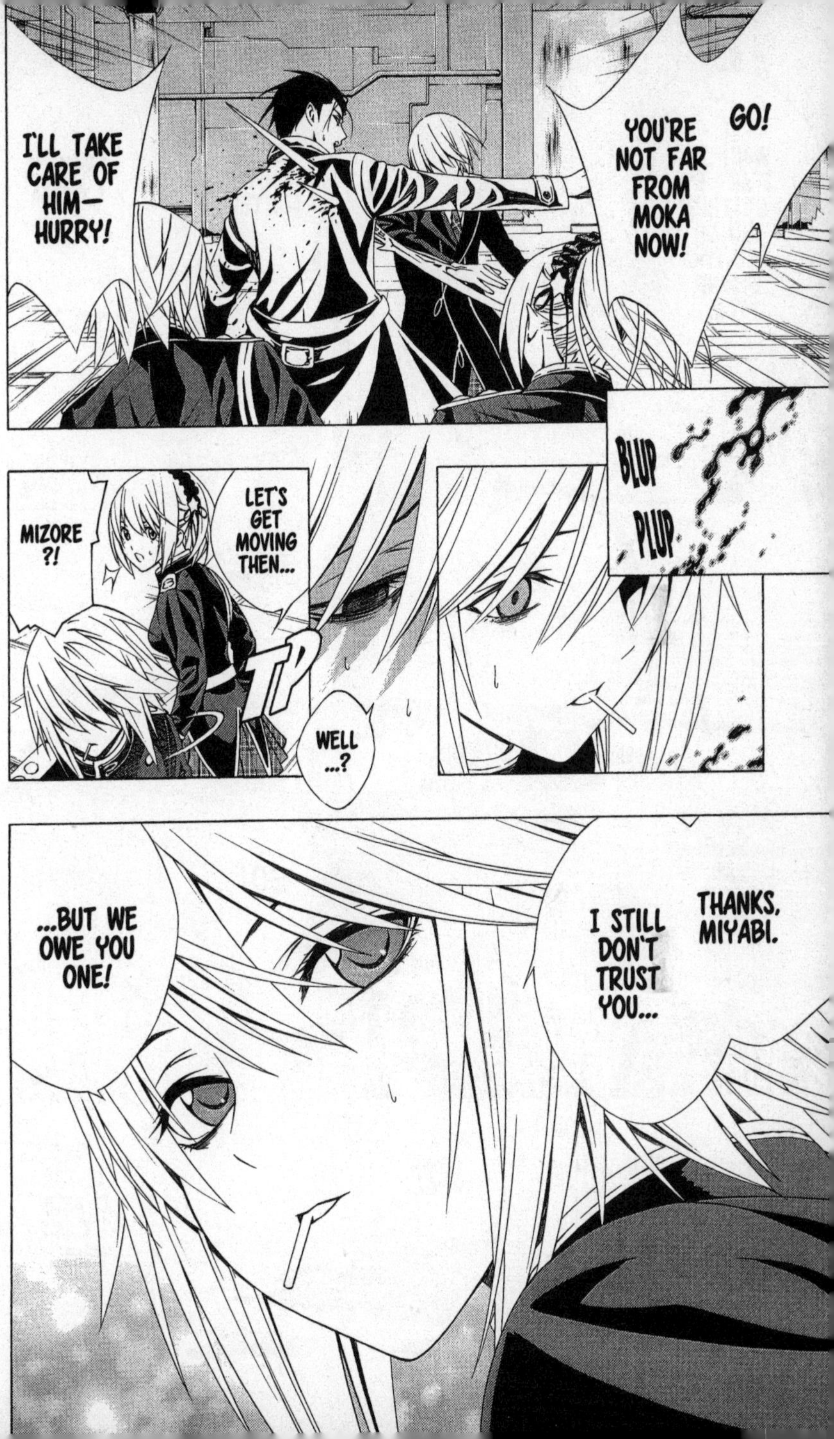
GO!
YOU'RE NOT FAR FROM MOKA NOW!
I'LL TAKE CARE OF HIM—HURRY!
BLUP
PLUP
WELL ...?
LET'S GET MOVING THEN...
MIZORE ?!
THANKS, MIYABI.
I STILL DON'T TRUST YOU...
...BUT WE OWE YOU ONE!

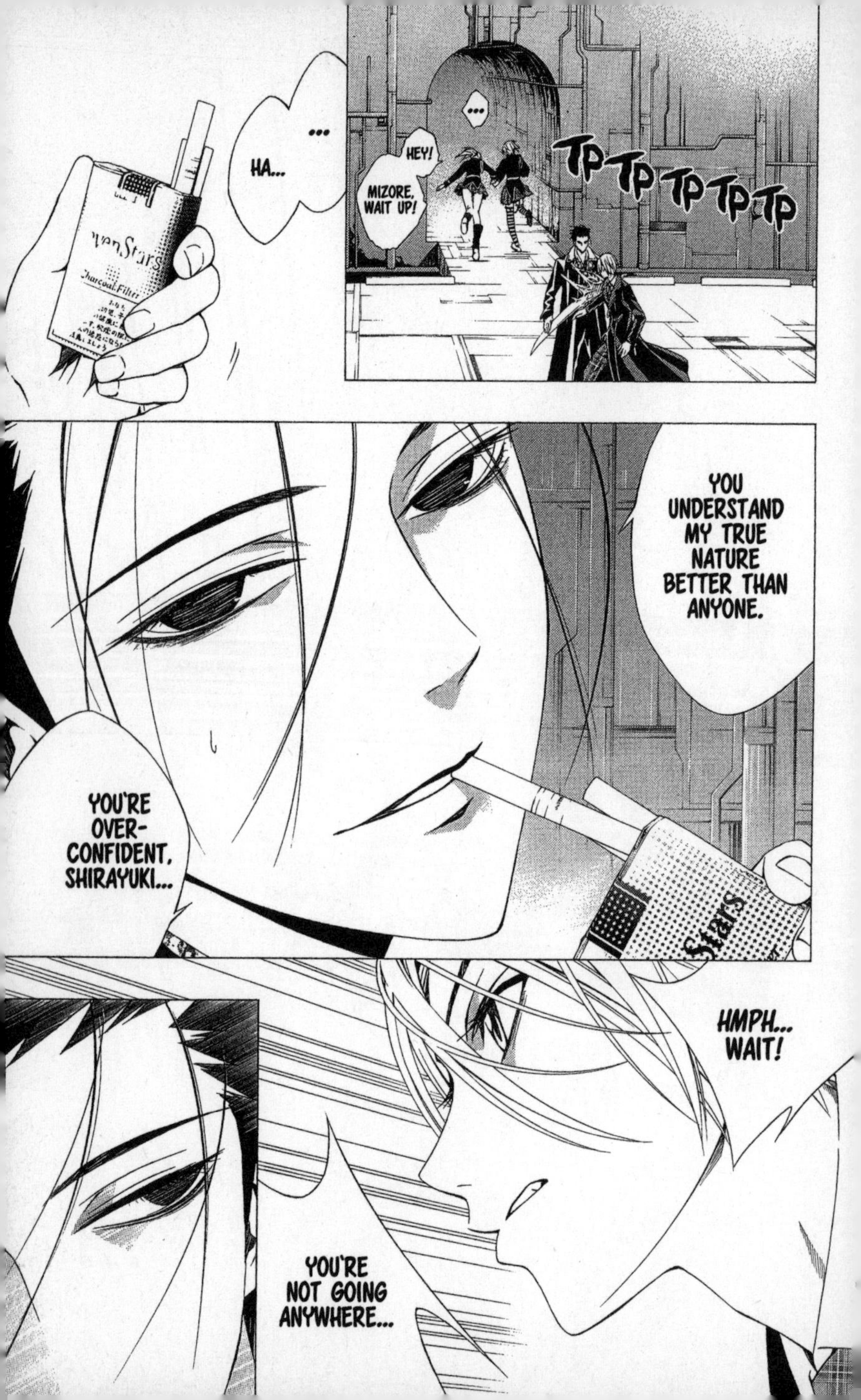
...
HEY!
MIZORE, WAIT UP!
TP TP TP TP TP
...
HA...
YOU UNDERSTAND MY TRUE NATURE BETTER THAN ANYONE.
YOU'RE OVER-CONFIDENT, SHIRAYUKI...
HMPH... WAIT!
YOU'RE NOT GOING ANYWHERE...

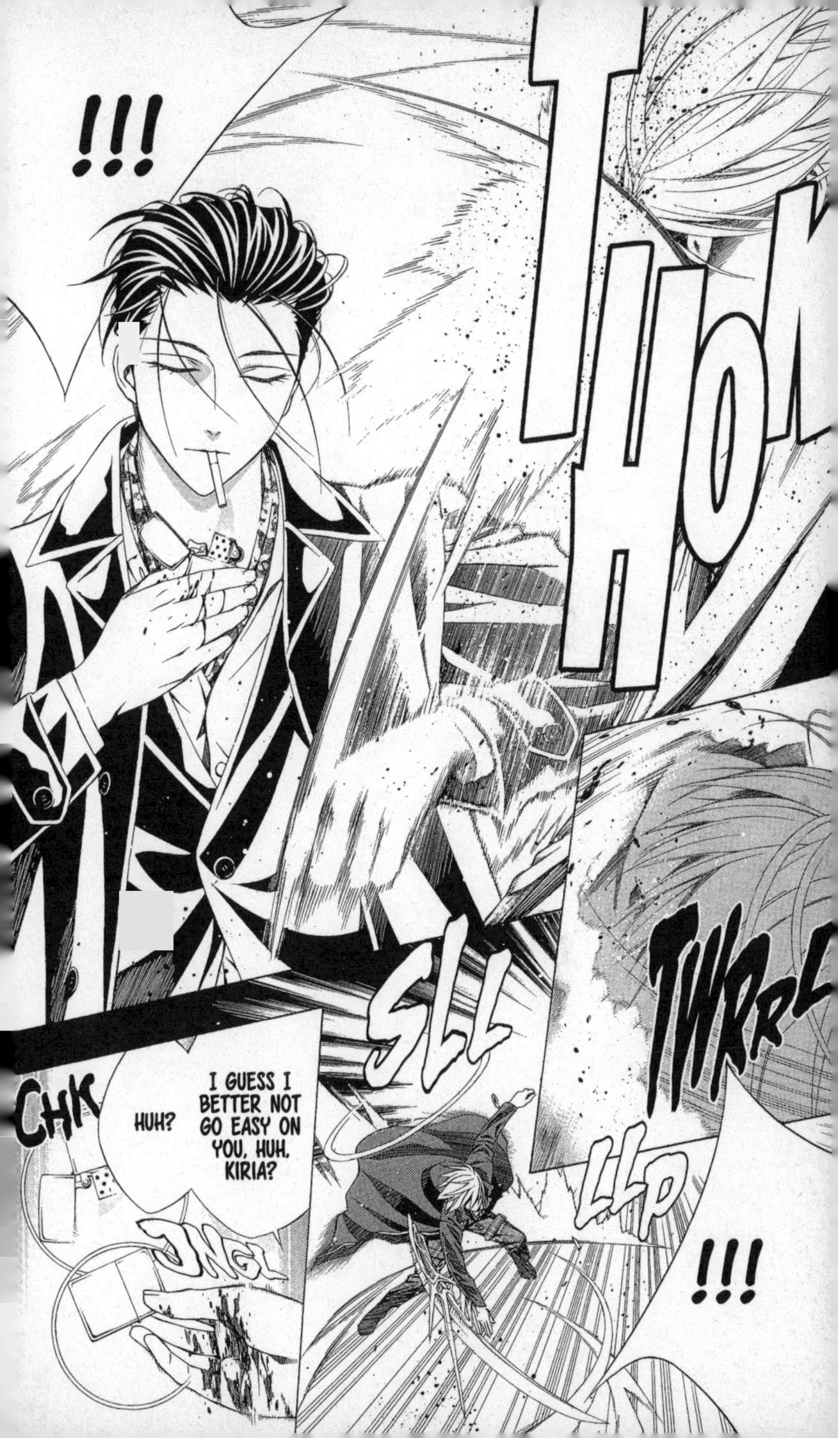
THO
!!!
TWRRL
SLL
LLP
!!!
I GUESS I BETTER NOT GO EASY ON YOU, HUH, KIRIA?
HUH?
CHK
JNGL

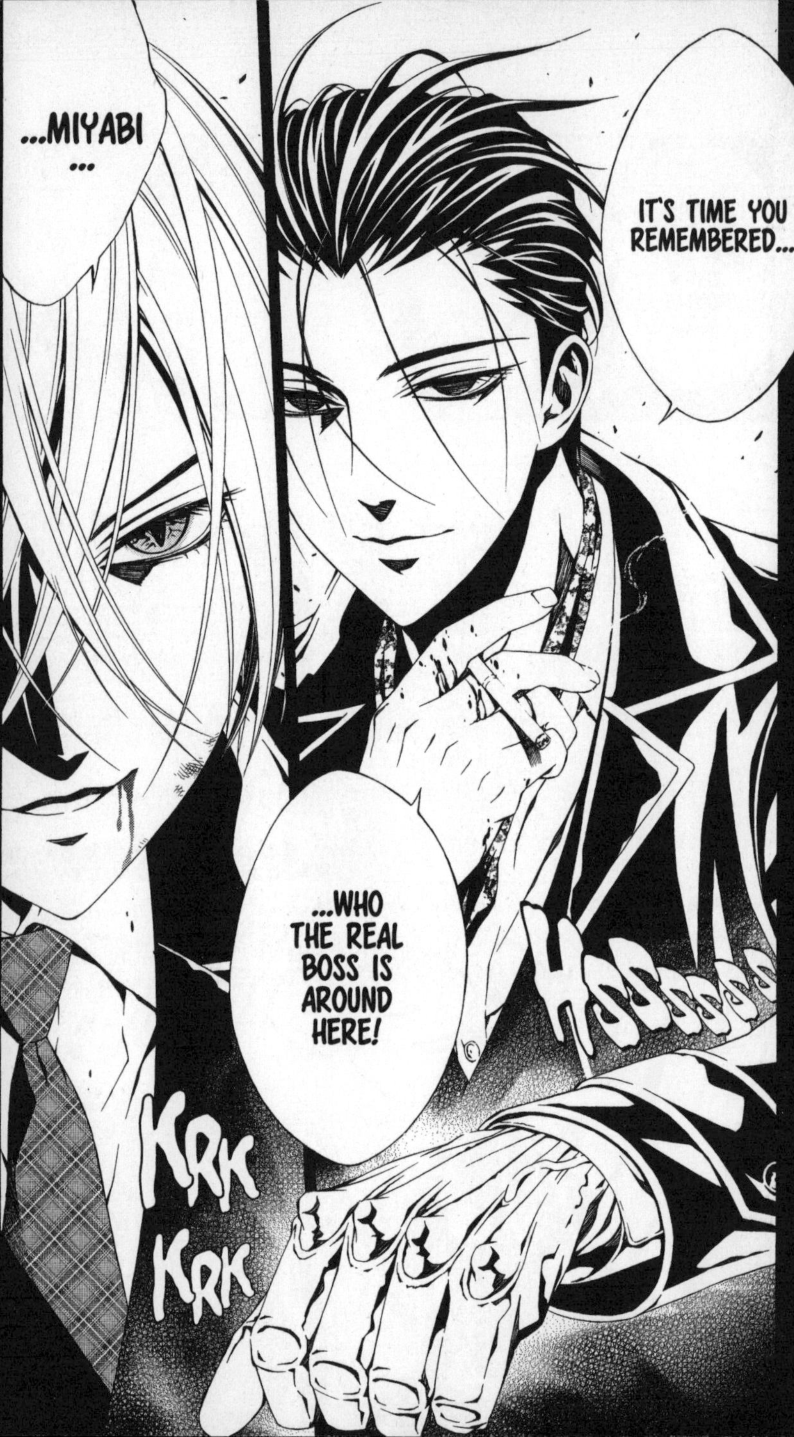
IT'S TIME YOU REMEMBERED...
...WHO THE REAL BOSS IS AROUND HERE!
HSSSSSS
...MIYABI ...
KRK KRK

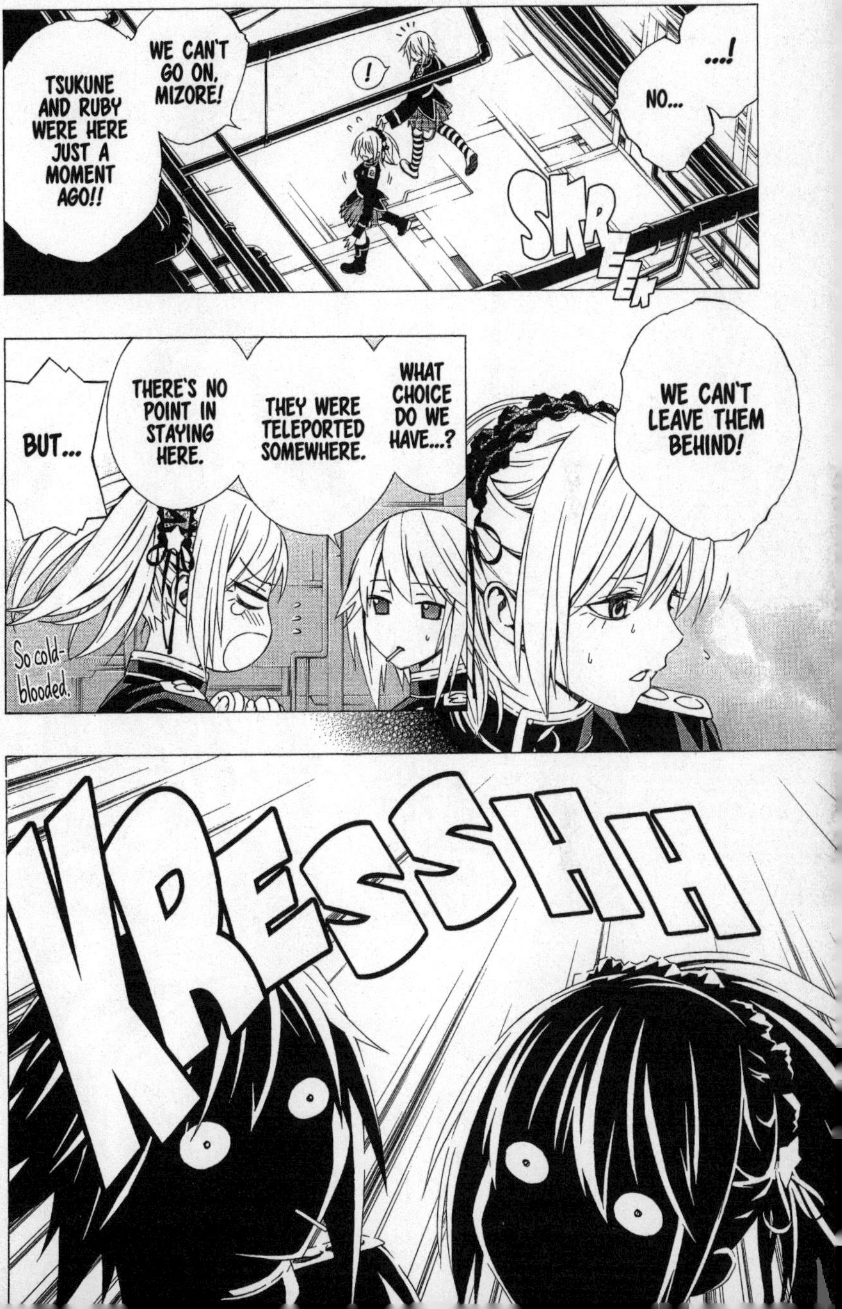
...!
NO...
SKREEK
!
WE CAN'T GO ON, MIZORE!
TSUKUNE AND RUBY WERE HERE JUST A MOMENT AGO!!
WE CAN'T LEAVE THEM BEHIND!
WHAT CHOICE DO WE HAVE...?
THEY WERE TELEPORTED SOMEWHERE.
THERE'S NO POINT IN STAYING HERE.
BUT...
So cold-blooded.
KRESSHH

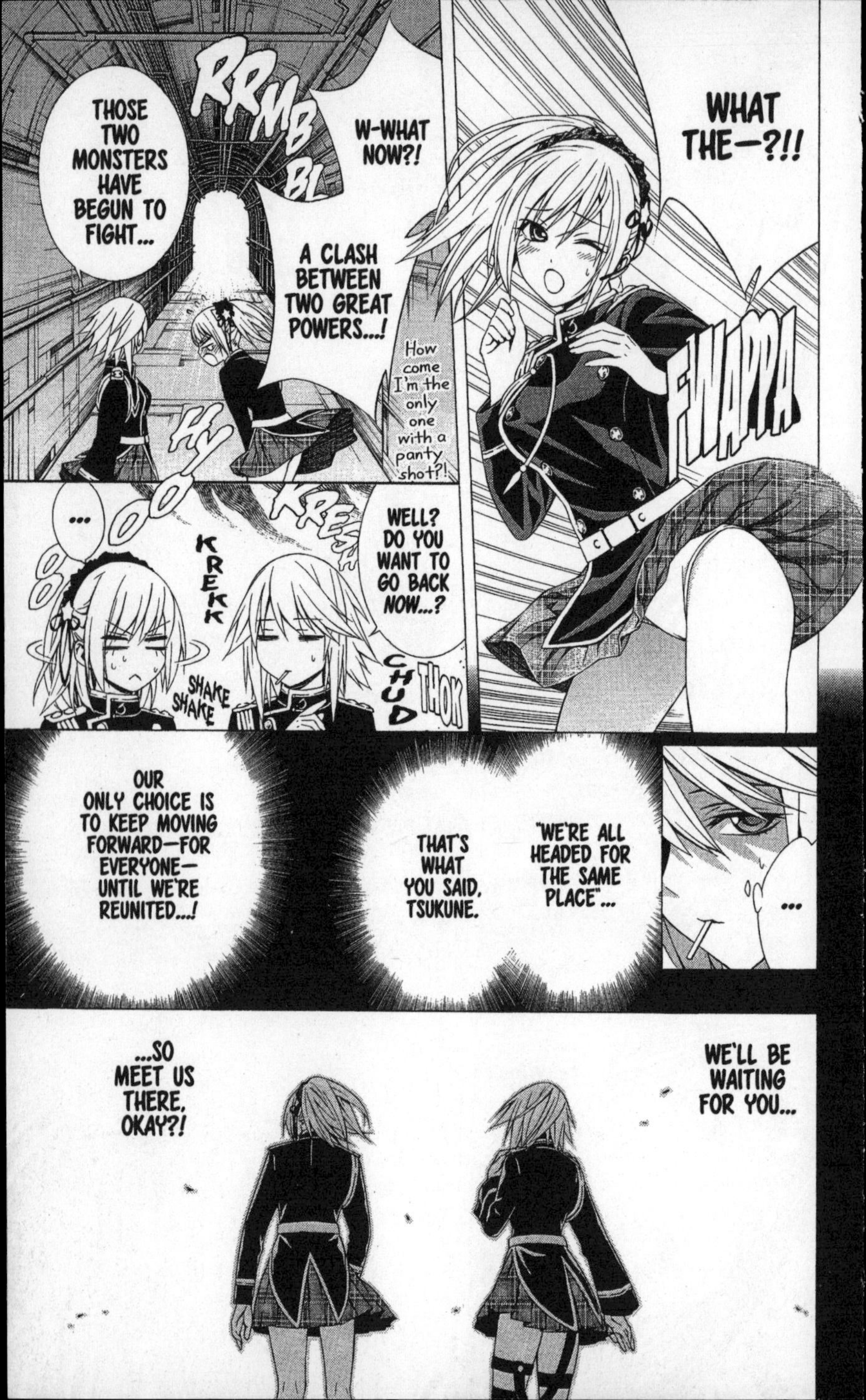
WHAT THE—?!!
FWAPPA
How come I'm the only one with a panty shot?!
RRMBBL
THOSE TWO MONSTERS HAVE BEGUN TO FIGHT...
W-WHAT NOW?!
A CLASH BETWEEN TWO GREAT POWERS...!
HYOOOO
KRESH
WELL? DO YOU WANT TO GO BACK NOW...?
KREKK
...
SHAKE SHAKE
CHUD
THOK
...
"WE'RE ALL HEADED FOR THE SAME PLACE"...
THAT'S WHAT YOU SAID, TSUKUNE.
OUR ONLY CHOICE IS TO KEEP MOVING FORWARD—FOR EVERYONE—UNTIL WE'RE REUNITED...!
WE'LL BE WAITING FOR YOU...
...SO MEET US THERE, OKAY?!

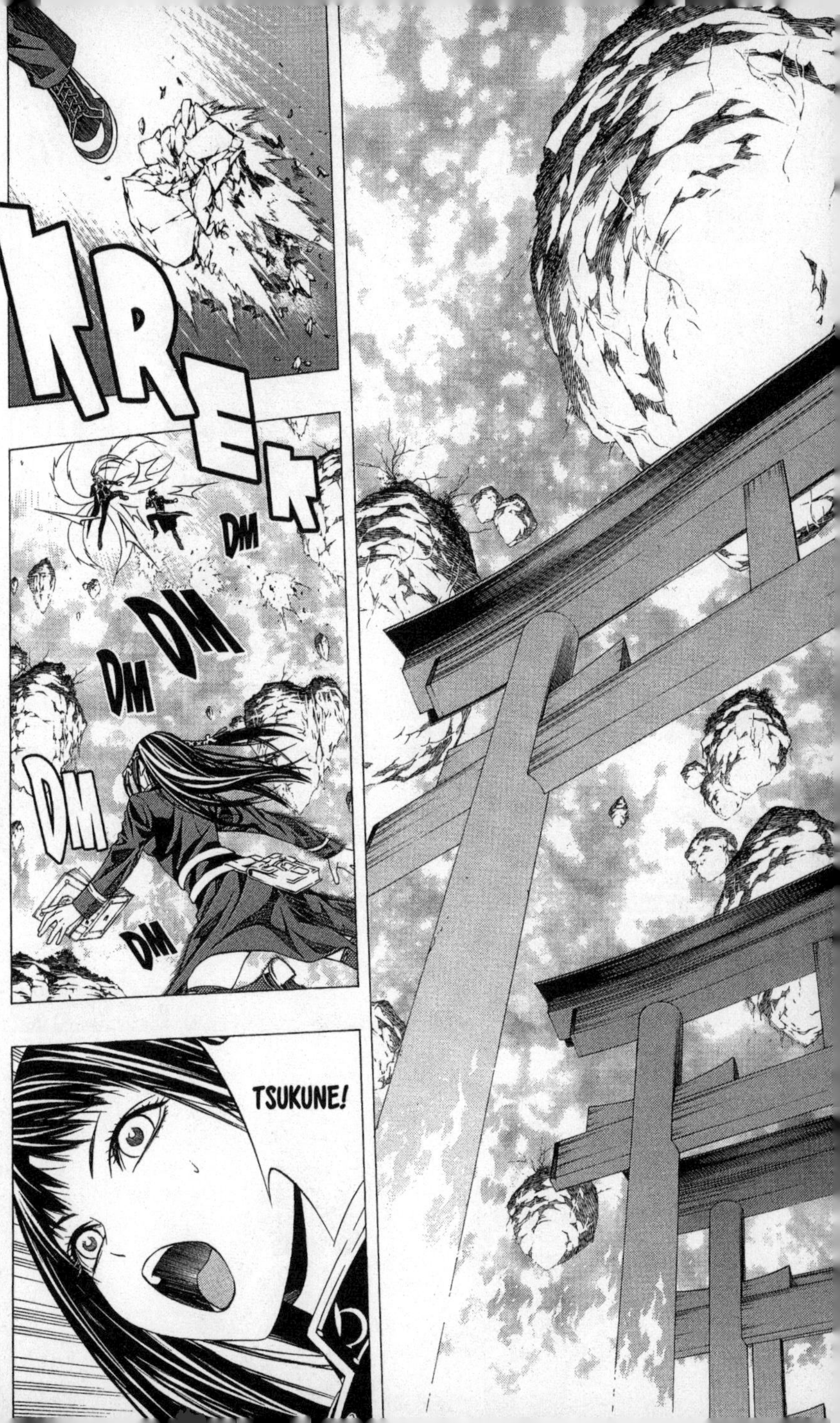
KRREK
DM
DM
DM
DM
DM
TSUKUNE!

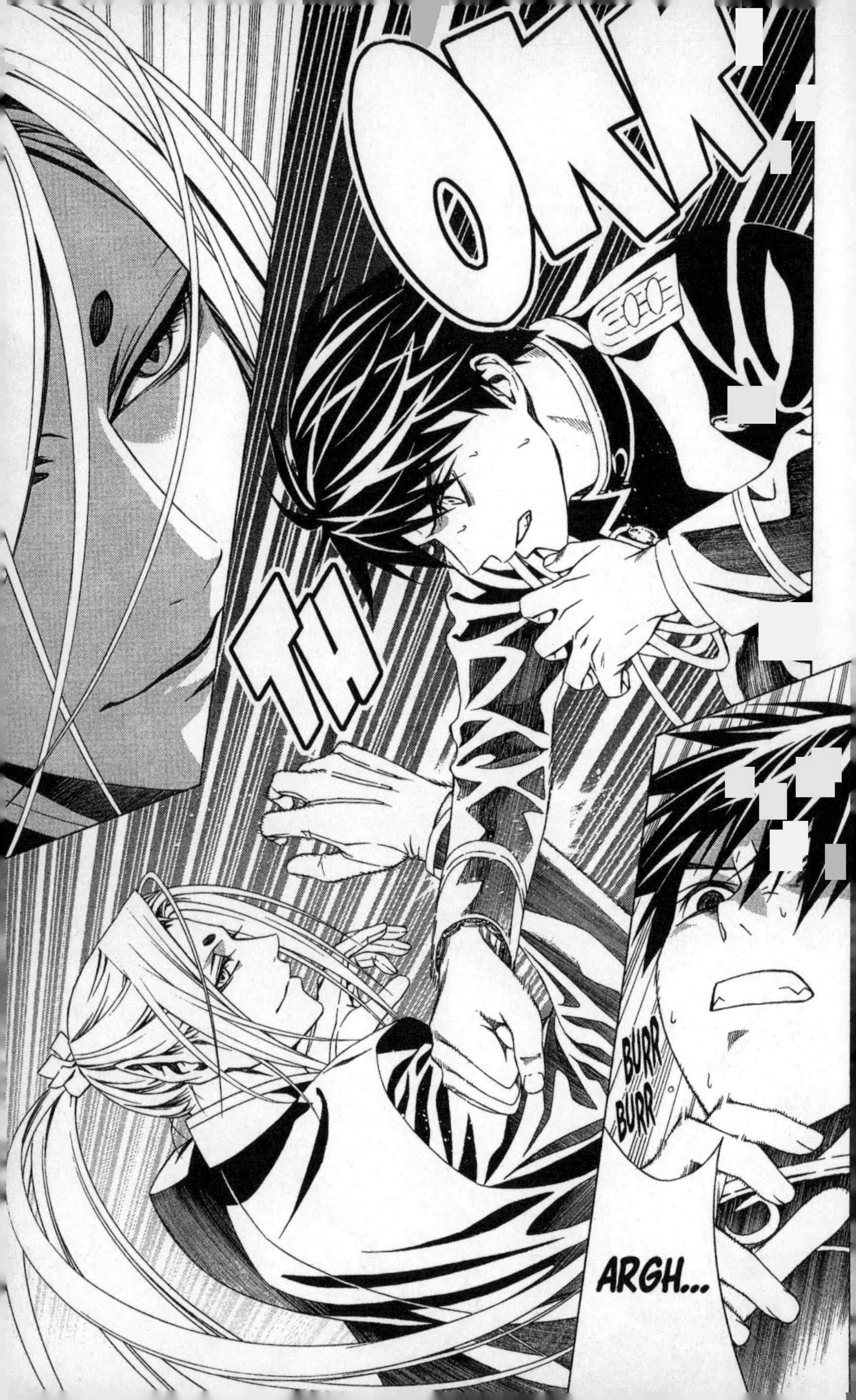
BURR BURR
ARGH...

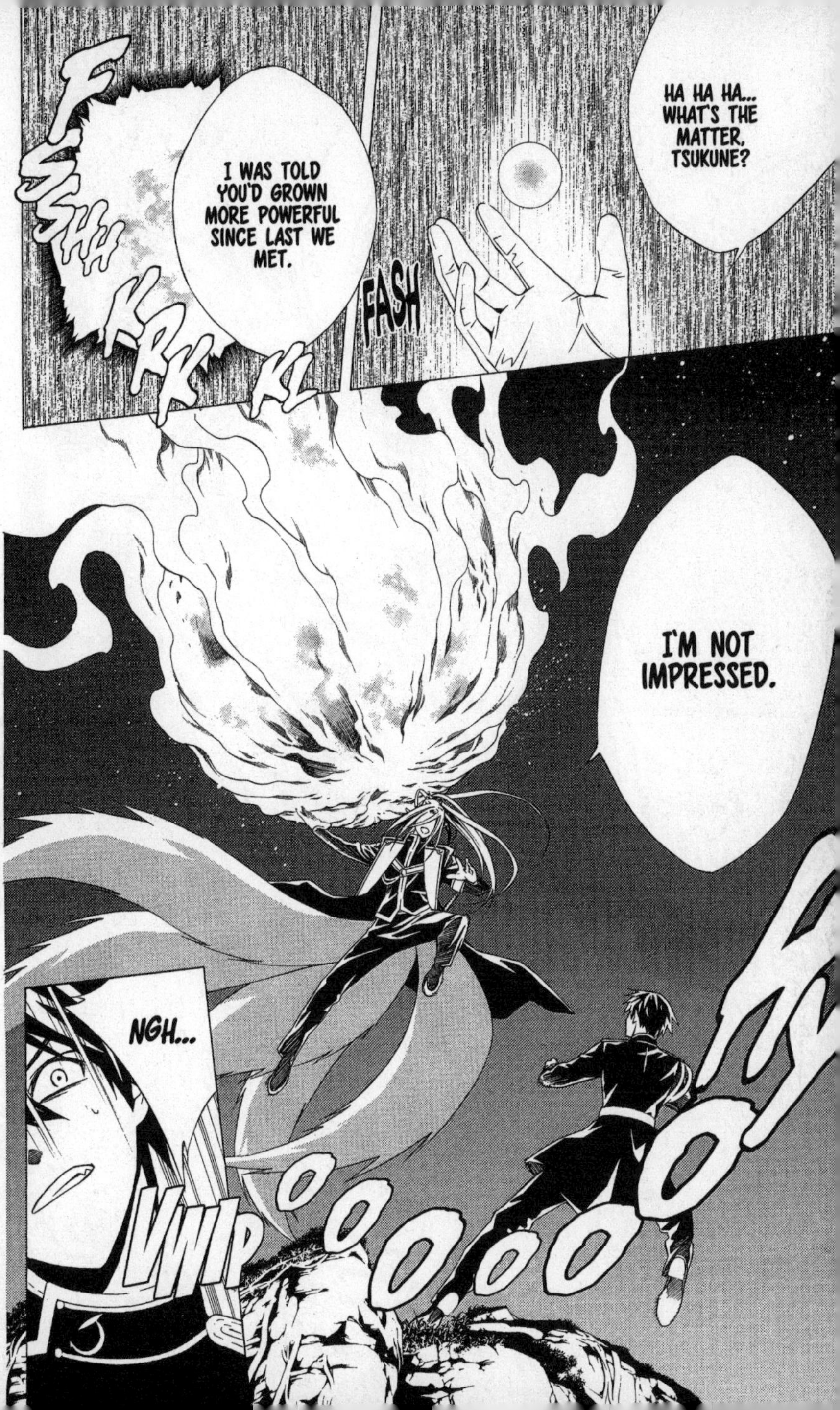
HA HA HA... WHAT'S THE MATTER, TSUKUNE?
FASH
I WAS TOLD YOU'D GROWN MORE POWERFUL SINCE LAST WE MET.
FSSHH
KRK KL
I'M NOT IMPRESSED.
VWIP
NGH...

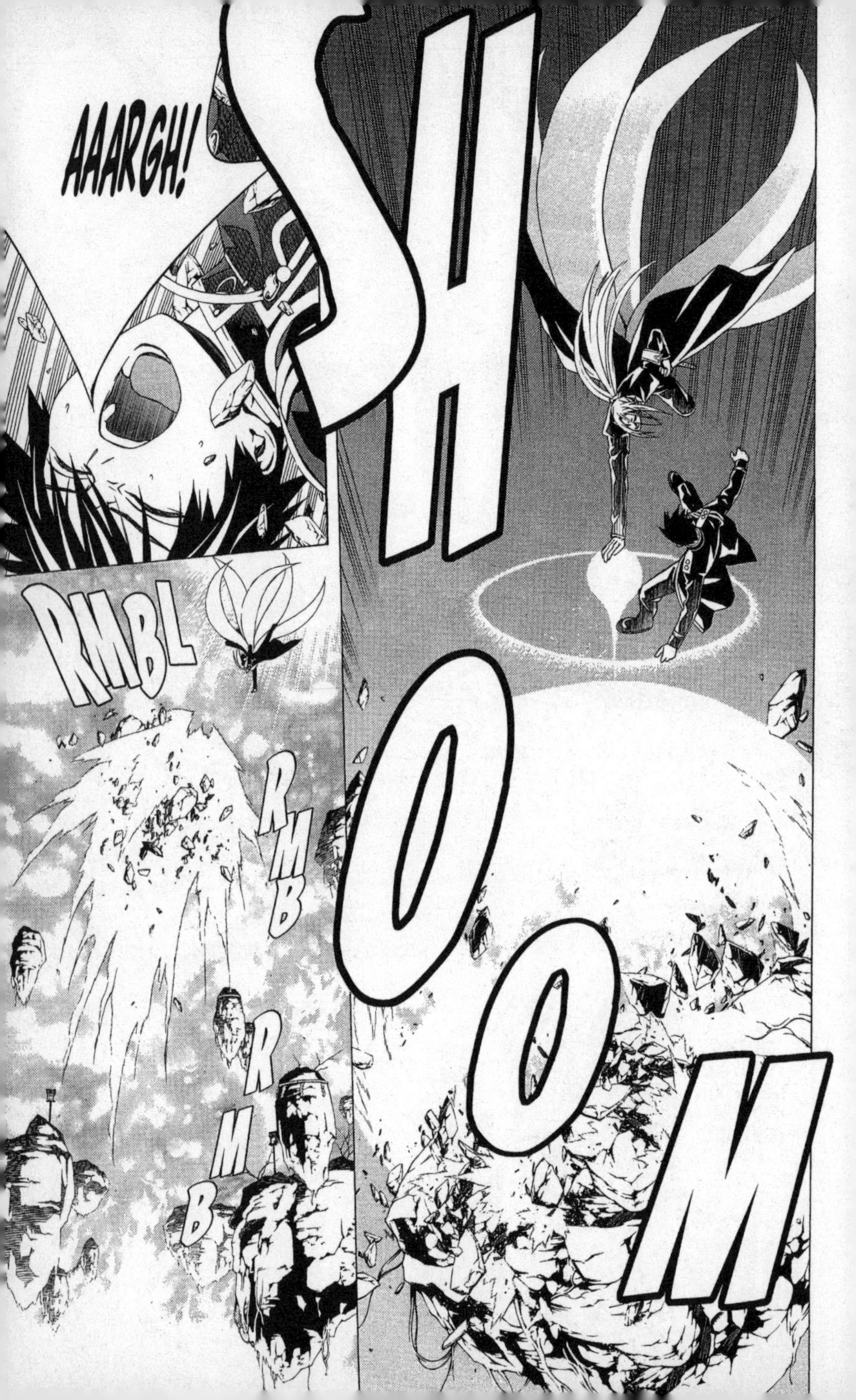
SHOOOM
AAARGH!
RMBL
RMB
RMB

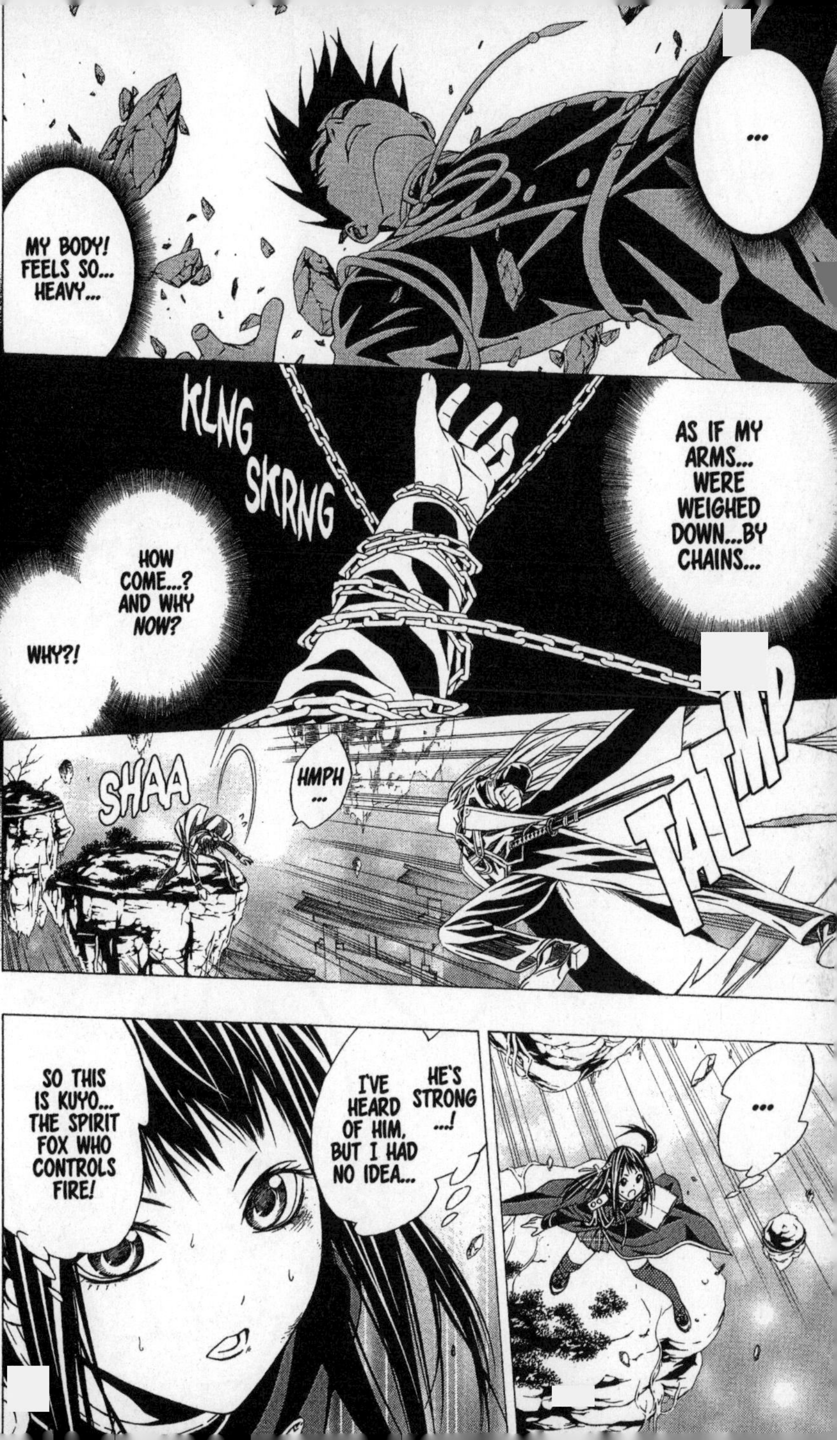
...
MY BODY! FEELS SO... HEAVY...
AS IF MY ARMS... WERE WEIGHED DOWN...BY CHAINS...
KLNG SKRNG
HOW COME...? AND WHY NOW?
WHY?!
TATMP
HMPH ...
SHAA
...
HE'S STRONG ...!
I'VE HEARD OF HIM, BUT I HAD NO IDEA...
SO THIS IS KUYO... THE SPIRIT FOX WHO CONTROLS FIRE!

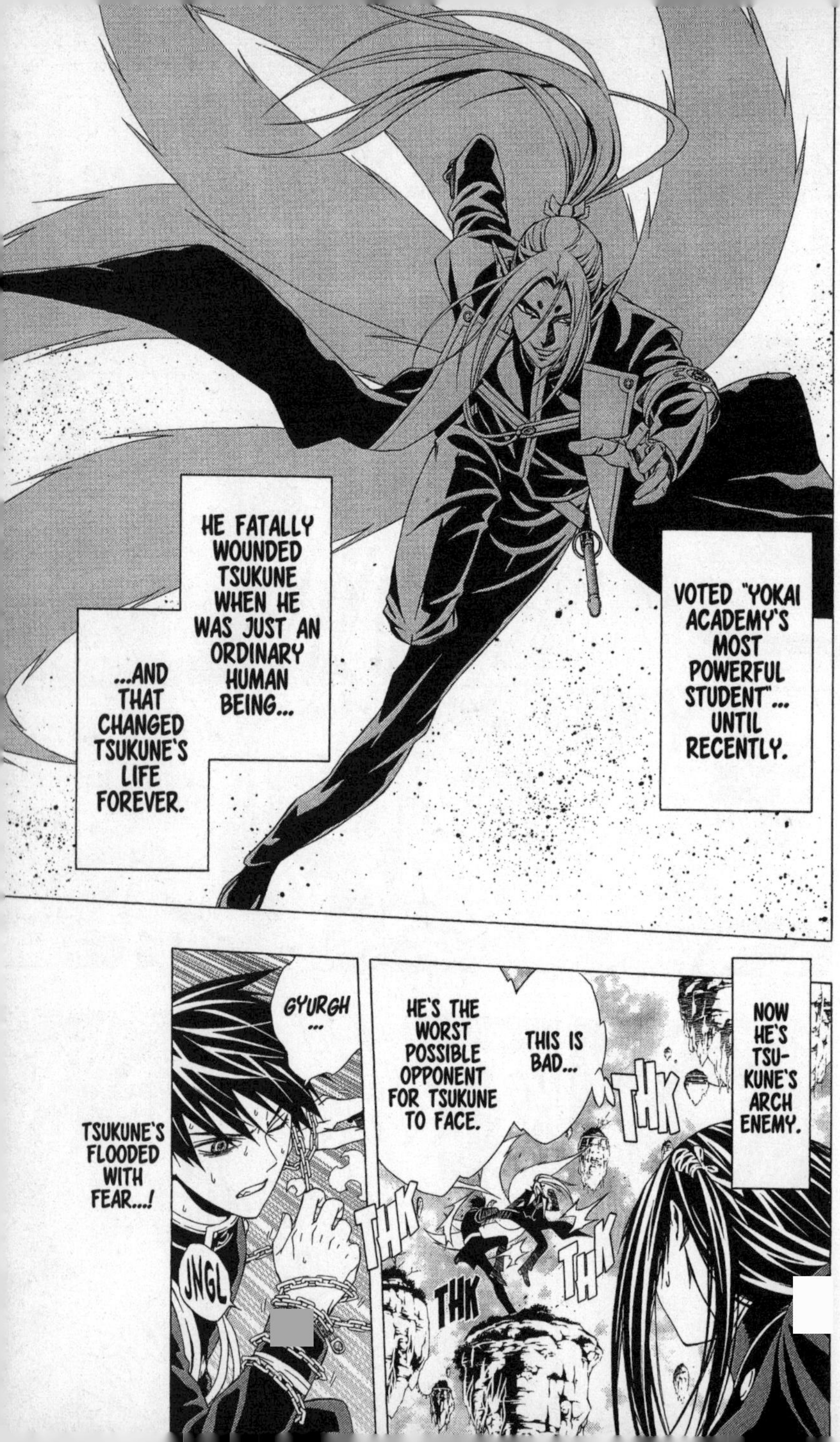
VOTED "YOKAI ACADEMY'S MOST POWERFUL STUDENT"... UNTIL RECENTLY.
HE FATALLY WOUNDED TSUKUNE WHEN HE WAS JUST AN ORDINARY HUMAN BEING...
...AND THAT CHANGED TSUKUNE'S LIFE FOREVER.
NOW HE'S TSU-KUNE'S ARCH ENEMY.
THK
THIS IS BAD...
HE'S THE WORST POSSIBLE OPPONENT FOR TSUKUNE TO FACE.
THK
THK
THK
GYURGH ...
TSUKUNE'S FLOODED WITH FEAR...!
JNGL

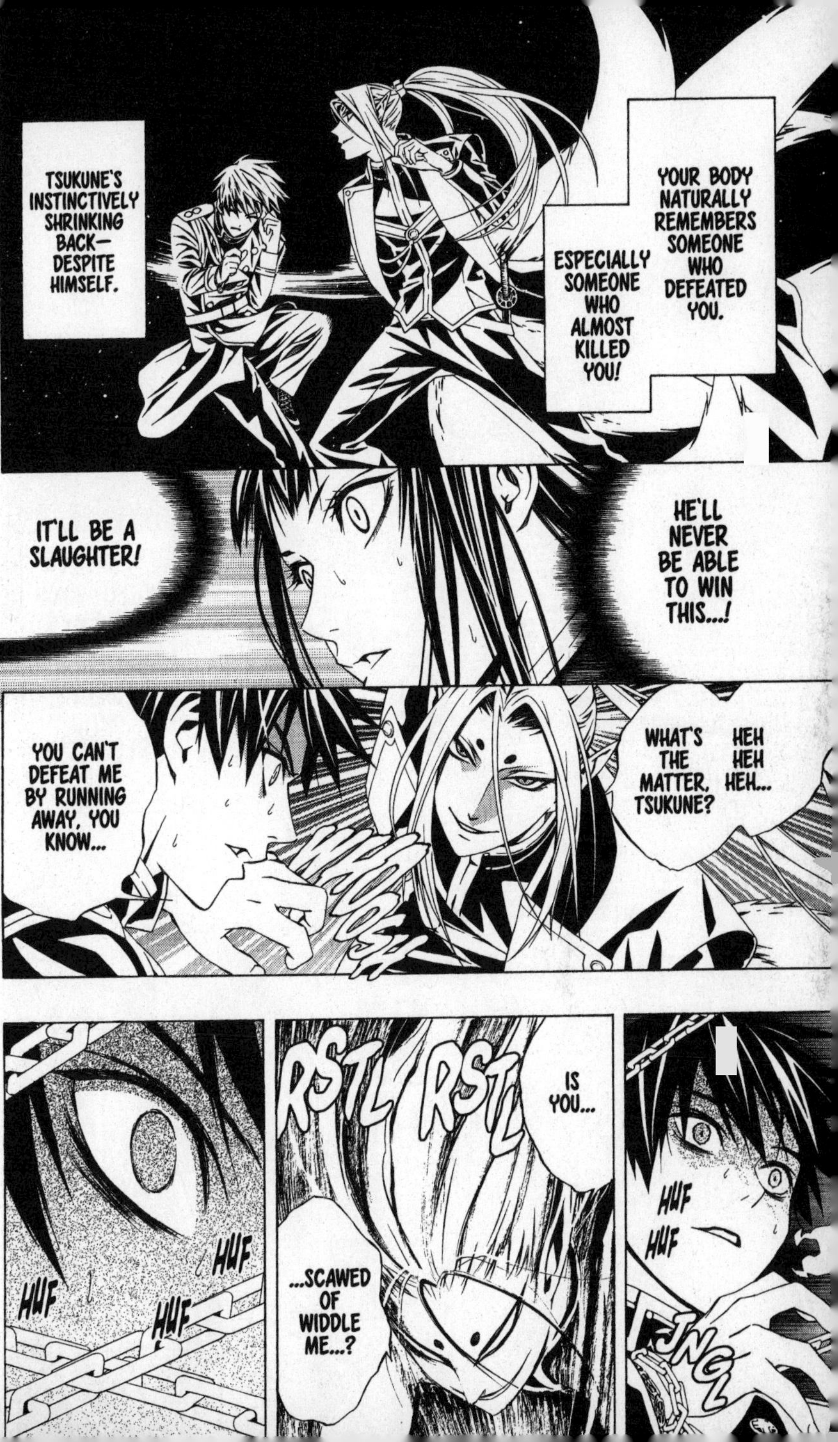
YOUR BODY NATURALLY REMEMBERS SOMEONE WHO DEFEATED YOU.
ESPECIALLY SOMEONE WHO ALMOST KILLED YOU!
TSUKUNE'S INSTINCTIVELY SHRINKING BACK—DESPITE HIMSELF.
HE'LL NEVER BE ABLE TO WIN THIS...!
IT'LL BE A SLAUGHTER!
HEH HEH HEH...
WHAT'S THE MATTER, TSUKUNE?
YOU CAN'T DEFEAT ME BY RUNNING AWAY, YOU KNOW...
HUF HUF
JNGL
IS YOU...
RSTL RSTL
...SCAWED OF WIDDLE ME...?
HUF HUF HUF

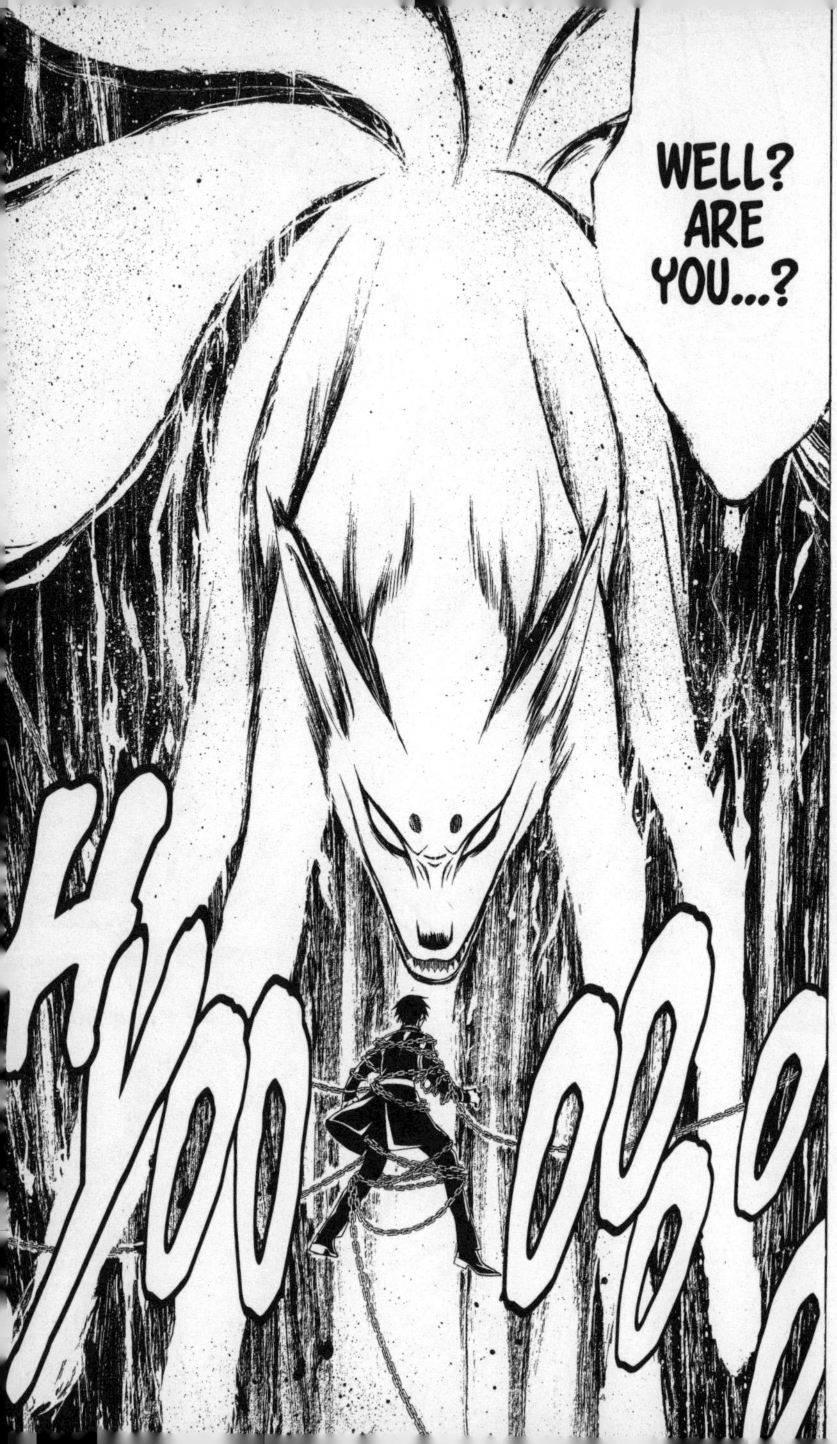
WELL? ARE YOU...?

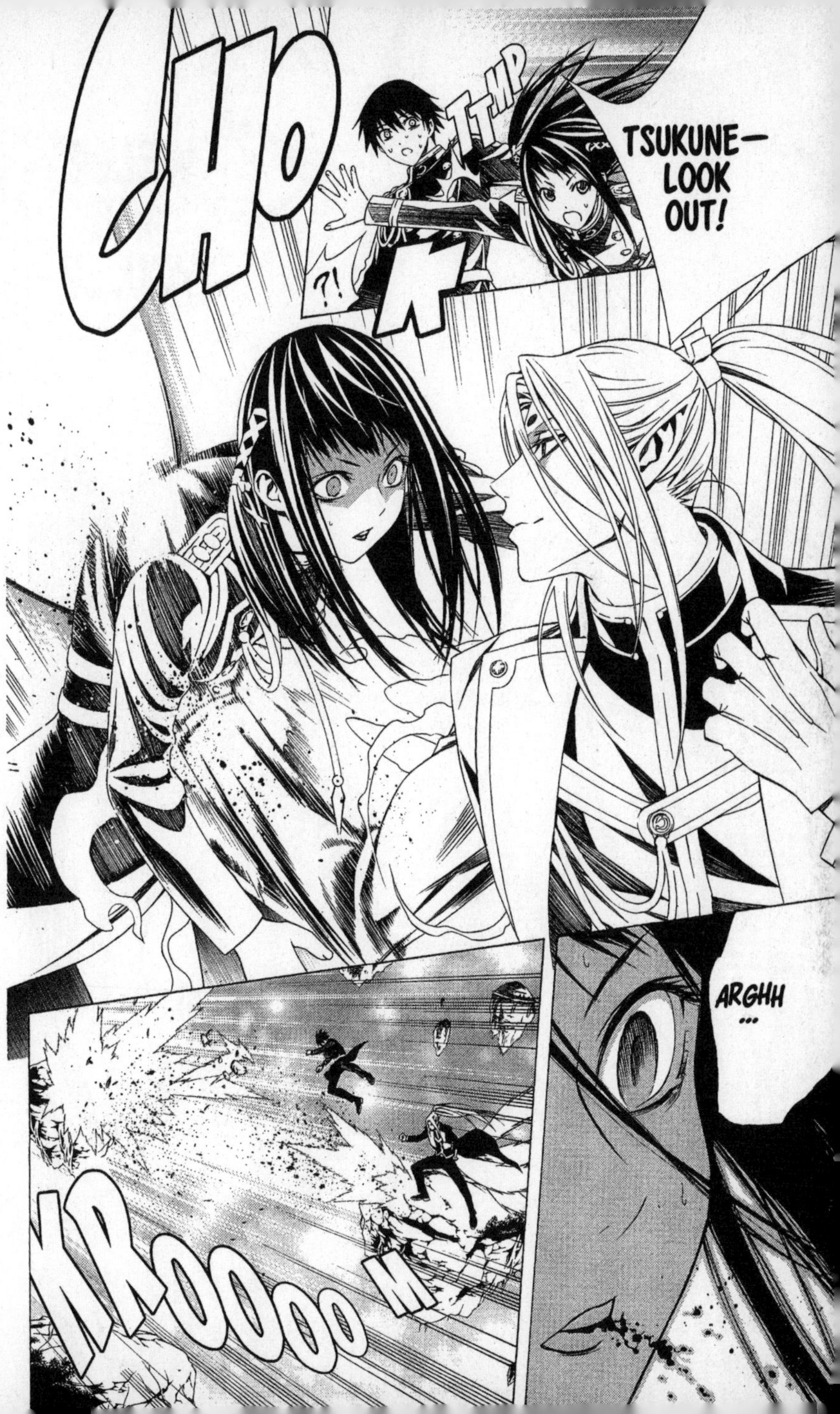
TSUKUNE—
LOOK
OUT!
TTMP
?!
CHOK
ARGHH
...
VROOOOOM

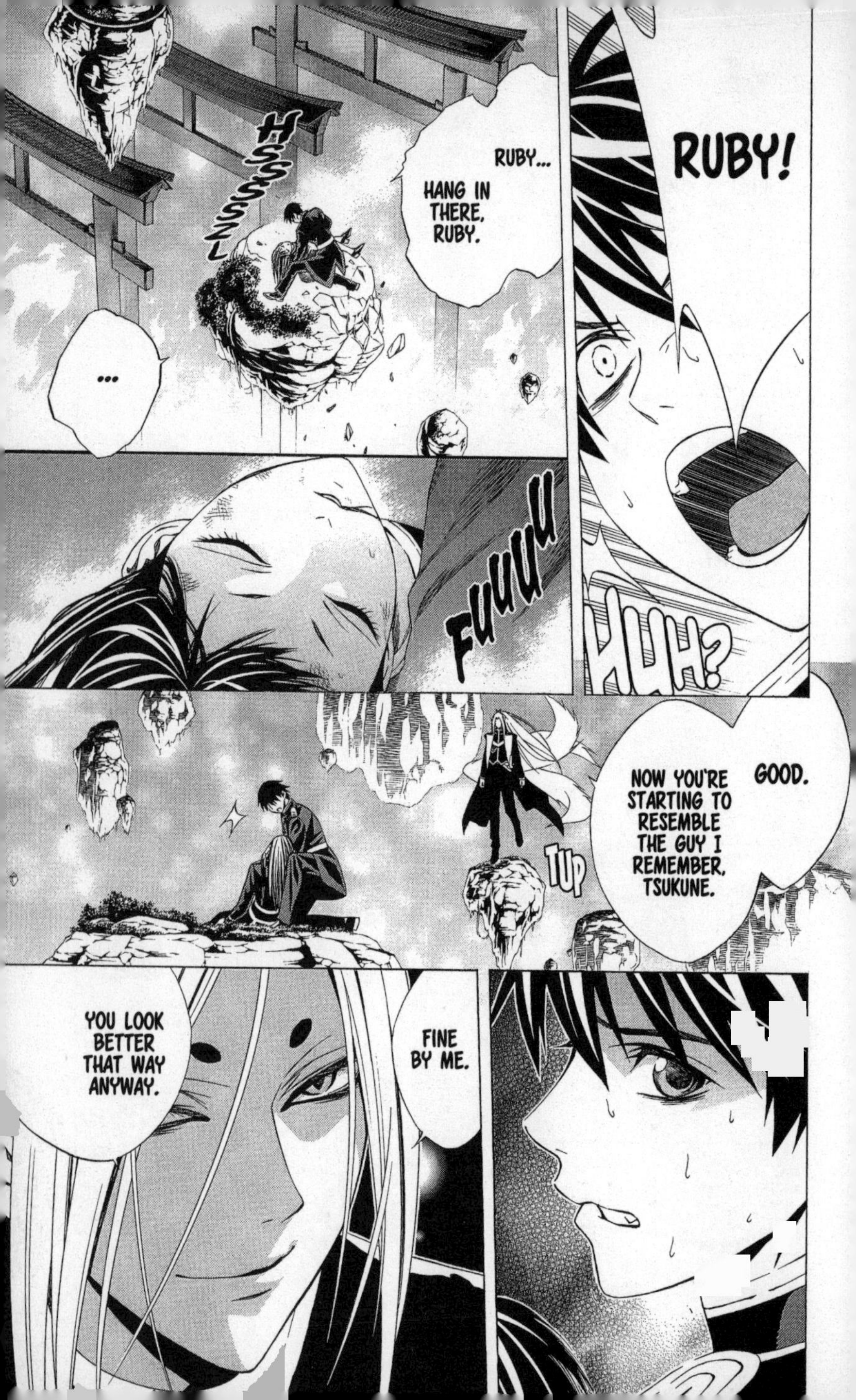
RUBY!
RUBY...
HANG IN THERE, RUBY.
HSSSSZL
...
HUH?
FUUUU
GOOD.
NOW YOU'RE STARTING TO RESEMBLE THE GUY I REMEMBER, TSUKUNE.
TUP
FINE BY ME.
YOU LOOK BETTER THAT WAY ANYWAY.

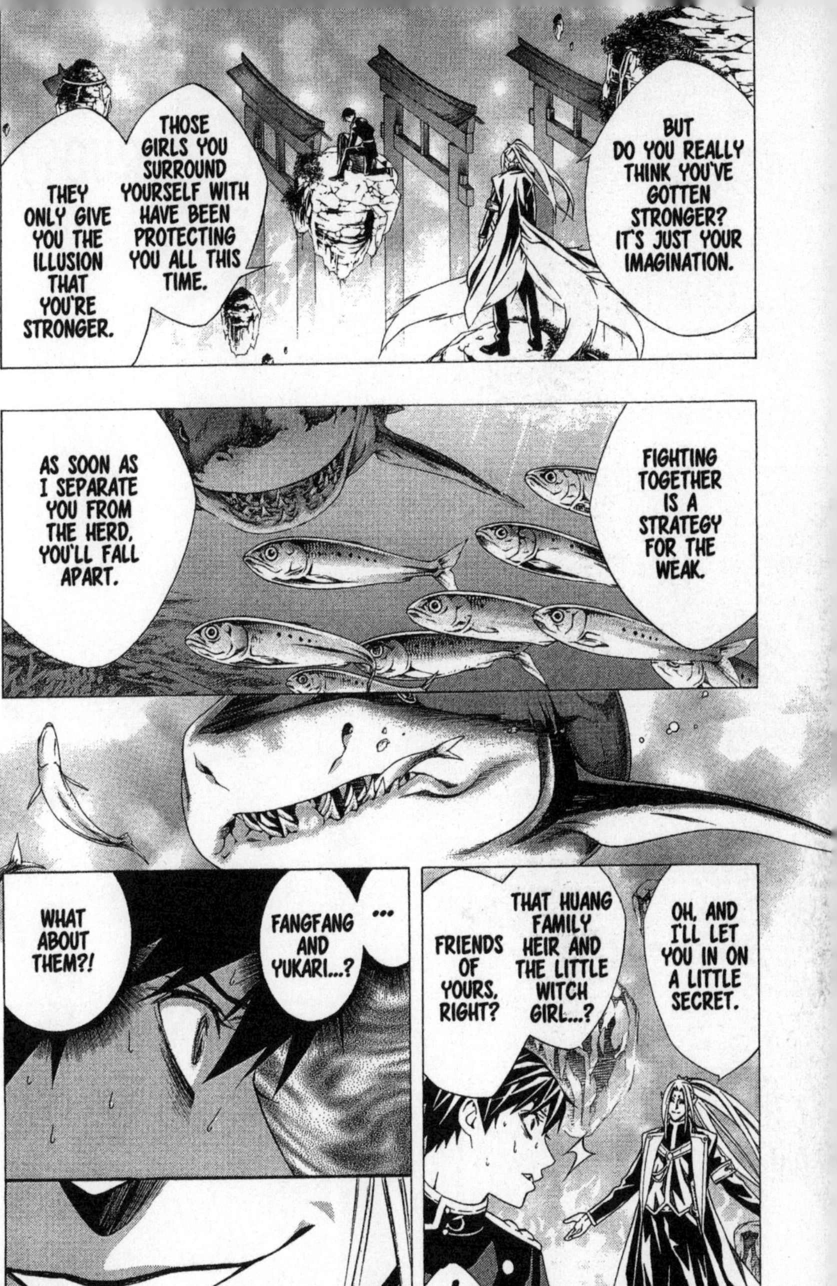
BUT DO YOU REALLY THINK YOU'VE GOTTEN STRONGER? IT'S JUST YOUR IMAGINATION.
THOSE GIRLS YOU SURROUND YOURSELF WITH HAVE BEEN PROTECTING YOU ALL THIS TIME.
THEY ONLY GIVE YOU THE ILLUSION THAT YOU'RE STRONGER.
FIGHTING TOGETHER IS A STRATEGY FOR THE WEAK.
AS SOON AS I SEPARATE YOU FROM THE HERD, YOU'LL FALL APART.
OH, AND I'LL LET YOU IN ON A LITTLE SECRET.
THAT HUANG FAMILY HEIR AND THE LITTLE WITCH GIRL...?
FRIENDS OF YOURS, RIGHT?
!
...
FANGFANG AND YUKARI...?
WHAT ABOUT THEM?!

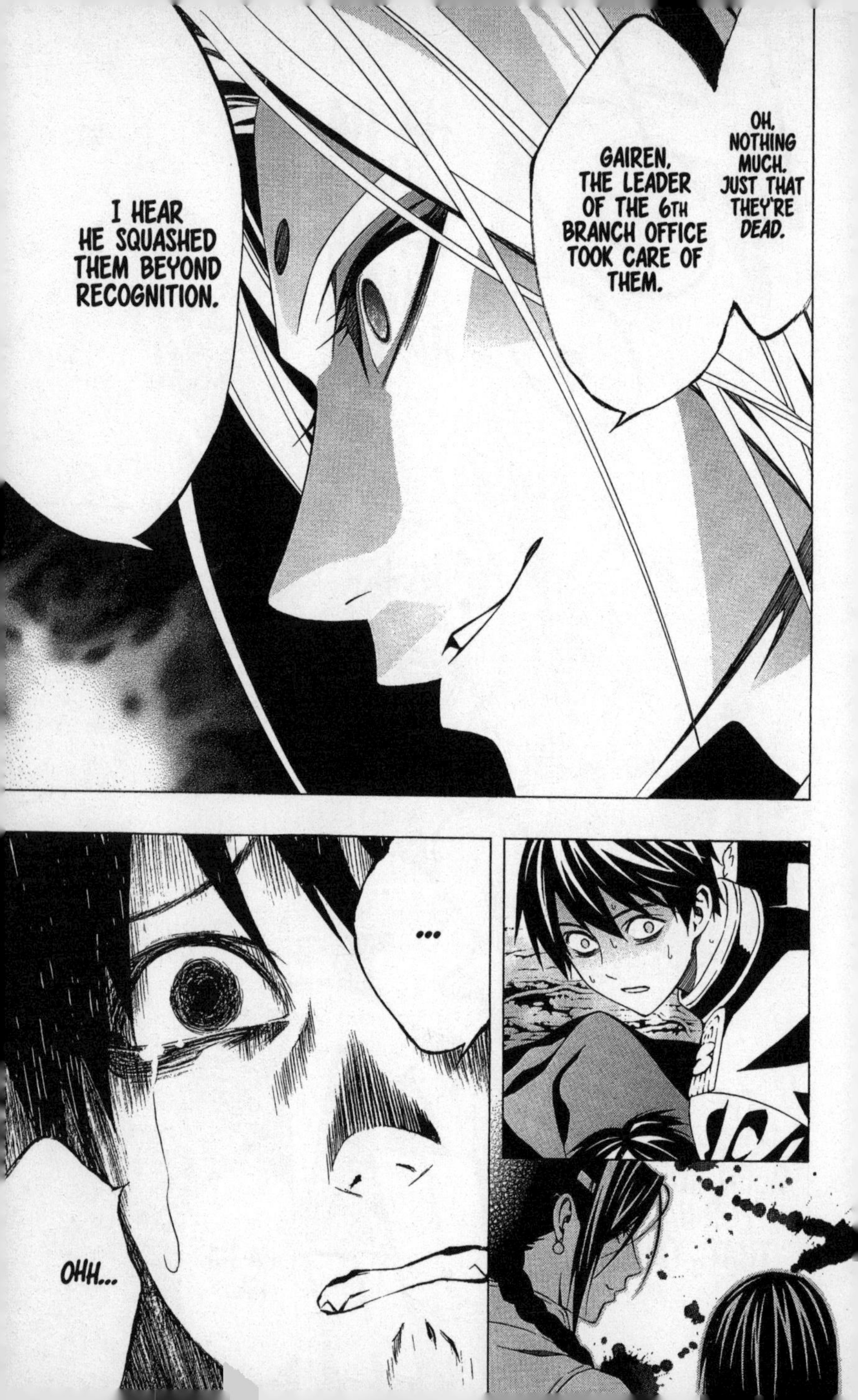
OH, NOTHING MUCH. JUST THAT THEY'RE DEAD.
GAIREN, THE LEADER OF THE 6TH BRANCH OFFICE TOOK CARE OF THEM.
I HEAR HE SQUASHED THEM BEYOND RECOGNITION.
...
OHH...

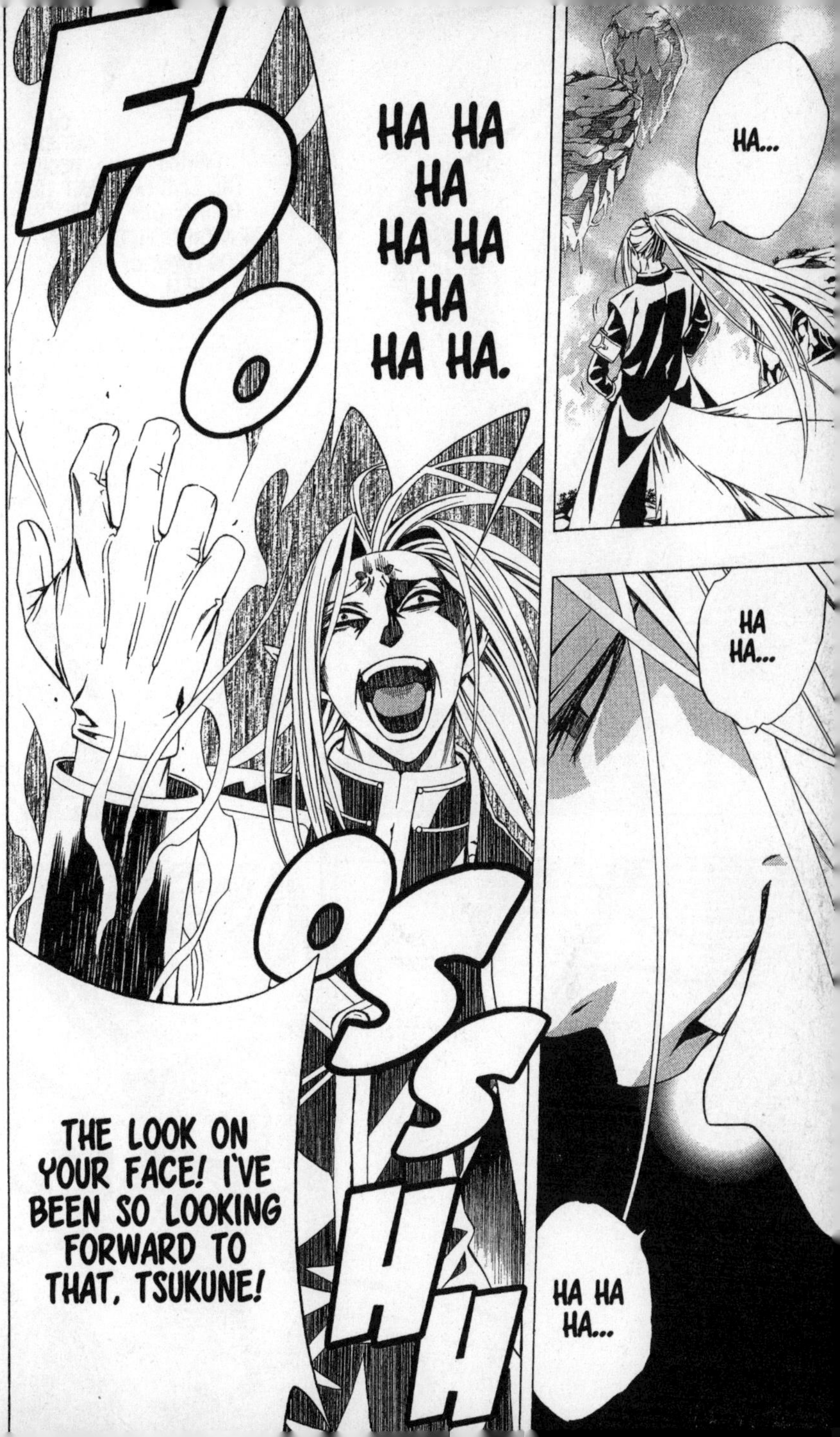
HA...
HA HA...
HA HA HA...
HA HA HA HA HA HA HA HA HA.
THE LOOK ON YOUR FACE! I'VE BEEN SO LOOKING FORWARD TO THAT, TSUKUNE!

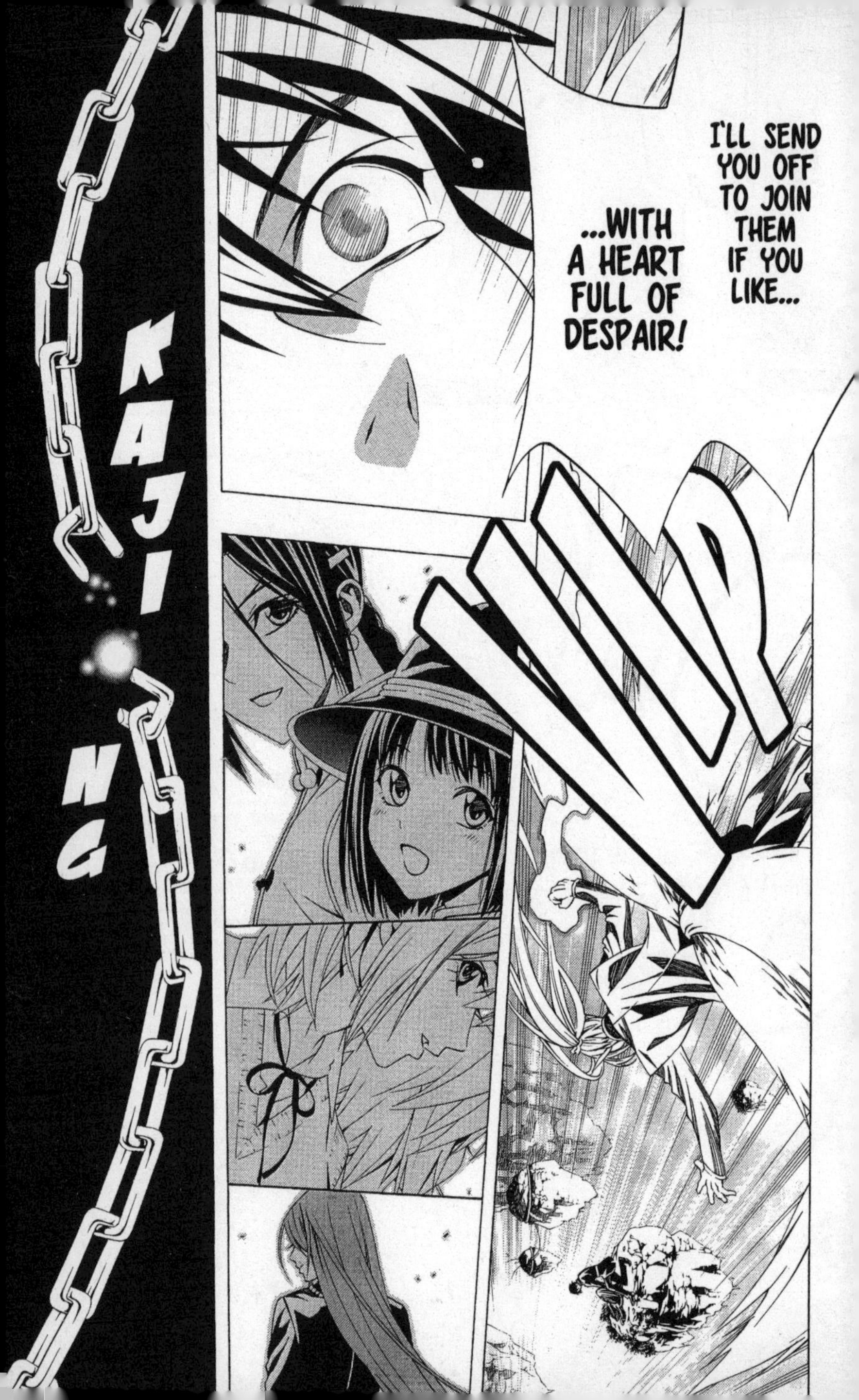
I'LL SEND YOU OFF TO JOIN THEM IF YOU LIKE...
...WITH A HEART FULL OF DESPAIR!
WHIP
KAJING

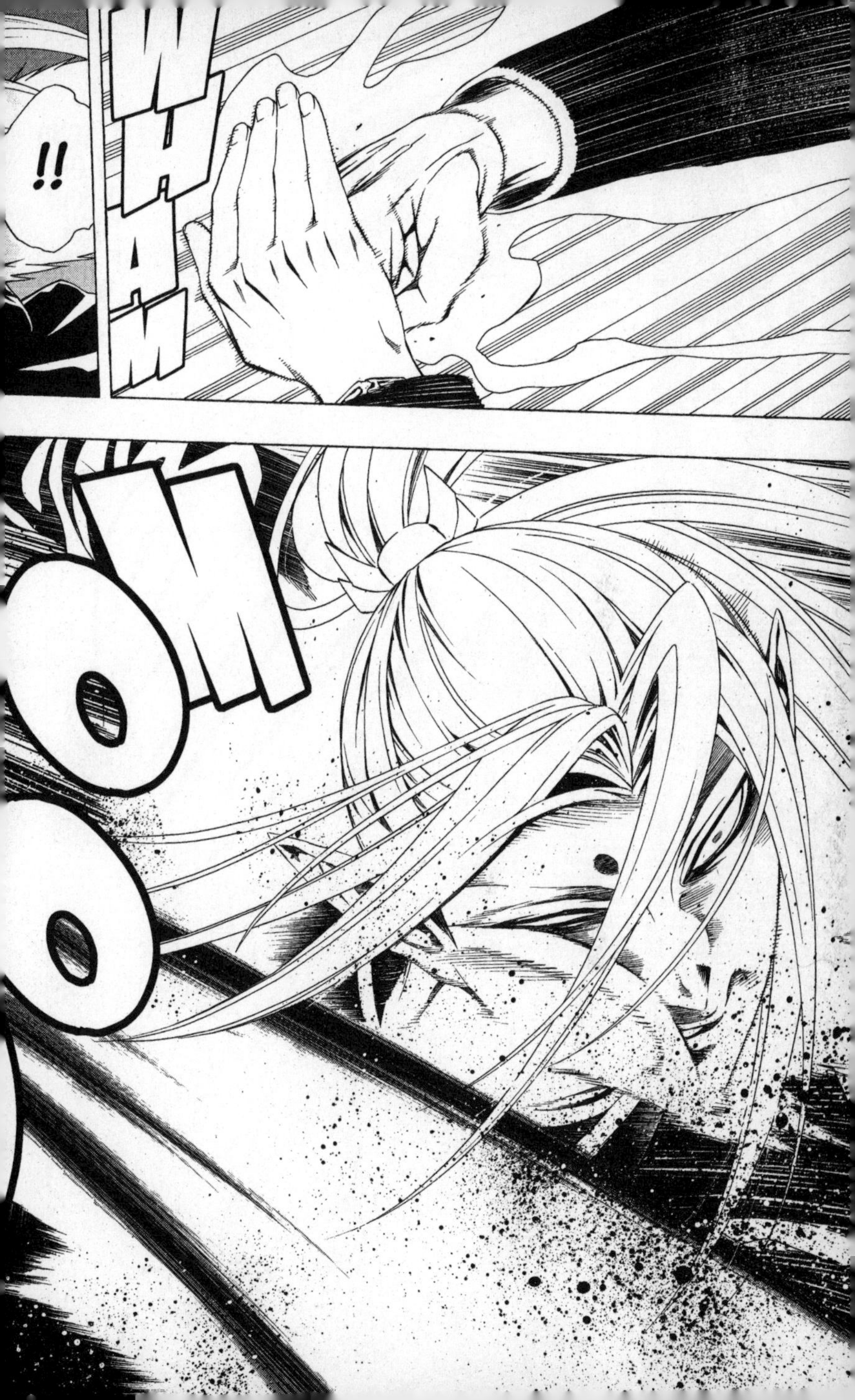
WHAM
!!

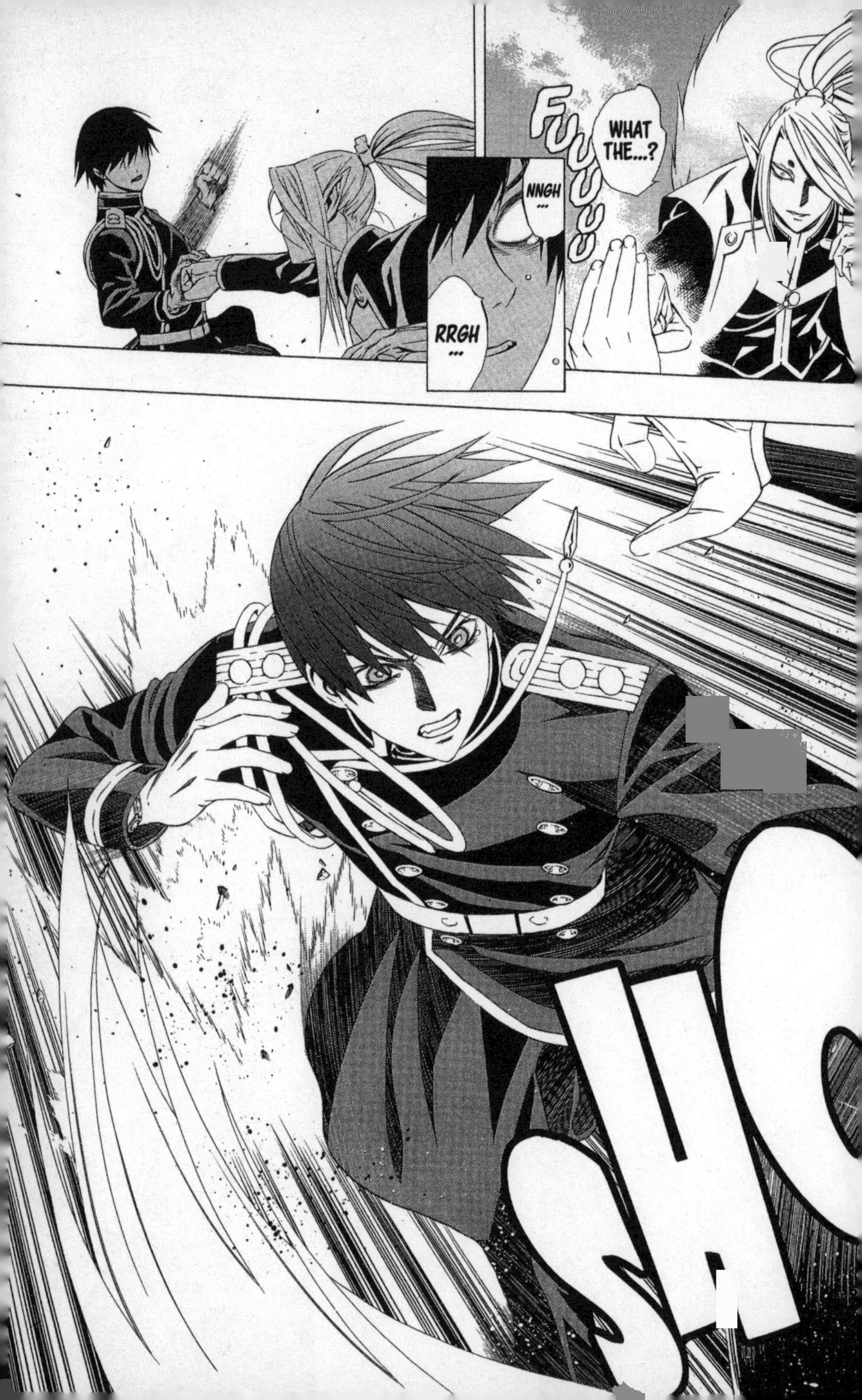
WHAT THE...?
FUUUUU
NNGH...
RRGH...
SHA

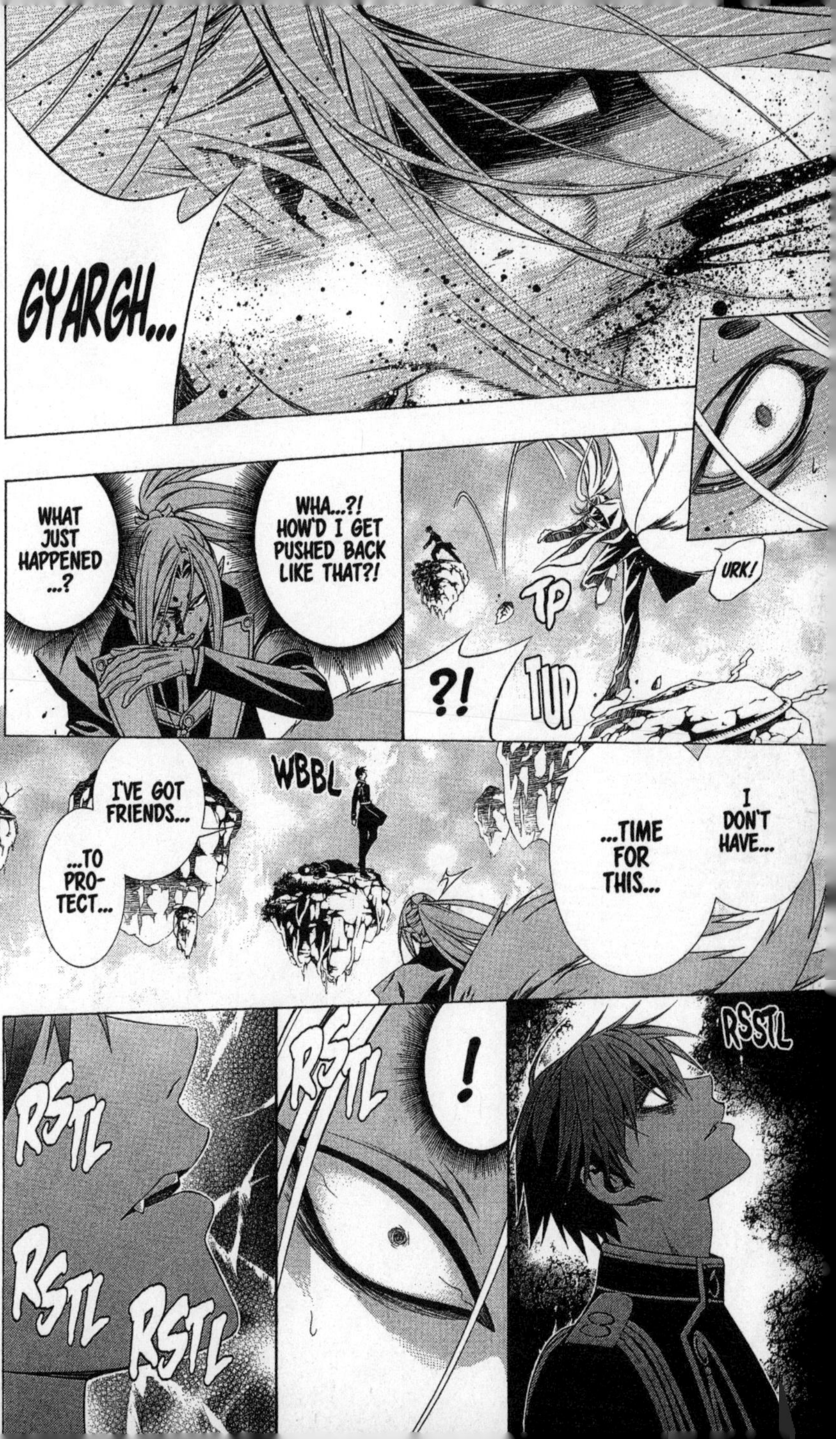
GYARGH...
URK!
TP
TUP
?!
WHA...?! HOW'D I GET PUSHED BACK LIKE THAT?!
WHAT JUST HAPPENED ...?
I DON'T HAVE...
...TIME FOR THIS...
WBBL
I'VE GOT FRIENDS...
...TO PRO-TECT...
RSSTL
!
RSTL
RSTL
RSTL
RSTL

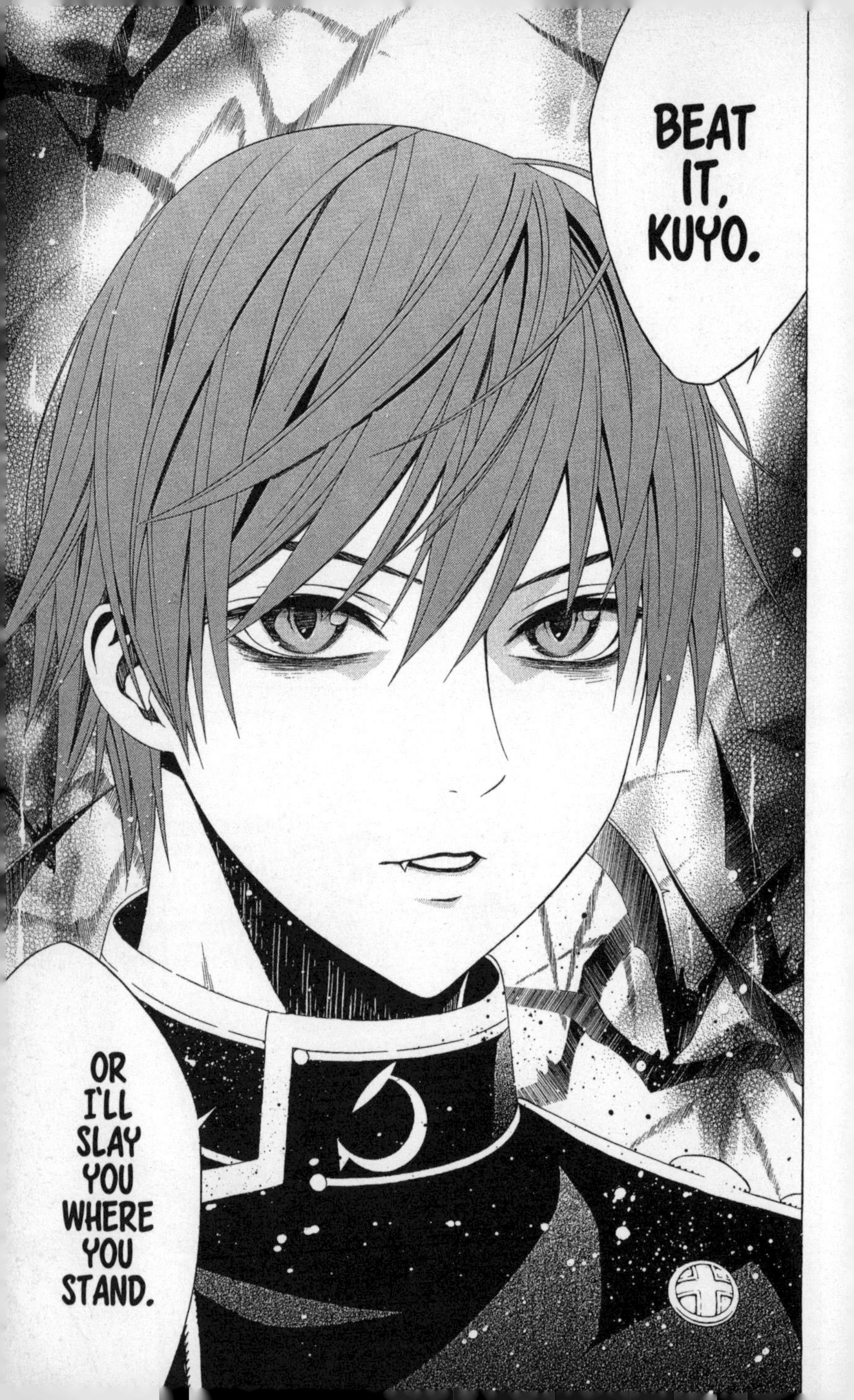
BEAT IT, KUYO.
OR I'LL SLAY YOU WHERE YOU STAND.

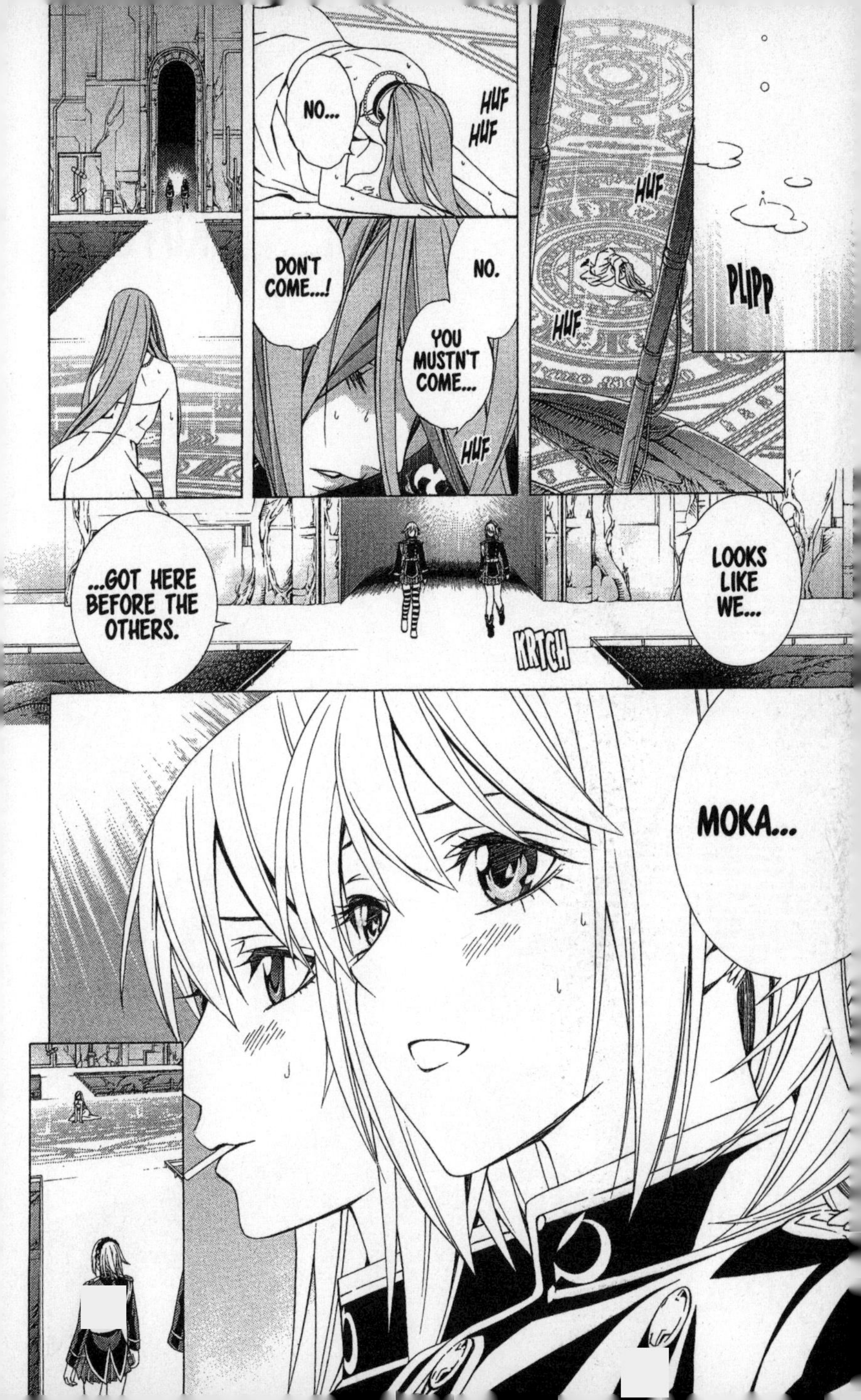
PLIPP
HUF
HUF
NO...
HUF HUF
NO.
YOU MUSTN'T COME...
DON'T COME...!
HUF
LOOKS LIKE WE...
KRTCH
...GOT HERE BEFORE THE OTHERS.
MOKA...

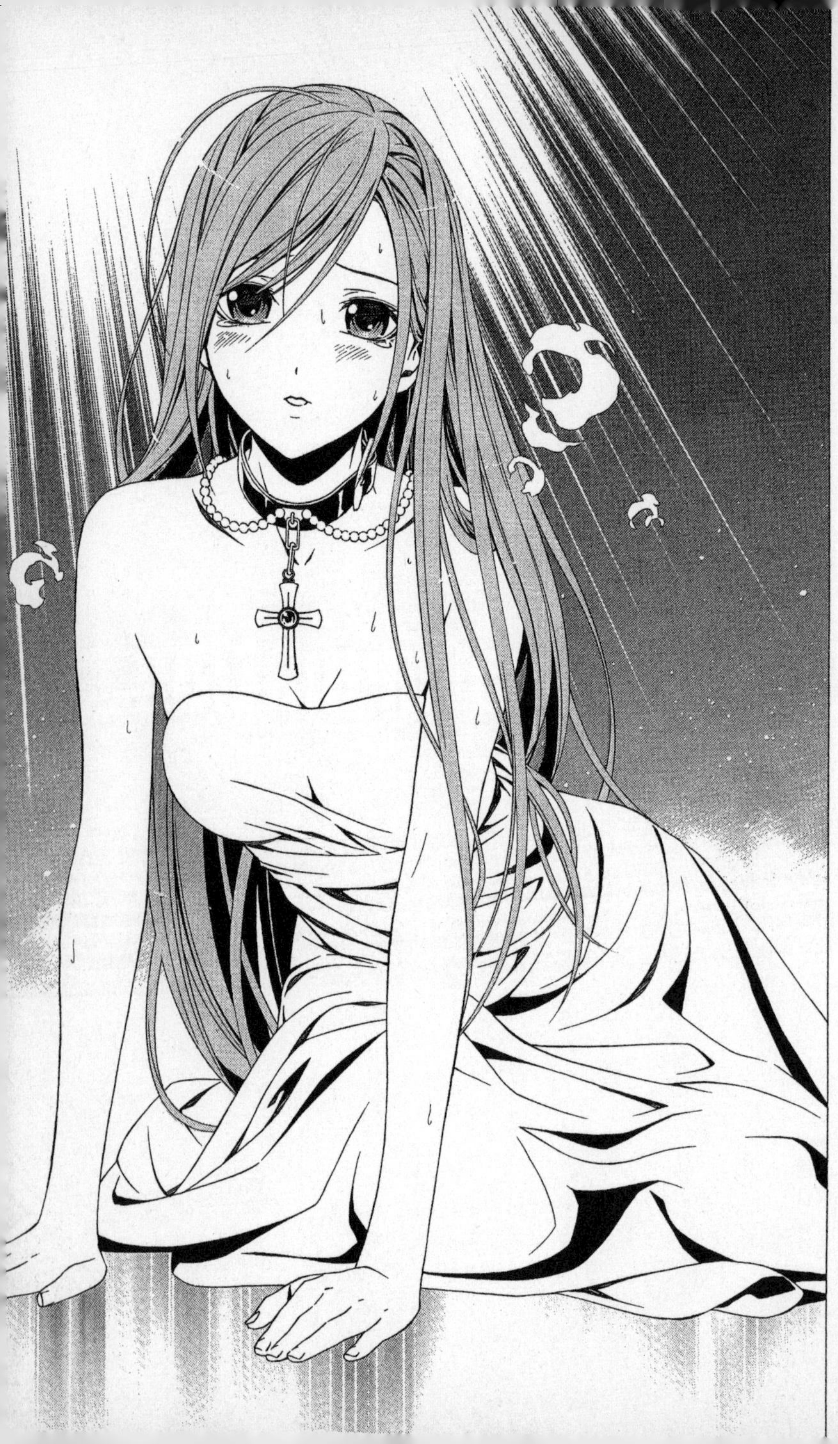

52: Transformation

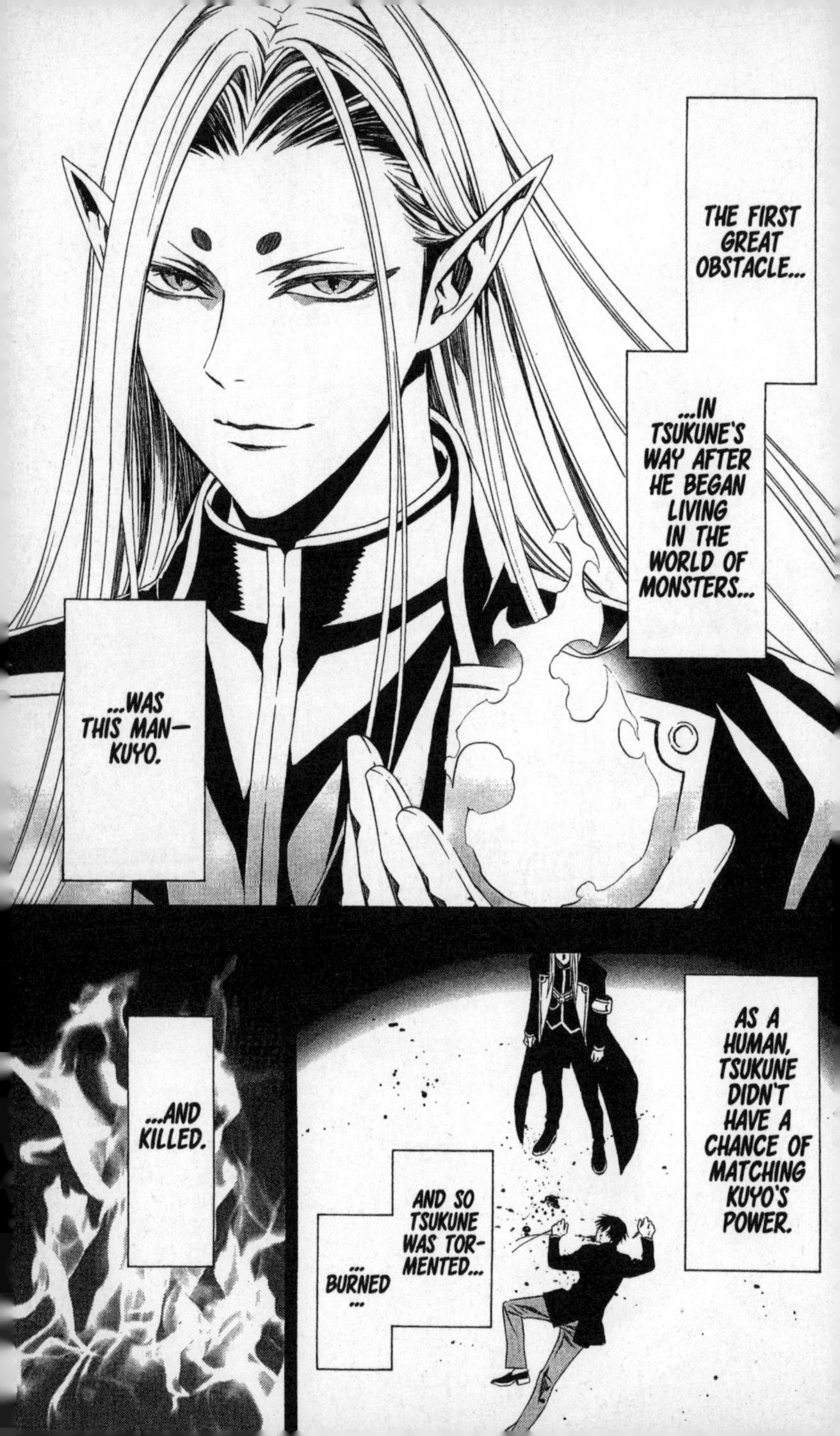
THE FIRST GREAT OBSTACLE...
...IN TSUKUNE'S WAY AFTER HE BEGAN LIVING IN THE WORLD OF MONSTERS...
...WAS THIS MAN—KUYO.
AS A HUMAN, TSUKUNE DIDN'T HAVE A CHANCE OF MATCHING KUYO'S POWER.
AND SO TSUKUNE WAS TOR-MENTED...
...BURNED...
...AND KILLED.

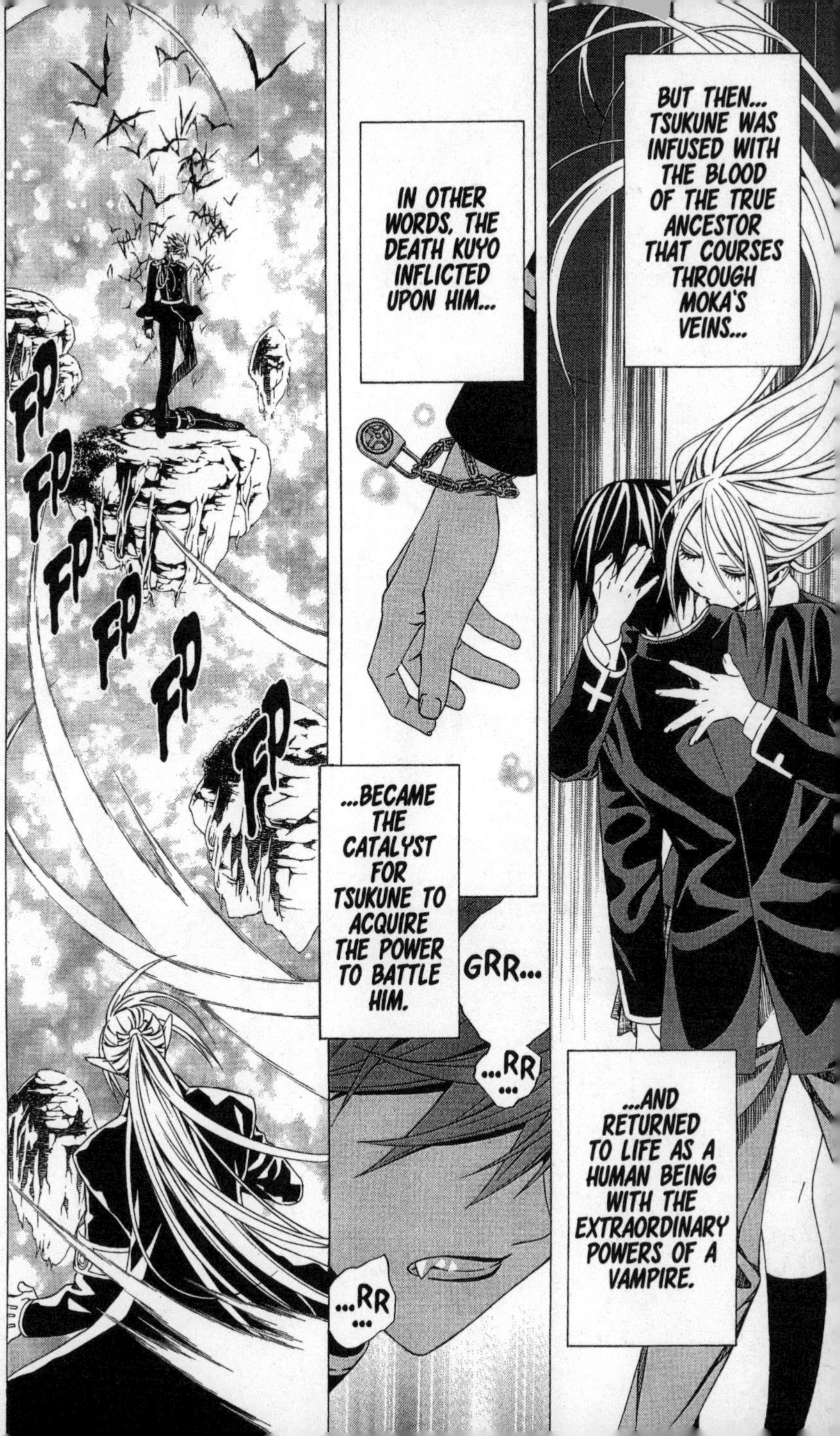
BUT THEN... TSUKUNE WAS INFUSED WITH THE BLOOD OF THE TRUE ANCESTOR THAT COURSES THROUGH MOKA'S VEINS...
...AND RETURNED TO LIFE AS A HUMAN BEING WITH THE EXTRAORDINARY POWERS OF A VAMPIRE.
IN OTHER WORDS, THE DEATH KUYO INFLICTED UPON HIM...
...BECAME THE CATALYST FOR TSUKUNE TO ACQUIRE THE POWER TO BATTLE HIM.
GRR...
...RR...
...RR...
FP FP FP FP FP FP

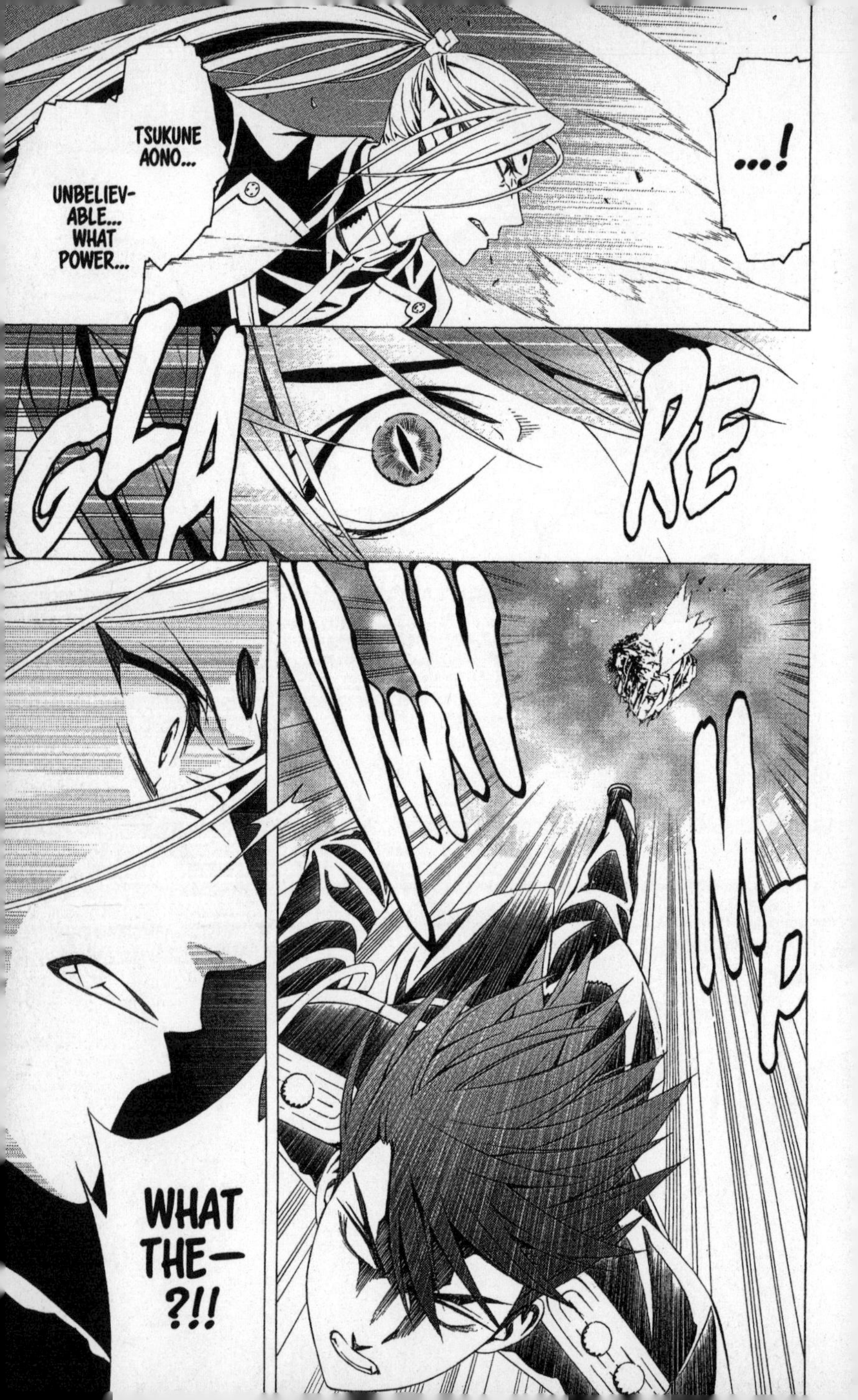
...!
TSUKUNE AONO...
UNBELIEVABLE... WHAT POWER...
GLARE
WHAT THE—?!!

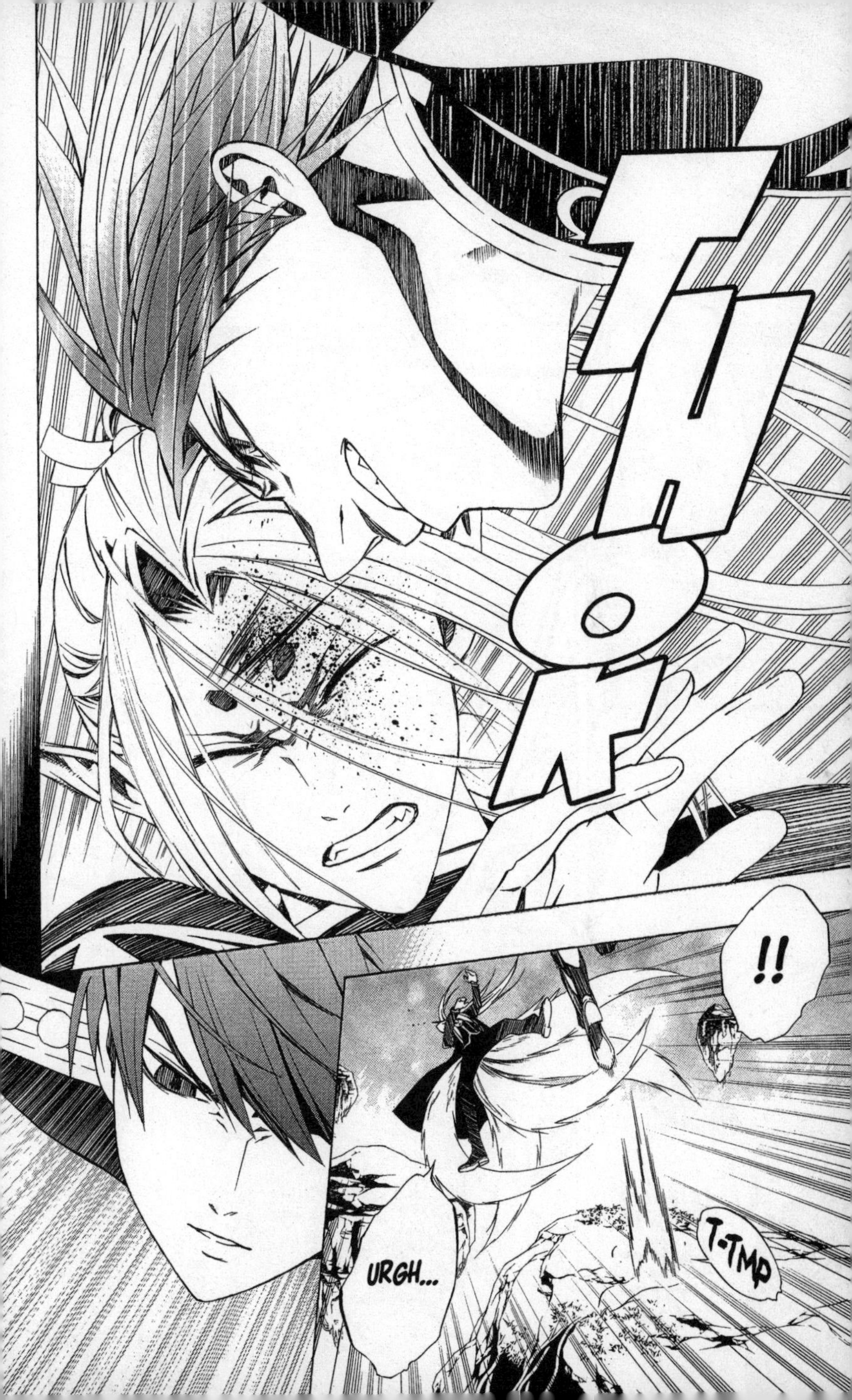
THOK
!!
T-TMP
URGH...

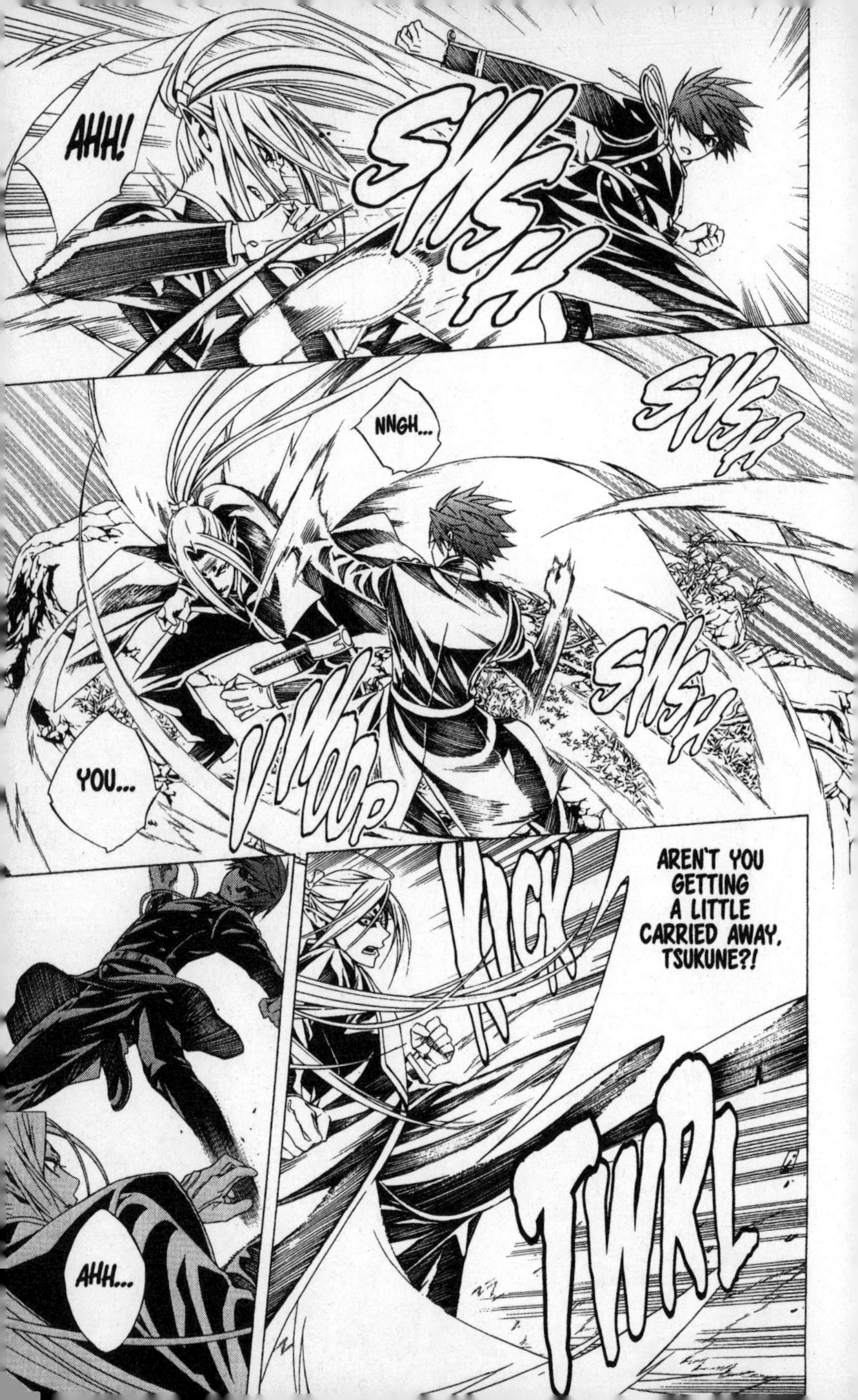
SWSH
AHH!
SWSH
NNGH...
SWSH
VWOOP
YOU...
AREN'T YOU GETTING A LITTLE CARRIED AWAY, TSUKUNE?!
WACK
TWIRL
AHH...

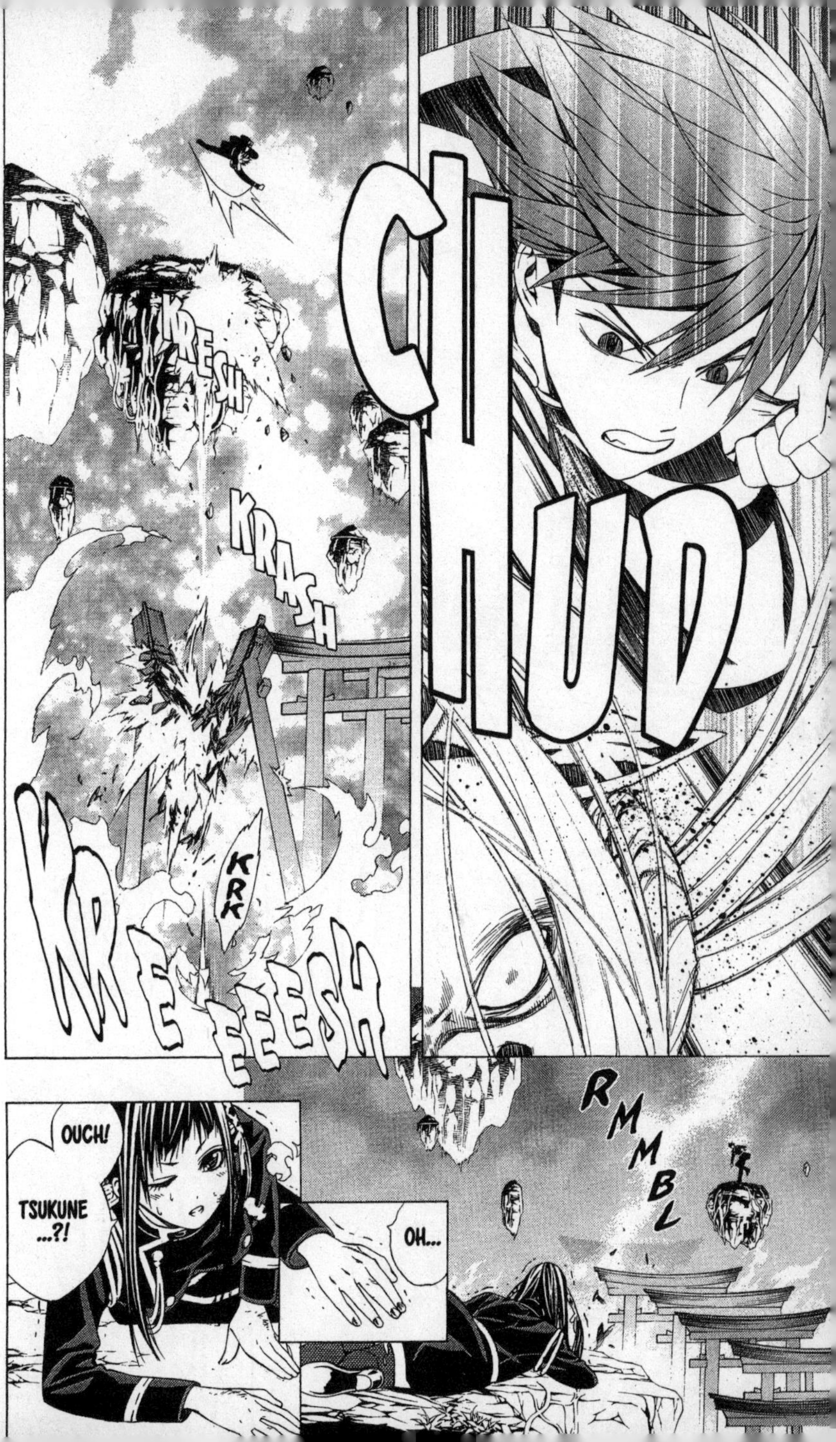
CHUD
KRESH
KRASH
KRK
KREEEESH
RMMBL
OH...
OUCH!
TSUKUNE ...?!

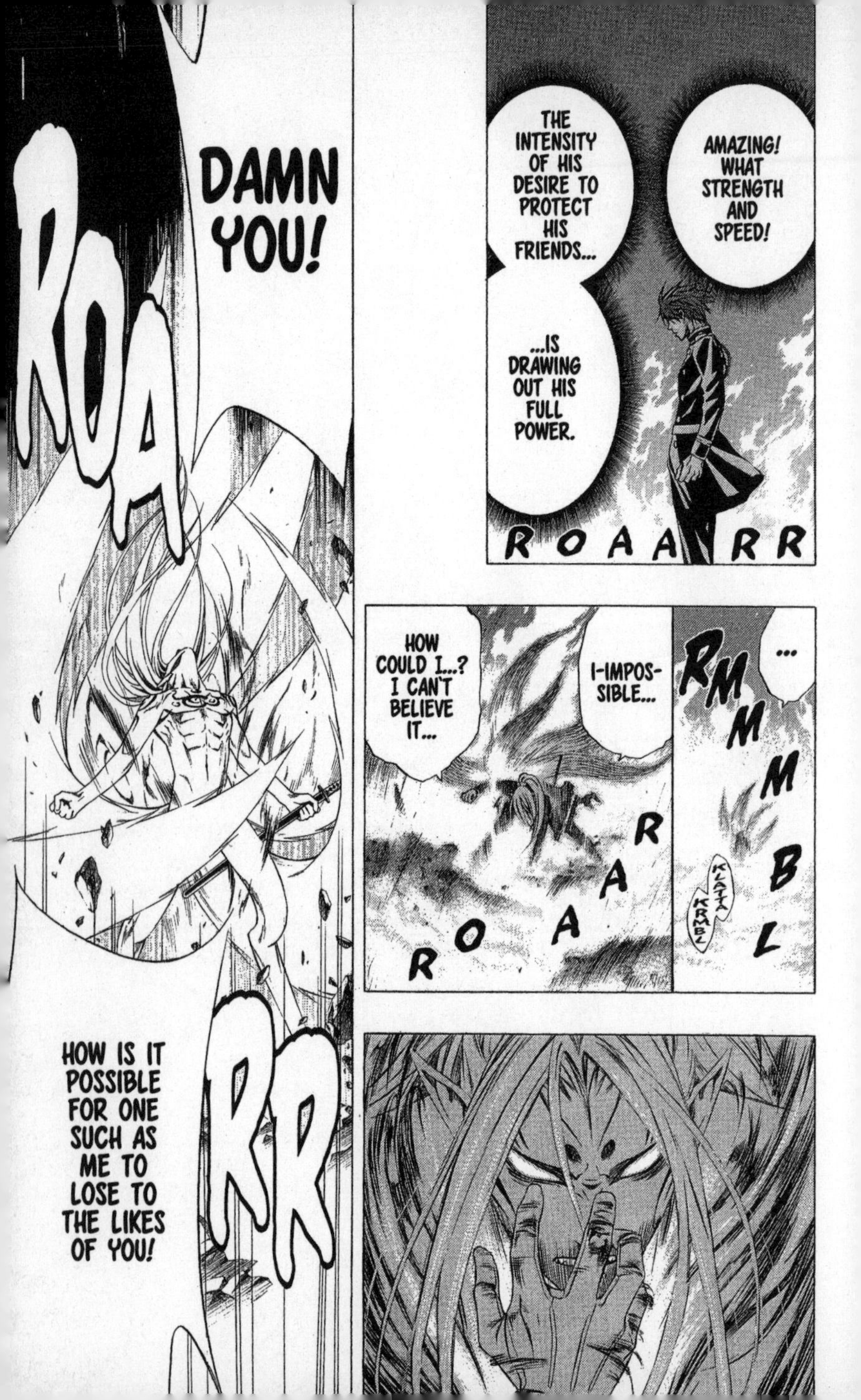
AMAZING! WHAT STRENGTH AND SPEED!
THE INTENSITY OF HIS DESIRE TO PROTECT HIS FRIENDS...
...IS DRAWING OUT HIS FULL POWER.
ROAARR
...
RMMMBL
KLATTA
KRMBL
I-IMPOS-SIBLE...
HOW COULD I...? I CAN'T BELIEVE IT...
ROAAR
DAMN YOU!
ROARR
HOW IS IT POSSIBLE FOR ONE SUCH AS ME TO LOSE TO THE LIKES OF YOU!

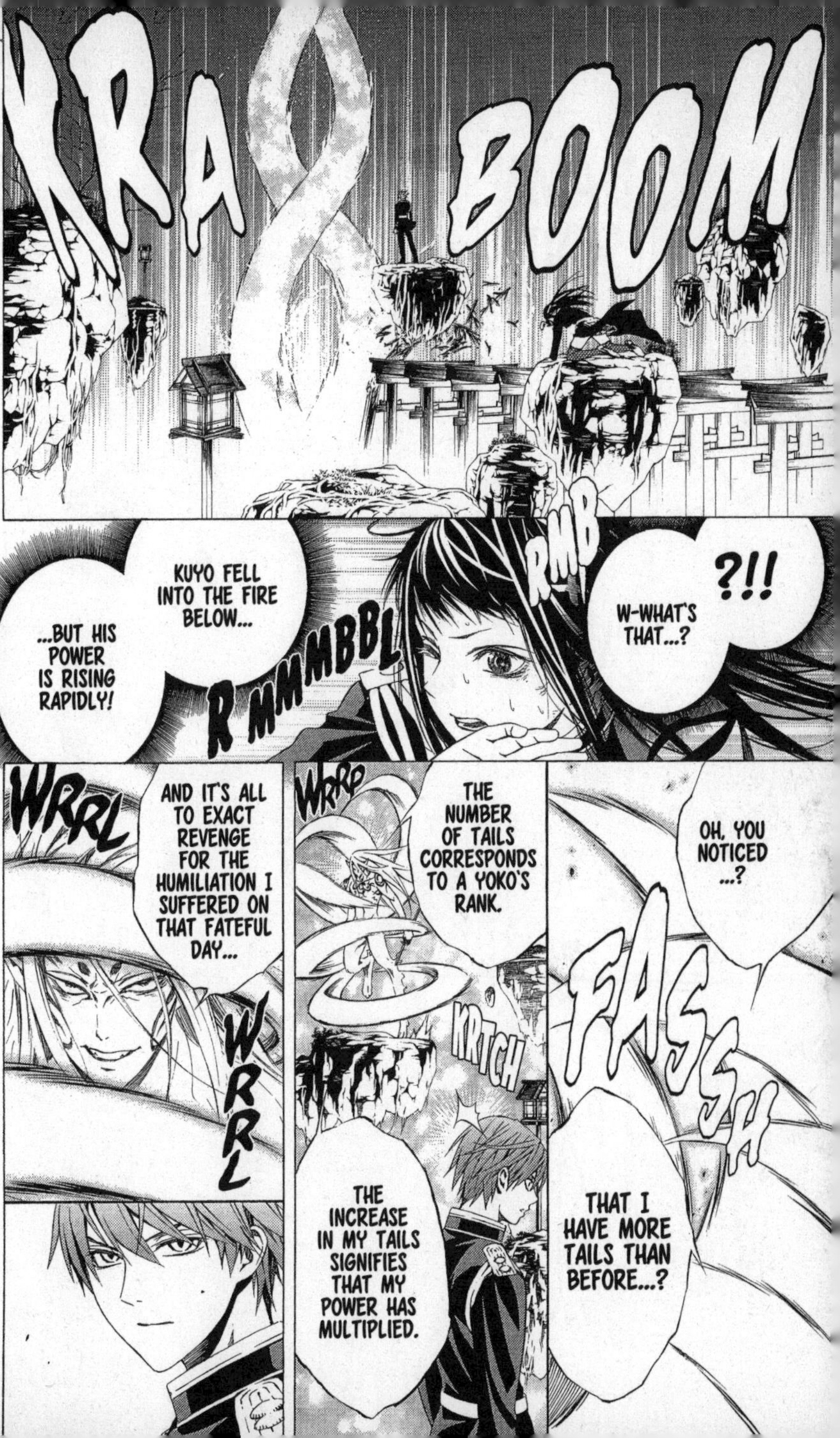
KRA BOOM
?!!
W-WHAT'S THAT...?
RMB
RMMMBBL
KUYO FELL INTO THE FIRE BELOW...
...BUT HIS POWER IS RISING RAPIDLY!
OH, YOU NOTICED...?
FASSH
THAT I HAVE MORE TAILS THAN BEFORE...?
WRRP
THE NUMBER OF TAILS CORRESPONDS TO A YOKO'S RANK.
KRTCH
THE INCREASE IN MY TAILS SIGNIFIES THAT MY POWER HAS MULTIPLIED.
WRRL
AND IT'S ALL TO EXACT REVENGE FOR THE HUMILIATION I SUFFERED ON THAT FATEFUL DAY...
WRRL

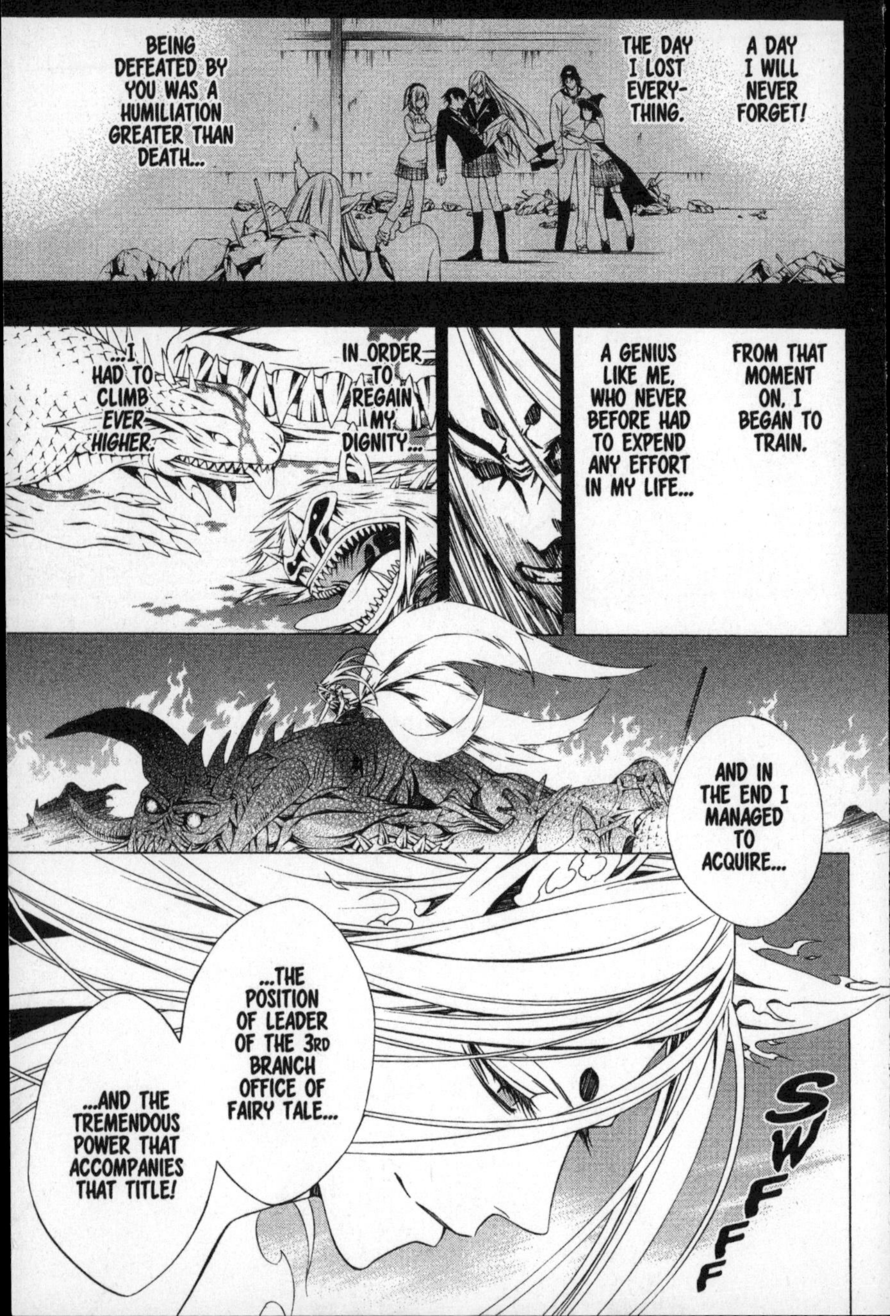
A DAY I WILL NEVER FORGET!
THE DAY I LOST EVERY-THING.
BEING DEFEATED BY YOU WAS A HUMILIATION GREATER THAN DEATH...
FROM THAT MOMENT ON, I BEGAN TO TRAIN.
A GENIUS LIKE ME, WHO NEVER BEFORE HAD TO EXPEND ANY EFFORT IN MY LIFE...
IN ORDER TO REGAIN MY DIGNITY...
...I HAD TO CLIMB EVER HIGHER.
AND IN THE END I MANAGED TO ACQUIRE...
SWFFFF
...THE POSITION OF LEADER OF THE 3RD BRANCH OFFICE OF FAIRY TALE...
...AND THE TREMENDOUS POWER THAT ACCOMPANIES THAT TITLE!

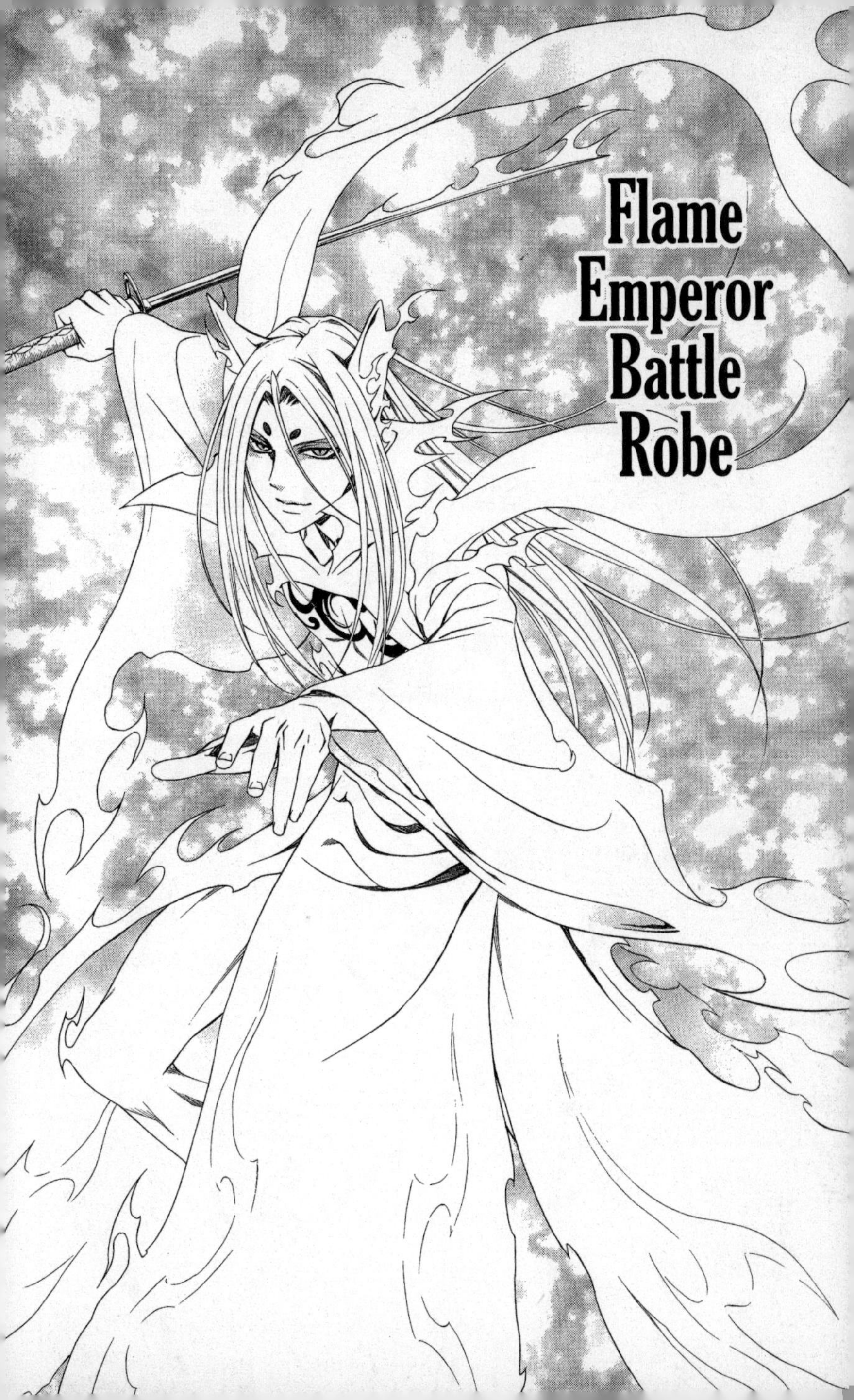
Flame Emperor Battle Robe

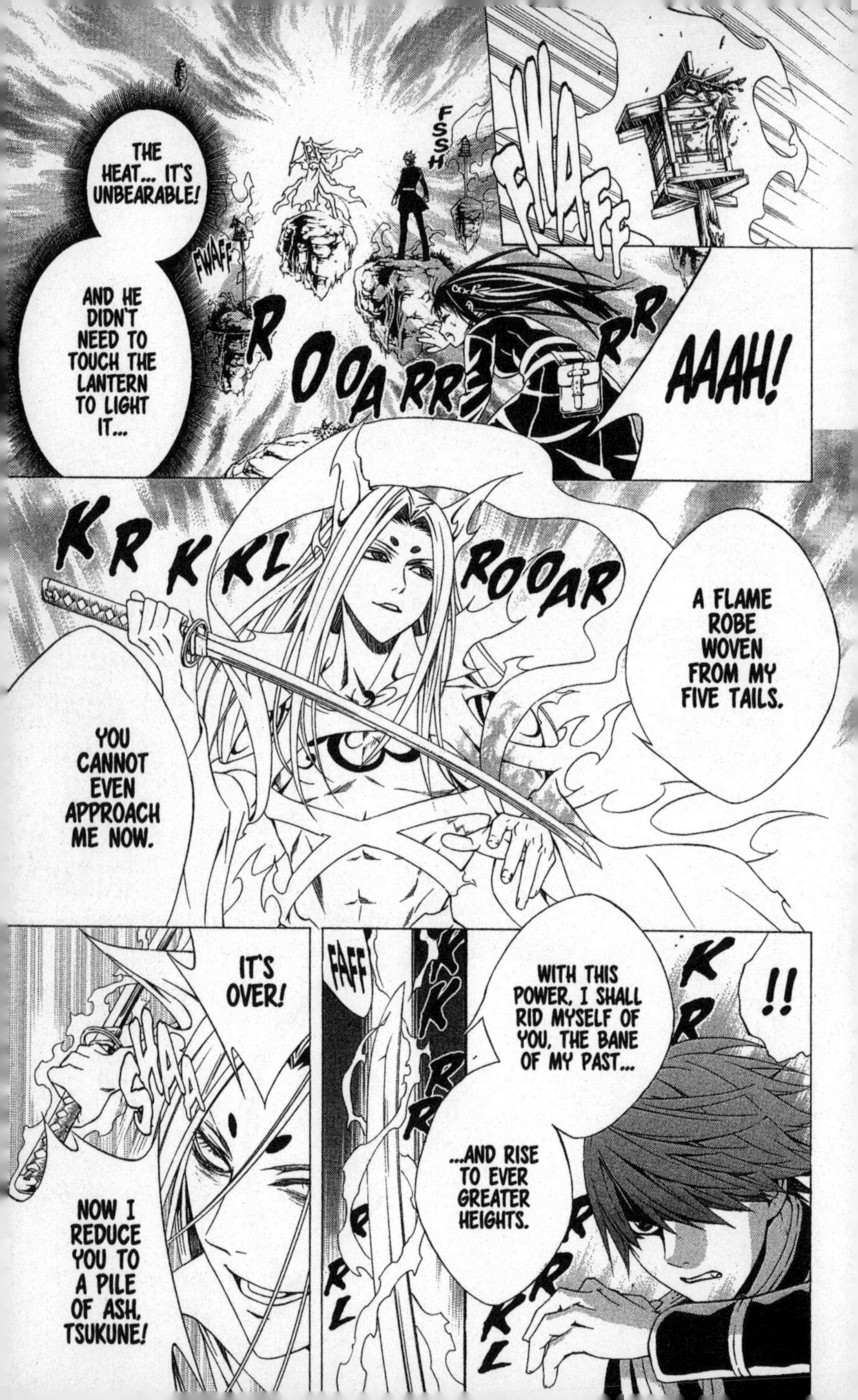
FWAFF
AAAH!
RRR
FSSH
THE HEAT... IT'S UNBEARABLE!
AND HE DIDN'T NEED TO TOUCH THE LANTERN TO LIGHT IT...
FWAFF
ROOARRR
A FLAME ROBE WOVEN FROM MY FIVE TAILS.
ROOAR
KRKKL
YOU CANNOT EVEN APPROACH ME NOW.
!!
KR
WITH THIS POWER, I SHALL RID MYSELF OF YOU, THE BANE OF MY PAST...
...AND RISE TO EVER GREATER HEIGHTS.
KRRRKL
FAFF
KRRRKL
IT'S OVER!
SHAA
NOW I REDUCE YOU TO A PILE OF ASH, TSUKUNE!

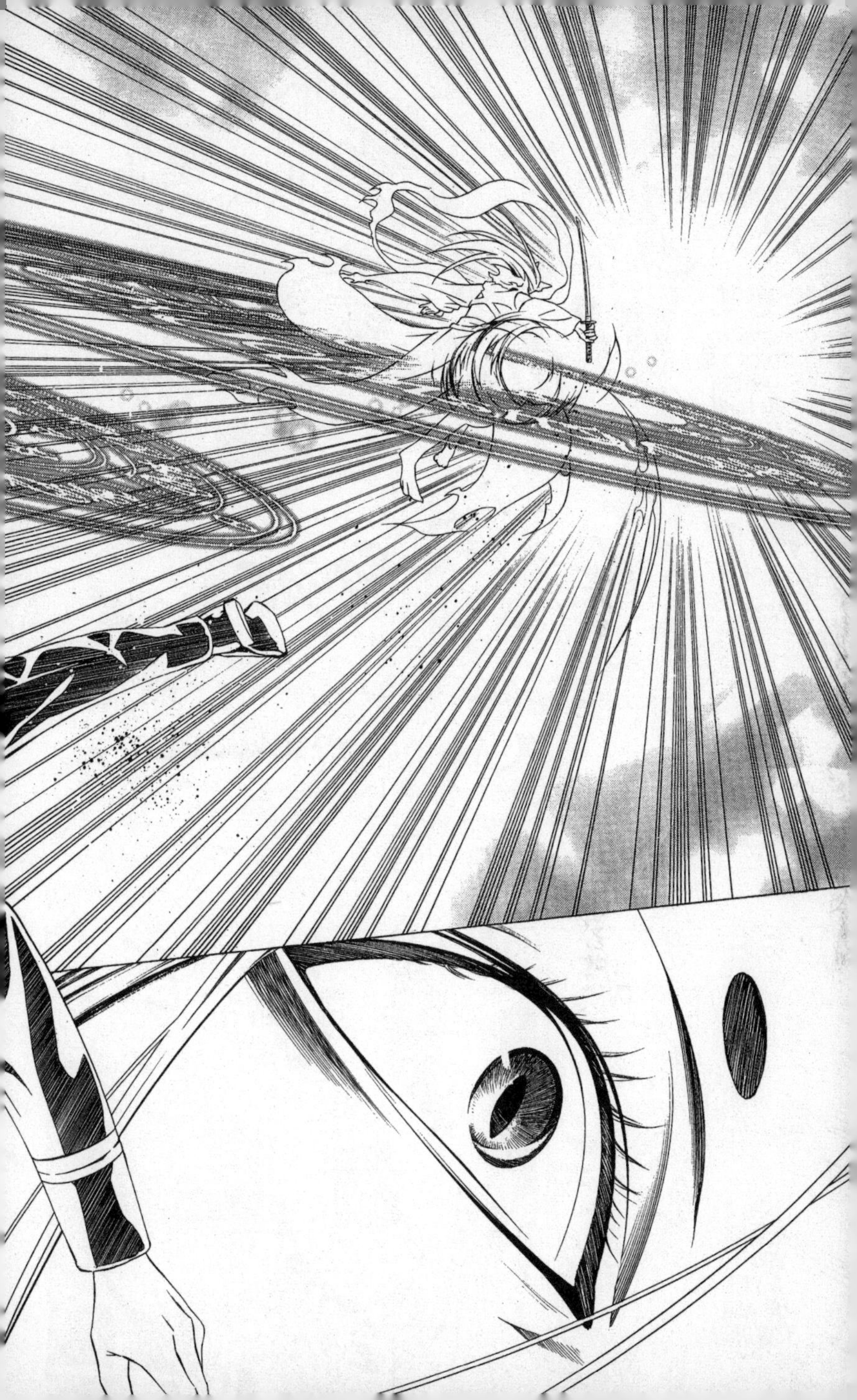

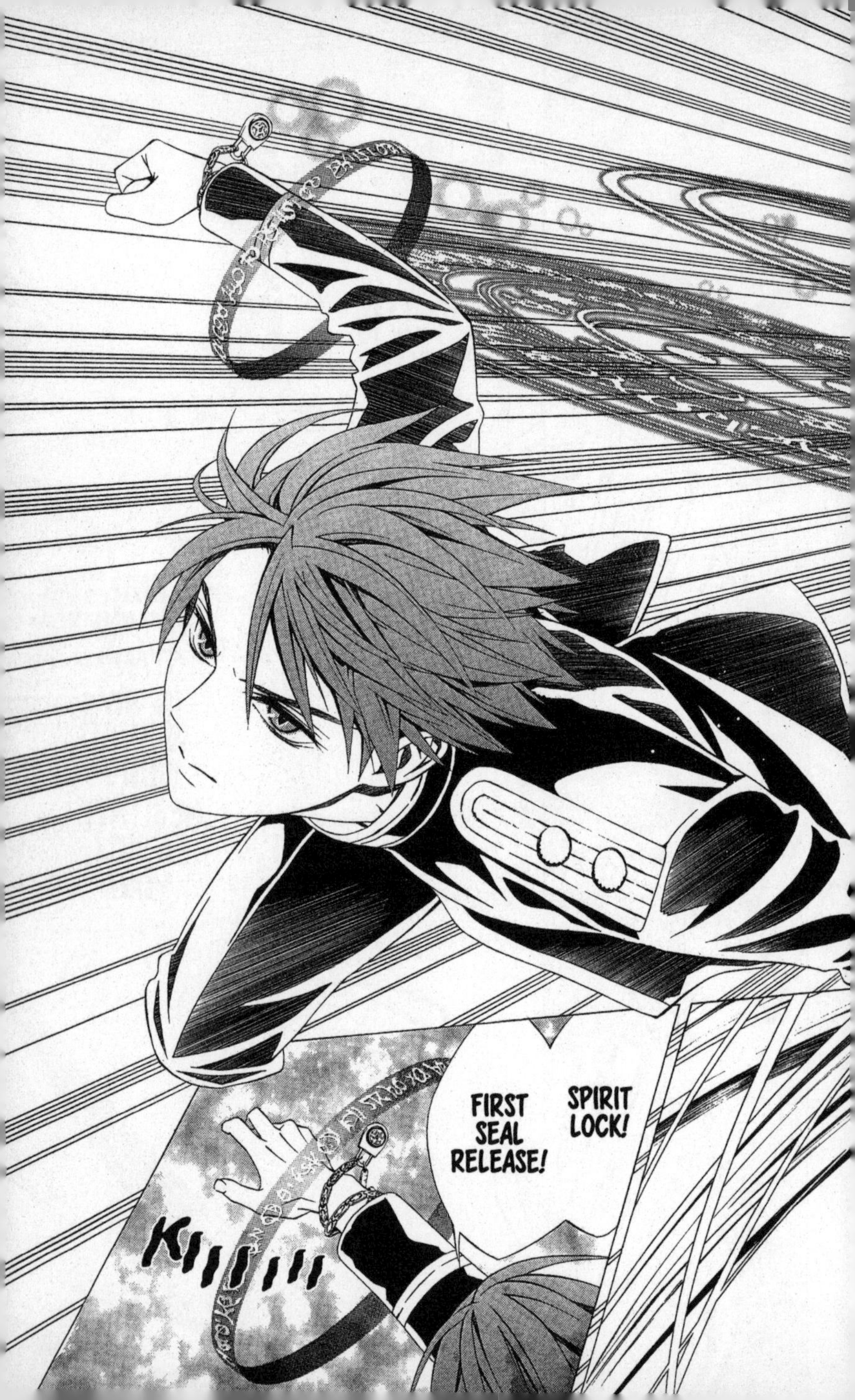
SPIRIT LOCK!
FIRST SEAL RELEASE!
KIIIIII

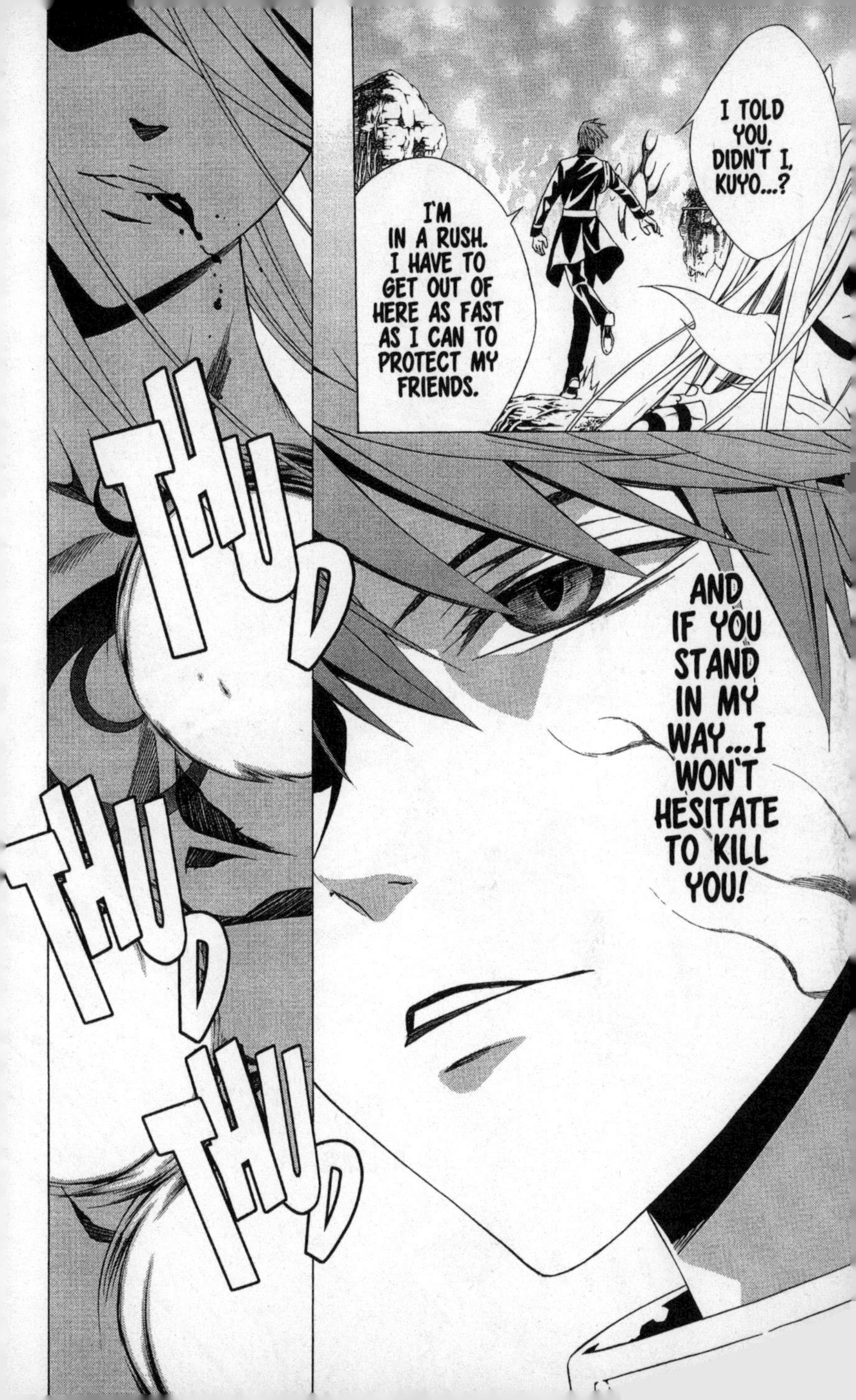
I TOLD YOU, DIDN'T I, KUYO...?
I'M IN A RUSH. I HAVE TO GET OUT OF HERE AS FAST AS I CAN TO PROTECT MY FRIENDS.
AND IF YOU STAND IN MY WAY...I WON'T HESITATE TO KILL YOU!
THUD
THUD
THUD

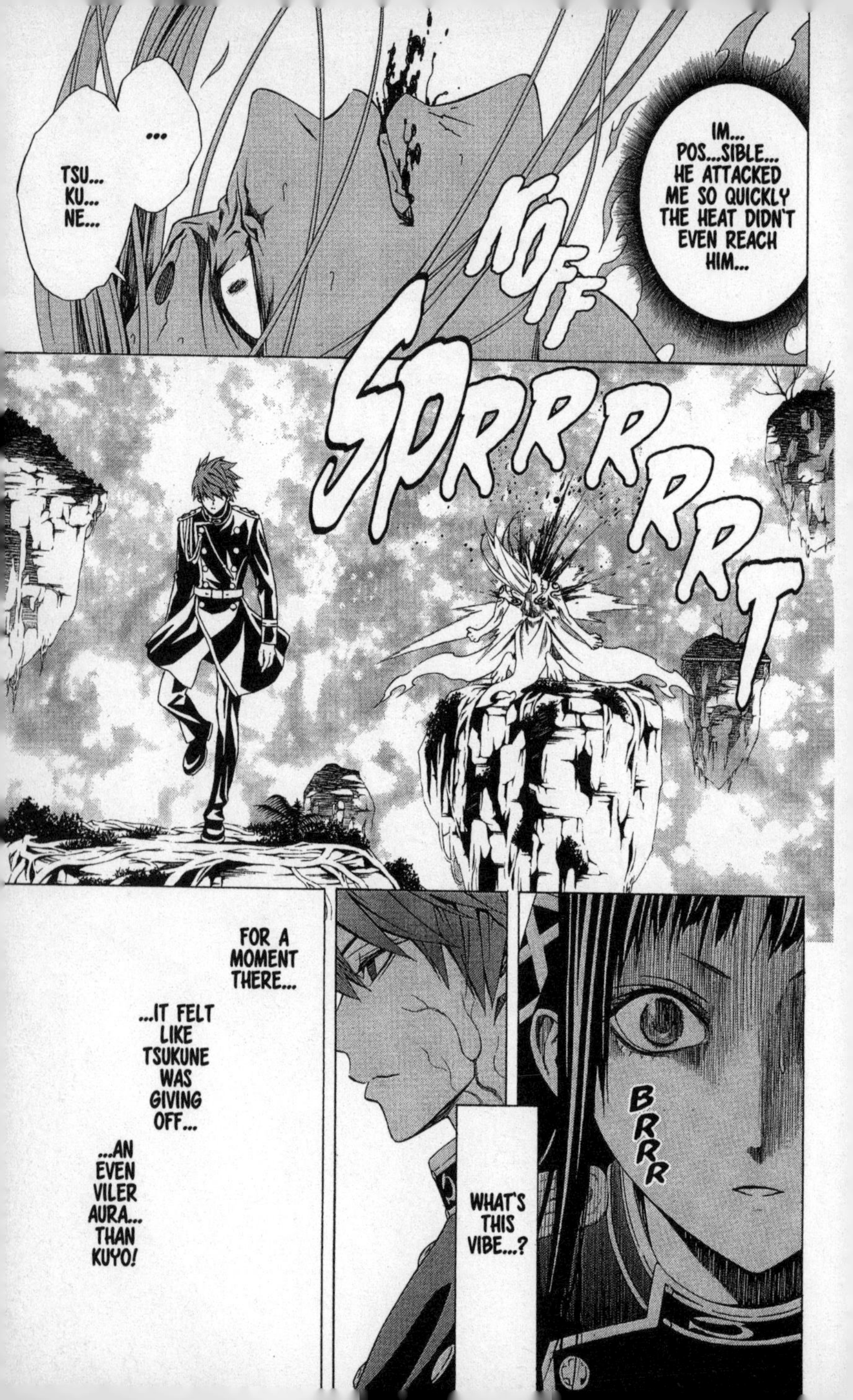
IM... POS...SIBLE... HE ATTACKED ME SO QUICKLY THE HEAT DIDN'T EVEN REACH HIM...
KOFF
...
TSU... KU... NE...
SPRRRRRRT
BRRR
WHAT'S THIS VIBE...?
FOR A MOMENT THERE...
...IT FELT LIKE TSUKUNE WAS GIVING OFF...
...AN EVEN VILER AURA... THAN KUYO!

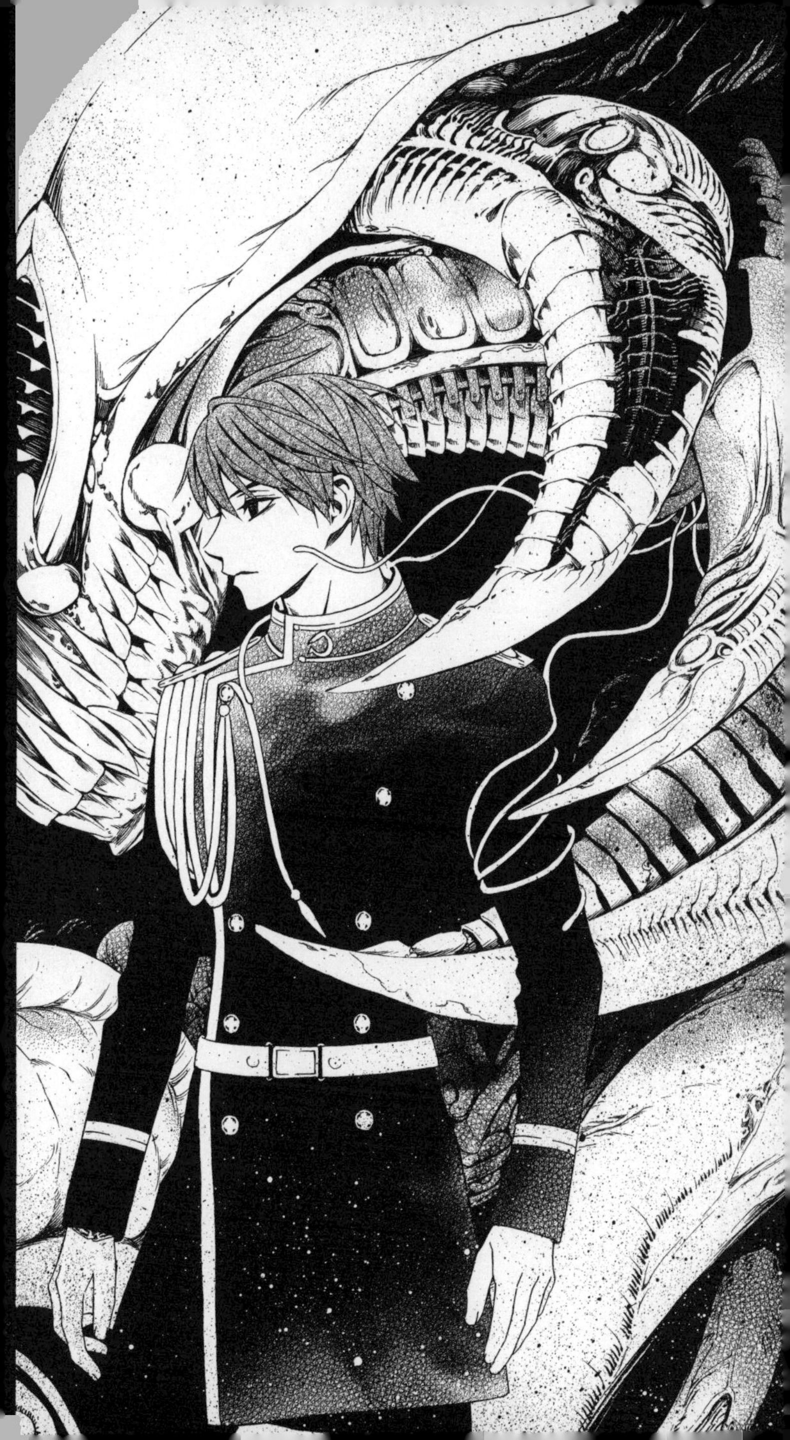

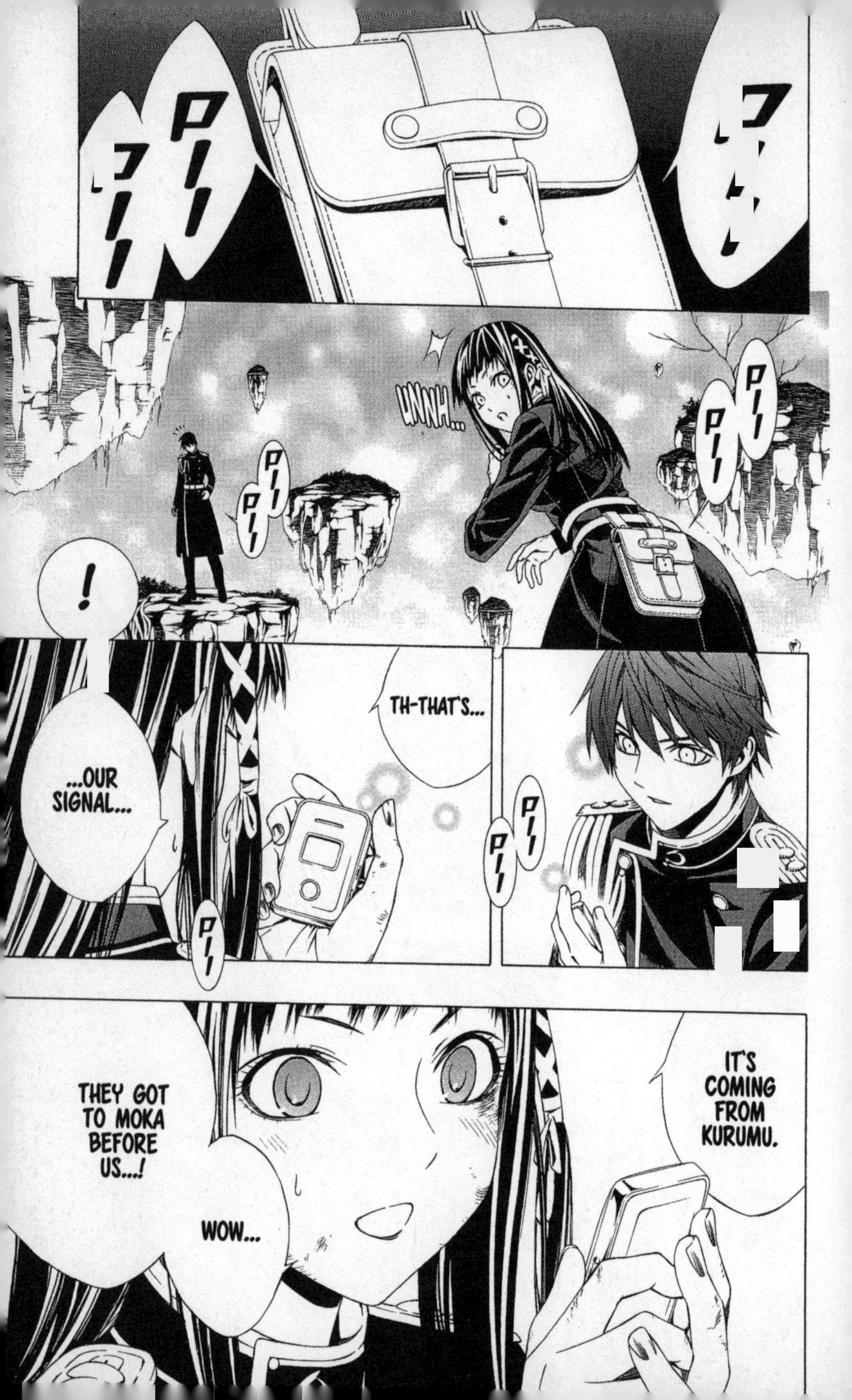
PI I
PI PI
UNNH...
PI PI
!
PI PI
TH-THAT'S...
...OUR SIGNAL...
PI
IT'S COMING FROM KURUMU.
THEY GOT TO MOKA BEFORE US...!
WOW...

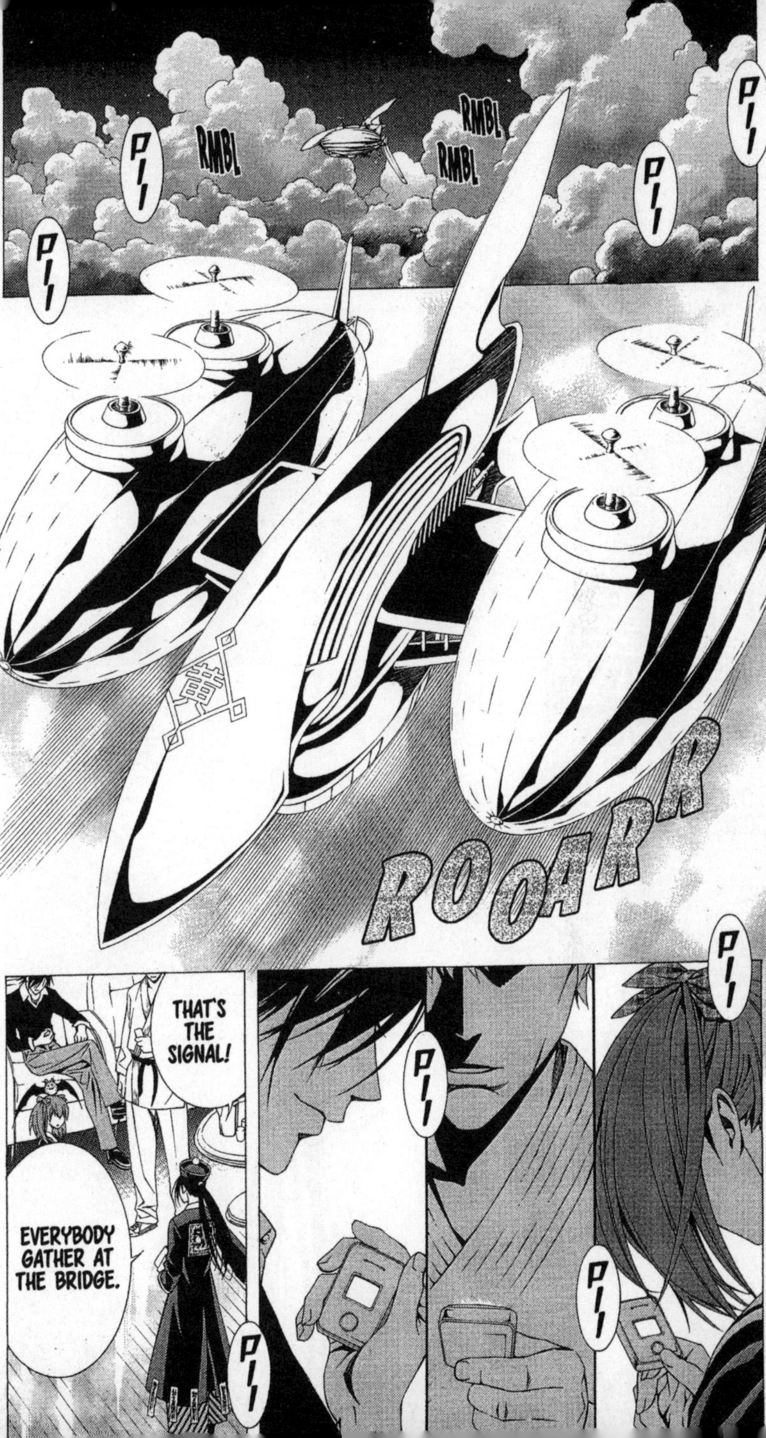
PII
PII
RMBL
RMBL
RMBL
PII
PII
ROOARR
PII
PII
PII
THAT'S THE SIGNAL!
EVERYBODY GATHER AT THE BRIDGE.
PII

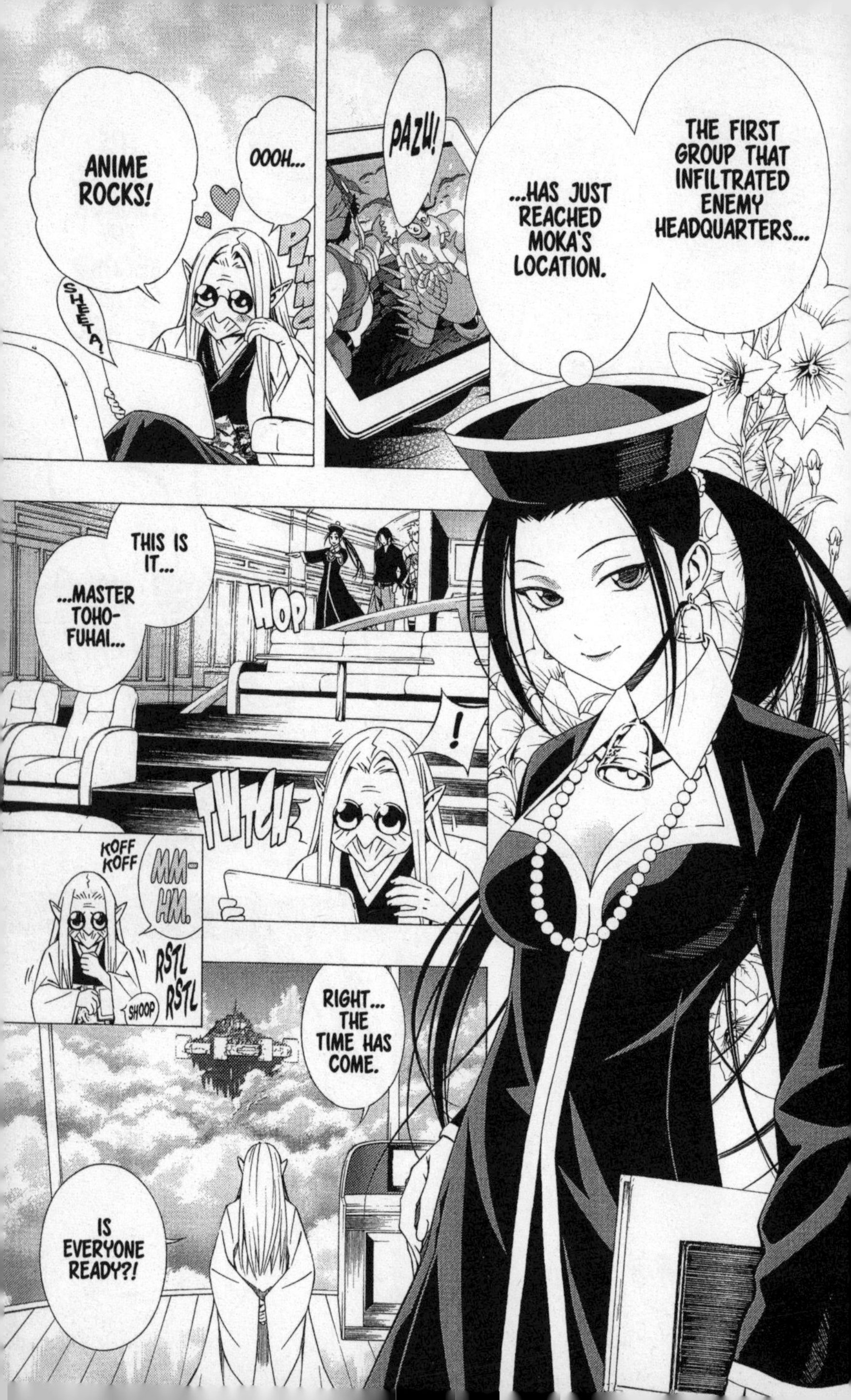
THE FIRST GROUP THAT INFILTRATED ENEMY HEADQUARTERS...
...HAS JUST REACHED MOKA'S LOCATION.
PAZU!
OOOH...
ANIME ROCKS!
SHEETA!
THIS IS IT...
...MASTER TOHO-FUHAI...
HOP
!
TWITCH
MM-HM.
KOFF KOFF
RSTL RSTL
SHOOP
RIGHT... THE TIME HAS COME.
IS EVERYONE READY?!

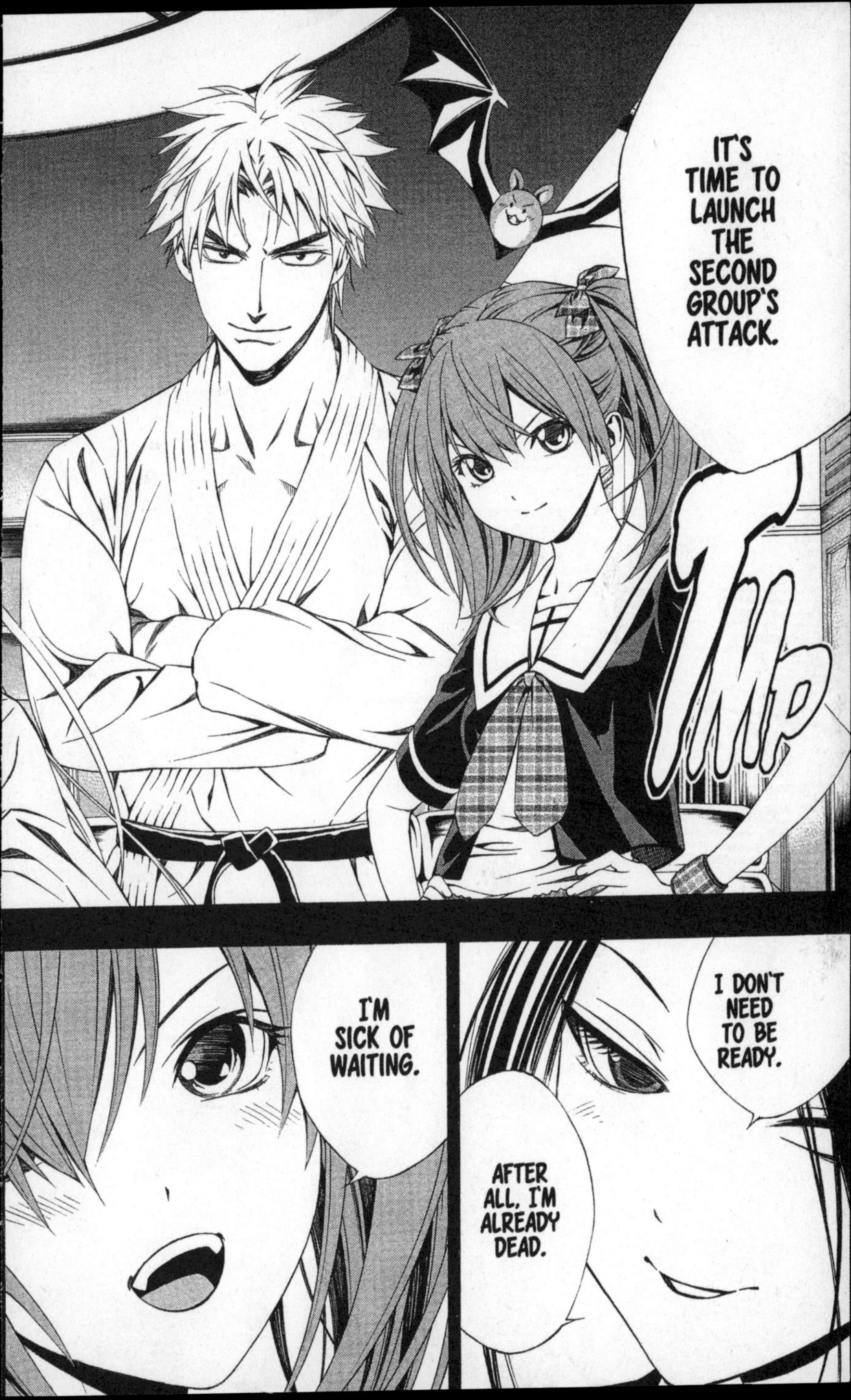
IT'S TIME TO LAUNCH THE SECOND GROUP'S ATTACK.
I DON'T NEED TO BE READY.
AFTER ALL, I'M ALREADY DEAD.
I'M SICK OF WAITING.

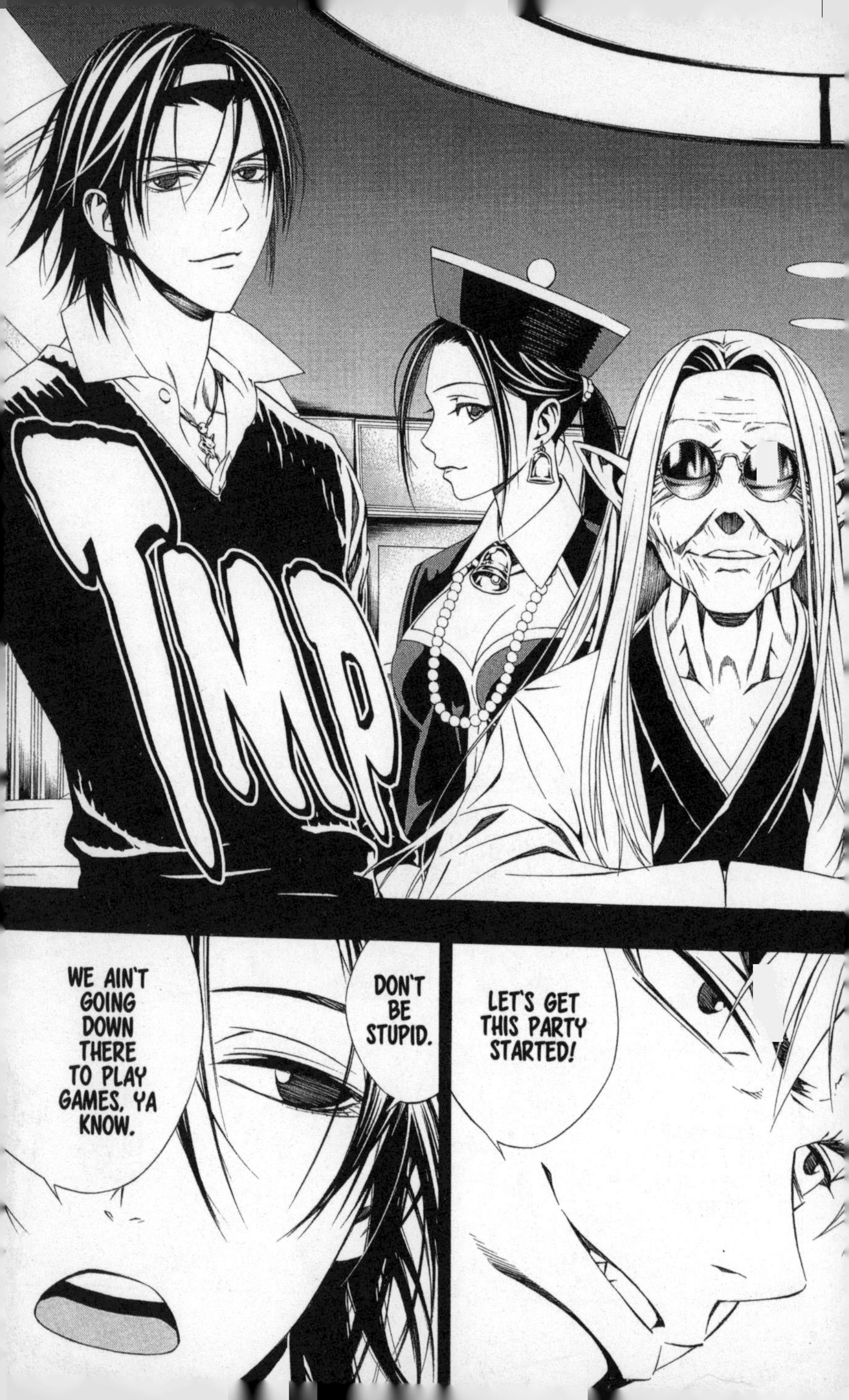
TMP
LET'S GET THIS PARTY STARTED!
DON'T BE STUPID.
WE AIN'T GOING DOWN THERE TO PLAY GAMES, YA KNOW.

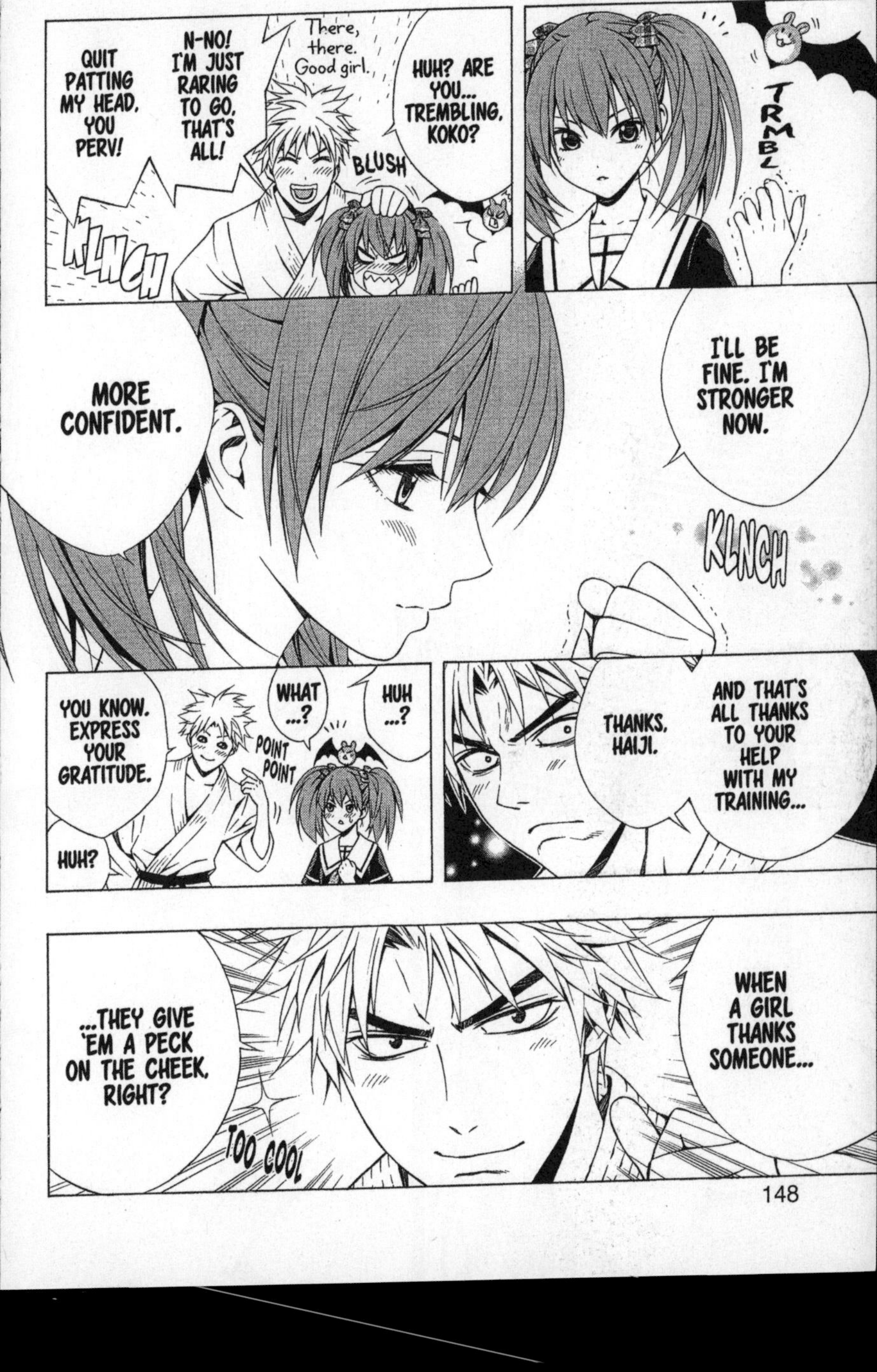
TRMBL
HUH? ARE YOU... TREMBLING, KOKO?
There, there. Good girl.
BLUSH
N-NO! I'M JUST RARING TO GO. THAT'S ALL!
QUIT PATTING MY HEAD, YOU PERV!
KLNCH
I'LL BE FINE. I'M STRONGER NOW.
KLNCH
MORE CONFIDENT.
AND THAT'S ALL THANKS TO YOUR HELP WITH MY TRAINING...
THANKS, HAIJI.
HUH ...?
WHAT ...?
POINT POINT
YOU KNOW. EXPRESS YOUR GRATITUDE.
HUH?
WHEN A GIRL THANKS SOMEONE...
...THEY GIVE 'EM A PECK ON THE CHEEK, RIGHT?
TOO COOL

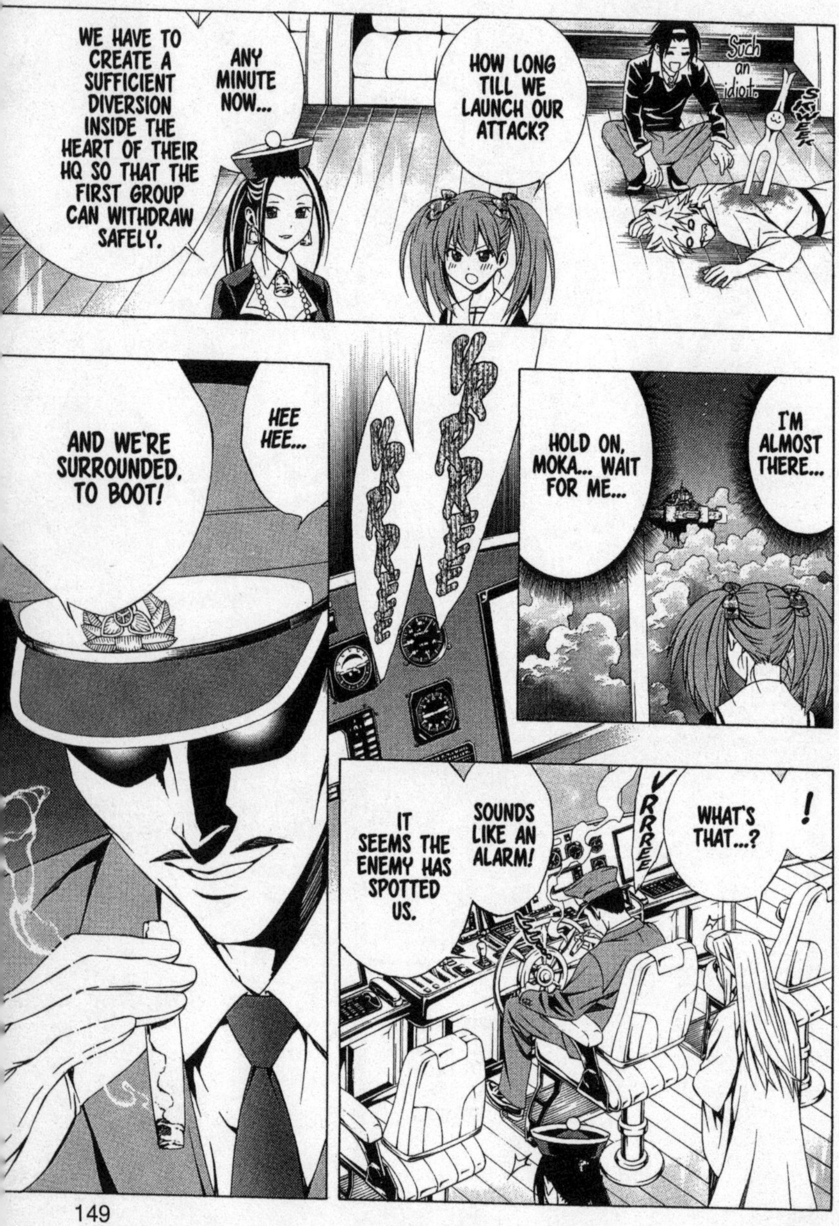
Such an idiot.
SKWEEK
HOW LONG TILL WE LAUNCH OUR ATTACK?
ANY MINUTE NOW...
WE HAVE TO CREATE A SUFFICIENT DIVERSION INSIDE THE HEART OF THEIR HQ SO THAT THE FIRST GROUP CAN WITHDRAW SAFELY.
I'M ALMOST THERE...
HOLD ON, MOKA... WAIT FOR ME...
!
WHAT'S THAT...?
VRRREE
SOUNDS LIKE AN ALARM!
IT SEEMS THE ENEMY HAS SPOTTED US.
HEE HEE...
AND WE'RE SURROUNDED, TO BOOT!

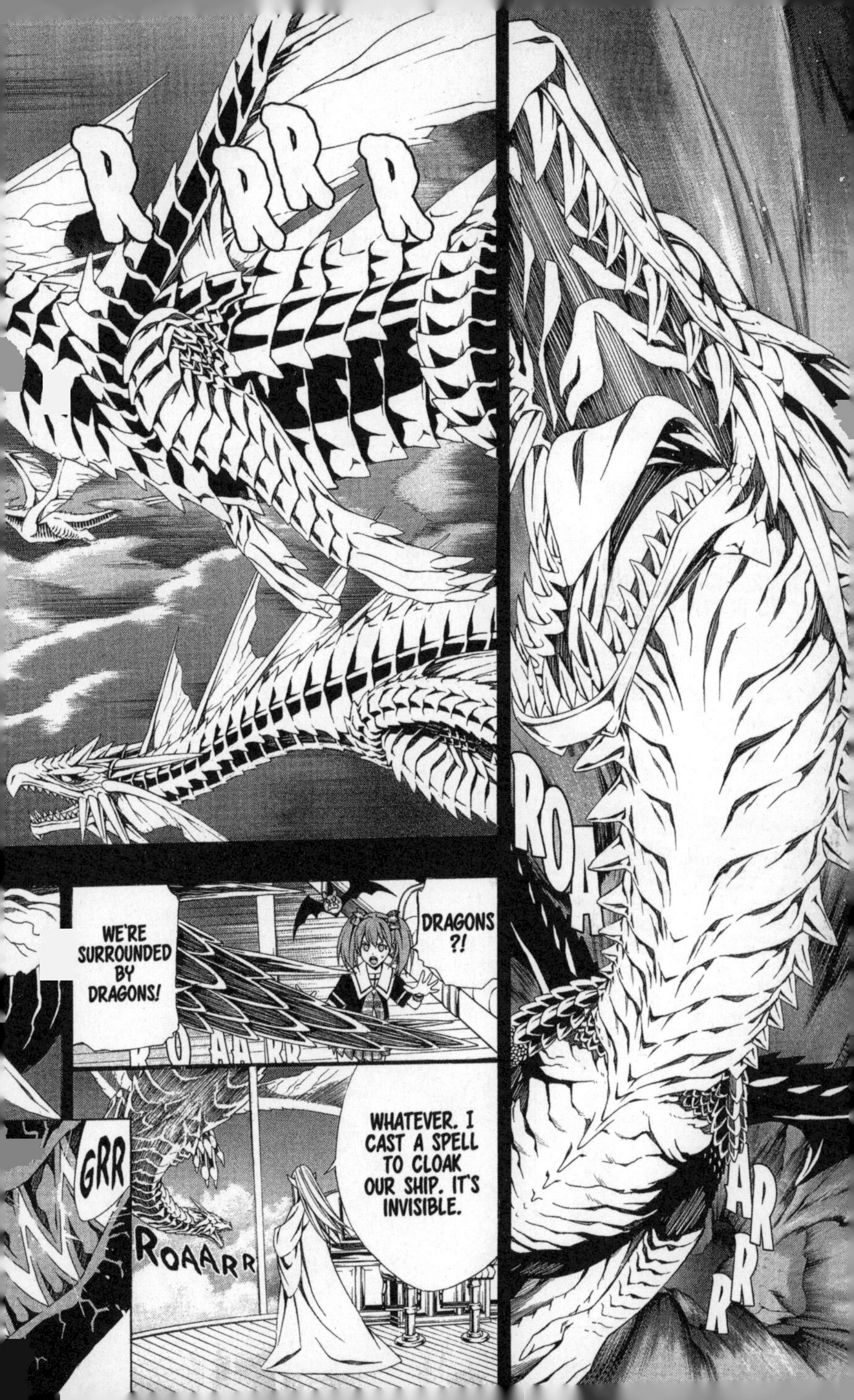
ROA
ARRR
RRRR
DRAGONS ?!
WE'RE SURROUNDED BY DRAGONS!
ROAARR
WHATEVER. I CAST A SPELL TO CLOAK OUR SHIP. IT'S INVISIBLE.
GRR
ROAARR

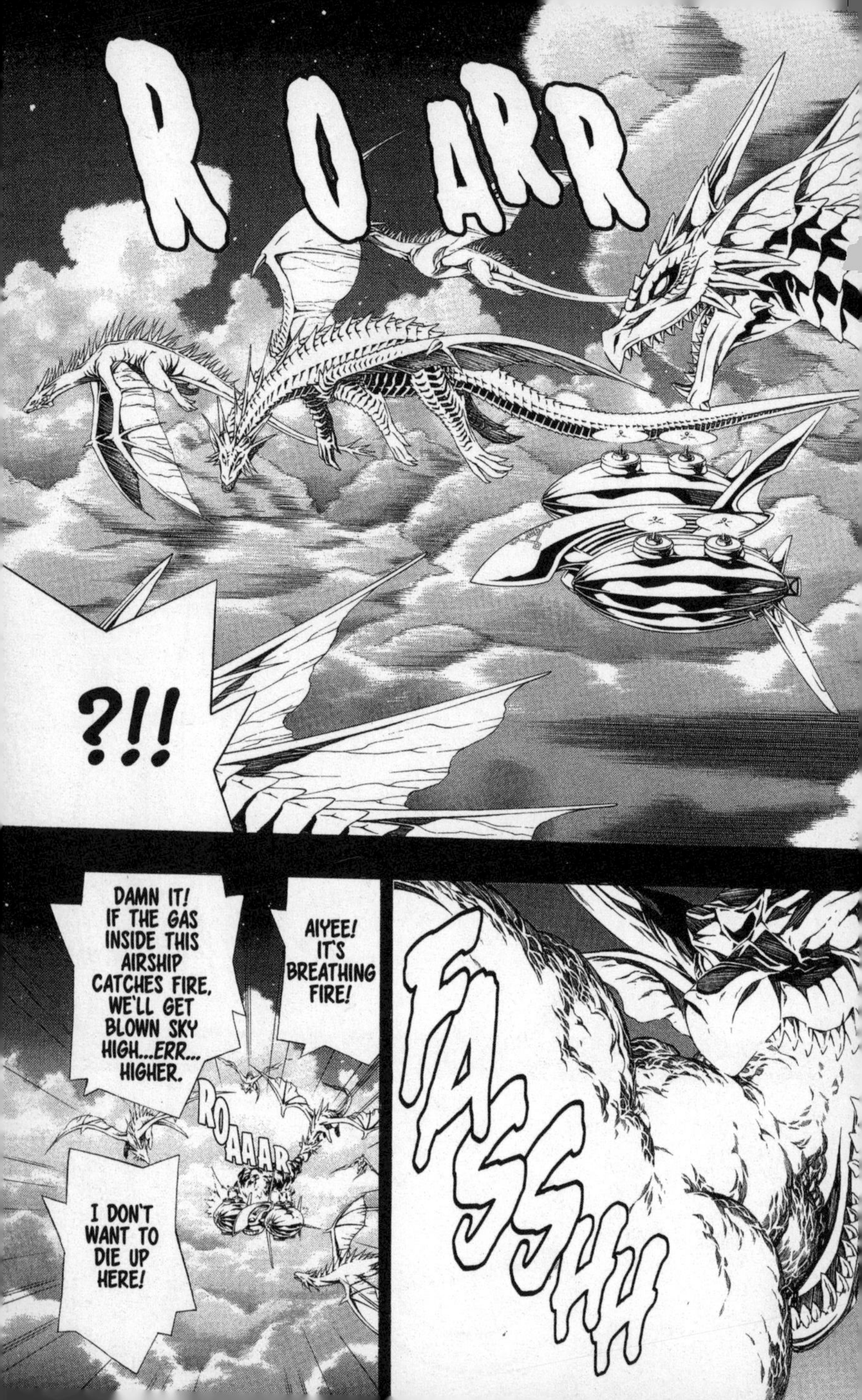
ROARR
?!!
FASSHH
AIYEE! IT'S BREATHING FIRE!
DAMN IT! IF THE GAS INSIDE THIS AIRSHIP CATCHES FIRE, WE'LL GET BLOWN SKY HIGH...ERR... HIGHER.
ROAAAR
I DON'T WANT TO DIE UP HERE!

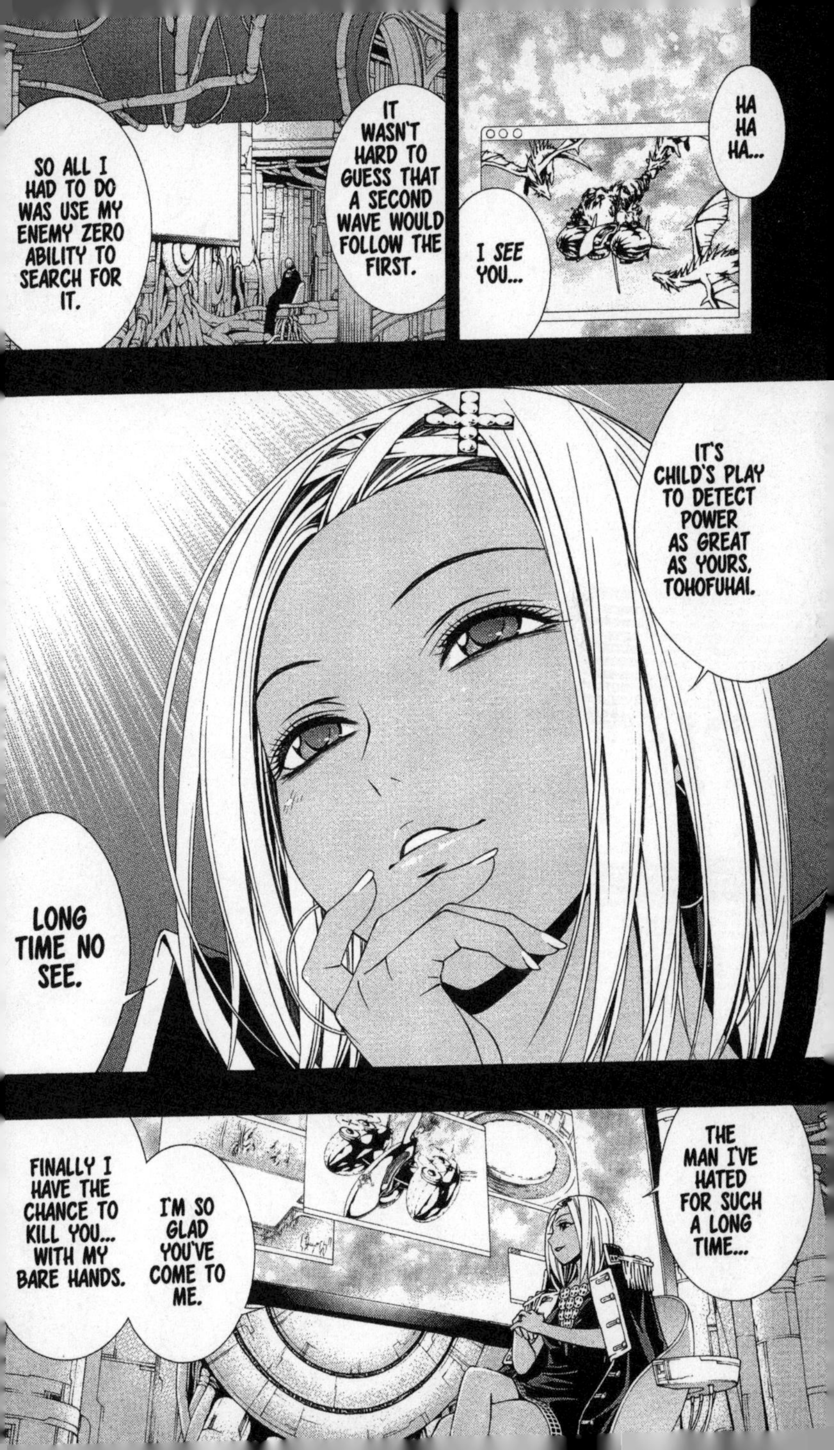
HA HA HA...
I SEE YOU...
IT WASN'T HARD TO GUESS THAT A SECOND WAVE WOULD FOLLOW THE FIRST.
SO ALL I HAD TO DO WAS USE MY ENEMY ZERO ABILITY TO SEARCH FOR IT.
IT'S CHILD'S PLAY TO DETECT POWER AS GREAT AS YOURS, TOHOFUHAI.
LONG TIME NO SEE.
THE MAN I'VE HATED FOR SUCH A LONG TIME...
I'M SO GLAD YOU'VE COME TO ME.
FINALLY I HAVE THE CHANCE TO KILL YOU... WITH MY BARE HANDS.

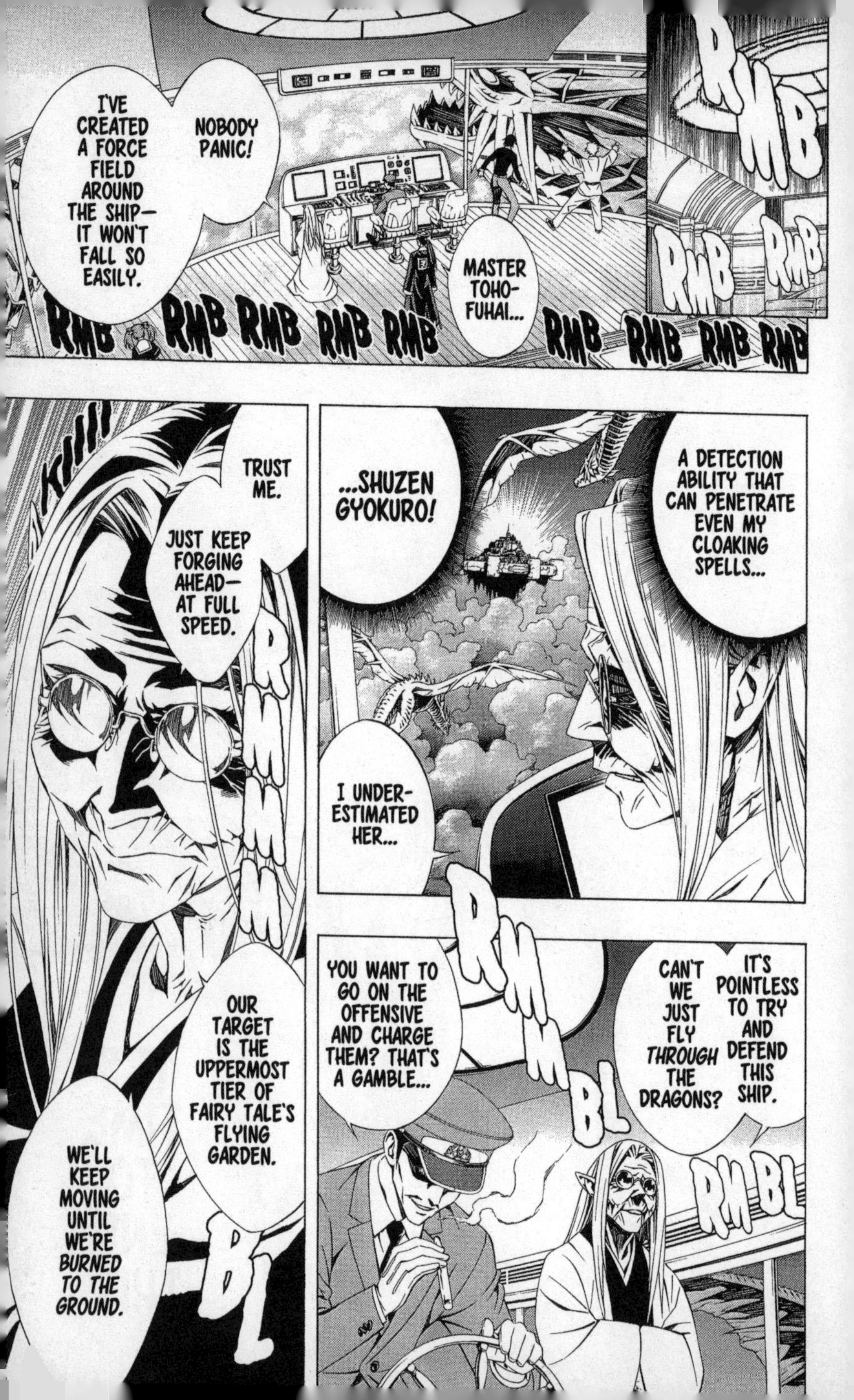
RMB
RMB
RMB
MASTER TOHO-FUHAI...
NOBODY PANIC!
I'VE CREATED A FORCE FIELD AROUND THE SHIP—IT WON'T FALL SO EASILY.
RMB RMB RMB RMB RMB RMB RMB RMB RMB
A DETECTION ABILITY THAT CAN PENETRATE EVEN MY CLOAKING SPELLS...
...SHUZEN GYOKURO!
I UNDER-ESTIMATED HER...
IT'S POINTLESS TO TRY AND DEFEND THIS SHIP.
CAN'T WE JUST FLY *THROUGH* THE DRAGONS?
YOU WANT TO GO ON THE OFFENSIVE AND CHARGE THEM? THAT'S A GAMBLE...
RMBL
RMBL
TRUST ME.
JUST KEEP FORGING AHEAD—AT FULL SPEED.
RMMM
OUR TARGET IS THE UPPERMOST TIER OF FAIRY TALE'S FLYING GARDEN.
WE'LL KEEP MOVING UNTIL WE'RE BURNED TO THE GROUND.

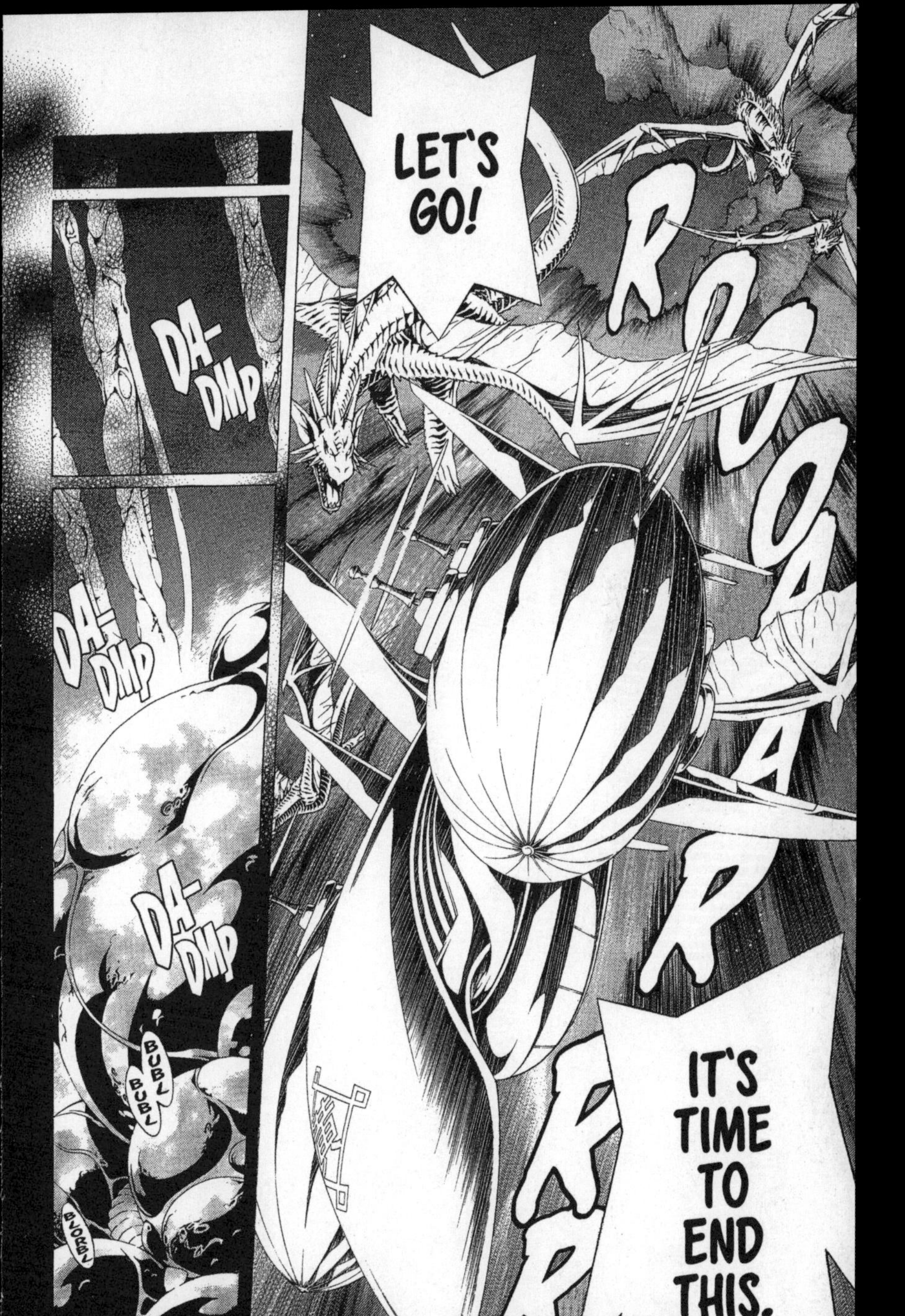
LET'S GO!
ROOOAARRRR
IT'S TIME TO END THIS.
DA-DMP
DA-DMP
DA-DMP
BUBL BUBL
BLORBL

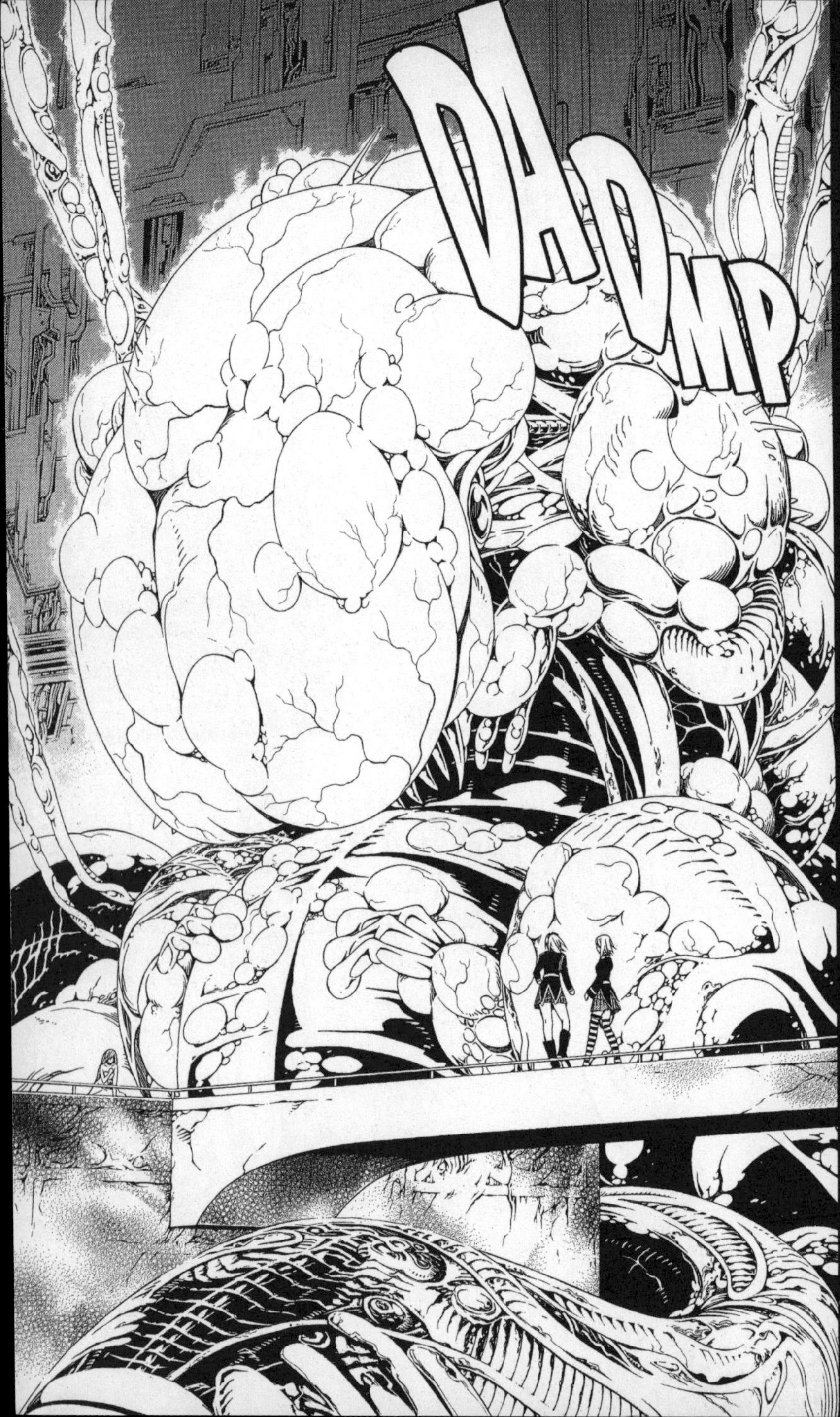
DADUMP

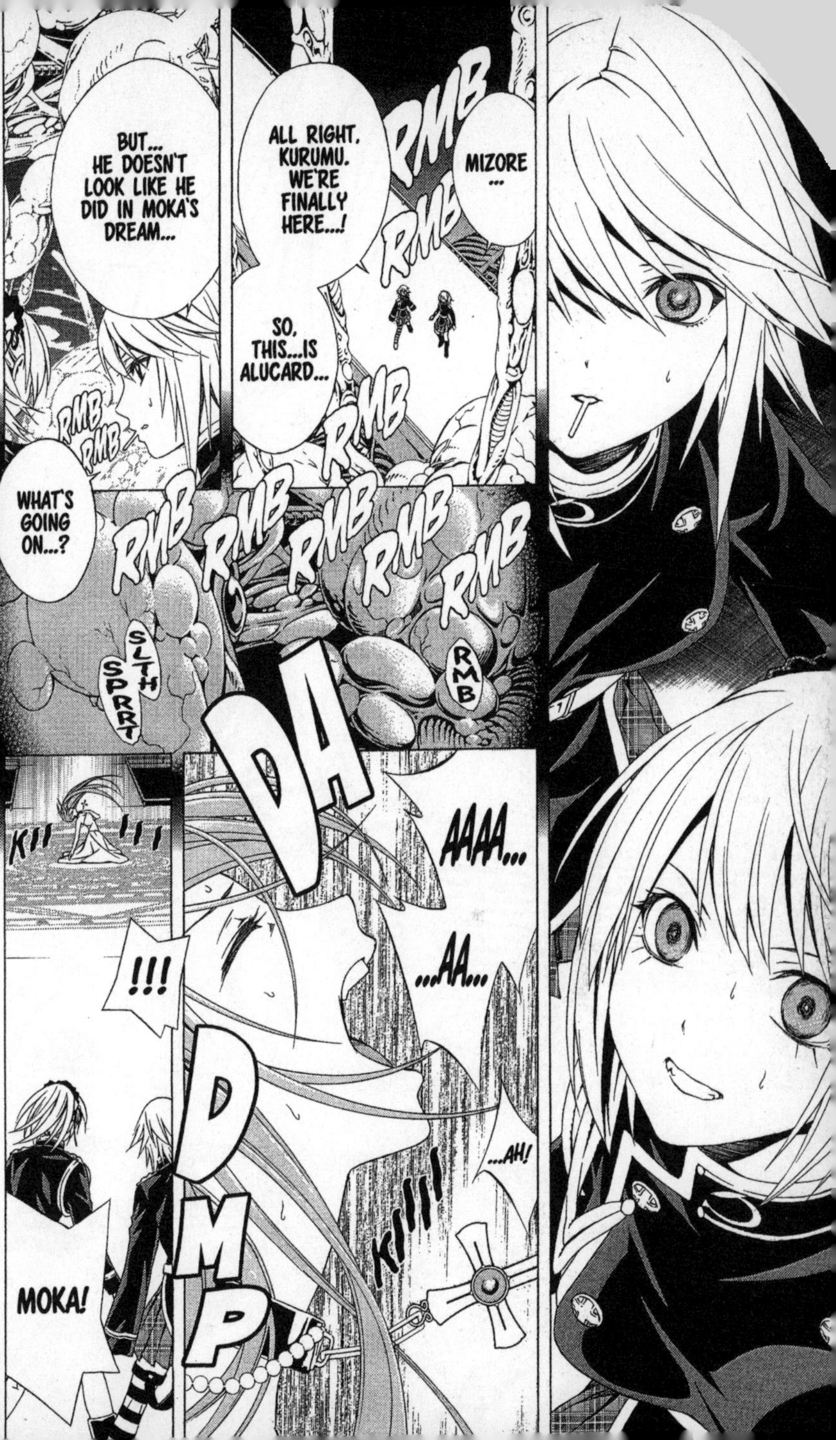
MIZORE ...
RMB
RMB
ALL RIGHT, KURUMU. WE'RE FINALLY HERE...!
SO, THIS...IS ALUCARD...
RMB
RMB
BUT... HE DOESN'T LOOK LIKE HE DID IN MOKA'S DREAM...
RMB
RMB
WHAT'S GOING ON...?
RMB
RMB
RMB
RMB
RMB
RMB
SLTH
SPRRT
DA
AAAA...
...AA...
...AH!
KIII
DMP
KII III
!!!
MOKA!

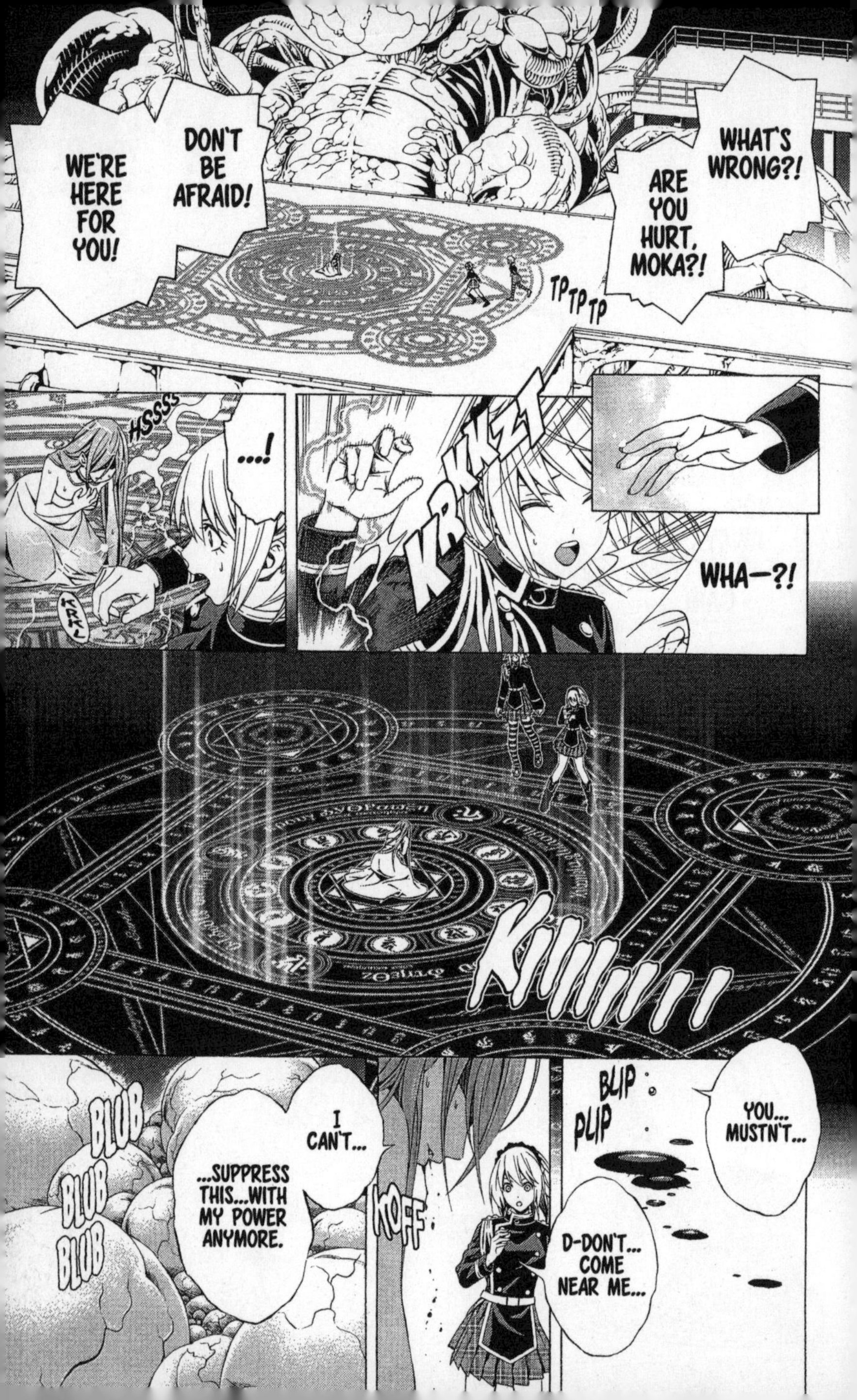
WHAT'S WRONG?!
ARE YOU HURT, MOKA?!
TP TP TP
DON'T BE AFRAID!
WE'RE HERE FOR YOU!
WHA—?!
KRKKZT
...!
HSSSS
KRKL
KIIIIIIII
YOU... MUSTN'T...
BLIP PLIP
D-DON'T... COME NEAR ME...
KOFF
I CAN'T...
...SUPPRESS THIS...WITH MY POWER ANYMORE.
BLUB BLUB BLUB

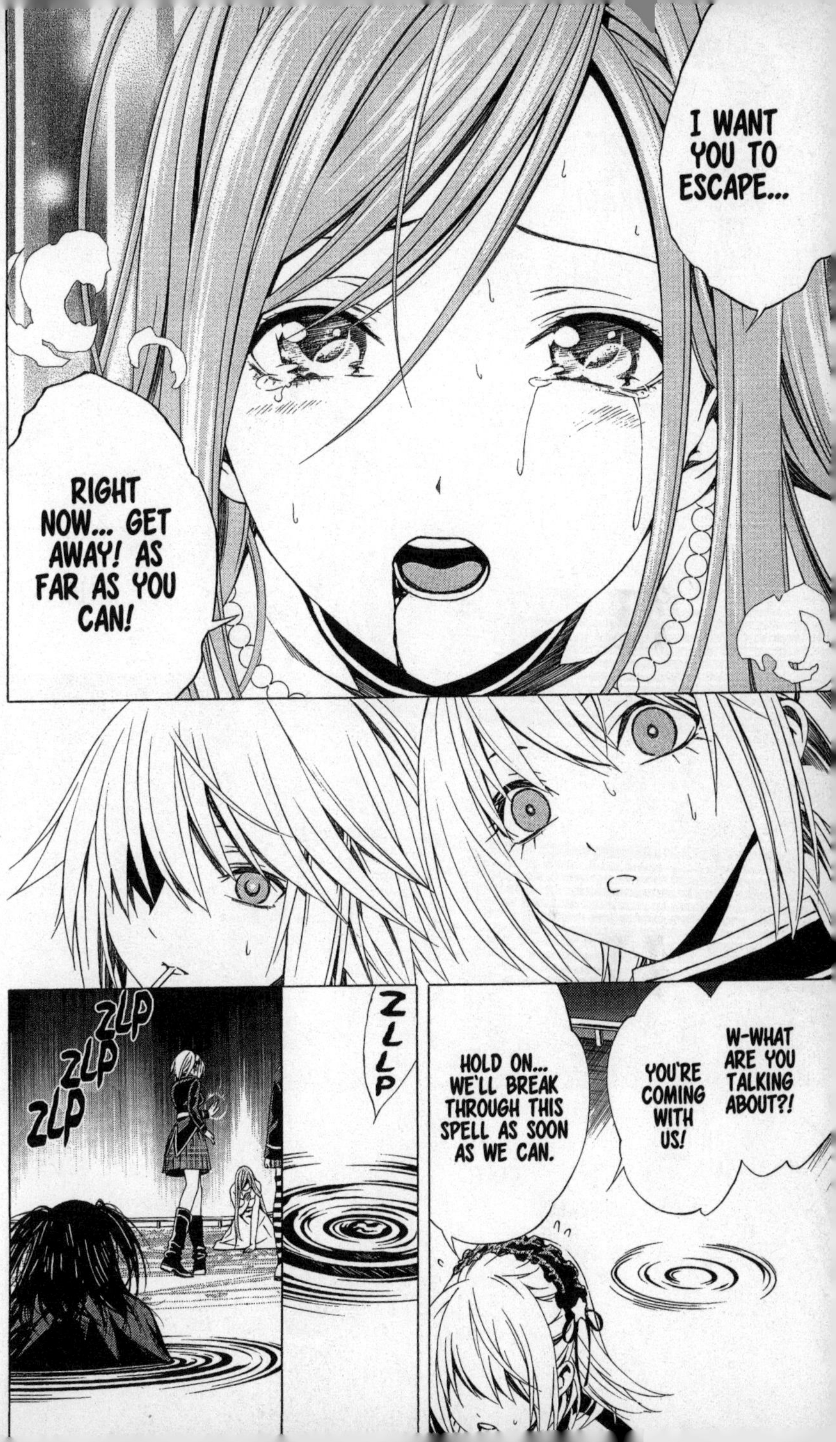
I WANT YOU TO ESCAPE...
RIGHT NOW... GET AWAY! AS FAR AS YOU CAN!
W-WHAT ARE YOU TALKING ABOUT?!
YOU'RE COMING WITH US!
HOLD ON... WE'LL BREAK THROUGH THIS SPELL AS SOON AS WE CAN.
ZLLP
ZLP
ZLP
ZLP

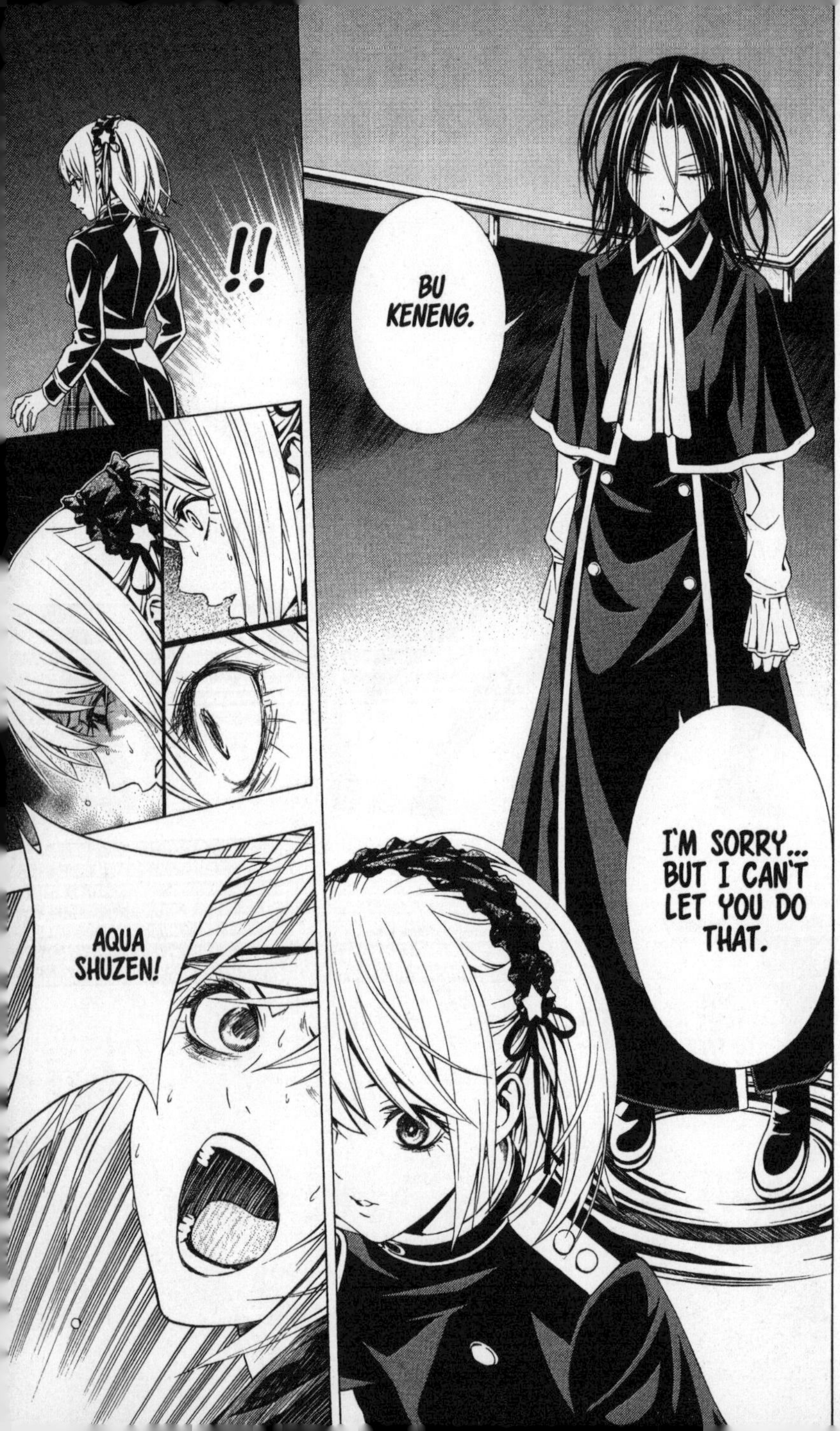
BU KENENG.
I'M SORRY... BUT I CAN'T LET YOU DO THAT.
!!
AQUA SHUZEN!

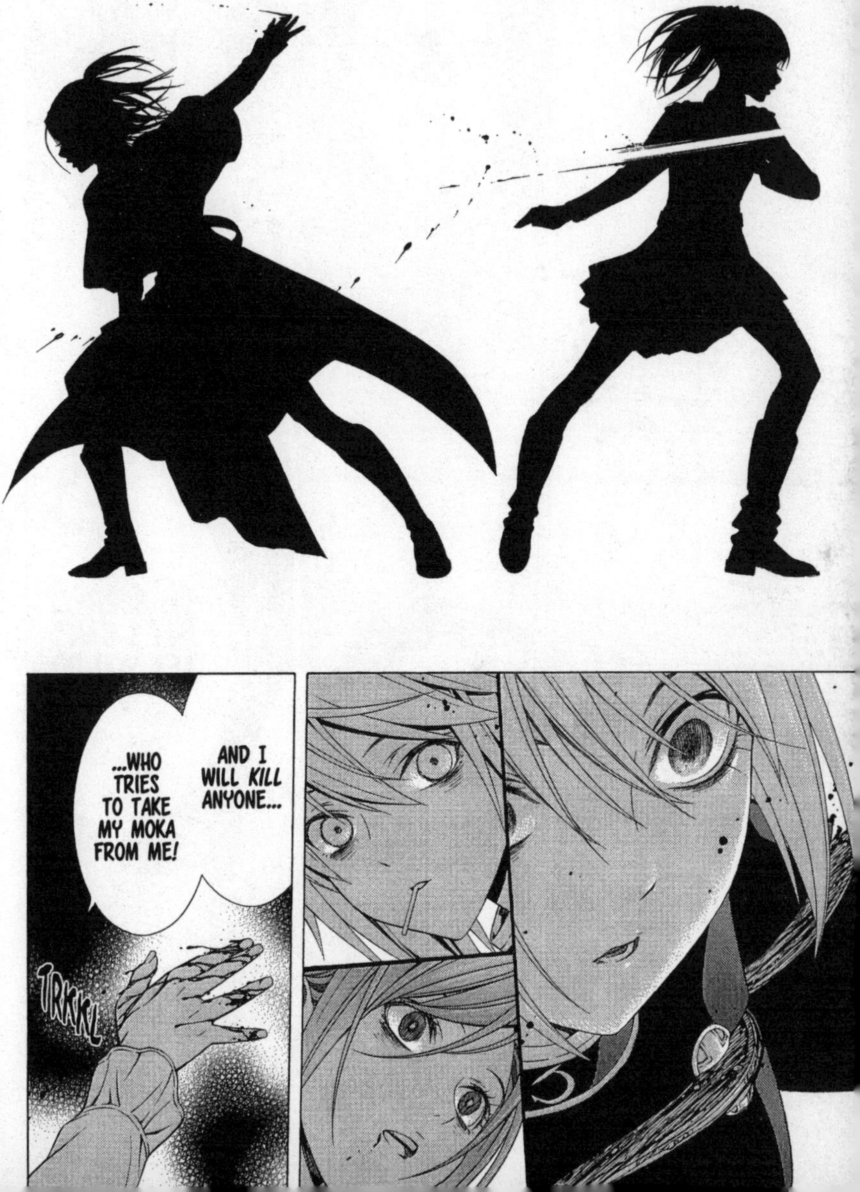
AND I WILL *KILL* ANYONE...
...WHO TRIES TO TAKE MY MOKA FROM ME!
TRKKL

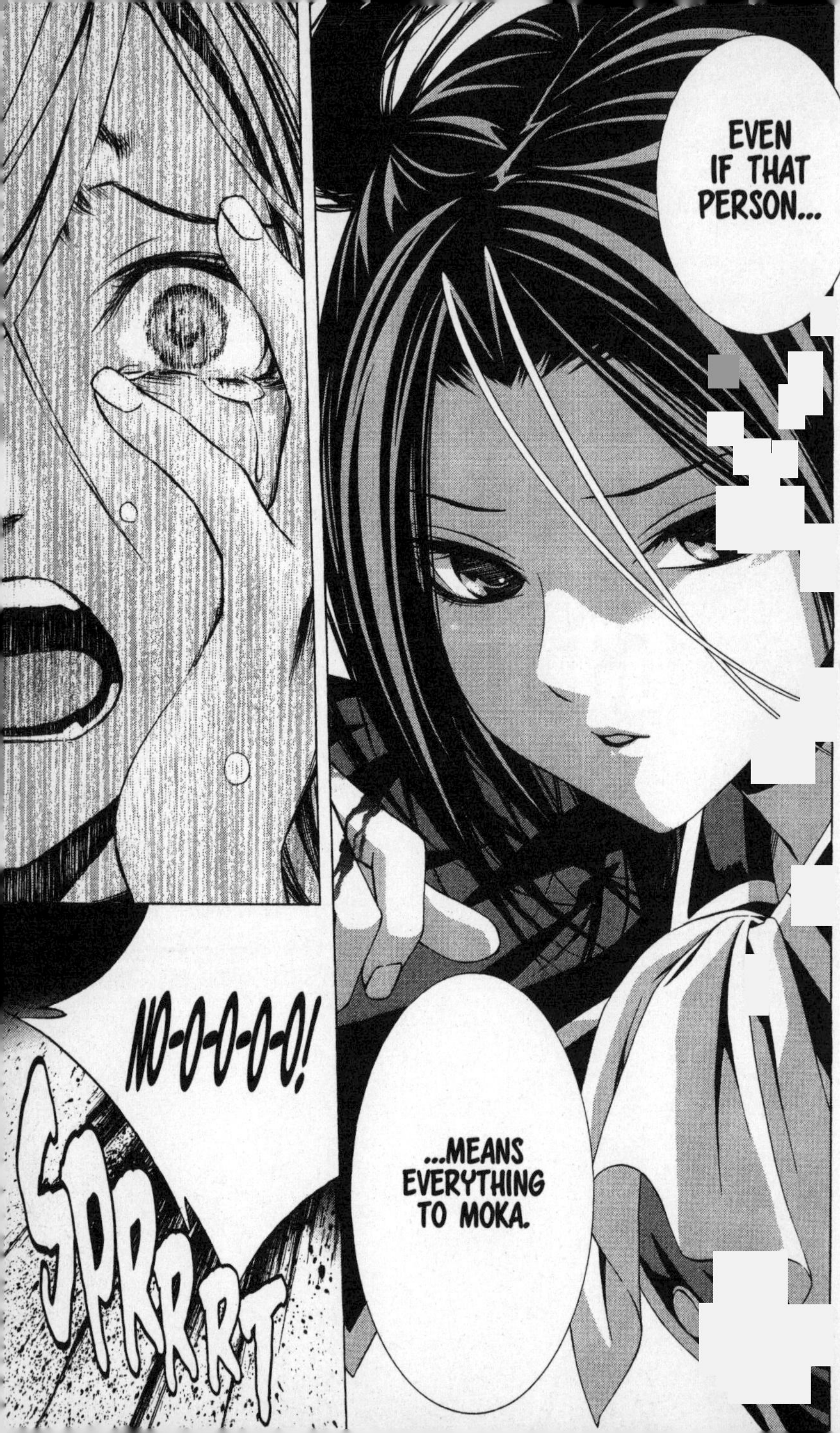
EVEN IF THAT PERSON...
...MEANS EVERYTHING TO MOKA.
NO-O-O-O-O!
SPRRRT

53: Replica

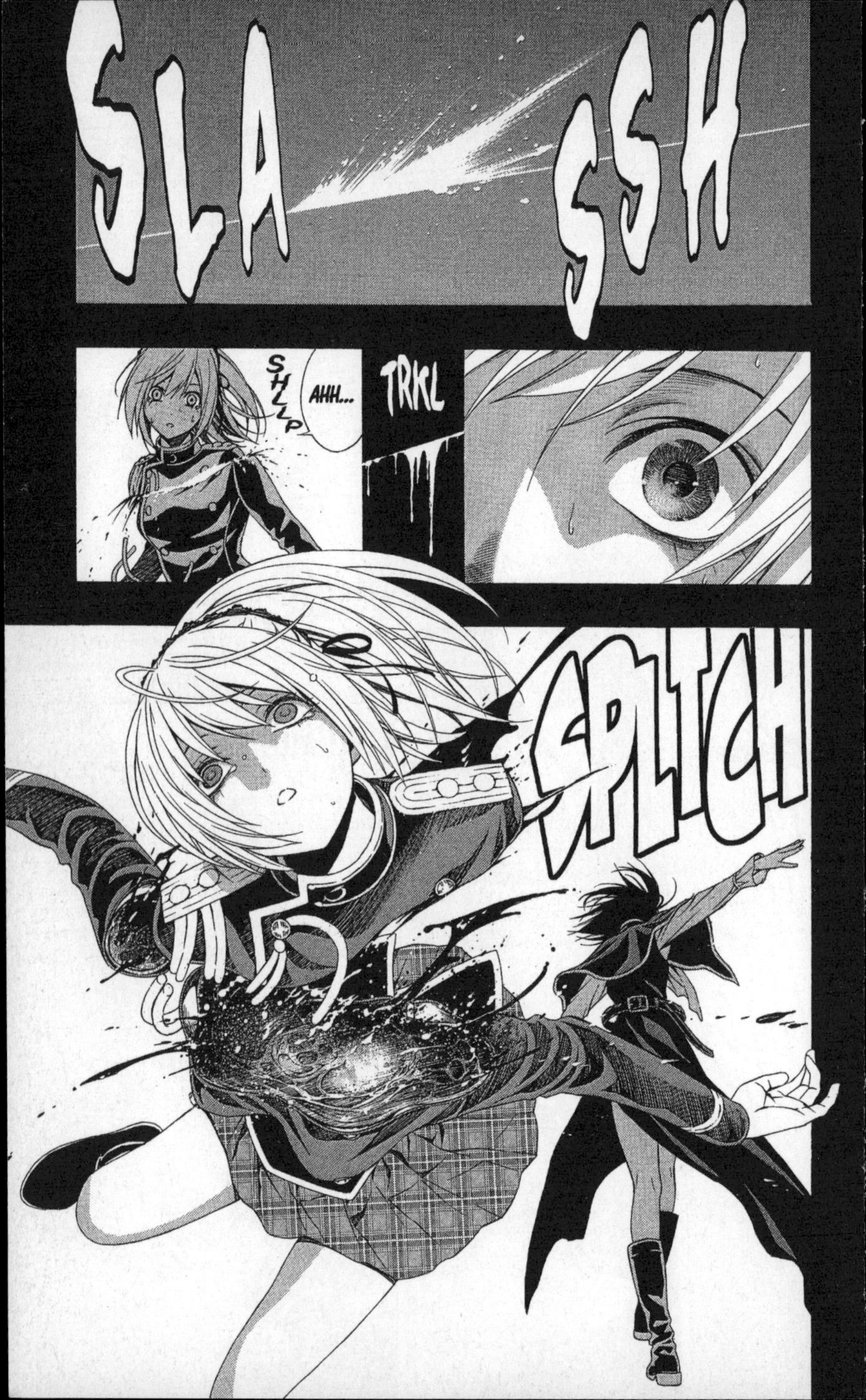
SLASSH
TRKL
AHH...
SHLLP
SPLTCH

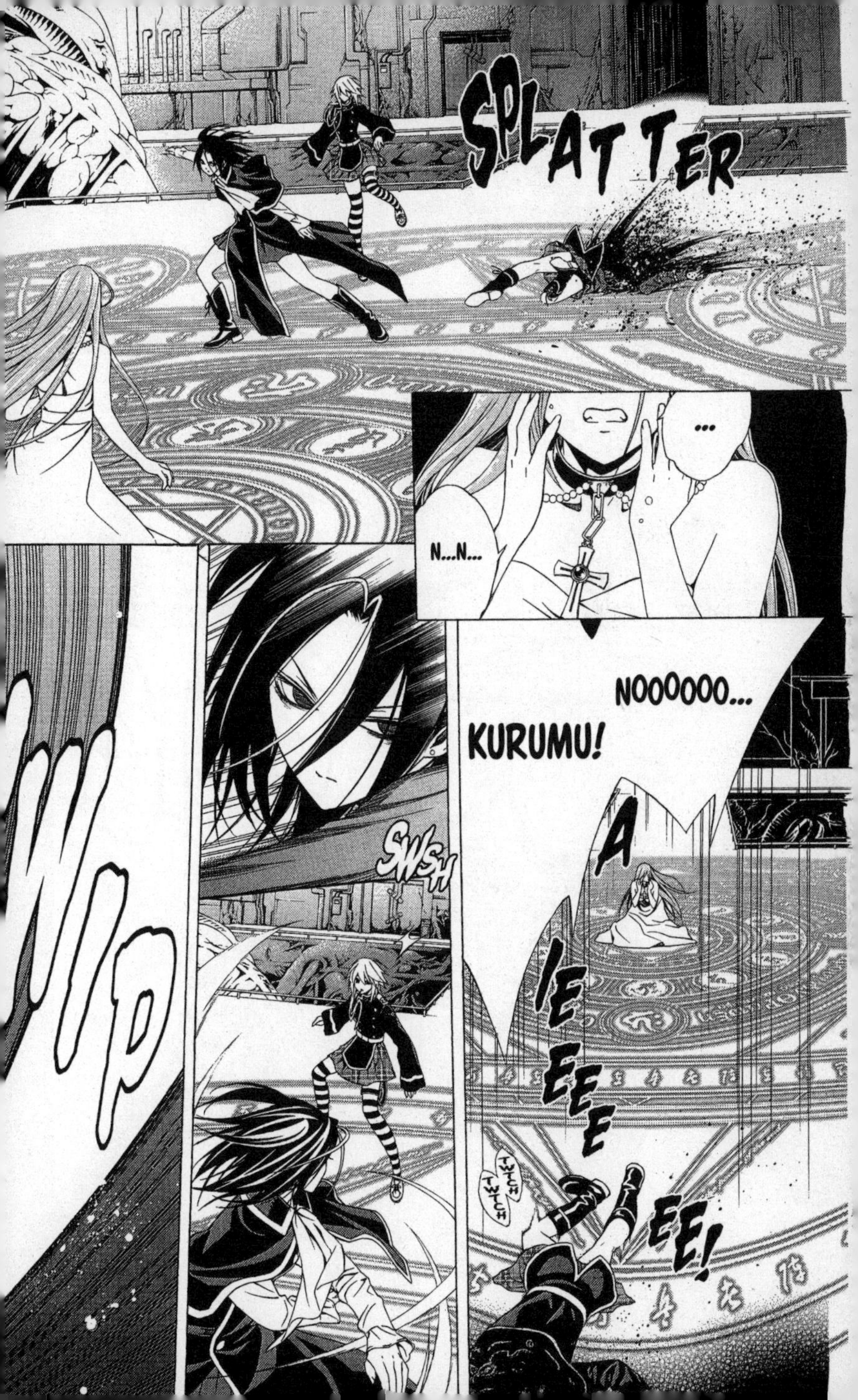
SPLATTER
...
N...N...
NOOOOOO...
KURUMU!
AIEEEEEE!
TWITCH
TWITCH
SWSH

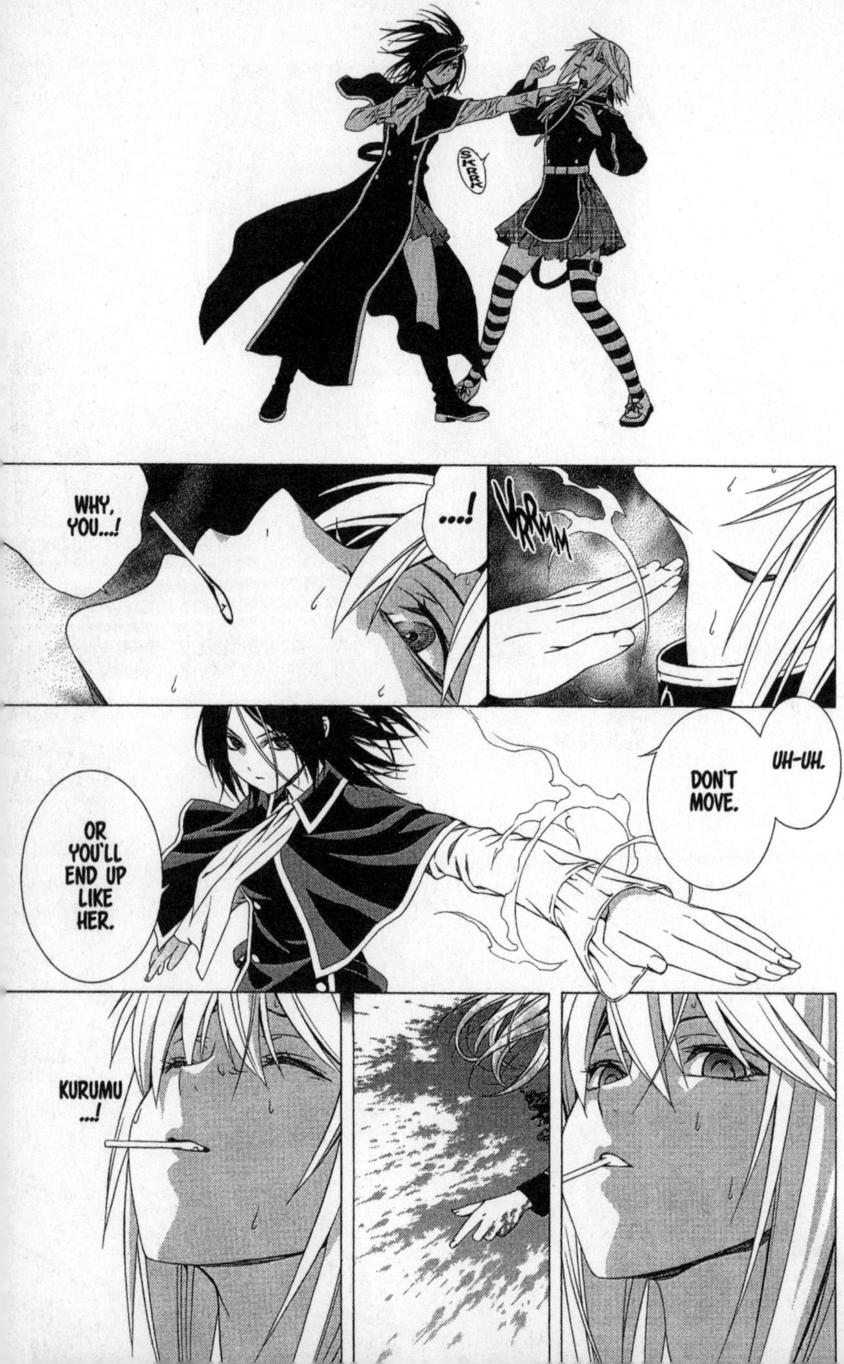
SKRRK
VRRMM
...!
WHY, YOU...!
UH-UH.
DON'T MOVE.
OR YOU'LL END UP LIKE HER.
KURUMU ...!

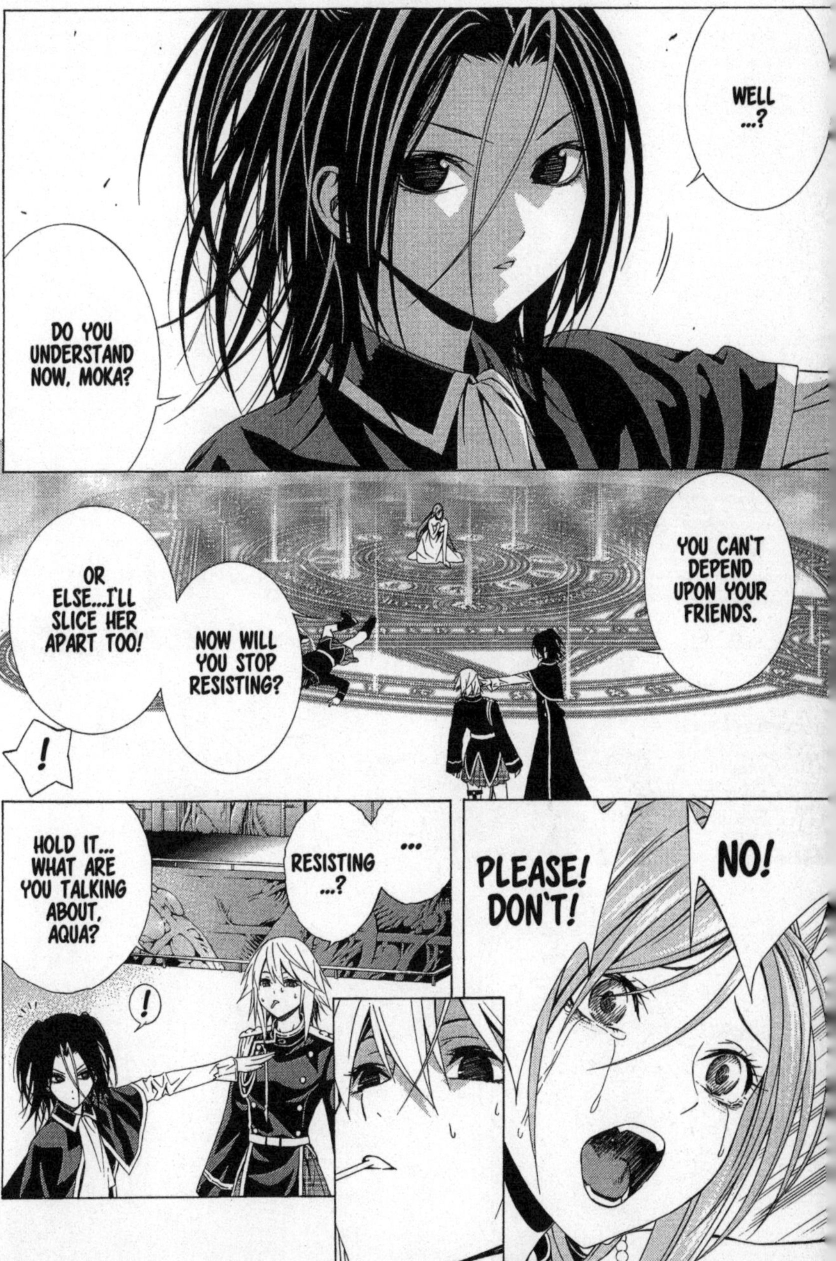
WELL ...?
DO YOU UNDERSTAND NOW, MOKA?
YOU CAN'T DEPEND UPON YOUR FRIENDS.
NOW WILL YOU STOP RESISTING?
OR ELSE...I'LL SLICE HER APART TOO!
!
NO!
PLEASE! DON'T!
...
RESISTING ...?
HOLD IT... WHAT ARE YOU TALKING ABOUT, AQUA?
!

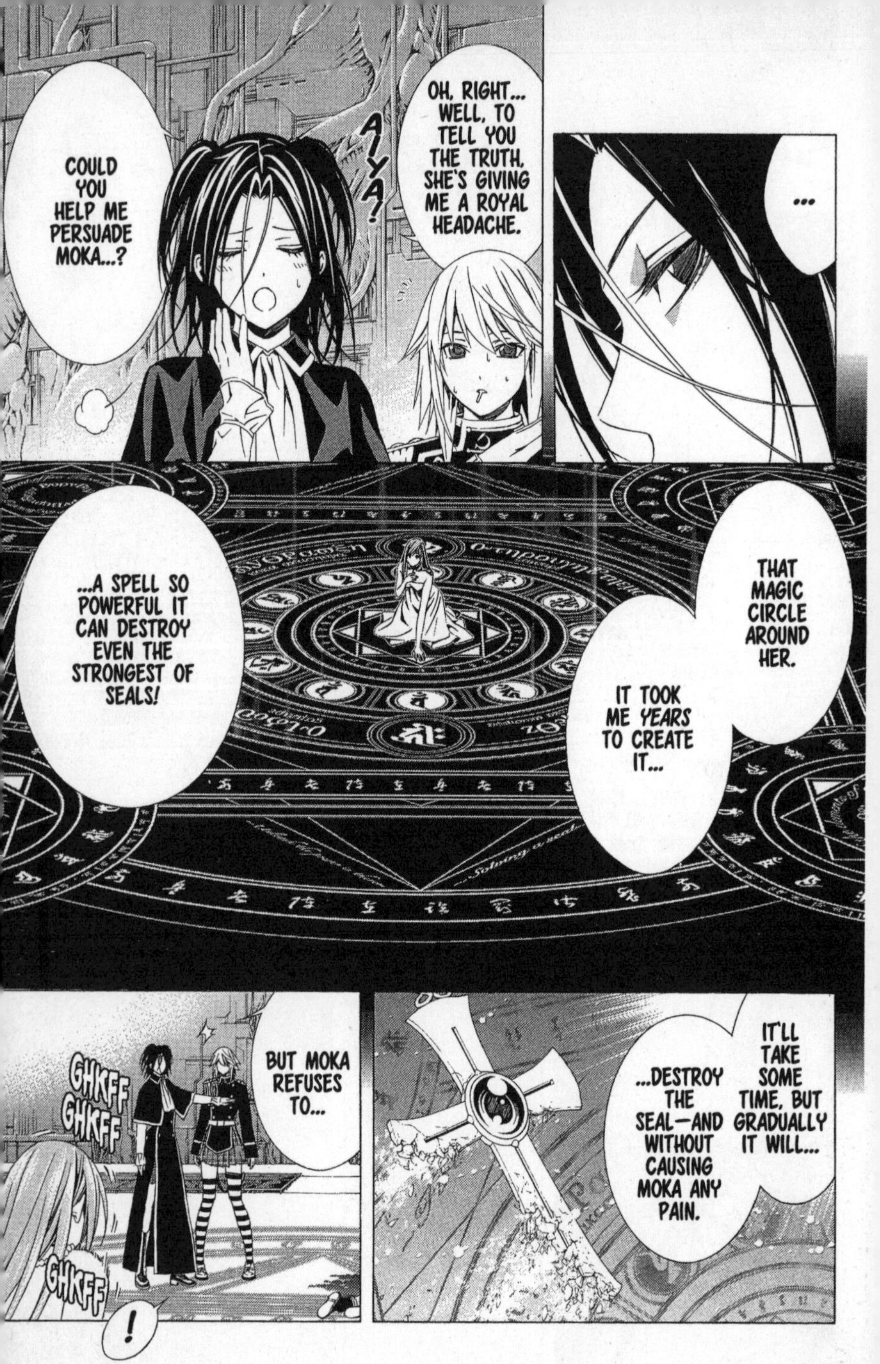
...
OH, RIGHT... WELL, TO TELL YOU THE TRUTH, SHE'S GIVING ME A ROYAL HEADACHE.
AIYA!
COULD YOU HELP ME PERSUADE MOKA...?
THAT MAGIC CIRCLE AROUND HER.
IT TOOK ME YEARS TO CREATE IT...
...A SPELL SO POWERFUL IT CAN DESTROY EVEN THE STRONGEST OF SEALS!
IT'LL TAKE SOME TIME, BUT GRADUALLY IT WILL...
...DESTROY THE SEAL—AND WITHOUT CAUSING MOKA ANY PAIN.
BUT MOKA REFUSES TO...
GHKFF GHKFF
GHKFF
!

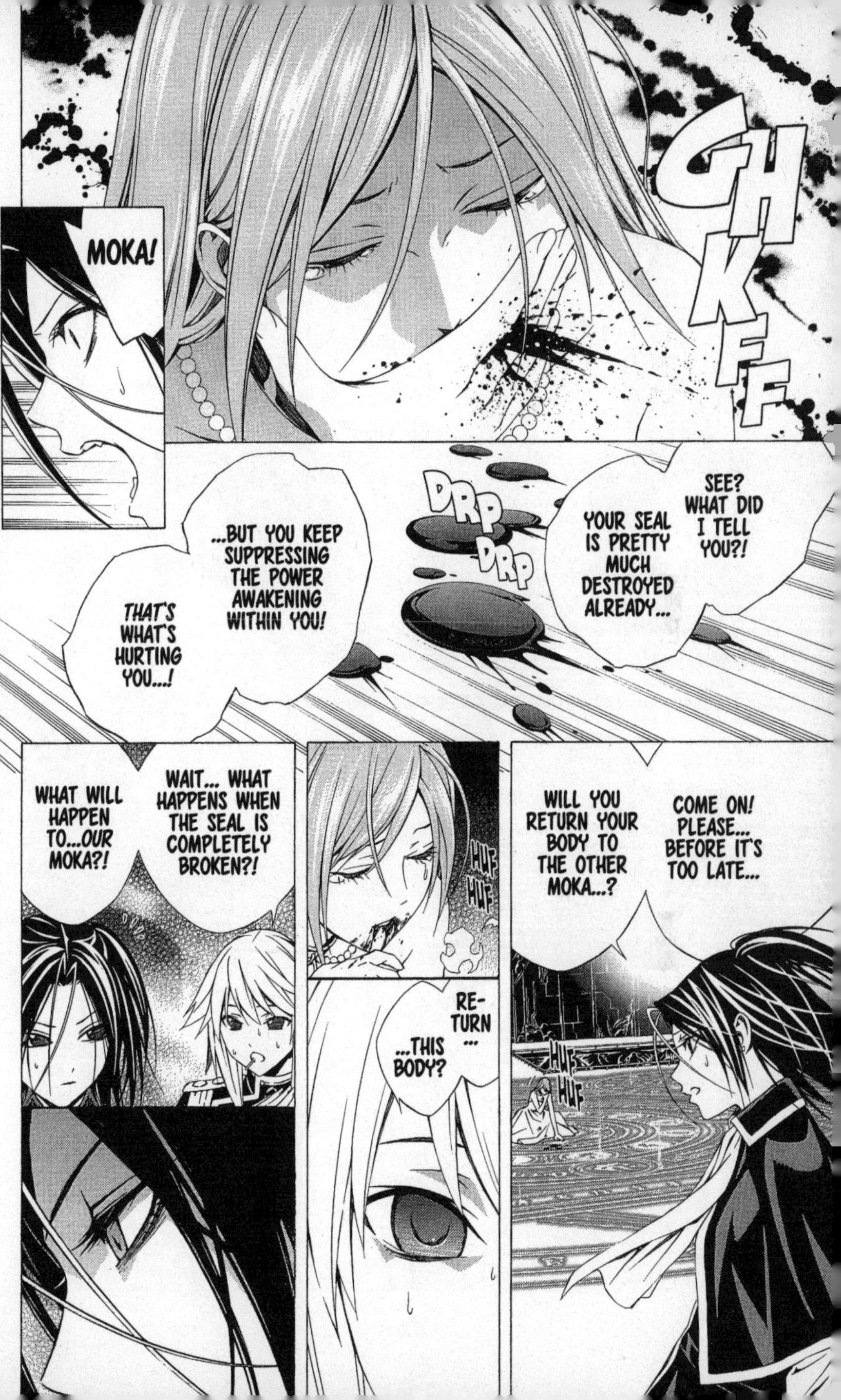
GHKFF
MOKA!
SEE? WHAT DID I TELL YOU?!
YOUR SEAL IS PRETTY MUCH DESTROYED ALREADY...
DRP DRP
...BUT YOU KEEP SUPPRESSING THE POWER AWAKENING WITHIN YOU!
THAT'S WHAT'S HURTING YOU...!
COME ON! PLEASE... BEFORE IT'S TOO LATE...
WILL YOU RETURN YOUR BODY TO THE OTHER MOKA...?
HUF HUF
HUF HUF
RE-TURN...
...THIS BODY?
WAIT... WHAT HAPPENS WHEN THE SEAL IS COMPLETELY BROKEN?!
WHAT WILL HAPPEN TO...OUR MOKA?!

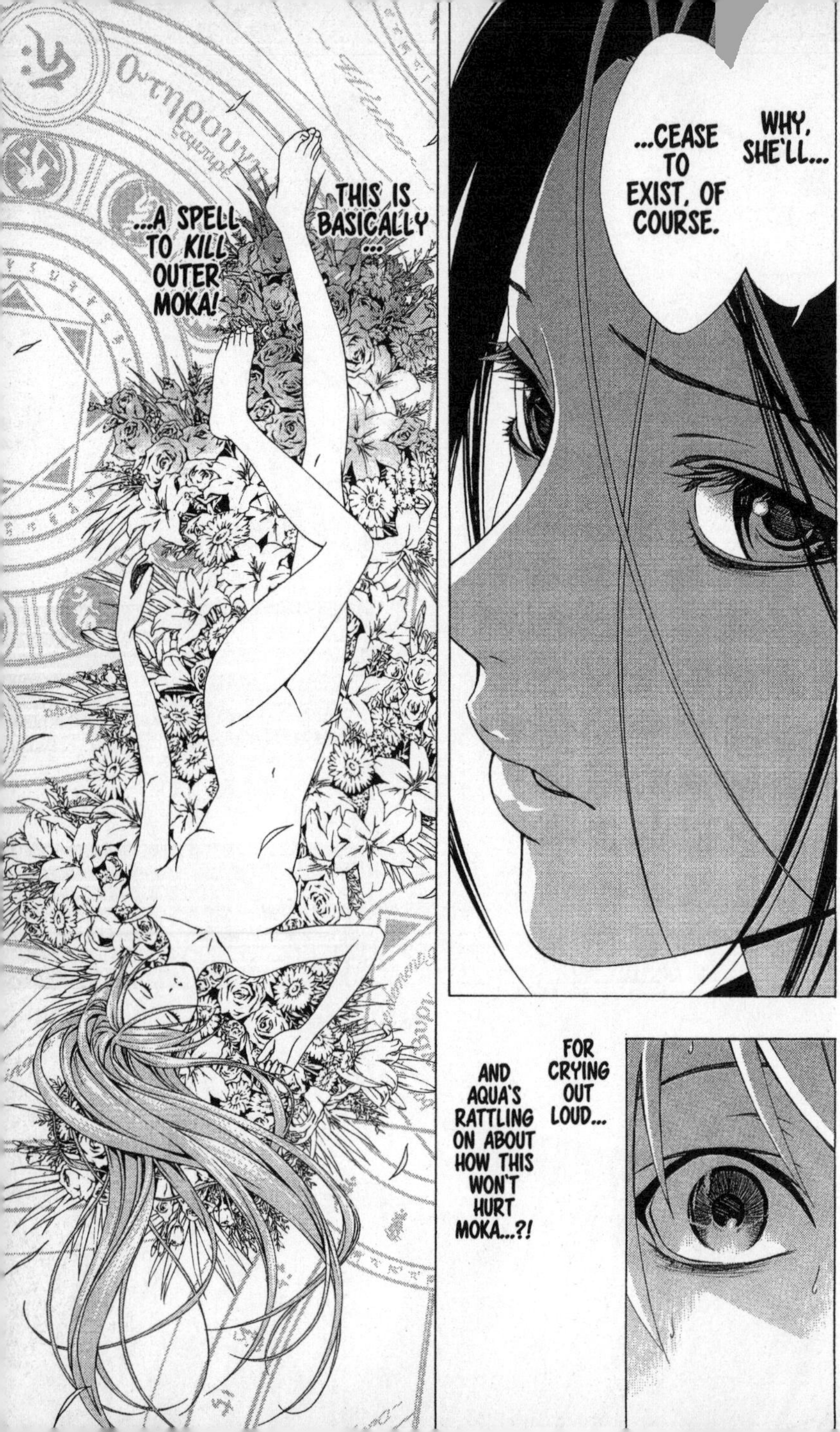
WHY, SHE'LL...
...CEASE TO EXIST, OF COURSE.
FOR CRYING OUT LOUD...
AND AQUA'S RATTLING ON ABOUT HOW THIS WON'T HURT MOKA...?!
THIS IS BASICALLY...
...A SPELL TO KILL OUTER MOKA!

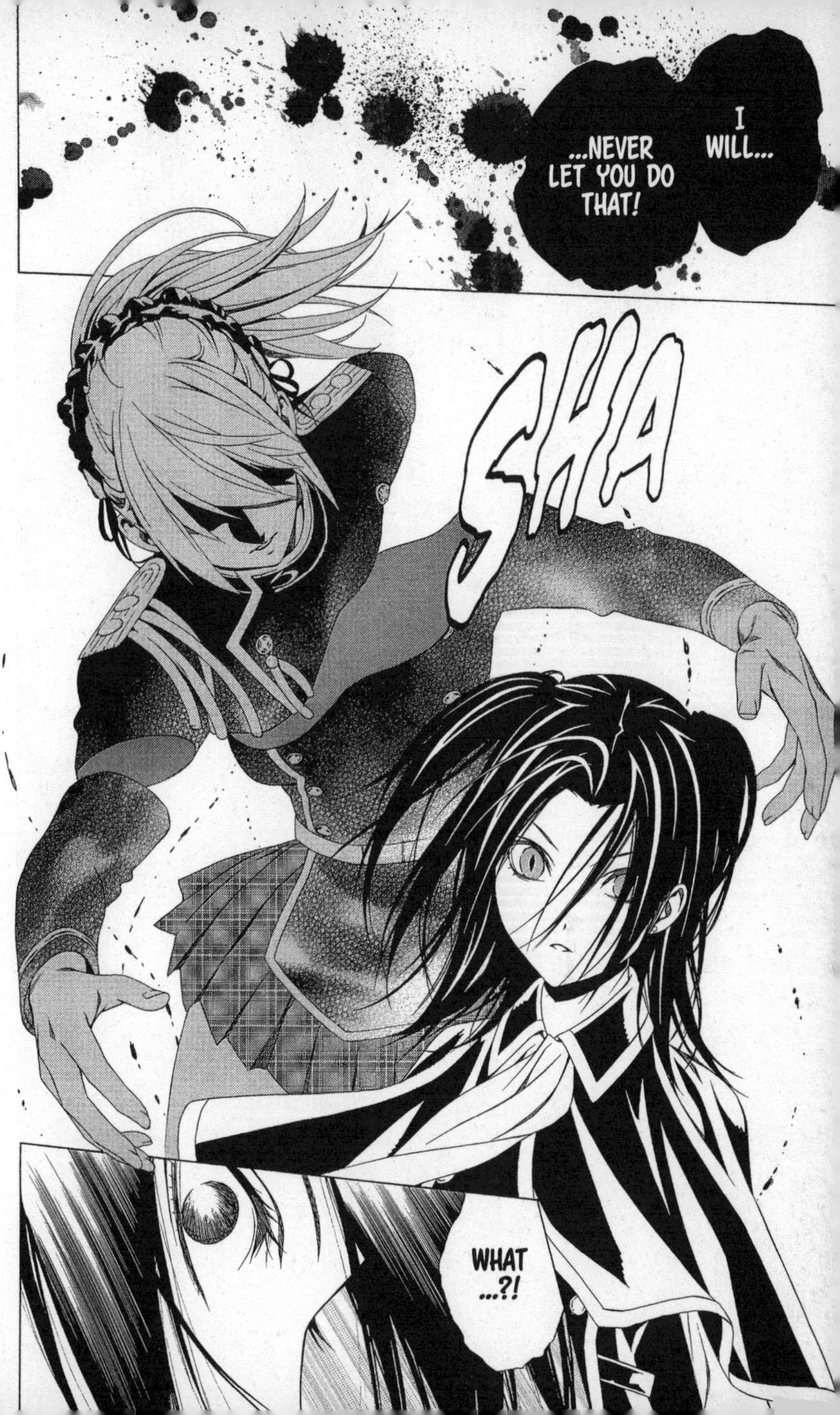
I WILL...
...NEVER LET YOU DO THAT!
SHA
WHAT ...?!

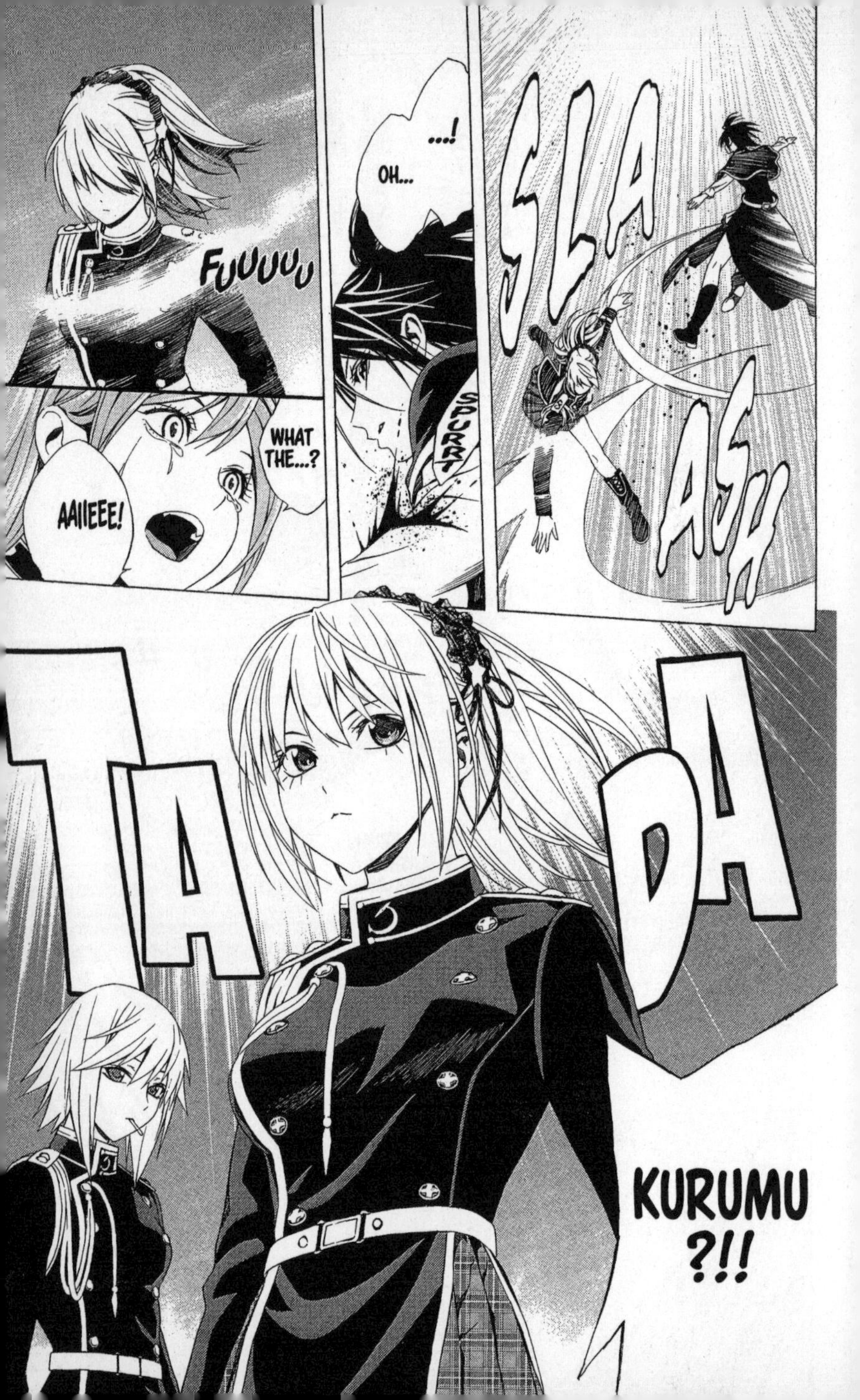
SLA
ASH
...!
OH...
SPURRT
FUUUUU
WHAT THE...?
AAIIEEE!
TA
DA
KURUMU ?!!

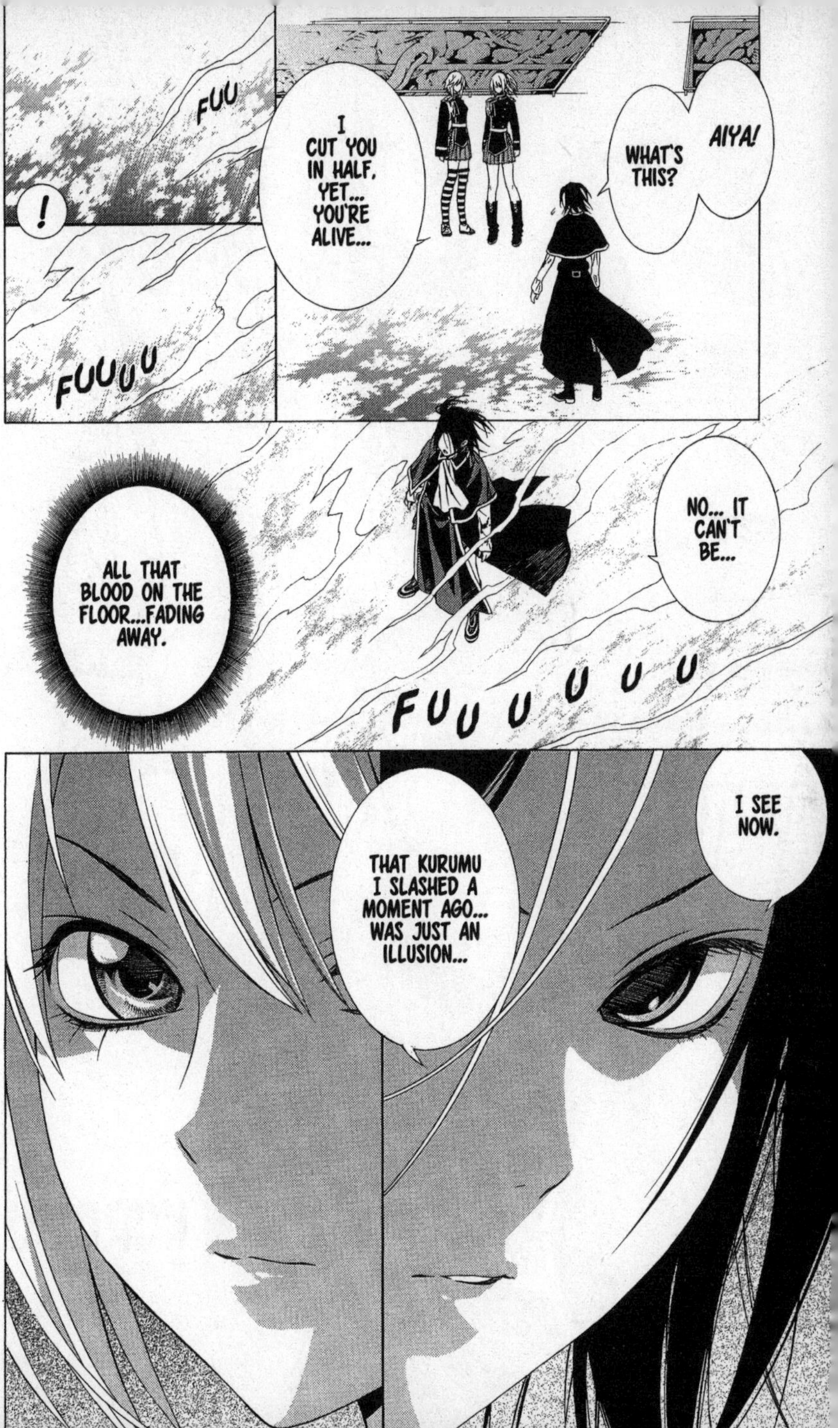
AIYA!
WHAT'S THIS?
I CUT YOU IN HALF, YET... YOU'RE ALIVE...
FUU
!
FUUUU
NO... IT CAN'T BE...
ALL THAT BLOOD ON THE FLOOR...FADING AWAY.
FUUUUUUU
I SEE NOW.
THAT KURUMU I SLASHED A MOMENT AGO... WAS JUST AN ILLUSION...

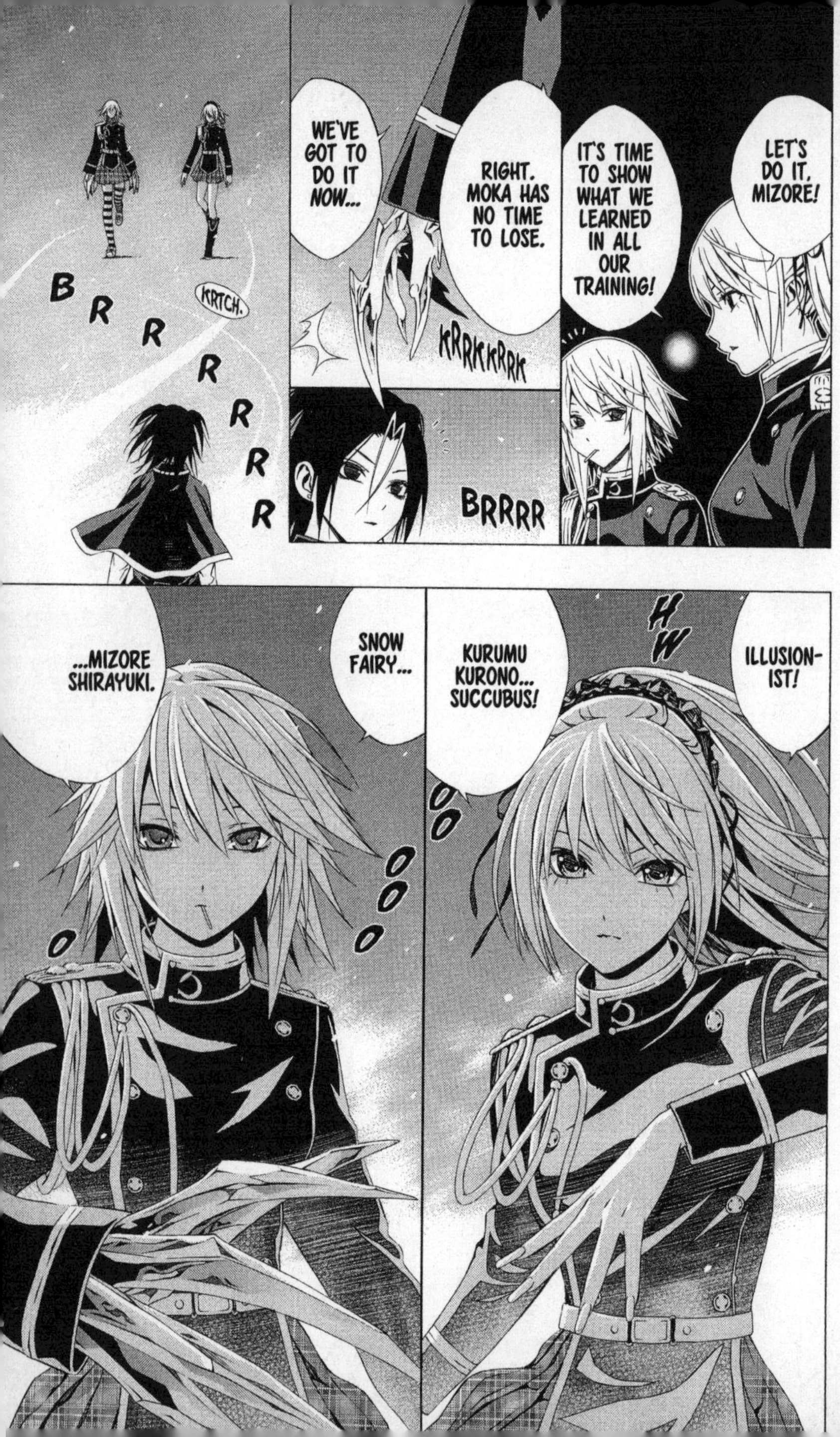
LET'S DO IT, MIZORE!
IT'S TIME TO SHOW WHAT WE LEARNED IN ALL OUR TRAINING!
RIGHT. MOKA HAS NO TIME TO LOSE.
WE'VE GOT TO DO IT NOW...
KRRKKRRK
BRRRR
KRTCH.
BRRRRRRR
ILLUSION-IST!
HW
KURUMU KURONO... SUCCUBUS!
OOO
SNOW FAIRY...
...MIZORE SHIRAYUKI.
OOOO
O

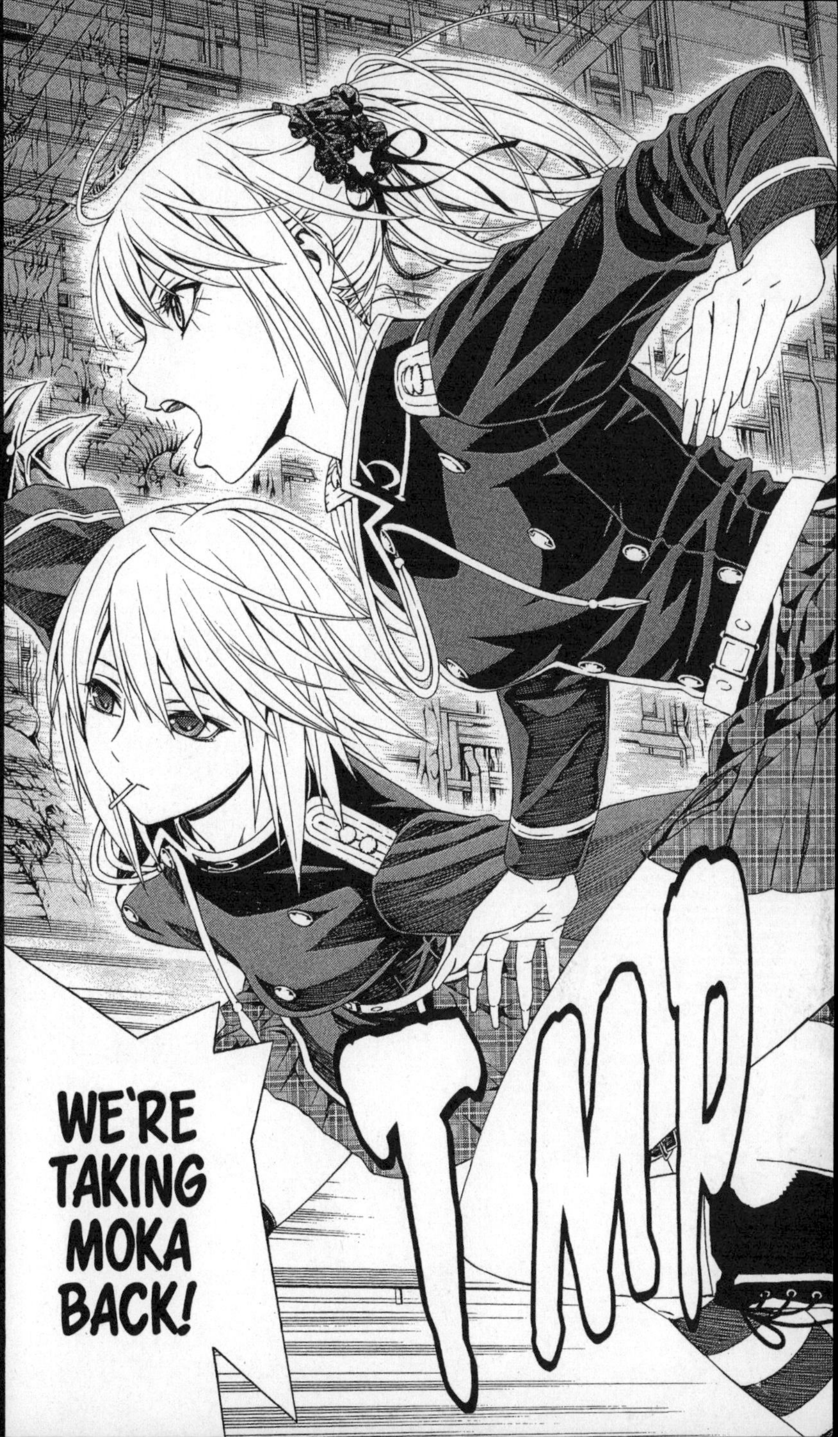
TMP
WE'RE TAKING MOKA BACK!

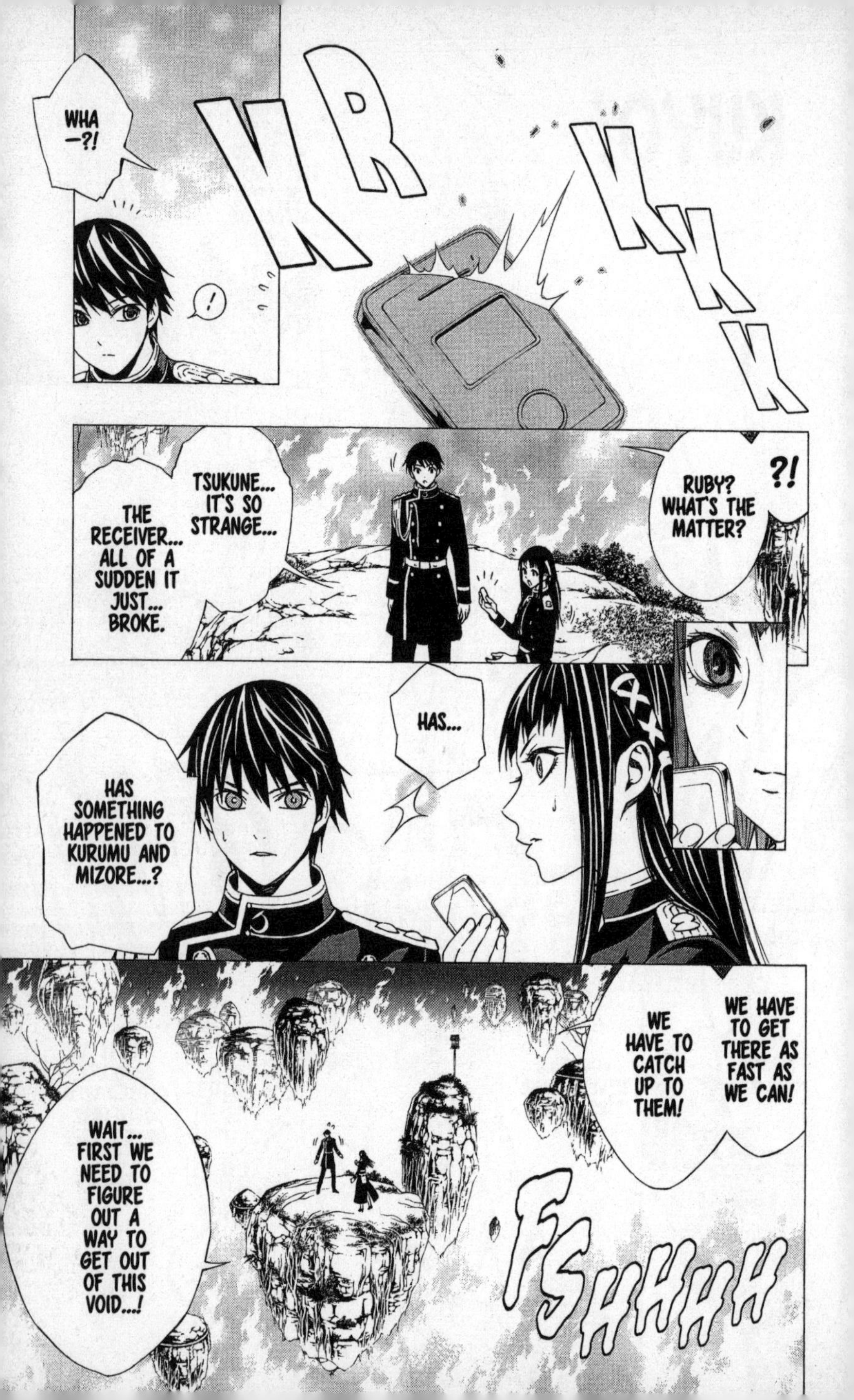
VRKKKK
WHA—?!
!
?!
RUBY? WHAT'S THE MATTER?
TSUKUNE... IT'S SO STRANGE...
THE RECEIVER... ALL OF A SUDDEN IT JUST... BROKE.
HAS...
HAS SOMETHING HAPPENED TO KURUMU AND MIZORE...?
WE HAVE TO GET THERE AS FAST AS WE CAN!
WE HAVE TO CATCH UP TO THEM!
FSHHHH
WAIT... FIRST WE NEED TO FIGURE OUT A WAY TO GET OUT OF THIS VOID...!

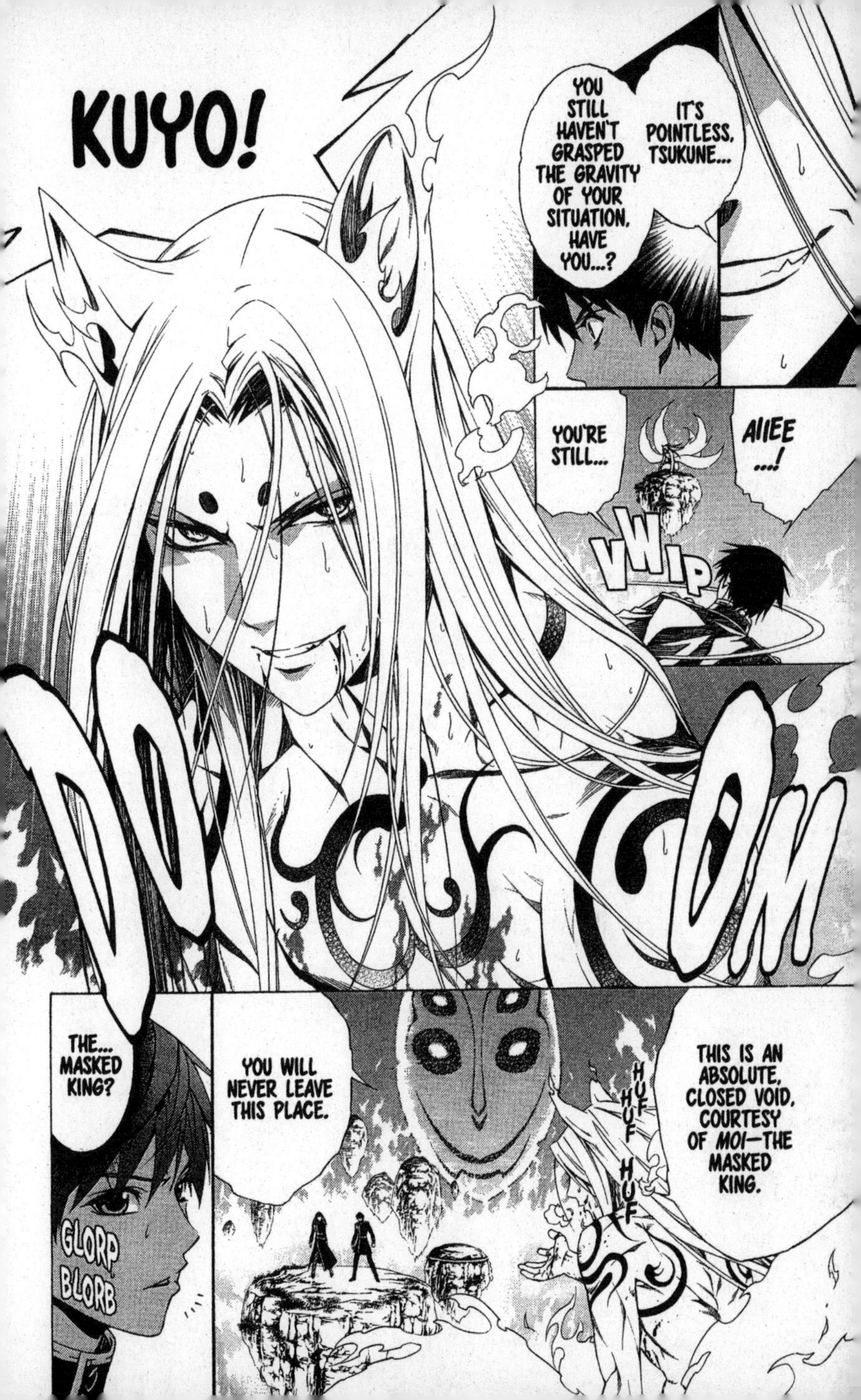
IT'S POINTLESS, TSUKUNE...
YOU STILL HAVEN'T GRASPED THE GRAVITY OF YOUR SITUATION, HAVE YOU...?
AIIEE ...!
YOU'RE STILL...
VWIP
KUYO!
DOOOM
THIS IS AN ABSOLUTE, CLOSED VOID, COURTESY OF *MOI*—THE MASKED KING.
HUF HUF
HUF HUF
YOU WILL NEVER LEAVE THIS PLACE.
THE... MASKED KING?
GLORP BLORB

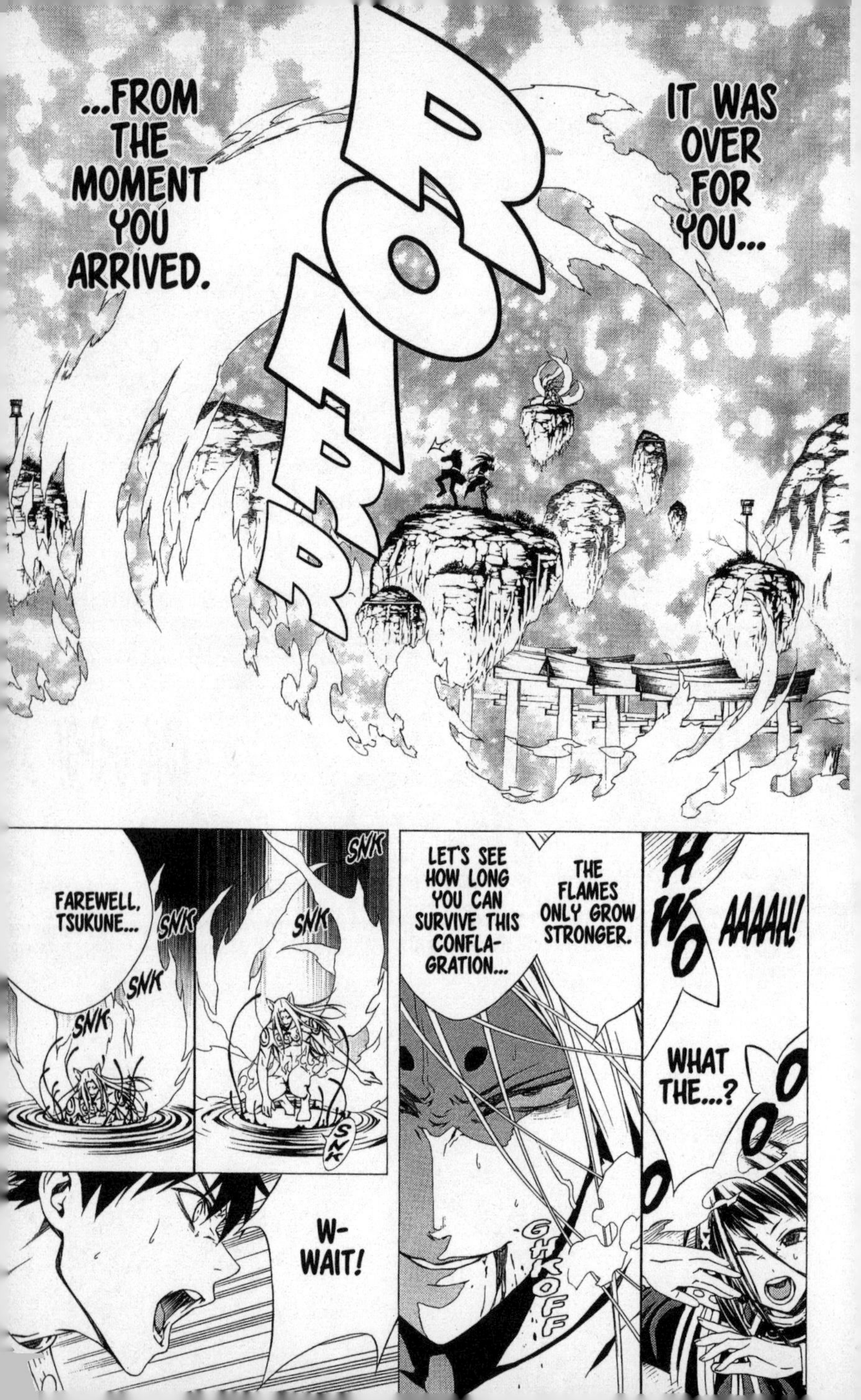
IT WAS OVER FOR YOU...
ROARR
...FROM THE MOMENT YOU ARRIVED.
HWOOOOO
AAAAH!
WHAT THE...?
THE FLAMES ONLY GROW STRONGER.
LET'S SEE HOW LONG YOU CAN SURVIVE THIS CONFLA-GRATION...
GHKOFF
SNK
SNK
SNK
FAREWELL, TSUKUNE...
SNK
SNK
SNK
W-WAIT!

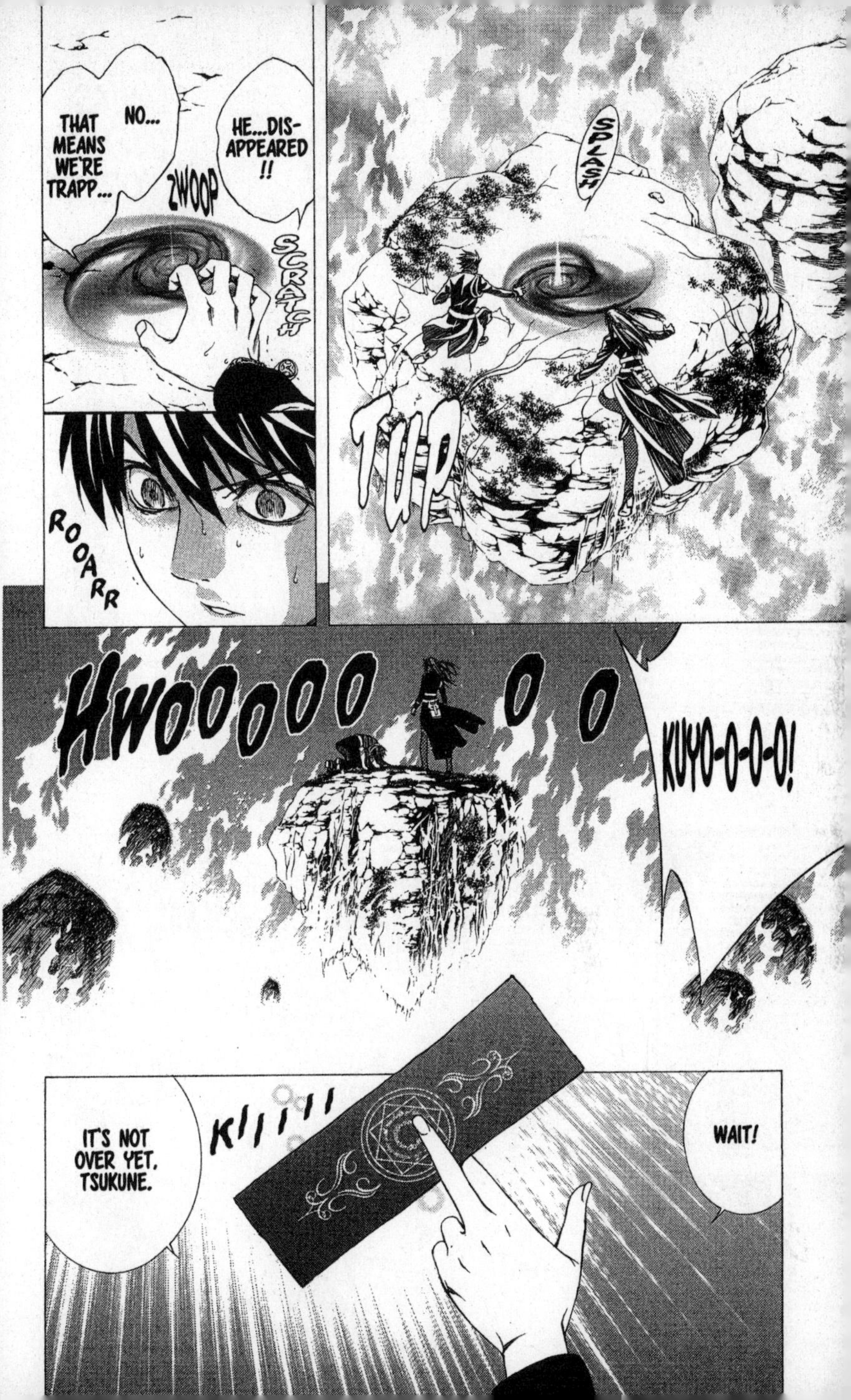
SPLASH
TUP
HE...DIS-APPEARED!!
NO...
THAT MEANS WE'RE TRAPP...
ZWOOP
SCRATCH
ROOARR
KUYO-O-O-O!
HWOOOOOO O O
WAIT!
KIIIII
IT'S NOT OVER YET, TSUKUNE.

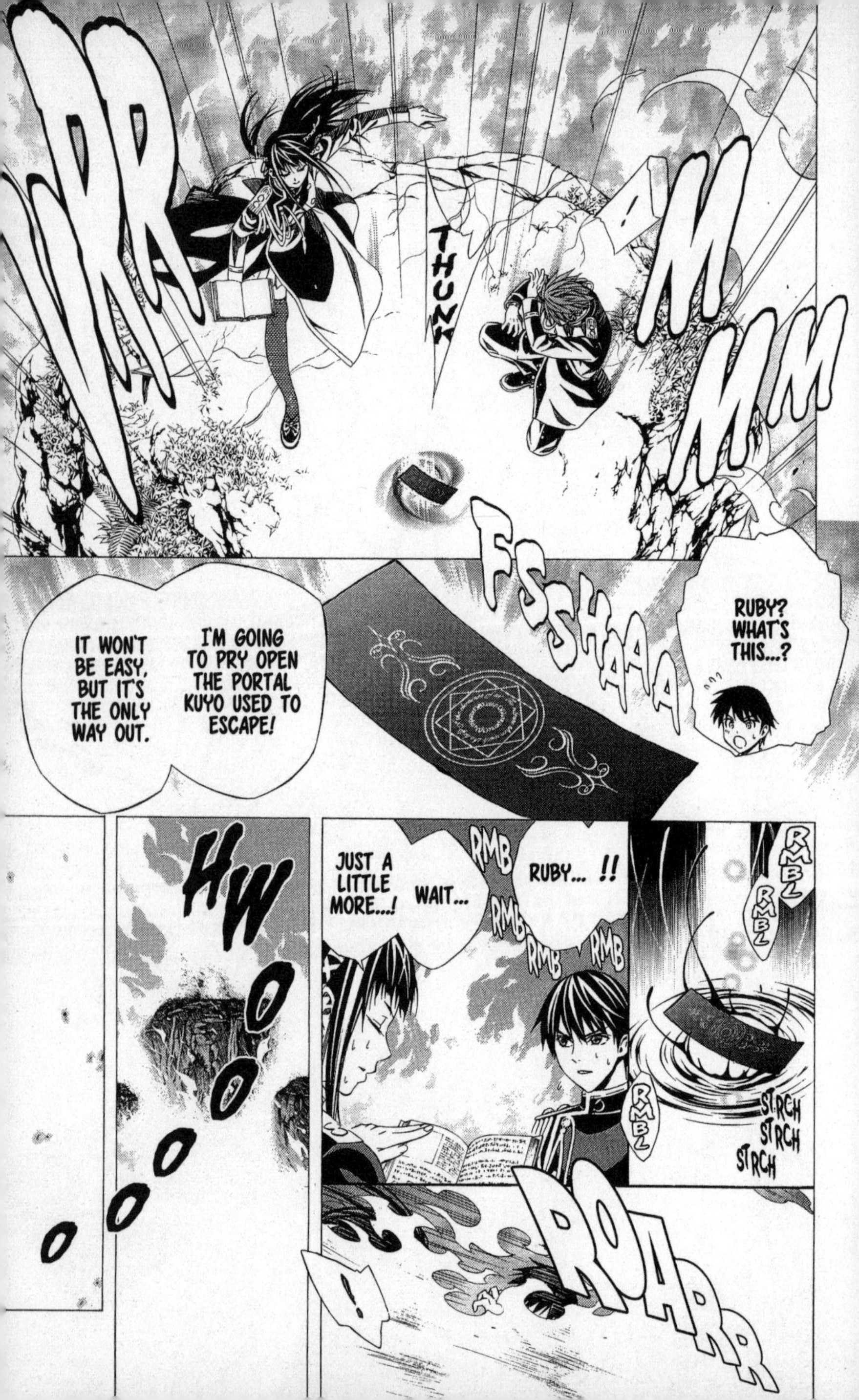
THUNK
RUBY? WHAT'S THIS...?
FSSHAAA
I'M GOING TO PRY OPEN THE PORTAL KUYO USED TO ESCAPE!
IT WON'T BE EASY, BUT IT'S THE ONLY WAY OUT.
RMBL
RMBL
RMBL
STRCH STRCH STRCH
RUBY... !!
RMB
RMB
RMB
RMB
WAIT...
JUST A LITTLE MORE...!
HWOOOOOOO
ROARRR
!

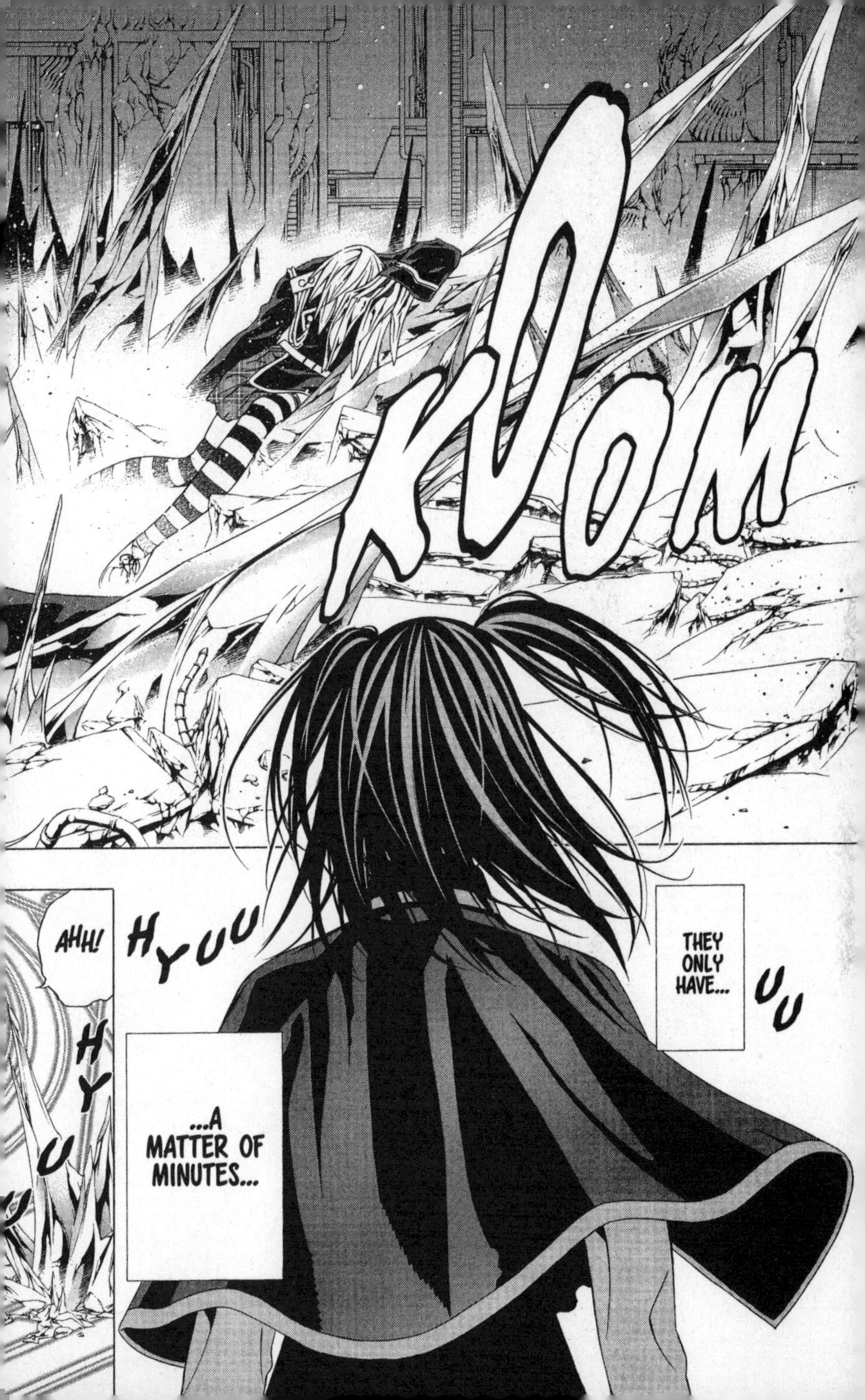
KVOOM
THEY ONLY HAVE...
HYUU UU
...A MATTER OF MINUTES...
AHH!
HYUU

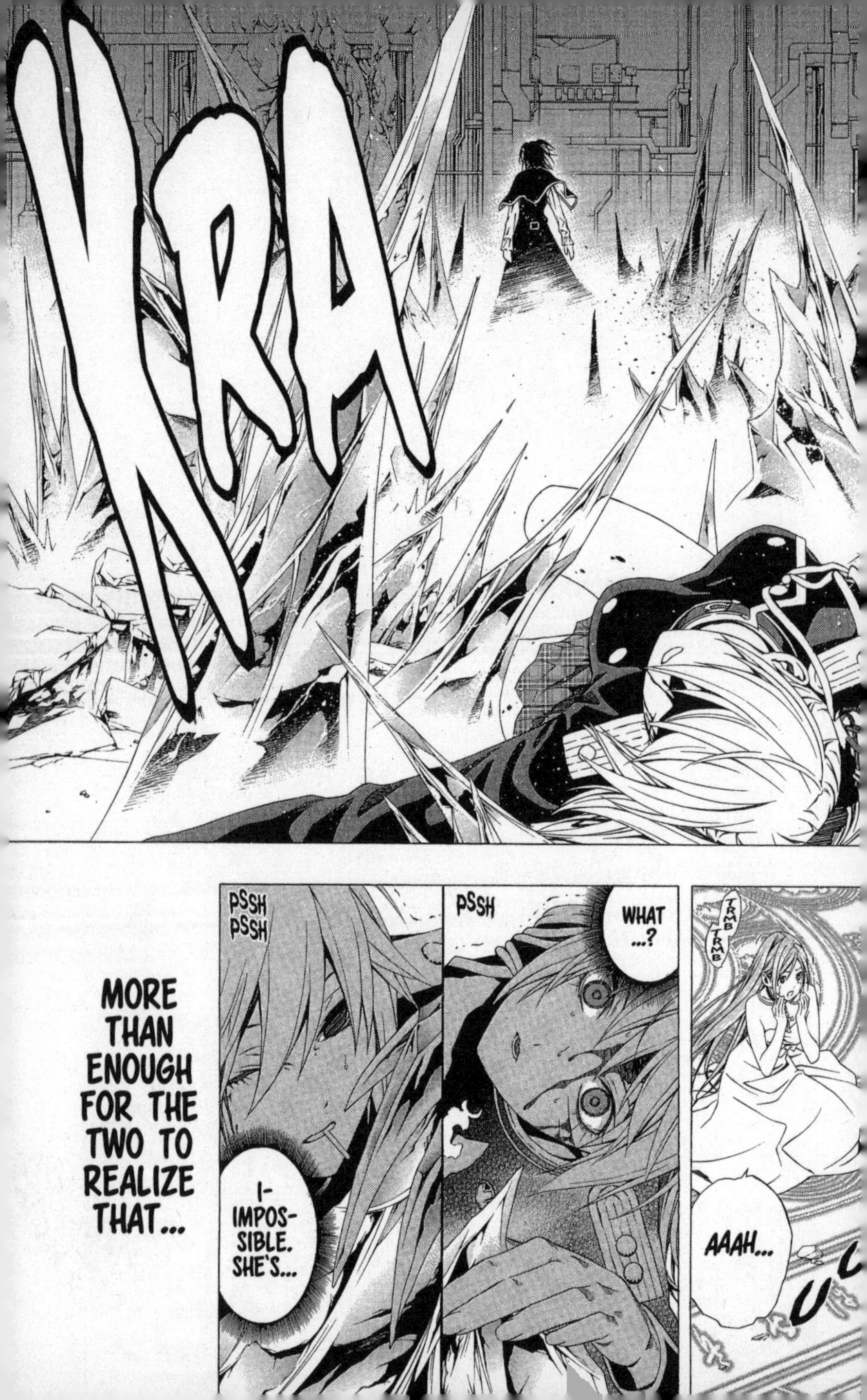
VRA
TRMB TRMB
AAAH...
PSSH
WHAT ...?
PSSH PSSH
I-IMPOSSIBLE. SHE'S...
MORE THAN ENOUGH FOR THE TWO TO REALIZE THAT...

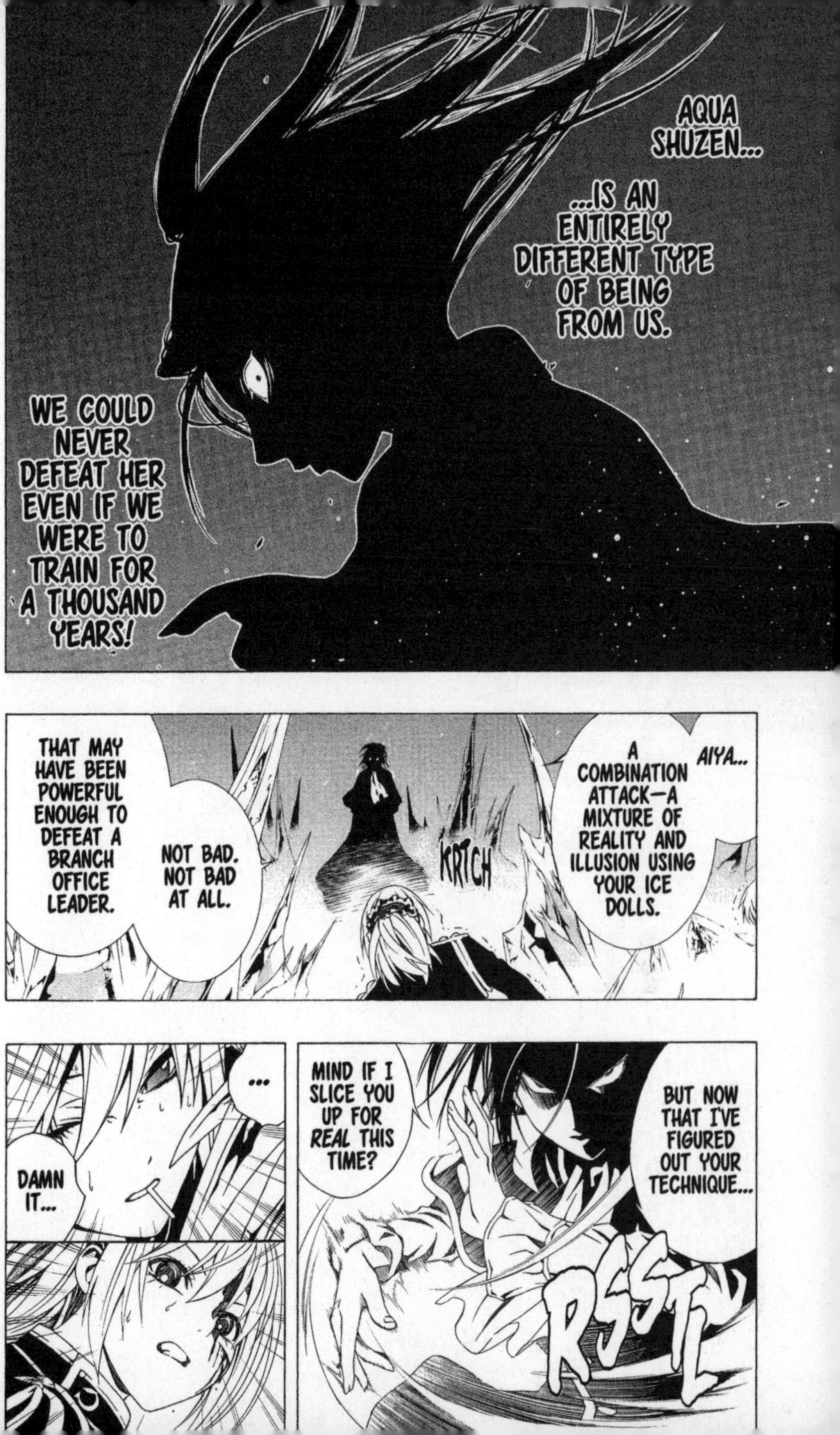
AQUA SHUZEN...
...IS AN ENTIRELY DIFFERENT TYPE OF BEING FROM US.
WE COULD NEVER DEFEAT HER EVEN IF WE WERE TO TRAIN FOR A THOUSAND YEARS!
AIYA...
A COMBINATION ATTACK—A MIXTURE OF REALITY AND ILLUSION USING YOUR ICE DOLLS.
KRTCH
NOT BAD. NOT BAD AT ALL.
THAT MAY HAVE BEEN POWERFUL ENOUGH TO DEFEAT A BRANCH OFFICE LEADER.
BUT NOW THAT I'VE FIGURED OUT YOUR TECHNIQUE...
MIND IF I SLICE YOU UP FOR *REAL* THIS TIME?
RSST
...
DAMN IT...

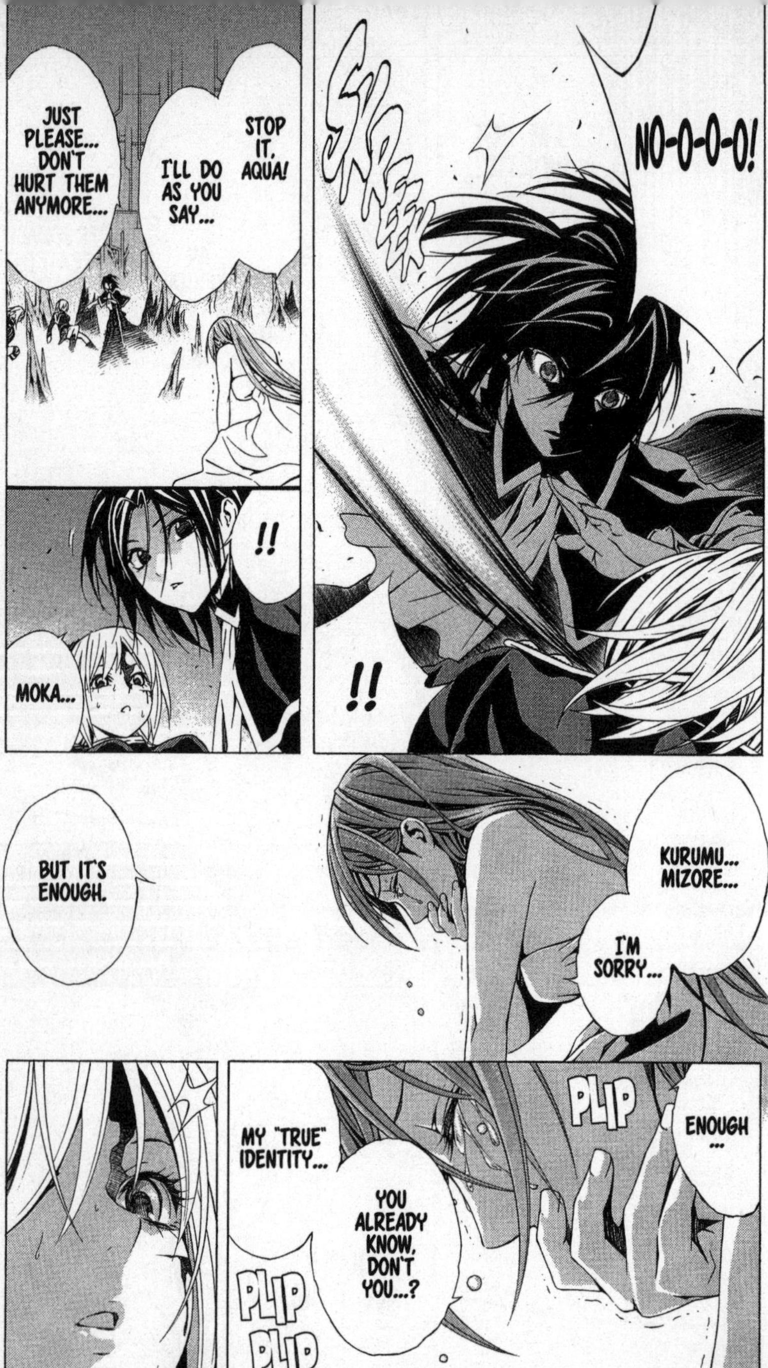
NO-O-O-O!
SKREEK
!!
STOP IT, AQUA!
I'LL DO AS YOU SAY...
JUST PLEASE... DON'T HURT THEM ANYMORE...
!!
MOKA...
KURUMU... MIZORE...
I'M SORRY...
BUT IT'S ENOUGH.
ENOUGH...
PLIP
MY "TRUE" IDENTITY...
YOU ALREADY KNOW, DON'T YOU...?
PLIP
PLIP

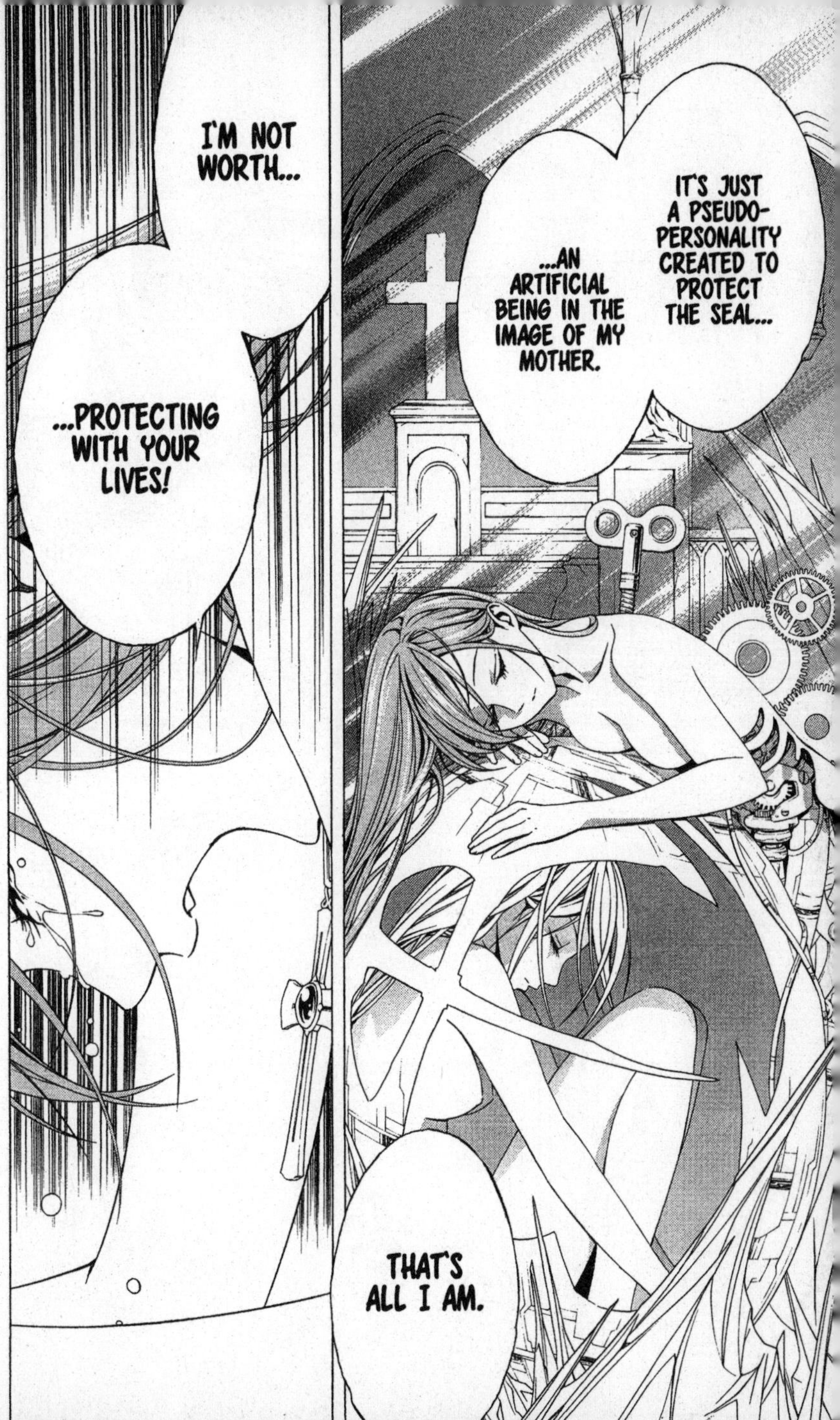
IT'S JUST A PSEUDO-PERSONALITY CREATED TO PROTECT THE SEAL...
...AN ARTIFICIAL BEING IN THE IMAGE OF MY MOTHER.
THAT'S ALL I AM.
I'M NOT WORTH...
...PROTECTING WITH YOUR LIVES!

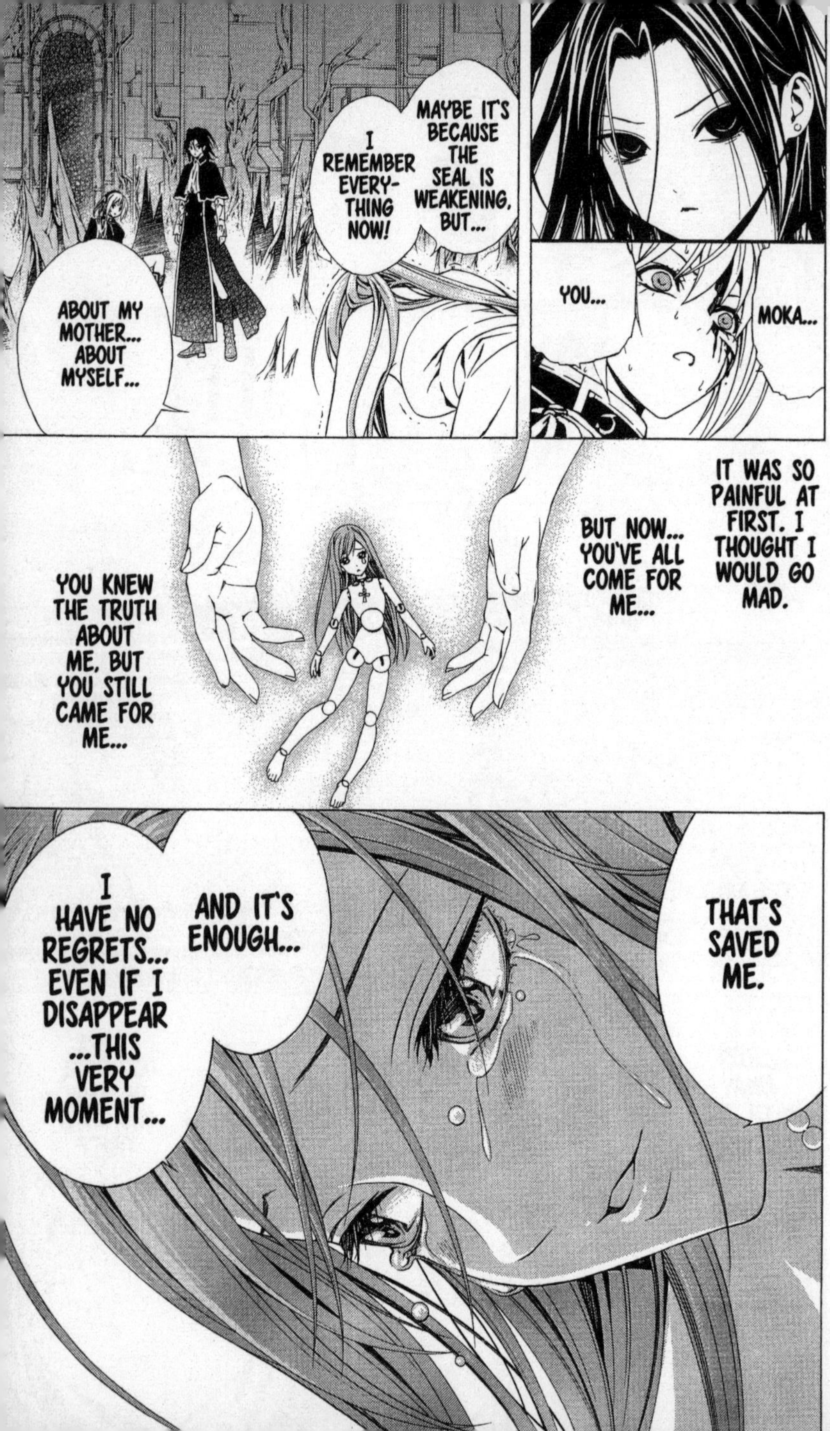
MOKA...
YOU...
MAYBE IT'S BECAUSE THE SEAL IS WEAKENING, BUT...
I REMEMBER EVERY-THING NOW!
ABOUT MY MOTHER... ABOUT MYSELF...
IT WAS SO PAINFUL AT FIRST. I THOUGHT I WOULD GO MAD.
BUT NOW... YOU'VE ALL COME FOR ME...
YOU KNEW THE TRUTH ABOUT ME, BUT YOU STILL CAME FOR ME...
THAT'S SAVED ME.
AND IT'S ENOUGH...
I HAVE NO REGRETS... EVEN IF I DISAPPEAR ...THIS VERY MOMENT...

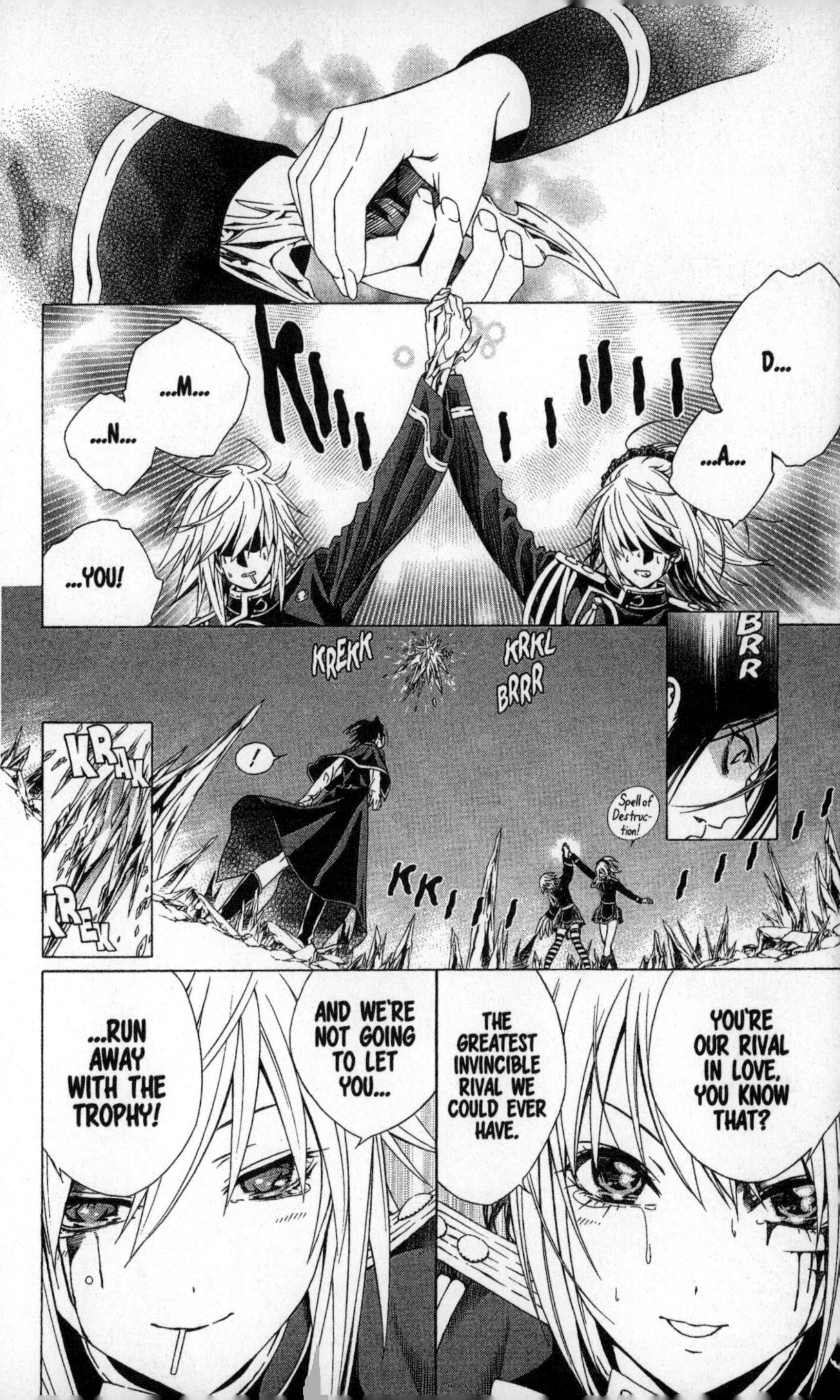
KRIIIIII
D...
...A...
...M...
...N...
...YOU!
BRRR
KRKL
BRRR
KREKK
!
Spell of Destruction!
KKIIII
KRAK
KREK
YOU'RE OUR RIVAL IN LOVE, YOU KNOW THAT?
THE GREATEST INVINCIBLE RIVAL WE COULD EVER HAVE.
AND WE'RE NOT GOING TO LET YOU...
...RUN AWAY WITH THE TROPHY!

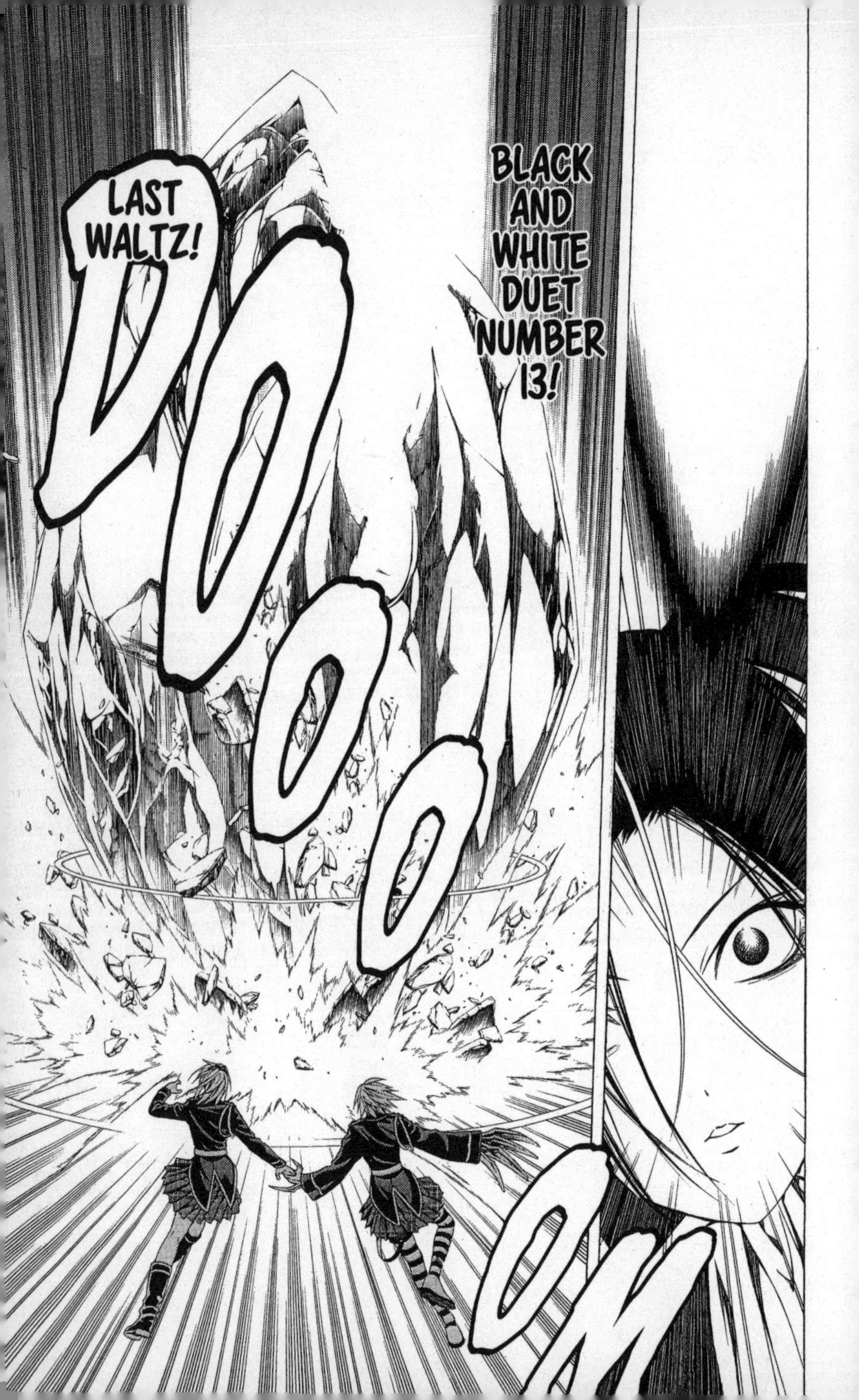
BLACK AND WHITE DUET NUMBER 13!
LAST WALTZ!
DOOOOOM

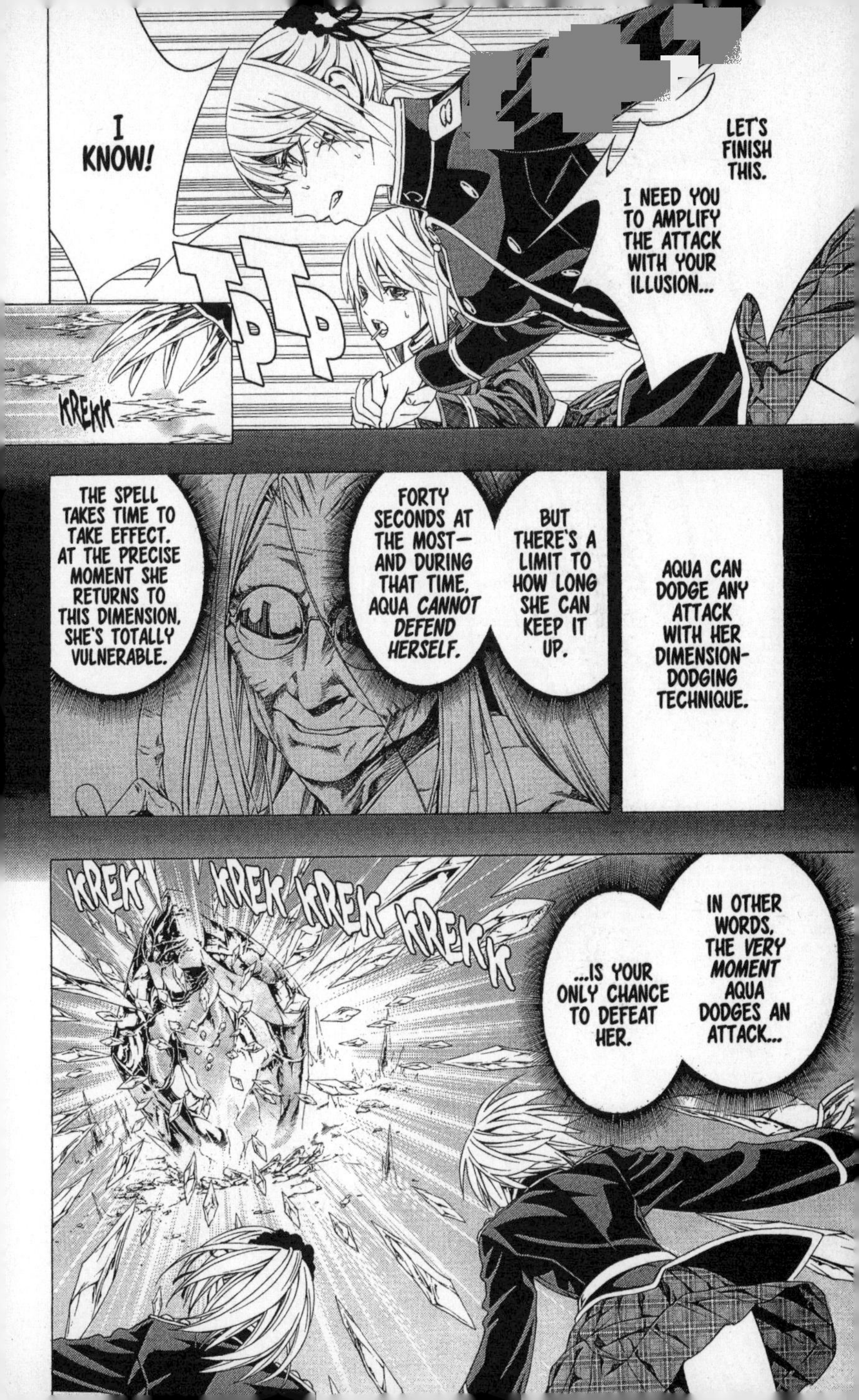
LET'S FINISH THIS.
I NEED YOU TO AMPLIFY THE ATTACK WITH YOUR ILLUSION...
I KNOW!
TP TP TP
KREKK
AQUA CAN DODGE ANY ATTACK WITH HER DIMENSION-DODGING TECHNIQUE.
BUT THERE'S A LIMIT TO HOW LONG SHE CAN KEEP IT UP.
FORTY SECONDS AT THE MOST— AND DURING THAT TIME, AQUA *CANNOT* DEFEND HERSELF.
THE SPELL TAKES TIME TO TAKE EFFECT. AT THE PRECISE MOMENT SHE RETURNS TO THIS DIMENSION, SHE'S TOTALLY VULNERABLE.
IN OTHER WORDS, THE *VERY MOMENT* AQUA DODGES AN ATTACK...
...IS YOUR ONLY CHANCE TO DEFEAT HER.
KREK KREK KREK KREKK

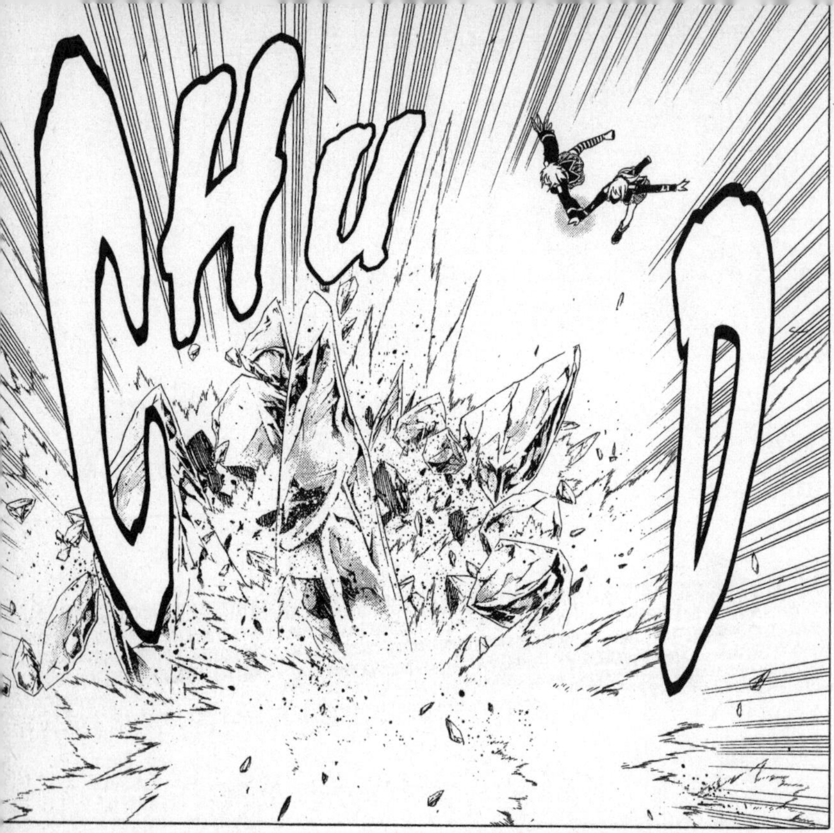
CHUD

"ARTIFICIAL"? DON'T MAKE ME LAUGH.

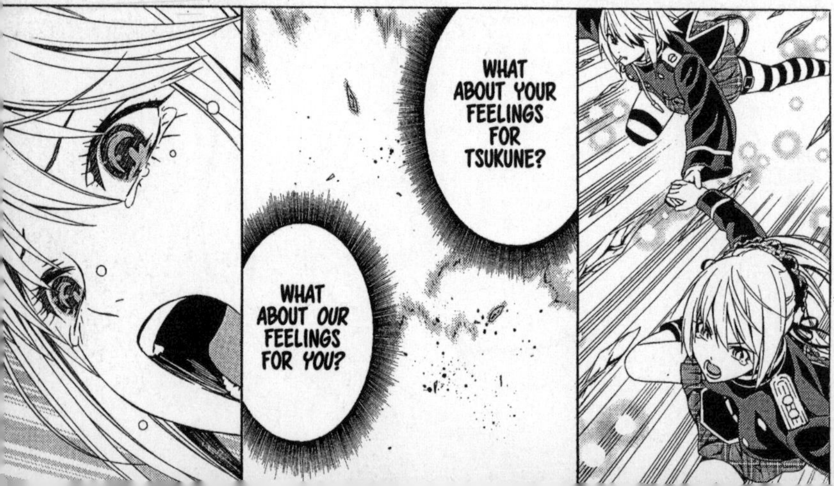
WHAT ABOUT YOUR FEELINGS FOR TSUKUNE?
WHAT ABOUT OUR FEELINGS FOR YOU?

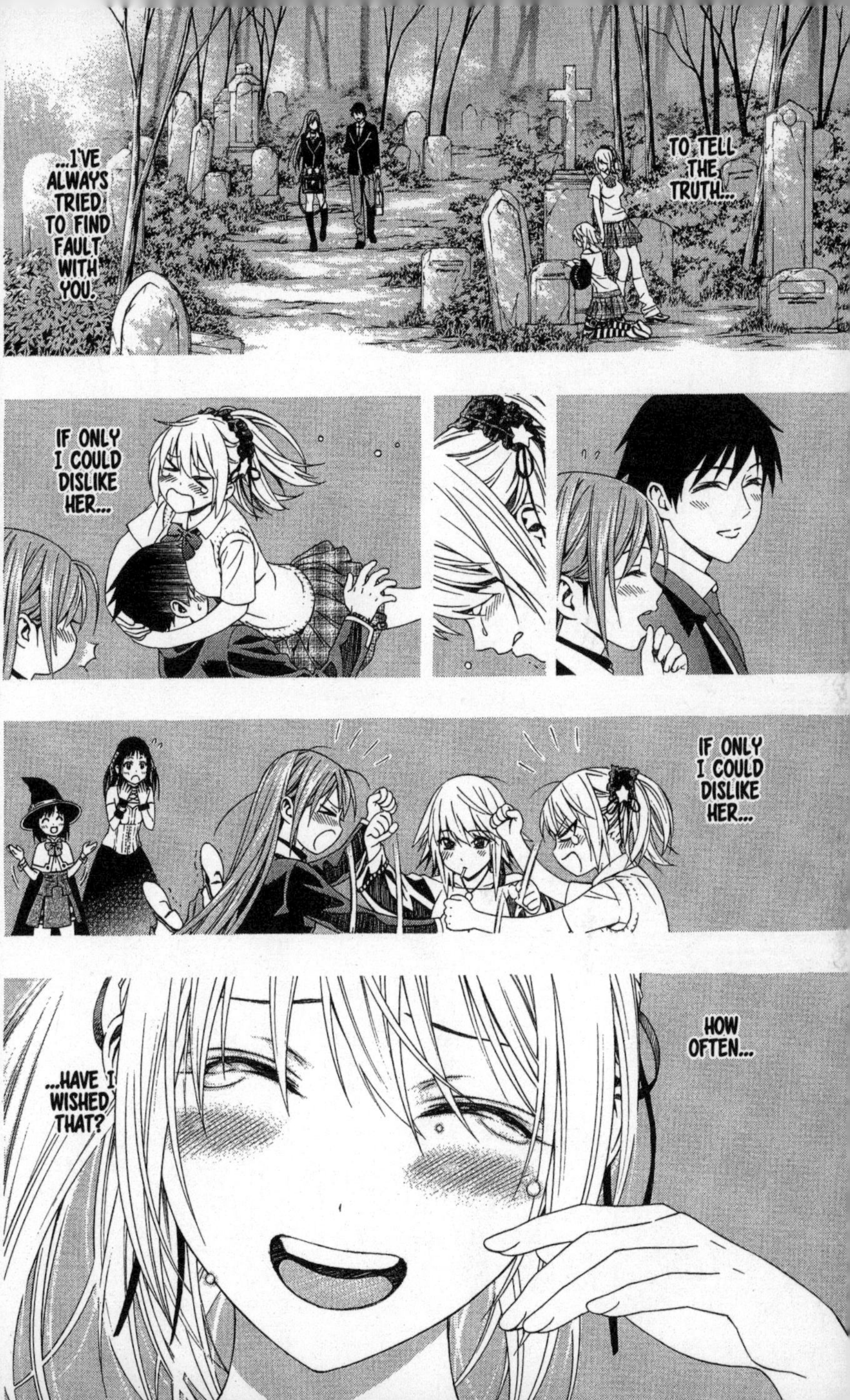
TO TELL THE TRUTH...
...I'VE ALWAYS TRIED TO FIND FAULT WITH YOU.
IF ONLY I COULD DISLIKE HER...
IF ONLY I COULD DISLIKE HER...
HOW OFTEN...
...HAVE I WISHED THAT?

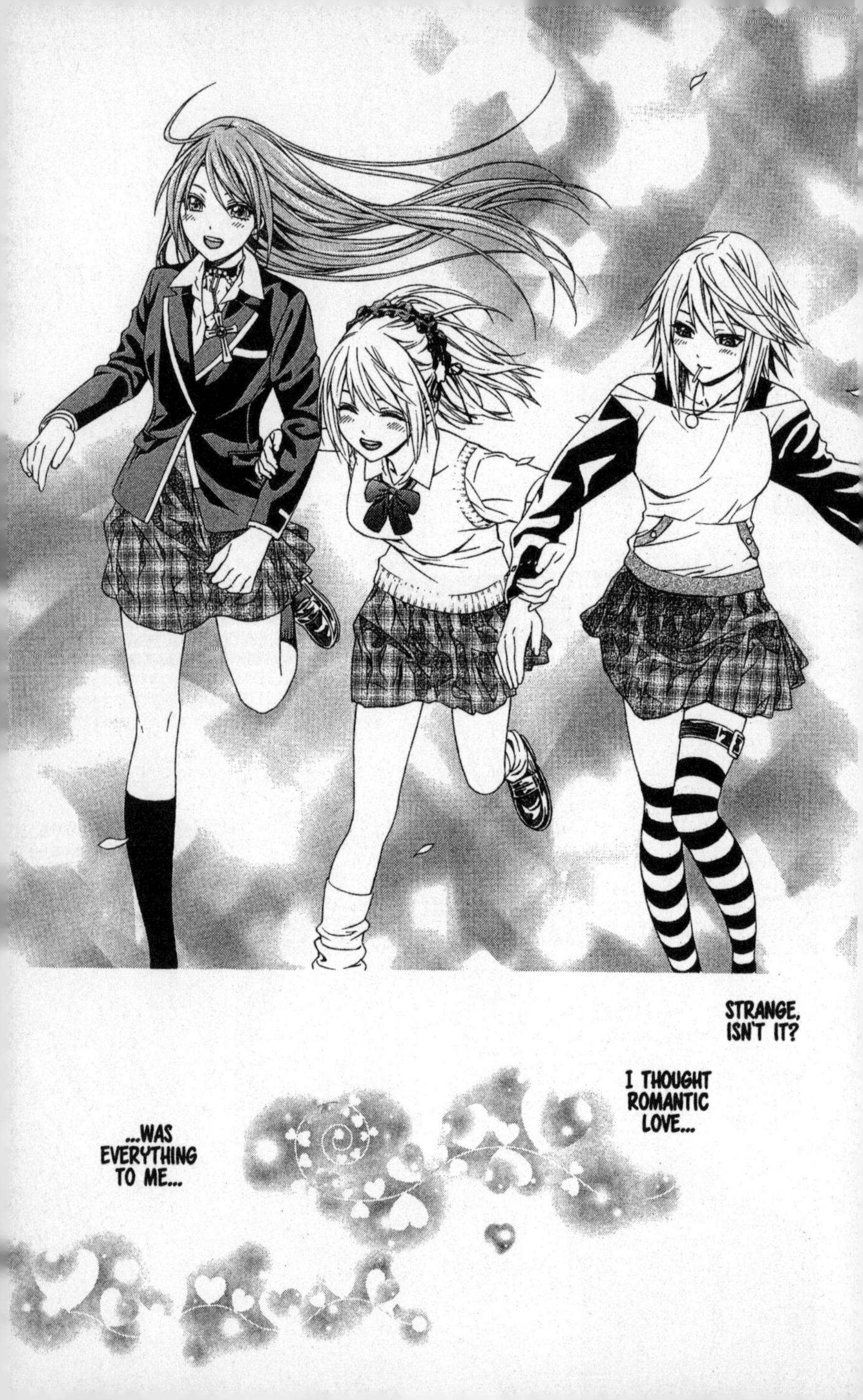
STRANGE, ISN'T IT?
I THOUGHT ROMANTIC LOVE...
...WAS EVERYTHING TO ME...

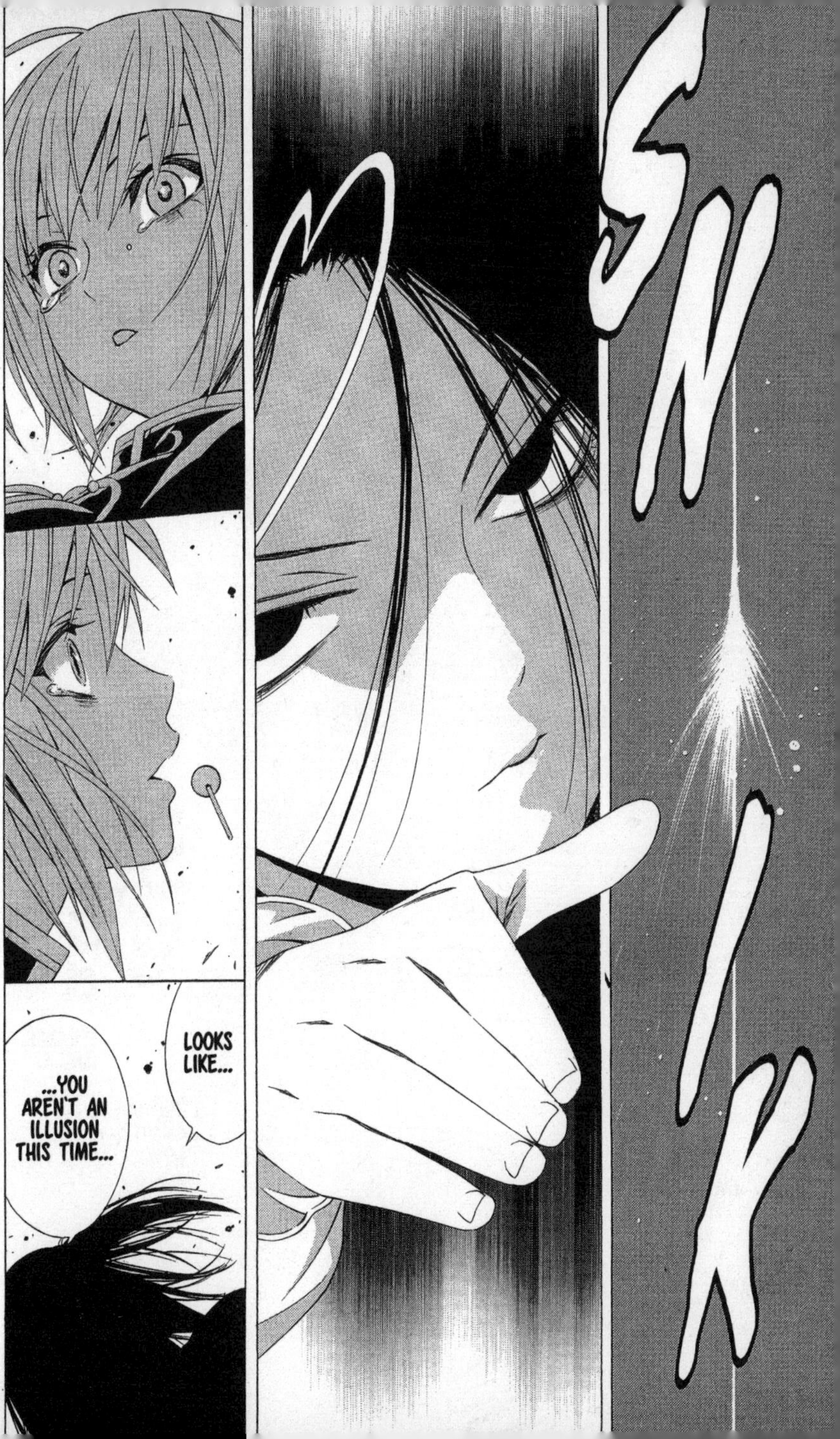
LOOKS LIKE...
...YOU AREN'T AN ILLUSION THIS TIME...

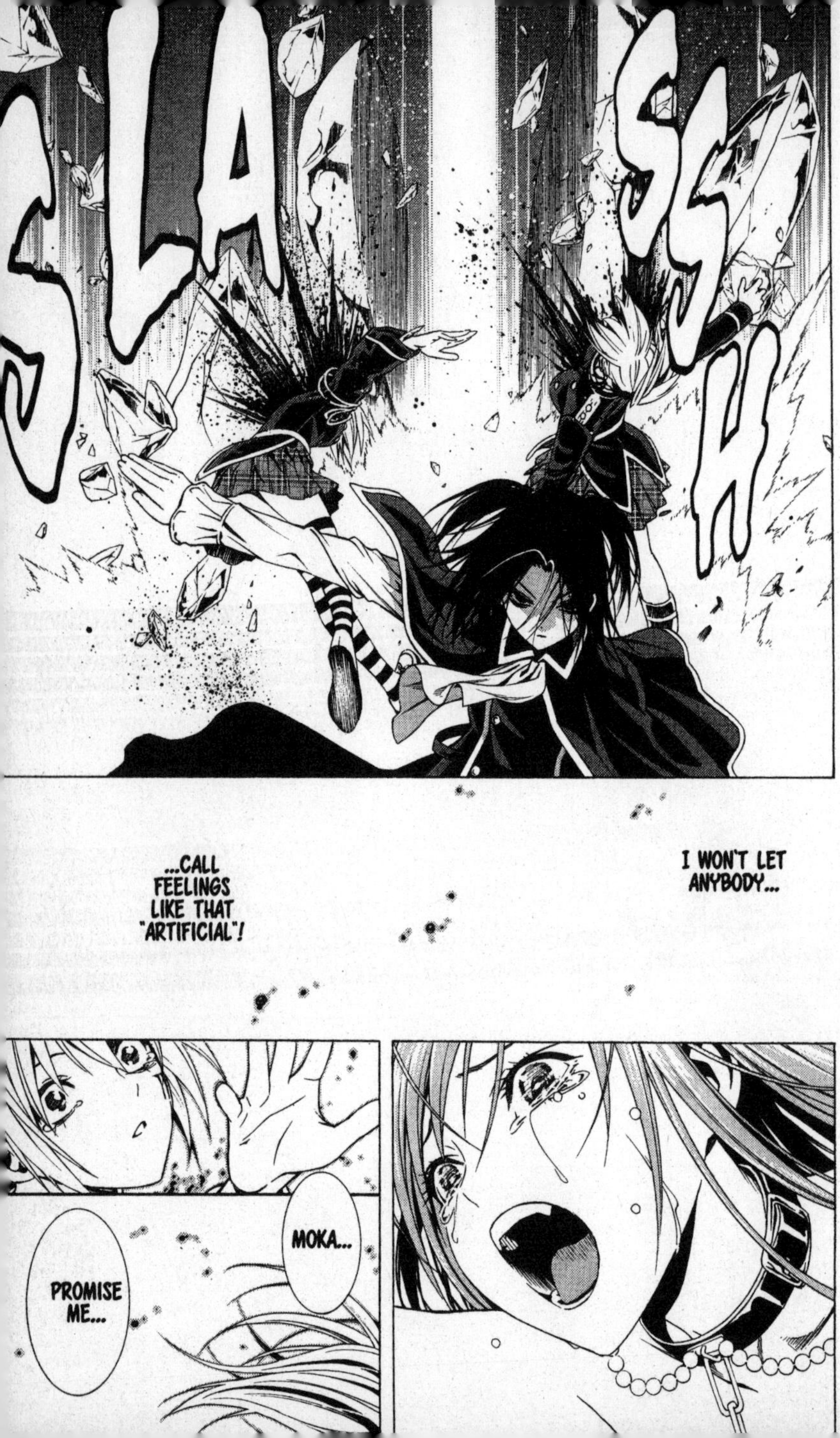
SLASH
I WON'T LET ANYBODY...
...CALL FEELINGS LIKE THAT "ARTIFICIAL"!
MOKA...
PROMISE ME...

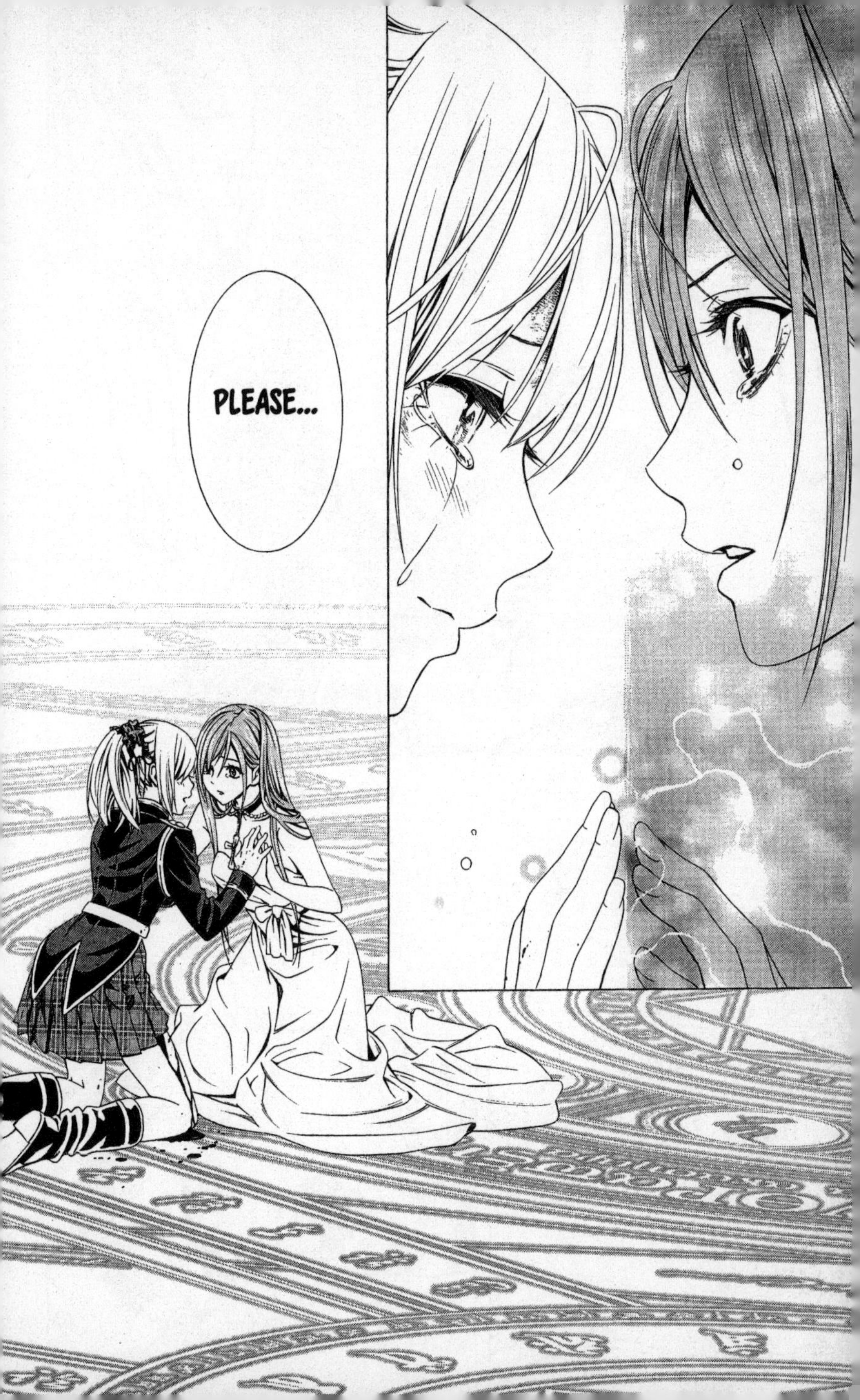
PLEASE...

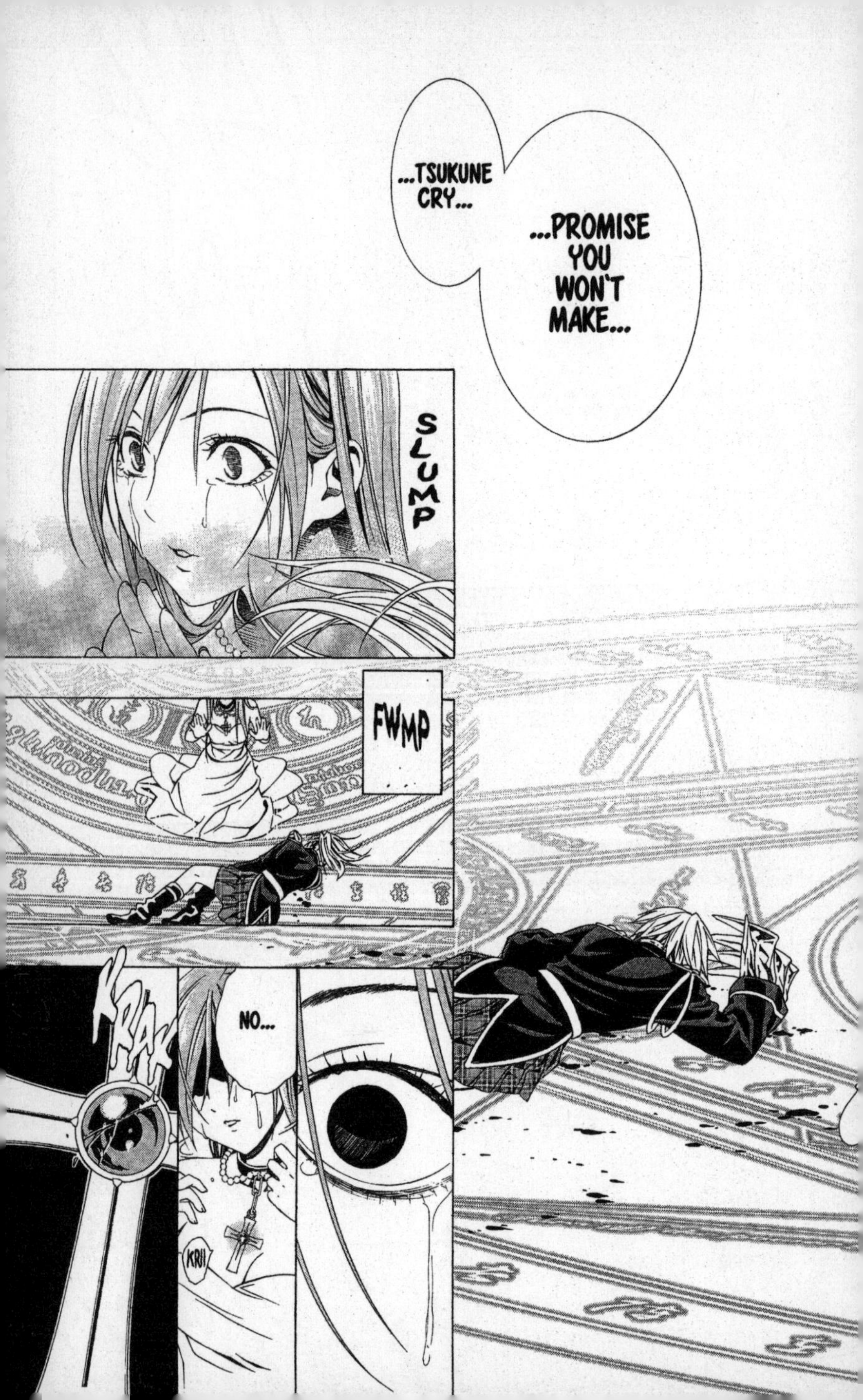
...TSUKUNE CRY...
...PROMISE YOU WON'T MAKE...
SLUMP
FWMP
NO...
KRAK
KRII

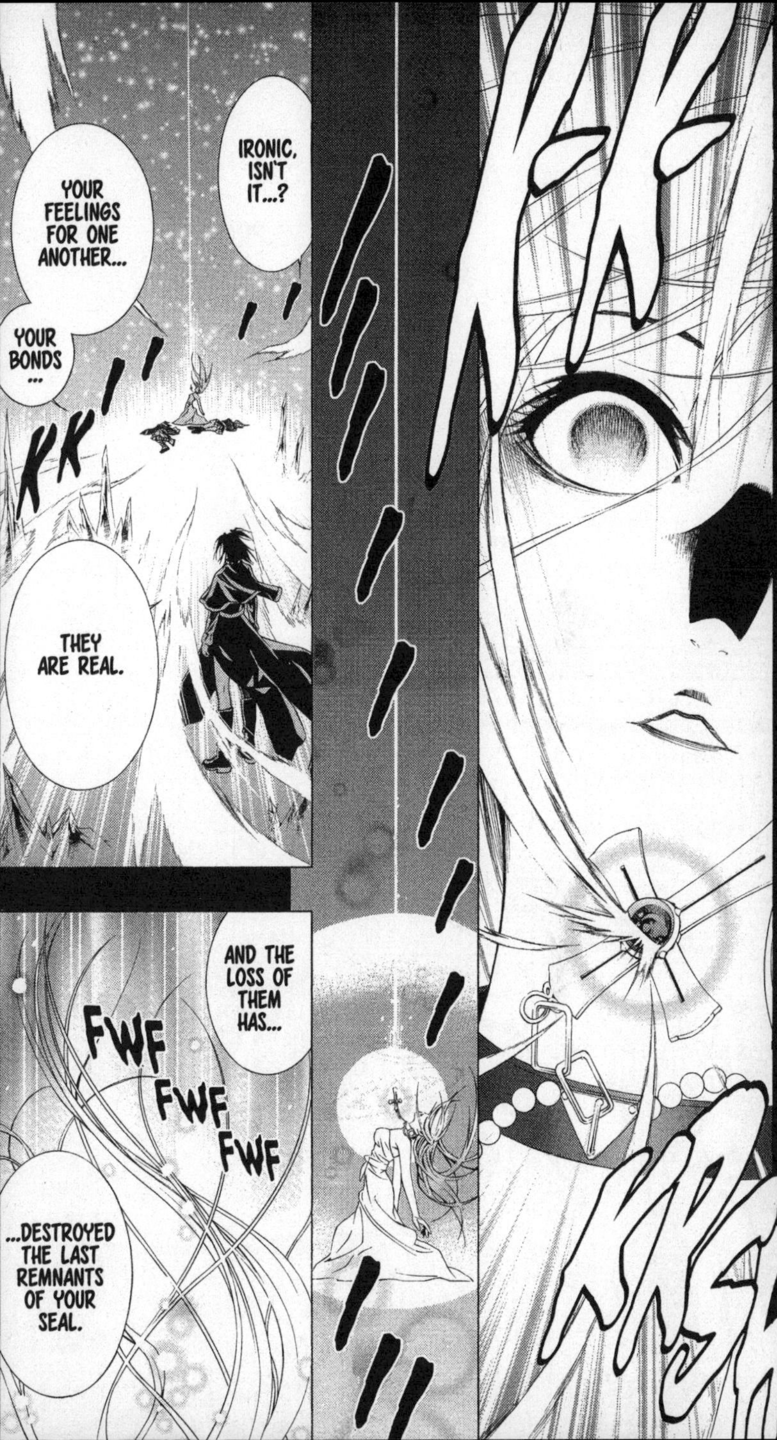
IRONIC, ISN'T IT...?
YOUR FEELINGS FOR ONE ANOTHER...
YOUR BONDS ...
KK
THEY ARE REAL.
AND THE LOSS OF THEM HAS...
FWF
FWF
FWF
...DESTROYED THE LAST REMNANTS OF YOUR SEAL.

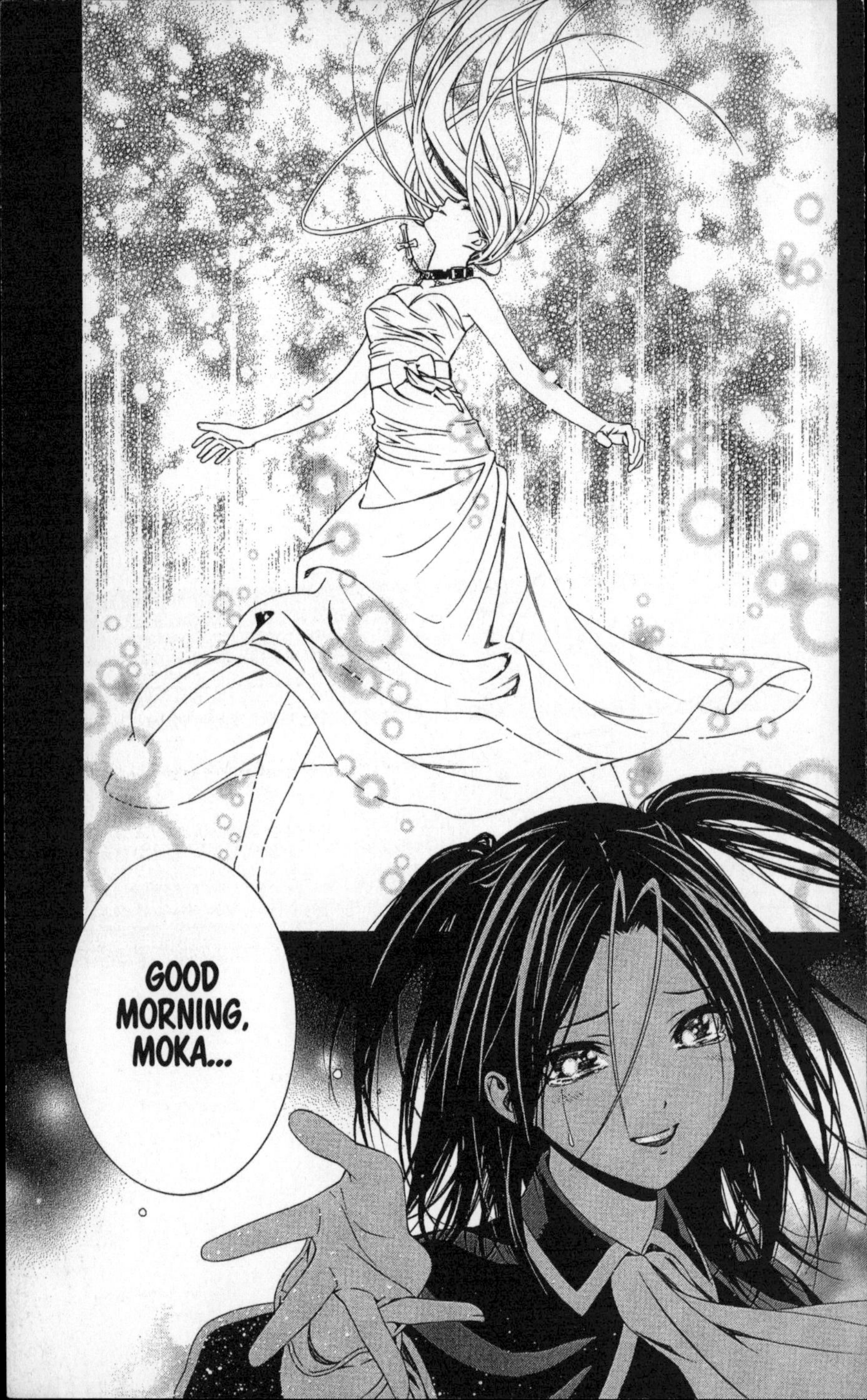
GOOD MORNING, MOKA...

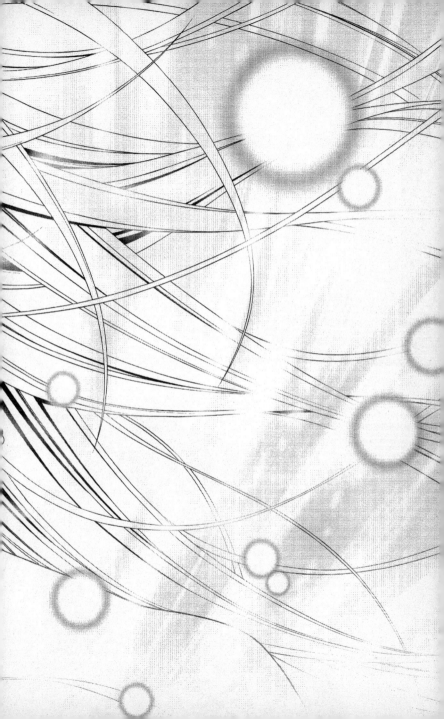

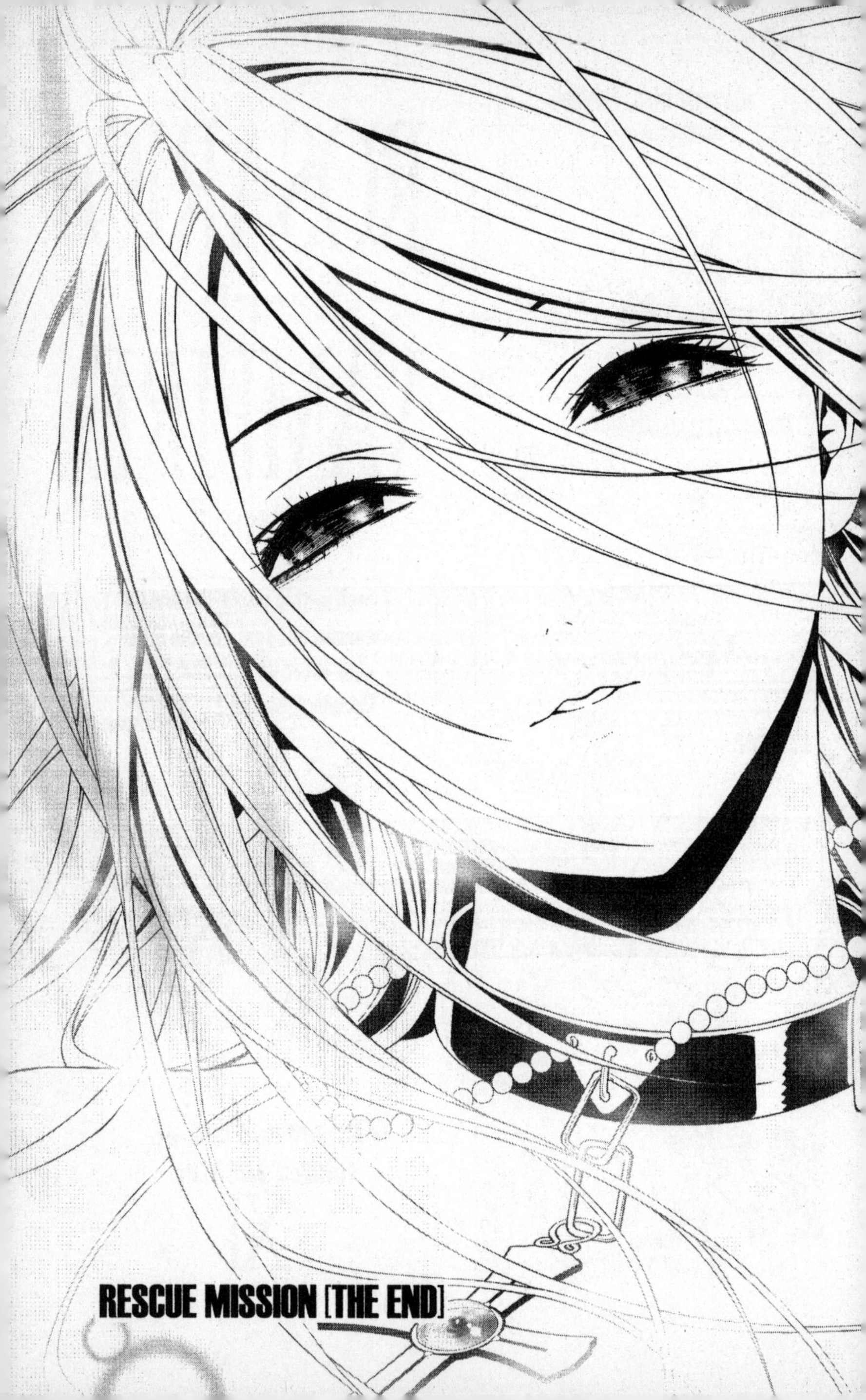
RESCUE MISSION [THE END]

ROSARIO + VAMPIRE

Season II

I realize this might seem a bit random, but Ludie is the main character of this volume's Meaningless End-of-Volume Theater.

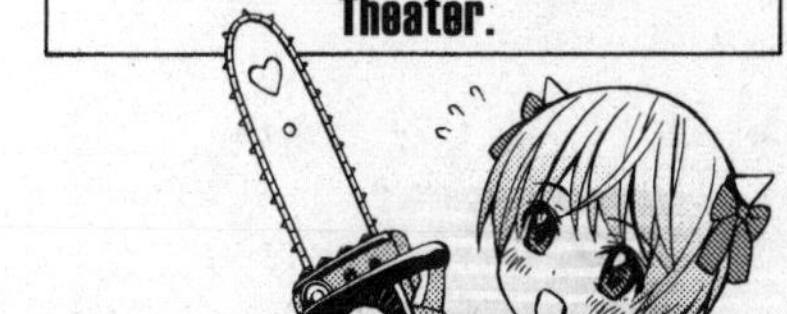
SPIN-OFF

Meaningless End-of-Volume Theater

XI

•Crush him, Ludie!•

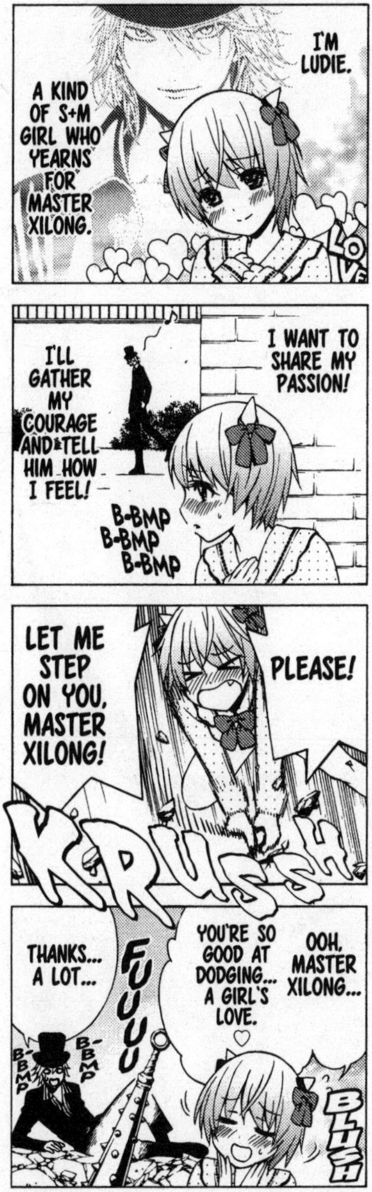
I'M LUDIE.
A KIND OF S+M GIRL WHO YEARNS FOR MASTER XILONG.
LOVE
I WANT TO SHARE MY PASSION!
I'LL GATHER MY COURAGE AND TELL HIM HOW I FEEL!
B-BMP B-BMP B-BMP
PLEASE!
LET ME STEP ON YOU, MASTER XILONG!
KRUSSH
OOH, MASTER XILONG...
YOU'RE SO GOOD AT DODGING... A GIRL'S LOVE.
BLUSH
FUUUUU
B-BMP
B-BMP
THANKS... A LOT...

•Heal Him, Ludie!•

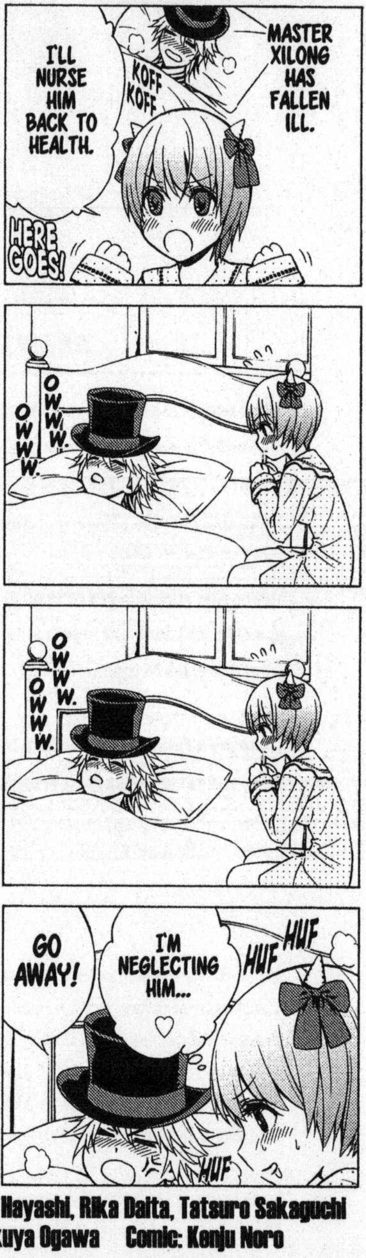
MASTER XILONG HAS FALLEN ILL.
KOFF KOFF
I'LL NURSE HIM BACK TO HEALTH.
HERE GOES!
OWWW.
OWWW.
OWWW.
OWWW.
HUF HUF
I'M NEGLECTING HIM...
GO AWAY!
HUF

•Everlasting, Ludie?•

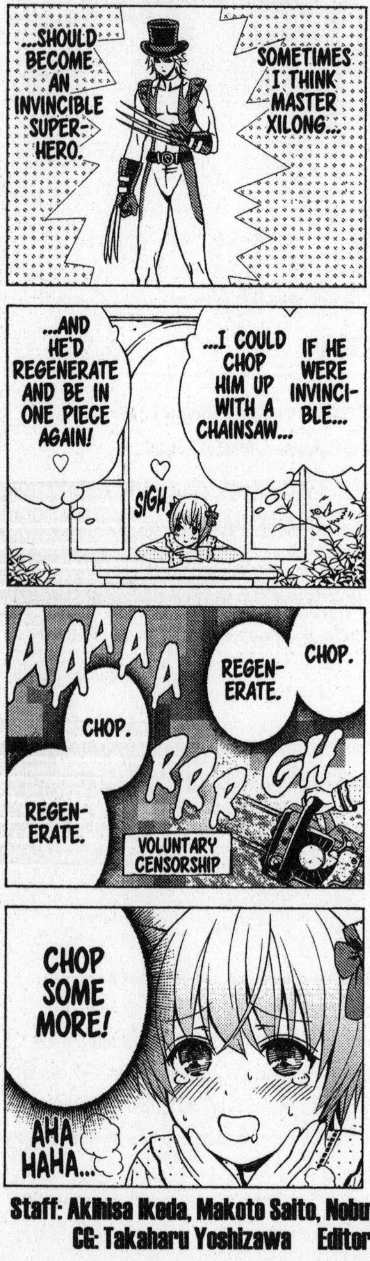
SOMETIMES I THINK MASTER XILONG...
...SHOULD BECOME AN INVINCIBLE SUPER-HERO.
IF HE WERE INVINCI-BLE...
...I COULD CHOP HIM UP WITH A CHAINSAW...
...AND HE'D REGENERATE AND BE IN ONE PIECE AGAIN!
SIGH
CHOP.
REGEN-ERATE.
AAAAA
CHOP.
RRRGH
REGEN-ERATE.
VOLUNTARY CENSORSHIP
CHOP SOME MORE!
AHA HAHA...

Staff: Akihisa Ikeda, Makoto Saito, Nobuyuki Hayashi, Rika Daita, Tatsuro Sakaguchi
CG: Takaharu Yoshizawa Editor: Takuya Ogawa Comic: Kenju Noro

AKIHISA IKEDA

When people ask me who my favorite characters are in other manga I have read, my answer is always the villains: Dio, Toguro, Hakumen, Master Kogan...*

*From *JoJo's Bizarre Adventure, Yu Yu Hakusho, Ushio To Tora,* and *Shigurui.*

I love super villains! They have an inimitable style and play by their own rules. They're powerful and dark, but there's something melancholy about them as well... And that's what draws me to them.

There are all manner of villains in the world of *Rosario+Vampire*: Aqua, Gyokuro, Miyabi, Kiria, and so on... I hope you're drawn to them too.

Akihisa Ikeda was born in 1976 in Miyazaki. He debuted as a mangaka with the four-volume magical warrior fantasy series *Kiruto* in 2002, which was serialized in *Monthly Shonen Jump*. *Rosario+Vampire* debuted in *Monthly Shonen Jump* in March of 2004 and is continuing in the magazine *Jump Square (Jump SQ)* as *Rosario+Vampire: Season II*. In Japan, *Rosario+Vampire* is also available as a drama CD. In 2008, the story was released as an anime. Season II is also available as an anime now. And in Japan, there is a Nintendo DS game based on the series.

Ikeda has been a huge fan of vampires and monsters since he was a little kid. He says one of the perks of being a manga artist is being able to go for walks during the day when everybody else is stuck in the office.

ROSARIO+VAMPIRE: Season II
11
SHONEN JUMP ADVANCED Manga Edition

STORY & ART BY AKIHISA IKEDA

Translation/Tetsuichiro Miyaki
English Adaptation/Annette Roman
Touch-up Art & Lettering/Stephen Dutro
Cover & Interior Design/Ronnie Casson
Editor/Annette Roman

ROSARIO + VAMPIRE SEASON II © 2007 by Akihisa Ikeda
All rights reserved. First published in Japan in 2007 by SHUEISHA Inc.,
Tokyo. English translation rights arranged by SHUEISHA Inc.

The stories, characters and incidents mentioned in this publication are
entirely fictional.

Printed in the U.S.A.

Published by VIZ Media, LLC
P.O. Box 77010
San Francisco, CA 94107

10 9 8 7 6 5 4 3 2
First printing, March 2013
Second printing, May 2015

www.viz.com

www.shonenjump.com

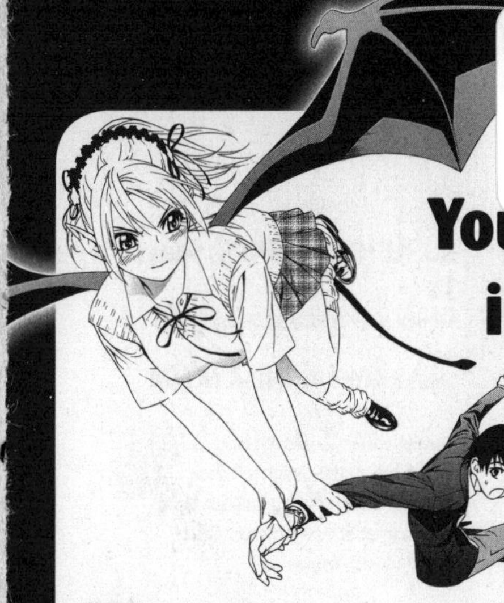

You're Reading in the Wrong Direction!!

Whoops! Guess what? You're starting at the wrong end of the comic!

...It's true! In keeping with the original Japanese format, **Rosario+Vampire** is meant to be read from right to left, starting in the upper-right corner.

Unlike English, which is read from left to right, Japanese is read from right to left, meaning action, sound effects and word-balloon order are completely reversed... something which can make readers unfamiliar with Japanese feel pretty backwards themselves. For this reason, manga or Japanese comics published in the U.S. in English have sometimes been published "flopped"—that is, printed in exact reverse order, as though seen from the other side of a mirror.

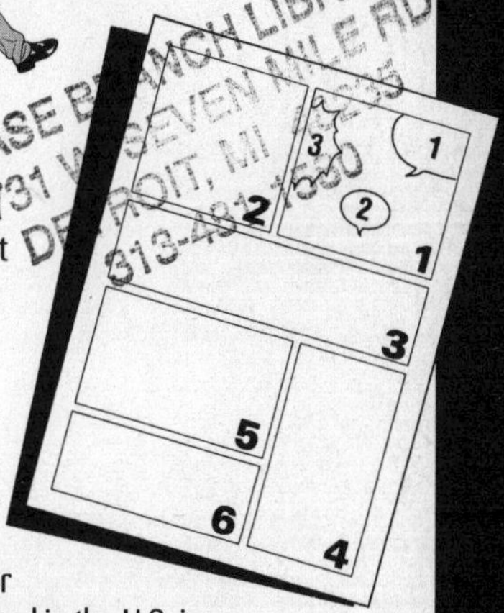
1
3
2
2
1
3
4
5
6

By flopping pages, U.S. publishers can avoid confusing readers, but the compromise is not without its downside. For one thing, a character in a flopped manga series who once wore in the original Japanese version a T-shirt emblazoned with "M A Y" (as in "the merry month of") now wears one which reads "Y A M"! Additionally, many manga creators in Japan are themselves unhappy with the process, as some feel the mirror-imaging of their art skews their original intentions.

We are proud to bring you Akihisa Ikeda's **Rosario+Vampire** in the original unflopped format. For now, though, turn to the other side of the book and let the haunting begin...!

—Editor